Working-Class Experience: The Rise and Reconstitution of Canadian Labour, 1800–1980

The serious and critical reader will not want a treacherous impartiality, which offers him a cup of conciliation with a well-settled poison of reactionary hate at the bottom, but a scientific conscientiousness, which for its sympathies and antipathies — open and undisguised — seeks support in an honest study of the facts, a determination of their real connections, an exposure of the causal laws of their movement.

Leon Trotsky, "Preface,"
History of the Russian Revolution (1932)

Bryan D. Palmer

WORKING-CLASS EXPERIENCE

THE RISE AND RECONSTITUTION OF CANADIAN LABOUR, 1800–1980

Working-Class Experience
© 1983—Butterworth & Co. (Canada) Ltd.

Printed and bound in Canada
5 4 3 2 1   3 4 5 6 7 8 9/8

Canadian Cataloguing in Publication Data
Palmer, Bryan D., 1951-
  Working-class experience

Bibliography: p.
ISBN 0-409-85767-X

1. Labor and laboring classes - Canada - History - 19th century. 2. Labor and laboring classes - Canada - History - 20th century. I. Title.

HD8104.P34   331'.0971   C83-094077-4

The Butterworth Group of Companies

Canada:
Butterworth & Co. (Canada) Ltd., Toronto and Vancouver

United Kingdom:
Butterworth & Co. (Publishers) Ltd., London

Australia:
Butterworths Pty. Ltd., Sydney

New Zealand:
Butterworths of New Zealand Ltd., Wellington

South Africa:
Butterworth & Co. (South Africa) Ltd., Durban

United States:
Butterworth (Publishers) Inc., Boston
Butterworth (Legal Publishers) Inc., Seattle
Mason Publishing Company, St. Paul

For D.H.A. and R.W.M.

Canadian Political Issues in Their Historical Perspective Series

Editors

Bruce Hodgins, Trent University
Bruce Rawlyk, Queen's University

This series attempts to deal with a variety of contemporary Canadian issues within a historical framework. Most volumes, it is expected, will be specifically oriented towards political problems. Emphasis will be placed not only on a sophisticated analysis of the present but also on how the past has impinged on the contemporary world. The volumes in the series will be original and sometimes controversial syntheses of existing literature and will raise, we hope, issues of fundamental importance regarding the essential nature of the Canadian experience. All the books in the series are written by acknowledged authorities and special emphasis is being placed upon sound scholarship, imaginative insight and clear and cogent writing.

By stressing the totality of working-class experience—political, cultural, institutional and economic, across different regions and over time, Bryan Palmer's WORKING CLASS EXPERIENCE provides invaluable insight into how this experience was forged and how the Canadian working-class has been made and remade over the last two centuries.

FORTHCOMING TITLES IN SERIES

Robert Paehlke: *Canadian Energy Policy in Historical Perspective*

Bernard Vigod: *French Canada*

Gillis and Roach: *Lost Initiatives*

Table of Contents

Tables, Figures, and Appendices

Acknowledgements

In a book such as this, covering a wide and interpretively problematic span of Canadian history, I have been sustained by a number of individuals who willingly shared sources and perspectives with me. Among the most generous have been Donald Akenson, Dale Chisamore, Michael Cross, Russell Hann, Peter de Lottinville, Robert Malcolmson, Ian McKay, Richard Rice, Wayne Roberts, Terry Ruddel, John Herd Thompson, and Brian Young. Debi Wells gave me access to her own research and took the time and trouble to read the manuscript in its entirety, as did Gregory S. Kealey and Allen Seager. George Rawlyk suggested that I do this book originally, forced me to rethink specific sections, and helped me to cut the manuscript down to a size that publishers deemed appropriate. My students in various seminars at Queen's and McGill Universities produced papers and remarkable criticisms of my own way of looking at working-class experience that have enabled me to write differently than I once would have. A Department of Labour grant provided research assistance, while the offices of the Dean of Arts and the History Department at Simon Fraser University facilitated the final typing of the manuscript. I am grateful to Bernice Ferrier, Jenny Alexander, and Wilma Whiffin, who typed with skill, patience, and good humour as we all struggled to meet deadlines.

I am also indebted to the many commentators whose published and unpublished writings form the foundation upon which this study rests. In the bibliography, I provide a comprehensive listing of those sources that inform the arguments of this book. Often, however, especially for the nineteenth-century material, I have drawn upon my own researches in newspapers and archival holdings. Those who require specific citations should feel free to contact me at the History Department, Simon Fraser University.

Finally, my deepest thanks go to two historians at Queen's University. Their support will never be forgotten.

Bryan D. Palmer
August, 1982

Introduction

The chief defect of all hitherto existing
materialism . . . is that the thing, . . . reality,
sensuousness, is conceived only in the form of
the *object* . . . or of contemplation . . ., but not
as *human sensuous activity, practice,* not subjec-
tively.

Karl Marx
"Theses on Feuerbach" (1845)

As I was preparing to pack this manuscript off to the publisher, Eugene
Forsey's monumental compilation of data on the workers' movement of
nineteenth-century Canada arrived in one morning's mail delivery.
Trade Unions in Canada presents, for the first time, a wealth of factual
information necessary to interpret important realms of labour's formative experiences. Unlike so many of his contemporaries and successors,
whose perspectives on the Canadian working class were influenced
directly or indirectly by the social-democratic milieu of the 1930s and
1940s, Forsey broke decisively from an explicitly political and implicitly
presentist concern with labour in its twentieth-century guise. Much of
recent working-class history has dealt with the more visible development of the labour movement in this century, and concentrates on a
specific set of questions: leadership, the emergence of collective
bargaining, the role of the state in "industrial relations," the development of unionism as an economic and political force, and the contest
between social democracy and communism for the allegiance of
Canadian workers in the 1930s and 1940s. However important such
issues may be, they inevitably focus our attention on labour's more
contemporary history, to the exclusion of an understanding of the
formative years of class formation and class conflict. Forsey, however,
has begun at the beginning, and his study provides a tacit critique of
those who have, for three decades, been implying that labour history
starts in 1919 with the Winnipeg General Strike. But his critique is,
understandably, a muffled one. Concentrating on unionism, he has

explored limited realms of working-class experience, and has presented, by his own admission, "few opinions or arguments" and "few analyses."

This book necessarily aims to be both something less and something more than Forsey's exhaustive history of trade unionism from 1812 to 1902. It is less, for it can of course make no pretence to fill the gaps in our factual knowledge in even one small corner of the vast field that encompasses working-class experience from 1800 to 1980. About unions, labour politics, family life, leisure activities, patterns of conflict, relations with the state, material circumstances, or a host of other facets of working-class life much more will have to be written than I have presented here. But this study is more, in that it is not simply a presentation of facts, a project always destined — given the nature of the sources — to be limited and inhibited. Unlike Forsey's *Trade Unions in Canada*, it is an attempt to generalize, to interpret, to locate periods of similarity in which working-class experience shared certain characteristics, and to separate them out from other epochs, in which the history appears to take turns in other directions. This book, then, is conceived as an argument about working-class experience, rather than a definitive chronicle of labour's history.

It is only by portraying the collective experience and by probing areas outside the realm of labour unions and politics that a sophisticated understanding of workers' experience can even be approached. Although political and union activities have both measured and influenced the tenor of the working-class experience, they are far from being its sole aspects. Likewise, the factual presentation of specific events and particular developments provide good starting points for study, but cannot stand as full characterizations of Canada's working class. This book attempts to create a unified portrait by bringing together diverse regional experiences and by drawing on many levels of working-class life. Two issues arise from such a treatment, and they have long been points of debate among historians of Canadian labour: the significance of regional disparity and the validity of examining the sparsely documented areas of working-class experience that lie outside labour organization and electoral activity.

First, as to *region* (and, by implication, *chronology*, for Canadian regions developed at an uneven pace and at different times): this book does not neglect regional peculiarities. But it does offer generalized arguments that may be developed out of attention to specific regional entities, as with, for instance, the focus on central Canada in the portrait of labour's early years. But throughout the book, the argument is developed as a "national" argument only where there is evidence that regional experiences shared certain similarities. Ironically enough, I would argue, this took place most prominently in the nineteenth century, prior to the erection of a Canadian state and the full impact of policies that might be construed as serving the interests of a central Canadian "imperialism." It was such policies and the class forces behind them — which always presented themselves as the embodiment and voice of "national" interest — that slowed development in the Maritimes and structured the west along particular paths. In the twentieth century, the consequences of such processes would be felt in the world of the working class, manifesting themselves in regional identification, different forms of organization or political practice, and divergent experiences, both materially and culturally. But in British North America or the early Canada of the immediate post-National Policy (1879) years, such divisions were less pronounced, and shared experiences were, to some extent, more prevalent.

Second, and perhaps even more contentious, is the way in which this book addresses working-class experience. Obviously the approach here breaks from previous attempts to survey the history of Canadian workers in its insistence that *working-class life extends beyond labour organizations and labour politics.* There is a need to study the place of workers in their communities and families, as well as in their unions and political parties, and this need has been insufficiently recognized by many labour historians. Church and tavern, printers' chapel (the name of the printing trade's organization), and election-night "treating" are all spheres of working-class life, interconnected and linked to the material realities of the workplace and the larger political economy. They are complex parts of a process of class formation that need to be analyzed in order to comprehend how workers came to see their interests as antagonistic to those of employers, and how workers whose experiences were constantly atomized through social institutions and ideologies came to embrace a collective response to the industrial-capitalist transformation of the late nineteenth century.

This book therefore differs from other labour history surveys in that it lays stress upon the totality of working-class experience. It is *class*, as embedded in the structural, primarily economic context of specific social formations, that is at the conceptual root of this study, not labour as an interest group fighting its way into a pluralist society by way of its unions and its political platform. The development of distinct working and nonworking classes was a protracted and contradictory process. It grew out of the economic relations of production, but was also clarified and reproduced over time in other formal and informal ways: through ritual and revelry, culture and conflict, family and funeral and, of course, through the strengths, weaknesses, and character of the workers' movement itself. At times new initiatives — from capital and/or the state — drove it into retreat, but its potential was never relinquished entirely.

None of this is to argue that workers' experiences inside and outside their unions and their political activities bore the distinct marks of class consciousness. Social and cultural life, like day-to-day developments at the workplace or in the political arena, were ambiguous, and class as an idealized, conscious expression of worker antagonism to capital and the state has been a rare phenomenon in Canada. But there are indications in the history that at specific moments there was an unprecedented merging of class institutions and perspectives, which produced organizational, political, and cultural ferment. To explore such activity, and to discover why it has been more intense at some moments than at others is one of the most difficult tasks before labour historians.

Part of the difficulty lies in the interpretive and historical divide that runs through our historiography, separating the history of the nineteenth century from that of the twentieth. These two periods have, for the most part, been studied by different kinds of historians. Nineteenth-century experience has been probed by those concerned with class, community, and, to a lesser extent, culture, while the twentieth century has been examined in terms of labour and the left (in its "syndicalist" face of the World War I years and its social democratic stance during the period of the Great Depression and the 1940s). So little is known of the explicitly cultural in the post-1900 years that it is impossible to make more than tentative statements in the discussion of such experience. Although historiographical developments have accentuated this rift, a part of its cause can be found in the history itself.

In earlier periods, workers lived far more localized and less commercialized lives than their more recent counterparts. Their politics, their unions, and their social and cultural experiences turned on community concerns and possibilities, and unfolded within specific settings. Later, by the 1920s, national markets, the presence of powerful North American states, monopoly capital, the potential expansion in consumer credit, and the rise of conspicuous consumption shifted workers' perspectives and moved labour in two complementary, if apparently divergent, directions. The class no longer lived in local communities, but in a larger, less personalized national or international community. At the same time, there was a retreat from the immediate community into the narrower unit of consumption represented by the family. In nineteenth-century workers' experience, family life was far more likely to have been integrated into neighbourhood activities and collective forms of working-class leisure than in the twentieth century, when the nuclear family probably became a haven, both psychological and consumer-oriented, in an increasingly alienating world.

But in the absence of any convincing discussion of this question and of countless others, it is necessary to proceed cautiously. There are, moreover, important discussions of organization and labour politics that can be used to address this twentieth-century experience. These facets of workers' lives may well have become more significant as the localized experiences of the nineteenth century gave way to the nationwide labour movements of the twentieth century. This is not to imply, of course, that labour's struggles to unionize and develop a political presence consumed, in its entirety, the experience of twentieth-century workers. Rather, they remained, as they had been in the nineteenth century (where they were undoubtedly weaker), but parts of a larger whole, and it is the understanding of this totality that is central. If it cannot yet be fully created because of immense gaps in our knowledge and conceptualization, we must nevertheless still try to gesture toward it, exploring the economic, institutional, political, and cultural experience of Canadian workers. This book attempts to suggest how this experience was forged, how the Canadian working class has been made and remade over the course of two centuries. In this rise and reconstitution of Canadian labour lies an interpretation of a part of our past and a suggestion of what must be attempted if the working class is again to reach toward its potential.

Chapter 1

Producing Classes, Paternalist Authority, 1800–1850

> Between the idea
> And the reality
> Between the motion
> And the Act
> Falls the Shadow
>
> T.S. Eliot,
> "The Hollow Men" (1925)

The Social Formation

The early history of the Canadian producing classes begins with the harvesters of the staples of fish and fur. Portuguese, Spanish, French, Irish, and English fishermen laboured to secure the cod that fed much of Catholic Europe and helped to keep the absolutist states of the seventeenth and eighteenth centuries financially afloat. Indian tribes hunted and bartered in the trade in furs that made the fortunes of European companies and American entrepreneurs. (It was estimated that by 1857 the Hudson's Bay Company had drawn £20,000,000 sterling in profit from the Canadas, while John Jacob Astor's yearly returns approached $500,000.) Finally, there were the voyageurs upon whose backs the Montreal and Quebec merchants relied, and who numbered approximately 2,500 between 1770 and 1820. Out of these experiences would be written the first paragraphs of resistance to authority and labour discipline, as well as introductory chapters in evolving relations of expropriation, exploitation, and subordination.

Such social relations of production extended into the nineteenth century, as did much of the history of craftsmen's associations and apprenticeship training in New France and shipyard labour in the port cities. However, the demise of the fish and fur empires occurred quite abruptly, and by the beginning of the nineteenth century, lumber and wheat had become the main staples of British North America. In New Brunswick, as Graeme Wynn has shown, a "timber colony" emerged, while wheat dominated central Canadian development. Outside the

Maritimes, and especially Newfoundland, where as late as 1857 those engaged in sealing and fishing comprised over 90 percent of the classifiable employed males, the years 1800 to 1850 saw the old staples give way to the new exports of square timber and wheat, both of which thrived under the protection of British mercantilist practice, but were forced into difficult years of readjustment, boom, and bust in the post-1846 repeal of the Corn Laws. Recent historical writing suggests that the "crisis on the land" in French Canada in these years has been overstated, but it would be foolish to dismiss the distress that characterized this period. As agriculture in Lower Canada stagnated under the seigneurial system and suffered further because of soil depletion, crop disease, escalating population pressure on the land, and decreasing wheat yields between 1802 and 1830, the timber trade helped to sustain an inherently unstable social structure in French Canada, and supplemented the expansive growth of the Upper Canadian and New Brunswick frontiers.

Imperial concerns over defending this developing region in the aftermath of the War of 1812, coupled with the transportation needs of the new staples, stimulated the improvement of the St. Lawrence rivers and lakes system of water transport, and between 1821 and 1848 a series of new and improved canals was completed. At Lachine (1821–48), Beauharnois (1842–45), Cornwall (1834–43), Williamsburg (1844–47), Chambly (1830–43), Rideau-Ottawa (1826–34), Welland (1824–29 and 1842–45) and other sites, canals were built, rebuilt, and enlarged.

The dimensions of such trade and construction were quite striking. The colonial debt accumulated through the creation of the canal system, which was completed in the 1840s at the precise moment that railways began to rival water transportation, approached £2,500,000 sterling. Wood exports from Quebec City were valued annually at between £600,000 and £871,000 sterling in the early 1830s (not a peak period), while at Saint John in 1826/27 the value of timber leaving the port was well over £230,000. Upper Canadian farmers shipped a total of 6,800,000 bushels of wheat and flour to Britain, the Maritimes, Quebec, and the United States at mid-century. On the east coast such activities were paralleled by the Halifax merchants' involvement in the trade in staples, their commercial connections to the West Indies and the United States, and their role in the construction of the Shubenacadie Canal.

These economic endeavours and public improvements turned on the demands of commercial capital as well as changing colonial imperatives. The extension of the market, in British North America, was thus a transatlantic process. Yet, ironically, its long-range implications and consequences would be more acute in Canada itself, where commerce and colonialism would sow the seeds of their own demise. For if the period prior to 1850 is justifiably regarded as the age of a predatory English commercialism brought internally to its knees in the 1840s, it was in these same years that the preconditions for an indigenous industrialism in the Canadas emerged. Prior to 1850, three distinct, but related, phenomena characterize the epoch as the culmination of a centuries-long prelude to Canada's Industrial Revolution: merchant capital, independent commodity production, and land policy laid the foundations for industrial capital's post-1850 surge.

The mercantile fortunes accumulated in the trade in staples sought speculative and investment outlets, searching for monopolistic advantage, but fostering the growth of productive capital and creating the internal development that would give rise to the basic structures of the home market. Hat manufacturing in Quebec City, of course, grew directly out of the fur trade. Even more dramatic was the case of shipbuilding, a logical extension of the timber trade, and a mammoth enterprise that employed over 3,350 workers in Quebec City alone in the peak production year of 1825. In its initial period of extended growth, as Richard Rice has shown, shipbuilding in the years 1809 to 1854 may have employed as many as one-quarter to one-half of the male workforce in Quebec city. One out of every five tons built in British North America over the course of the nineteenth century was constructed there, where large yards employed 180 to 190 hands, in contrast to the smaller concentrations of shipworkers in Saint John, along the Mirimachi River, or in the rude schooner and sloop-producing outports and rural yards of eastern Canada. Naval dockyards in Halifax and Kingston also produced ships, most notably at the latter locale during the War of 1812, when over a thousand "artificers" were recruited from Quebec and Great Britain to be transported to the Upper Canadian centre from 1813 to 1815.

Often the mercantile pursuit of development extended beyond a simple link to the traditional staples. In Halifax, commercial waterfront capital sought productive opportunity through the creation of the Stanyan Rope Works in 1826/27, where 21 Scottish immigrants found employment. Montreal businessmen, as Gerald Tulchinsky shows in *The River Barons*, exemplified this process, and Peter McGill, George Moffatt, Joseph Masson, James Ferrier, and the Molson family all embraced diverse economic interests during the first half of the century. Like these entrepreneurs from Montreal, Upper Canadians such as William H. Merritt in St. Catharines played a vital role in the construction of the St. Lawrence canal system. This, as much as any other factor, partially overcame some of the impediments blocking the creation of an integrated home market. Merchant capital, then, in varied ways and uncertainly, to be sure, provided one path to industrial development.

The second path was a more modest one. Independent commodity producers — saw and grist millers, carpenters, shoemakers, tailors, iron forgers, and others — captured local markets and expanded productive concerns. Apparently most pronounced in emerging industrial cities like Montreal, Toronto, and Hamilton, this rise of the independent commodity producer also occurred in a host of Upper Canadian communities from London in the west to Gananoque in the east. Battling restrictive mercantilist doctrine and practice, American competition, and chronic shortages of skilled labour in the early years, aspiring central Canadian capitalists operated in far from ideal circumstances in this pre-1850 period. A 1799 petition to establish an iron works in Chippewa, Upper Canada, commenced, "Your honours are knowing how difficult it will be to get labourers." Ephraim Jones promised to supply government demands for iron by constructing a foundry at Gananoque in 1815, but requested "that from the troops in this garrison I may have such mechanicks as the different departments can spare with a sufficient number of labourers." Technological advances, particularly the rise of machinery and steam engines in the post-1820 years, stimulated development, and by the 1840s capitalist handicraft production was established in metropolitan centres such as Toronto and Montreal. Upper Canadian manufactories of this period operated on a small scale and were concentrated in artisan trades such as cabinet making and foundry production of machinery, castings, and stoves. They seldom employed more than ten workers. A large paper mill in Belleville and the Cobourg woollen mill that employed 170 workers were exceptions, and in 1850 the average manufactory employed 3.32 workers. Of the 3,300 manufacturing establishments in Upper Canada at mid-century, 88 percent consisted of gristmills, sawmills, carding and fulling mills, woollen factories, distilleries, breweries, tanneries, foundries, and oat meal mills, collectively employing close to 10,000 hands, while the remaining 12 percent of productive enterprises employed about 1,300 workers in shingle, carriage, cabinet, and boot-and-shoe factories. Table 1.1 shows the average number of workers in these establishments in 1851. Out of these handicraft-dominated manufactories would emerge the fully mechanized, larger factories of the industrial age. Like merchant capital, independent commodity production provided a varied and uncertain path to capitalist development. Both paths to capitalist industrialization led, of course, to the burgeoning towns of the pre-1850 period, and it was there that the early producing classes were concentrated.

Yet developments in rural areas were not without a role to play. Upper and Lower Canada were approximately 85 percent rural at mid-century, but land policy and practice ensured that by the 1840s access to the land was restricted, forcing farm families on to increasingly constricted plots and newly arrived immigrants into wage labour.

The workforce thus obtained help to overcome barriers to the creation of a capitalistic labour market and was therefore essential to the economic development of the Canadas. This was not only a vital

TABLE 1.1   Industrial establishments and average number of workers in 1851, South-Central Canada West

	Employees per establishment	Establishments	Number of individual workers
Gristmills	3.5	283	990
Sawmills	2.4	756	2,570
Carding and fulling mills	1.7	56	151
Woollen factories	9.6	42	445
Distilleries	2.2	37	118
Tanneries	1.5	91	500
Foundries	14.6	34	530
Breweries	4.1	16	82
TOTAL		1,315	5,386

SOURCE: Jacob Spelt, *Urban Development in South-Central Ontario* (Reprinted with the permission of Carleton University Press), p. 74.

prerequisite to the large public-works projects of the canal era, it was also a central component in the emerging social relations of urban life (where servants were much in demand), in early manufacturing and construction, on the docks of a commercially oriented society, and in the fields and forests of a wheat-and-timber economy.

The barriers to effective land settlement emerged with stark swiftness from east to west. Agriculture and permanent settlement were discouraged in Newfoundland, where it was felt that ownership of the land would undermine allegiance to the fishery, threatening monopolistic profit and striking a blow at the training ground for the Empire's seamen. Settlement proceeded, but slowly and unevenly. The whole of Prince Edward Island was granted to a handful of absentee landlords in 1767, while extensive grants alienated significant tracts of suitable land in Nova Scotia and New Brunswick before 1800. Township granting and the longstanding practice of seigneurial tenure (not abolished until 1854) in Lower Canada contributed to an agricultural crisis that produced declining average farm sizes, a growing ratio of landless inhabitants to landowners, and population migration to the cities, the United States, and the barren lands of the northern shield. On the Upper Canadian frontier, a crisis on the land would not develop until well after 1840, but early speculators held much of the best land, while church and state each took their appropriate one-seventh of the province's acreage. Free land grants, originally designed to attract settlers, were turned back in 1826, assisted emigration efforts were curtailed, and immigrants and prospective landowners had to pay for their passages and purchase their lots. The rationale behind these moves was expressed in a speech by Lord Goderich, the Colonial Secretary, in 1831: "Without some division of labour, without a class of persons willing to work for wages, how can society be prevented from falling into a state of almost primitive rudeness, and how are the comforts and refinements of civilized life to be procured?''

By the mid-1830s, Goderich's insistence that "there should be in every society a class of Laborers as well as a class of Capitalists or Landowners" (echoing Edward Gibbon Wakefield's 1833 theory of "systematic colonisation") was bearing fruit: an irate Kingston mechanic complained in the midst of a severe depression that "country mechanics, like birds of passage, this summer are pouring into undertakers, working late and early for *twelve dollars a month* subject to be hired out again like slaves, to others at advanced wages — a degradation that the meanest bushwacker swaying an axe, who neither spent years nor months in practice or study of his calling seldom submits to.'' By 1851, in the rural areas of the Home District to the east of Toronto, some 10,172 out of 14,994 labouring-age males (67.8 percent) were landless, and wage rates had plummeted across the Canadas.

The early nineteenth-century social formation was therefore based on commercial capital structures that were undoubtedly a hegemonic and a social structure unquestioningly agricultural. At the same time, however, a manufacturing sector was coming into being and the process of class formation was underway. (See Table 1.2.) Such a perspective underscores the close link between town and country, and reveals the importance of the home market and of the early producing classes — aspects often obscured by the stress upon the mercantile and rural essence of Canadian society before 1850. Moreover, in approaching the social formation in this manner, we are led toward an understanding of the economic dislocations and political instability that influenced developments during the years from 1800 to 1850. Given these disruptive realities, what were the elements that helped to stabilize early Canadian society?

Paternalism

Few attempts have been made to come to grips with the character of social and productive relations in early Canada. Perhaps the only significant statement is that of the economic historian and labour economist H.C. Pentland, in his long-completed but only recently released *Labour and Capital in Canada*. Where Pentland's argument has particular force, and where it demands extension, is in the assertion that social relations before 1850 developed within a system of "status, hierarchies, symbols, privileges, and loyalties," where a particular style of leadership and coordination evolved out of an understanding that human motivation was a complex process reaching past the purely economic.

To look at the years 1800 to 1850 in this way is to argue that

TABLE 1.2 Occupational census, 1851

Population		Agricultural	Commercial	Domestic	Industrial	Professional	Not Classified
952,004	Upper Canada	86,637	9,297	18,013	44,950	6,798	80,773
890,261	Lower Canada	78,437	8,831	17,095	26,273	4,780	67,739
193,800	New Brunswick	18,601	1,292	—	8,276	456	11,113
276,854	Nova Scotia	31,604	7,728	—	22,819	556	—
14,112	Hamilton	82	517	608	1,645	228	782
30,775	Toronto	183	1,447	1,815	3,270	454	1,584
7,035	London	62	206	137	884	71	400
11,697	Kingston	47	606	785	1,292	186	706
7,760	Bytown	47	271	479	747	72	624
57,715	Montreal	40	2,458	1,622	4,659	451	1,333
42,052	Quebec City	86	1,571	1,323	3,604	458	1,387
38,475	Saint John (city & country)	764	720	—	3,166	87	3,713
39,914	Halifax (city & country)	2,099	1,117	—	4,191	132	—
25,587	Pictou County	3,463	418	—	1,387	41	—

SOURCE: *Census of Canada*, 1871, vol. 4 (Ottawa, 1876).

paternalism was the dominant form of social relationship. As a prevailing ethos that defined relations of superordination and subordination in an age of commercial capital and nascent industrialism, paternalism grew out of the necessity to justify exploitation and mediate inherently irreconcilable interests. It rationalized inequality and provided for a hierarchical order, but did so in diverse ways. In its historical manifestations, it included kindness and affection of superiors toward subordinates, as well as cruelty, harshness, and gross insensitivity. But paternalism's ultimate significance, regardless of its character, lay in undermining the collectivity of the oppressed by linking them to their "social superiors." This did not necessarily imply an absence of social, even overtly class, conflict, however, for not a little of the sustaining power of paternalism was its recognition of its Subject's humanity and of the master's responsibilities. Out of this could come resistance as well as accommodation.

The history of paternalism in British North America from 1800 to 1850 is thus a varied and complex one. Although it began to recede as bourgeois forms and capitalist structures encroached upon social and economic life, paternalism defined much of social relationships in this period. Regionally, it offered various faces, from the disgruntled seigneur displeased with his *censitaire's* disregard for authority to the oldest ship fisherman in a Newfoundland outport, who appropriated the title of "king" as a measure of his authority. Capable of benevolence when obeyed, paternalist figures were all too willing to revert to barbaric forms of repression.

At the St. Maurice forges, the aristocratic paternalism of a Scots "monarch", Mathew Bell, overcame the desultory habits of the French ironworkers originally imported from Burgundy. A tradition-bound, superstitious, quarrelling, bad-mannered, cursing lot, according to Benjamin Sulte, these immigrants were at first reluctant to succumb to Bell's authority and grieved about conditions and costs of provisions in the iron-producing community. But by providing "certain and uniform labour" and encouraging marriage among the imported craftsmen and local women, Bell guided his workers in the direction of stability. Eventually, the workers of St. Maurice sustained an insular community of "more than a thousand persons accustomed from their childhood to a particular branch of labour" and apparently contented with their lives. At the other end of the paternalist spectrum, the hatter Mathew Hall secured the imprisonment of a disobedient female apprentice, who was seven months pregnant. After nine years of service, Isabel Webster had violated her apprentice's agreement by committing fornication, which, along with playing at "Cards, Dice, or Tables," was one of the many activities outlawed for workers. While Hall's reaction was anything but fatherly, his legal rights were eminently patriarchial.

Such examples of paternalist practices, both malign and charitable, could be reproduced extensively, and they drew their meaning not so much from the isolated instances of rebellion and resistance as from the cultivation of a notion that authority was constituted in the hands of people who were born to rule or who had earned the right to rule. To be sure, when that rule was exercised poorly, a price was paid in open discontent. More often than not, however, dissatisfaction with the paternalist right to rule led to negotiation, rather than aggressive challenge in these pre-1850 years.

As work commenced on the Lachine Canal in July 1821, a celebration was held in which French and Irish labourers were treated to a dressed ox and plenty of beer, allowed to brawl harmlessly, and sent on their way so that the contractors and local gentlemen could retire to a nearby inn for their own ample dinner. Such a ceremonial beginning (or ending) to a construction project was commonplace and reinforced a sense of the social structure, leaving no room for doubt as to the particular responsibilities of masters and men. Almost three decades later, 150 carpenters met in Saint John in 1849 to give "three hearty cheers . . . to the British Ship Owners" and to establish the ten-hour day. The hours of labour were a more substantial claim than a piece of meat and a barrel of beer, and the ship carpenters, craftsmen with the bargaining power provided by a commercial boom, were in a better position to extract concessions than a heterogeneous group of unskilled labourers. But their cheers for their employers hinted that they, too, lived within the paternalist confines of connection and separation.

In Upper Canada, a society hierarchically ordered since the first settlement of the 1780s, the paternalist structures were of three discrete sorts: economic, political, and socio-cultural (ethnic and religious). At root a noneconomic legitimation of economic ends, Upper Canadian paternalism expressed itself within its society's three critical sectors: merchant capital, petty production, and landed property.

It was, of course, strongest when all these sectors were interconnected, as in the case of the Garden Island timbering community at the junction of Lake Ontario and the St. Lawrence River. There, the merchant-manufacturer "Governor" Dileno Dexter Calvin built an empire that encompassed timbering, shipbuilding, merchandising, lake and river towing, freighting, and salvaging, employing approximately 300 settled and highly skilled workmen and an equal number of transient (often Indian or French Canadian) raftsmen. Calvin's enterprises commenced in 1836, founded on monopolistic control of the St. Lawrence and the trade in hardwood, and came to a close in the late nineteenth century with his death in 1884. Fervently opposed to unions, drink, and ostentatious living, Calvin concerned himself with all aspects of life on "his" island, where he was patron, employer, employee, and neighbour, the spiritual leader and first citizen of a self-enclosed community that knew few of the divisions of race, ethnicity, status, and religion so common in the early nineteenth century. Cash was seldom needed, accounts being settled "on the books." With wages authoritatively established by Calvin's concerned hand, and goods and services (food, lodging, banking, education, and health care) dispensed according to his judgment of need, Calvin was lord of a 65-acre timbering manor. Workers remained with him for their entire lives, as did their children and grandchildren, who, like their fathers and mothers, shared in the company profits on a small scale. Three generations of sailmakers worked for the Governor. Calvin's arbitrary dislikes (which extended to dogs and short men) and unquestioned authority (manifesting itself in charges for lost or broken tools), as well as the gruelling pace of work dictated by the seasonal arrival of ships, meant that Garden Island was no haven for the small of stature, the independent minded, or the work shy. But his paternalist practices succeeded because they provided a continuity and security that proved attractive. When an American visitor stopped at the island in the 1870s, he noted that life "seemed saturated in traditions and memories" and spoke of a "simple well-ordered village where employers and workmen dwelt together and in the government of which they co-operated in harmony."

One part of the loyalties elicited by Calvin's paternalism was his visible involvement in all work operations and social events: he could be seen captaining river tugboats, shaping morality in the local Baptist church, or advocating temperance in the island's Mechanics' Hall. Familiarity bred respect for authority, rather than contempt. In workshops across the country, this same kind of bond was reproduced on a smaller scale. The intimacy of handicraft production and the promise of mobility up the ladder of craftsmanship — from apprentice to journeyman to master — strengthened the ties between employers and workers. Houses built to accommodate working families, and the staging of festivals, dinners, and parades championing the virtues of producers reinforced such tendencies.

Paternalist figures like Calvin may have exerted considerable influence by controlling access to work, but in other settings it was an uncompromising grip on property itself, in the form of land, that was paramount. Colonel Thomas Talbot, settler of the St. Thomas-London area, was a typical landed paternalist. Known as the "Baron," Talbot used his land as a final bargaining tool, granting it freely to incoming settlers, but retaining ultimate control, merely pencilling in settlers' names on a survey, so that they could later be erased at his whim. Gruff and unconcerned with commercial activities or administrative functions at York, he projected the style of the eighteenth-century gentry. Like Bishop John Strachan at York, who toured with a ponderous state coach, valet, and elegant casette with a dozen glasses, out of which the finest wines were ceremoniously drunk, Talbot was capable of using an impersonal commodity like drink to reflect the paternalist ethos and its firm understanding of social place. Those who bought their liquor by the barrel, rather than the jar, and those who took their spirits with style and couth, rather than debauched indiscipline, lived their superiority. This kind of ritualized display of authority was coupled with occasional and well-placed acts of kindness, awe, and respect. Talbot ruled his "principality" for over 30 years.

In an age characterized by the dominance of merchant capital, paternalism also reached beyond petty production and the estate to embrace wider constituencies. On large public projects such as the construction of the Niagara dockyards, the passing of Sir John Colborne in a steamboat might draw a salute from the works, followed "by the cheers of about 200 workmen, mechanics and others employed thereon." *The Long Point Advocate* (Simcoe), reported an 1842 meeting of the mechanics of the Talbot district that ended with a toast to the Queen, Sir Charles Bagot, and themselves:

> May commerce flourish, troubles cease,
> And Tradesmen smoke their pipes in peace.

Kingston mechanics, in closing an 1841 address to Charles Poulett Thomson, the future Lord Sydenham, expressed hope that "all classes will unite with your Excellency in placing the Government . . . upon such a firm basis that it cannot be shaken from the affections of the People and an unwavering allegiance to Her Majesty's Throne."

Such ideological and social relations reveal how economic forms of paternal authority were inseparable from the whole context of political rule. Indeed, across the Canadas, paternalism functioned not simply as an outgrowth of economic relations, but as a political practice. While even dissident political figures might be advised to follow the paternalist "guidelines" — one controversial candidate for office was advised in an 1806 election to "have Liquor in some convenient spot for the people to drink (and perhaps something to eat)" — it was in Tory circles that paternalism worked its forms, language, and consequences most obviously. It is true that no uniform Toryism existed before 1850. This was a period of faction, rather than party, and forms of paternalism varied according to the different socio-economic contexts from which they emerged. A strident and bureaucratized official culture developed early in the administrative Tory stronghold of York, where a small but influential military-administrative élite began to take control of Upper Canadian society.

Outside York, other Tory strongholds emerged, often more secure in their paternal authority because they were more firmly rooted in their particular locales. Such settings moulded diverse paternalist forms, but all had certain political functions in common. Tories were meant to be elected, and elected they often were. In the 1860s, a descendant of D.D. Calvin noted that all his grandfather's workmen "wisely voted

Conservative," and a Liberal vote on the island was a sure sign that "there was a newcomer in the village." Talbot, too, exercised a similar pervasive and deeply embedded political authority. Rarely forced to intervene actively in elections, he was capable of replying to challenge with an unveiled power that usually secured its intended end. In 1812, for instance, a dissident Methodist lay preacher named Benjamin Mallory defied the Colonel and opposed his candidate. Talbot managed to have the polls set up a mere 60 miles from his opponent's home. After Mallory and his supporters tramped through the woods to the hustings they found "the 'Father of the Settlement' providing votes for his favourite with as much expedition as the Yankee's manufacture their cut nails — by furnishing all who were willing to support the claims of the Young Aspirant to office and who were not already qualified — with Location Tickets [an informal granting of the right to use land that did not establish legal title]." In the 1836 election, one pensioner was asked who he voted for. "How the devil do I know . . . when the Colonel is not here to tell me," he replied. Variations on these themes were common in the 1820s and 1830s as Tory factions competed for the support of their plebeian constituencies, rolling the rum and whiskey barrels into the streets or mounting the platform to put the wheels of the Orange Order in motion. By the early 1830s, with the Reform threat a decade old, the Orangemen were being used to ride roughshod over all comers, and in constituencies like Leeds–Grenville, every electoral contest in the years 1833 to 1836 saw riotous Orangemen clash with those standing in opposition to the local compact.

So pervasive was the authority of local compacts that there is a danger of regarding the Canadas in this period as a "one-class society," and in discussions of power and privilege during these years that conclusion is drawn all too often. But a complete examination of historical events reveals that paternalist authority was not always accepted as part of the natural order. In fact, paternalist influence was often achieved through negotiation. Deference to authority was there, but so too were polite, and not so polite, demands. In the midst of widespread opposition to the Kingston Penitentiary's practice of teaching inmates craft skills and marketing their wares, thereby undermining honest labour and glutting the local market with shoddy goods, one Tory leader wrote to another to assure him that, Christopher "Hagerman ha[d] made all right here with the Mechanics and is sure of his election." When Cornwall canallers, known for their riotous behaviour, settled into a "very orderly and quiet mannered" posture, a special Act of the House of Assembly provided for their winter relief and 632 of their number were employed throughout the off-season, rather than being dismissed in the usual peremptory fashion. Paternalism responded to the tug at its arm or the poke in its face as much as it noted the bowed head and the doffed cap.

A final aspect of the paternalist presence in early Canada is even more amorphous than the diverse manifestations of economic and political forms and substance. Turning on an ethnocultural axis, this paternalism could work within the parameters of order and hierarchy as defined by the official culture, or it could march defiantly against it. Ogle Gowan's Orangeism (which claimed 11,000 to 12,000 members in the early 1830s), for instance, while ultimately pressed into service for the Tory cause, united Irish Protestants, among them mechanics and labourers, in ways that disrupted local élites, social order, and political authority. Priests among the Scots Catholics of Glengarry or the Irish Catholic canallers were often a stabilizing force, imposing their own authority in the face of the obvious weaknesses of a removed and Anglican Toryism. And in the Ottawa Valley, minor skirmishes between French Canadian and Irish raftsmen escalated in the 1830s into the Shiners' Wars. Orchestrating the every move of these seemingly uncontrollable Irish timberers was their patrician "King," Peter Aylen, defender of the oppressed Irish race at the same time that he was lining his own pockets with the surplus he extracted from their overworked hides. He would eventually move the Shiners beyond brawls on the river banks and into the very arena's of symbolic authority, defying the staid and outraged Bytown gentry. Led by Aylen, the Shiners terrorized local residents, disrupted the annual meeting of the Bytown Horticultural Society, and forced a split in the ranks of the local magistrates. Ultimately driven back, and abandoned by the opportunistic Aylen, the Shiners raised the spectre of social disorder. These and other developments indicate that where Tory compacts could not sustain paternalism through economic and political means, others might well step into the breach, playing upon ethnic and religious loyalties to weave together their own small organic communities.

In all of this, paternalism was one part self-conscious creation by the merchants, independent producers, and landed gentry, and one part negotiated acceptance by the various plebeian subjects of the producing classes. But these two parts did not constitute the whole. Paternalism was reinforced by the material constraints of the social formation that had spawned it. For much of paternalism's sustaining power lay in the unique economics, politics, and culture of each locality in early Canadian society. Paternal authority gained strength from physical separation, diverse subeconomies, and the realities of wielding power in an age that predated the establishment of a powerful state, welfare services, and an impersonal labour market. Equally significant was the social fragmentation that ensured that this very same authority would not be challenged decisively, either through class conflict or in the political arena. It must not be forgotten, however, that the paternalism briefly sketched above was in constant evolution, adapting to social and economic change. And although localism and social fragmentation dominated life in the early nineteenth century, trends toward greater unity did exist. Paternalism was an ethos marking time; the men who practised it, a passing breed. In bringing about the demise of paternalism, the emergence of class division in society and the resulting tensions and conflicts would not be an unimportant factor.

Divergent Cultures, Convergent Experiences

Workers during the pre-1850 years were hardly a unified class. They lacked self-definition and clarity of purpose; their organizations, when they did exist, were immature and locally based, although they could, on occasion, appeal to trade groupings across the country. Attached to their craft, their religion, their ethnic experience, perhaps even to their city, town, or region, workers in this period remained part of a broad amalgam cut off from the paternalist élite, but isolated within various social classifications that ranged from age, gender, and status (apprentices, female labourer, journeymen), to style of life (rough and respectable). Fragmentation, rather than collectivity and solidarity, was at the centre of daily labouring life in the early Canadas. Whole cultures were created anew out of the social formation of the epoch. Canallers from the destitute farms of French Canada or the villages and fields of Cork, Connaught, and Munster huddled in temporary shanties along the Lachine and Welland canals, they and their families numbering in the hundreds or thousands. At the same time, the shipwrights of countless small yards exhibited a settled continuity that embraced generations. Out of such divergent cultures, no clear and categorical class experience could emerge, and it is therefore impossible to compile a history of the working class in this period. Instead, we will look at the varied histories of components of the producing classes.

These histories, with their particularities of region and status, were rooted in material circumstances. Robert Tremblay has found that in Montreal in the years 1790–1830, the producing classes were stratified according to level of earning power. At the top of the wage hierarchy were skilled tradesmen and river pilots who commanded sufficient wages to keep them among the best-paid workers in the city. But well below them was a stratum of voyageurs, domestics, and day labourers, among whom could be found a high proportion of immigrants, unskilled workers, women, and children. Tremblay suggests that in a sample of approximately 430 Montreal workers, 20 percent earned less than £2 monthly, 61 percent between £2 and £5, 14 percent between £5 and £10, and 5 percent over £10. Those whose wages fluctuated around £2 monthly obviously lived in a situation of advanced poverty, expending 60 percent of their income on food and the remaining 40 percent on lodging, clothing, and health, but the select few with incomes exceeding £10 a month faced little of this financial pressure and insecurity. The social structure of mid-nineteenth century Hamilton, studied in detail by Michael Katz, reveals a comparable social ordering. Of the 342 labourers in the city, 75.5 percent were among the poorest residents, while less than 1 percent of such unskilled workers accumulated sufficient wealth to place them among the upper 20 percent of Hamilton's well-to-do. But among tradesmen like printers and bakers, the upper ranks were more easily attained, approximately 30 percent achieving this status. Forty-four percent of the bakers were also among the city's poor, however, indicating that even within a single trade the range of possibilities was wide, extending from employing and property-owning craftsmen to journeymen and apprentices. While Hamilton's 100 machinists, masons, and molders were never as poverty-stricken as labourers, neither were they likely to join the rich: more than 40 percent of these mechanics were among the city's poor in 1851, while less than 5 percent of their number achieved significant wealth.

Wage differentials were thus a fundamental feature of early Canadian class experience, dividing labourers from craft workers. Gender and age also figured strongly in such hierarchies, the worst-paid labour being that provided by women and children. If male labourers could never expect much more than half the wage of the skilled craftsman (and often less, especially when board, lodging, or military compulsion were involved), female servants were even more badly off. When, in 1840, farm labourers in the Toronto area were reportedly receiving 3 shillings/9 pence, female cooks' wages hovered around 2 shillings/5 pence while domestics were paid a mere 2 shillings. Over the course of the first half of the nineteenth century, moreover, servants' wages dropped (as did male labourers' from the 1820s to the 1840s) from 3 shillings/6 pence to 2 shillings/6 pence. Robert Gourlay, agitator and early critic of the Upper Canadian élite, reported that female servants could expect from 20 to 30 shillings a month, plus board and lodging, in 1818. By the 1830s, however, newspaper reports indicated a decline to 15 to 20 shillings, a rate that would not rise appreciably higher in the 1840s. The daily mason in Quebec earned 7 shillings in 1845, the cooper in Hamilton, $2.00 in 1840, and the miner in Albion Mines, Pictou County, received 10 shillings during the 1840s. But even these meagre wages were beyond the reach of the Irish canaller struggling throughout the 1840s to keep his wage up to 2 shillings/6 pence in the face of employer reductions. They were even farther beyond the reach of the dairy women of Ottawa, who received 1 shilling/1 pence, or of Toronto, who earned 2 shillings. Semiskilled female labour — dressmakers and milliners — managed only an average of 2 shillings/6½ pence across Upper Canada in 1840, and in Portsmouth (near Kingston), women toiling in the shirt and stay-making industries were said to be subjected to "female slavery . . . to the manifest detriment of the poor rates and the morals of [those] employed." Of the young "advantageously hired

TABLE 1.3   Daily wage rates (shillings/pence) for unskilled labour and craft workers (carpenters), 1800–1850

Occupation	Date	Rate	Place
1. Labourers	1809	1/3	Amherstburg, U.C.
(military)	1809	0/9	Amherstburg, U.C.
(surveyor's)	1810	1/6	York
(military)	1812	0/10	Quebec
(surveyor's)	1815	2/6	York
(farm harvest)	1818	5/0	Western District, U.C.
(farm harvest)	1818	3–5/0	Eastern District, U.C.
(day)	1820	2/6–3/9	Upper Canada
(canaller)	1826	2/3	Rideau
(canaller)	1832	3/0	Rideau
(day)	1840	3/6–4/0	Kingston
(farm)	1840	3/8½	Average Upper Canada
(canaller)	1843	2/0–2/6	Lachine-Beauharnois
2. Carpenters	1809	5/0 + rum	Amherstburg, U.C.
	1818	7/9	Average Upper Canada
(foreman)	1826	7/6	Upper Canada
(canal foreman)	1832	7/6	Rideau
	1840	6/11¾	Average Upper Canada
	1845	5/6	Quebec

out" but not formally apprenticed, we know little. In the mines of Pictou County, boys might make as much as 3 shillings a day if they were over 14 years of age, but a mere 1 shilling/6 pence if between 12 and 14. In Lower and Upper Canada and in the port cities of the Maritimes, they undoubtedly worked for much less, when and if they could find paid employment. Table 1.3 shows regional and occupational variations in wages earned.

Such differences separated skilled from unskilled, male from female, and child from adult, although the collective wages of family members, a not uncommon necessity in this age, could bring these strata together in the face of common need. Among the skilled group, of course, there was also fluctuation, but generally it was not great. The more obvious wage differential was regional, for subeconomies existed in specific locales, where population concentrations, agricultural specialization, labour demands, and stages of economic development all varied, creating wide discrepancies in the cost of living. This is revealed most dramatically in an average wage ratio compilation for selected occupations in the various districts of Upper Canada in 1840. Constructed by Leo Johnson, this data indicates that if the provincial average was set at 100, wage rates would have fluctuated from a low of 87 in Ottawa to a high of 111 in Niagara. Such a static picture, of course, does not take into account important variations over time, and especially early in the century labour scarcity often pushed wages up to unprecedented levels. Even seasonal adjustments widened the range of rates. Not only were wages different among various sectors of the producing classes, then, but they also differed markedly from place to place, and changed over time. In the absence of precise data on the cost of living — over time and across regions and subregions — differences in wage rates cannot be easily interpreted. They do, however, point to marked separations among various strata of the labouring people.

If there were divergent material realities within the producing classes sufficient to warrant recognition of a variety of cultures, there were also commonalities of experience that appear to be important. Many workers, isolated in their own trades or callings and locales, had similar experiences, but geographical separation prevented them from recognizing the fact. All workers, as Judith Fingard has shown, were subjected to the seasonal work stoppages and harsh winter climate that led to wintertime poverty and hardship for British North American workers. The growing incursions of the market and the beginnings of an impersonal and exploitative division of labour took its toll on canaller and petty producer, dispossessed habitant and youthful apprentice. In Montreal, manufacturing nailers, hatters, and founders brought employees together by creating specialized divisions of labour as early as the second decade of the nineteenth century, and even in highly traditional work spheres such as the Gaspé fisheries, villagers from St. Thomas (near Quebec) were orchestrated into discrete work routines of cutting, salting, and packing. Paternalism may have played off old divisions and entrenched allegiances for a time in settings like these, but the gathering of large numbers of workers on the impersonalized canal sites of the 1830s and 1840s was a precursor to the collectivization of labour that marked future productive relations.

Out of converging experiences would come the first recognition of class structure and of common discontents. Manifested in desertions, turn-outs, riots, worker organization, and other collective efforts, the grievances of the producing classes first made themselves felt in the years from 1800 to 1850. The voice of the labouring poor emerged in a petition circulated in Merrickville, Upper Canada, in June 1837: "The Monopoly being Enjoyed by the owners of Mills in this place is such as to cause General Dissatisfaction and in the present state of the country, the poor destitute inhabitants have greatly suffered through want of bread, when at the same time, there was plenty at the above mills . . . and the owners would not sell in small quantities for the accommodation of the poor, even for money." In the early history of Canada's producing classes, the shocked indignation of this settler would be reproduced in diverse and diverging contexts. As the moral economy of the paternalist order deteriorated to the point that bread itself was hoarded for profit, a conception of class distinctions began to be formed among those various groups who provided the human material fashioning the country's first generation of workers.

The Irish and Others: Some Quantities

Canadian workers, like all workers, had to be recruited, a process that entailed an unusual amount of disruption and displacement. Unlike the English experience, for instance, Canadian labour recruitment involved much more than severing the peasantry from the land. It was premised upon an original expropriation, the aboriginal peoples having been subjected to a three-centuries-long contact with Europeans that culminated in the obliteration of their way of life. Ravaged by disease, liquor, the cultural disruption of superior technologies, and religious imports, Indian peoples suffered severe dislocations and depopulation. Reduced to a state of dependency by 1850, they were, for the most part, marginalized, and over the course of the nineteenth century were shunted into increasingly restricted areas within the reserve system.

Canada's first producers were therefore Indian, but its first working class was not. Workers were instead drawn from the ranks of English Canadian farmers and, more importantly, from European fields and factory towns, the United States to the south, and the distressed, subdivided rotures of the St. Lawrence seigneuries.

English and Scots immigrants provided one early source of labour, especially the Highland Scots, the most important group prior to 1816, when perhaps 10,000 had come to the Canadas. Of these, approximately 5,000 remained, the rest departing for the United States. After 1816, the English became more numerous, and 5,000 to 10,000 arrived yearly at the port of Quebec between 1823 and 1850, although many would, once more, find their way to the cities and farms of the United States. In Nova Scotia, the Scots remained the predominant immigrant stream; 22,000 landed there between 1815 and 1838, and many of these went to Cape Breton. Such figures are rough measures at best, and the statistics do not allow for much precision. Nor do they tell us much about the nature of the migrations, and even basic occupational information is lacking. A small sample of British immigrants directed to Upper Canada from New York by James Buchanan from 1817 to 1819 indicates a preponderance of farmers (one-third), and significant numbers of labourers (slightly less than one-twelfth), blacksmiths, carpenters, masons, tailors, and weavers. By mid-century, such English and Scots immigrants comprised approximately 36 percent of the more than 400,000 British-born in Upper and Lower Canada.

If we are to believe the reports of chagrined landowners and other paternalist figures, such English and Scots migrants easily adapted to the ways of the other significant immigrant group, the Americans. In fact, it is likely that American ideas and social practice had such influence on the new immigrants simply because of the vast numbers of Americans crossing the border to the Canadas. In the late eighteenth century, United Empire Loyalists had settled in Nova Scotia, Prince

Edward Island, New Brunswick, the Eastern townships of old Quebec, and the western frontier of Upper Canada. Before the War of 1812, thousands of so-called "late loyalists" crashed the Canadian landmarket, taking advantage of available plots. It is estimated that by 1815 there were more than 100,000 American-born inhabitants in Upper and Lower Canada; they accounted for as much as 80 percent of the English-speaking population. Many of these early immigrants settled on the land, but free movement across the border ensured that mechanics and labourers of American background remained a presence in certain locales, especially the expanding Upper Canadian towns. One anonymous observer thought that this American presence accounted for much of the political turmoil of the period, writing to the lieutenant-governor that "The very chips of democracy are those Mechanicks from the United States. . . . And no sooner do they arrive here than they list the Corps of rebellious miscreants and sow the seeds of discord and disaffection and were it not for them, the faction of which Mackenzie, Ryerson, and Bidwell are the heads would have died away long since." This conception of American influence was also evident in a newspaper's reaction when the clerks of Kingston initiated a shorter-hours campaign in 1837. (Workers in Cobourg and Belleville also sought regulation of their hours in these years.) The sarcastic rebuke of the press ran as follows:

> Whereas it has been further represented that the above recited graceless proceedings . . . have been originated by certain calculating Yankees, for the purposes of propagating and disseminating in this our loyal town the pernicious, treasonable, and democratical doctrines of Atheism, Republicanism, and Revolution . . . NOW KNOW YE, . . . all shops and warehouses be closed at those hours only, which their respective proprietors may themselves select.

American workmen were obviously regarded as a troublesome lot, given to independence of action and riotous celebration of the 4th of July: Gananoque tanners in 1816 and Norfolk ironworkers in 1825 were but two groups reprimanded for such behaviour.

Another source of labour recruitment was the natural increase of the *canadien* population, descendants of the indentured labourers, soldiers, salt smugglers, and marriageable women from the orphanages and brothels of France who had emigrated to the Canadas before 1760. These provided the demographic basis of the *habitant* class, which began to be driven from the land during the agricultural crisis of the post-1815 years. As early as 1800, Kingston-area farmers were hiring French Canadian harvest help, and many raftsmen were drawn from agricultural areas that could no longer support the entire farming population. As Fernand Ouellet has shown, rural communities "ceased to be simple pastoral collectivities led by curés and seigneurs," and the fragmentation of farms consolidated a rural proletariat. As conditions worsened in the years after 1820, many habitants were driven to the New England milltowns, but this migration was essentially a post-1860 phenomenon, as many as 500,000 French Canadians escaping to the United States in the years from 1860 to 1890. Far less momentous were the migrations to the Eastern Townships and the northern shield. All told, throughout the 1840s, French Canadian population movement to these destinations could not have exceeded 4,000 per year, and the drift to the cities did not begin in any numbers until after mid-century. This is confirmed in examinations of the social structure of Montreal and Quebec in the pre-1850 years. While both the Montreal and Quebec districts contained large percentages of landless rural labourers in 1842 (38 percent and 28 percent, respectively), the French-speaking percentage of the producing classes was actually declining over time, the competition of immigrant labour exerting pressures that helped to keep many of these rural workers on the land. Having once constituted the majority of the producing classes (51 percent in 1831), Montreal's French-speaking workers had been reduced to a minority (42 percent) 11 years later. As unpublished research by Joanne Burgess suggests, certain Montreal trades, like shoemaking, might actually have reversed this trend toward British dominance, but it is unlikely that this situation prevailed across the crafts. Thus, in spite of a surplus of low-paid, impoverished French Canadian workers, they remained at best a secondary or tertiary source of labour recruitment.

The group that provided the most awesome numbers to the newly developing class of producers was the Irish. Comprising anywhere from 47 percent to 85 percent of the total number of immigrants landing at Quebec and Montreal between 1817 and 1847, the Irish stocked the labour pool of early Canadian society. As Terrence Punch has shown in an unpublished study of the Irish in Halifax, they comprised approximately 40 percent of the city's producing classes in 1838, *before* the famine migrations of the late 1840s. Fully 55 percent of the city's labourers, 77 percent of its servants, and 85 percent of its truckmen were Irish in 1838, and among the skilled, the number of Irish, although less, was also substantial: between 20 and 25 percent of Halifax's carpenters, hatters, masons, shoemakers, and tailors were Irish in 1838. As Katz has shown, Irish Catholics were a significant presence in Hamilton, Canada West, in the same period. They made up 24.1 percent of the city's skilled artisans and a majority of its labourers (57 percent). In Montreal, the Irish numbered over 9,500 in 1844, congregated in working-class neighbourhoods such as "Little Dublin" and "Griffintown," establishing themselves in key work sectors like canal labouring and carting.

Many have studied the movement of the Irish into the Canadas in the years before 1850, but the most significant findings are those of Donald Akenson, an Irish historian who has systematically delineated the dimensions of the migration, differentiating the prefamine migrations from the famine-induced migration of 1846–54, clarifying the religion (Protestant or Catholic) of the migrants, and tracing their Upper Canadian destinations. From 1815 to 1845 the flow of Irish immigrants was closely related to the economic cycles associated with the timber trade, and by 1842, 27.6 percent of the population of Upper Canada was Irish or born in Canada of Irish parents. The famine migrations commenced in 1846, with 104,518 destitute Irish landing in Canada in 1847, causing an upheaval that rocked the social structure of Upper Canada. Akenson has established that the majority of the impoverished Irish who found their way to Upper Canada settled in rural areas. As late as 1861, 75 percent of the Irish lived on the land or in small villages. It is nevertheless clear that the Irish (and especially Irish Catholics) provided the sheer numbers and raw muscle of an impersonal, urban-based labour market. While Irish Catholics comprised only 18.59 percent of the total Upper Canadian population in 1851, they made up 34.49 percent of the urban population. And in the cities they were likely to be found among the poorest people. Katz notes that between 1851 and 1861, for instance, the economic status of Irish Catholics in Hamilton deteriorated greatly, the percentage among the poorest 20 percent of the population more than doubling from 20.1 to 44.6.

Although the cities may not have been the main destination of Upper Canadian Irish immigrants, the Irish, and especially the Roman Catholics, were thus vital to the cities. In Halifax, where access to Nova Scotia's farms had long since been closed, baptismal registers from 1827 to 1847 suggest that a mere 5 percent of the Irish headed for the land, while 48.3 percent remained in Halifax and 46.7 percent migrated to the "Boston states." Had they been able to find their way to New Brunswick, they might have fared better, but a study of Charlotte County reveals that while Irish Protestants represented 54 percent of all farmers in 1861, the Irish Catholic percentage was much less — about 28 percent. And to be on the land was not necessarily to be propertied, especially in the case of Catholic immigrants. While Irish Protestants constituted 15 percent of the landless labourers, Catholics made up a far greater proportion, at 43 percent.

In Lower Canada, where the seigneurial system and loyalist settlements in the Eastern Townships imposed some restrictions on the choices before Irish immigrants, the Irish would have been more likely to gravitate to urban centres, and especially to Montreal. As Akenson shows, the Irish in Upper Canada were able to secure land, especially if they were Protestant, but arriving precisely at the moment when Upper Canadian agriculture was itself on the verge of a crisis, with declining wheat yields and increasing population pressures on the land, the famine Irish would likely have led a precarious existence. Many would be dependent on marginal holdings or seasonal wage labour: if not themselves recruited to unskilled labour, their children likely would be.

Across the Canadas, then, the Irish became a major presence among the early Canadian labouring poor. This was especially true in the cities, where the Irish comprised 37 percent, 32 percent, and 35 percent of the populations of Toronto, Hamilton, and Halifax in 1851.

Apprenticeship

Before the Irish appeared on the Canadian scene in great numbers, urban newspapers often carried advertisements offering rewards for apprentices who had deserted their masters. Apprenticeship was a binding relation, in which both master and apprenticed youth had established rights and responsibilities. The nineteenth-century legal agreement remained substantially unaltered in form from its eighteenth-century antecedents. A typical turn-of-the century agreement would have seen a widowed mother or a father bind son or daughter to be taught a said "Trade, Science, Or Occupation," to "dwell continue and serve" with a particular master for a set period of time (anywhere from three to ten years) or until the age of 21 years. Moreover, the apprentice was to keep the craftsman's "secrets and trade commands" and not to "imbezil or waste" the master's goods nor suffer him to be wronged. In addition to these work-related responsibilities, the apprentice could not commit fornication, contract matrimony, haunt taverns or playhouses, frequent dice tables, play cards, secure unlawful gains, or absent him/herself without the master's leave. These duties fulfilled, the apprentice was to be "well and sufficiently taught and instructed," provided with meat, drink, washing, lodging, apparel, and all other necessities, in sickness and in health. An additional suit of clothes, "as is fit and usual for such an Apprentice," was to be provided, and masters might be legally responsible for fines levied against mischievous apprentices. At the completion of his or her time (when all days lost to absence, misconduct, or negligence had to be made good), the apprentice might expect a parting gift of clothing, tools, or money.

Recent studies of apprenticeship by Jean-Pierre Hardy and David-Thiery Ruddell (Quebec City) and Pierre H. Audet (Montreal) indicate that changes in work relations were underway as early as the period from 1790 to 1815. A once highly personalized form of craft training and work organization was becoming impersonal, giving rise to discontent among apprentices. One measure of this was the rising number of desertions. More than 200 young apprentices deserted their Quebec masters in these years, while in Montreal the number of desertions rose appreciably after 1805. In Upper Canada, as well, newspapers regularly offered rewards for escaped apprentices, with servants, tailors, carpenters, labourers, and shoemakers taking to their heels. Despite the formalities of apprenticeship, it was clear that paternal authority was not without opposition.

This opposition proceeded from the escalating economic rationality of these years, as apprenticeship became less craft training supplemented by moral and educational supervision and more a form of bound labour. As masters accumulated capital, stepped up production demands because of market considerations, and hired increasing numbers of apprentices to do the heavy and often unskilled labour needed in the shop, apprentices began to see only the tyranny of their obligations and grew resentful of the master's failure or refusal to fulfill his responsibilities adequately. Signs of this deterioration in the master-apprentice relationship were readily apparent by the turn of the century and were even more obvious by 1810.

New forms of apprenticeship would emerge in the post-1860 years as new skills came into being and international craft unions formed around them. Printing, for instance, would point to the way of the future as early as the 1830s. But the essentially eighteenth-century form of apprenticeship, although surviving into the nineteenth century, was a traditional practice about to be superseded by the new social formation of the 1800–1850 years. At Halifax, in 1845, a record of indenture marked this transformation of the apprenticeship agreement:

> I agree with the consent of my father Robert Cose to serve Messrs. Temple & Lewis Piers from the first day of June 1845 till the first day of June 1851 and to be obedient to their commands, conducting myself in a sober honest and respectful manner, and to be obedient to the Foreman of their Rope Works, or to any person under him who may have authority to direct me. It being understood that I am to have the privilege of learning to spin before the expiration of the above term, and that I am to be paid for my services at the following rates, viz: 5/a week till the 1st day of June 1846 . . . 18/a week to 1 June 1851. Said Piers being bound by this Agreement, while they continue the manufacturing of Cordage, provided I conduct myself to their satisfaction.

Witness	"James Cose"
"Alex Carson"	"Robert Cose"
[Foreman]	"T. & L. Piers"

Masters thus began to exempt themselves from responsibilities and traditional apprenticeship was replaced with a more market-oriented variant. The protections once offered by masters disappeared, but the proprietary and authoritative aspects of apprenticeship remained.

The Respectable

Young apprentices reacted to this deteriorating paternalist order and its waning sense of responsibility with acts of individualistic rebellion. Desertion was one part of this process, dissolute behaviour yet another, way of challenging the master's attempt to retain total control over the

TABLE 1.4   Partial list of early Canadian unions

Date	Craft	Place
1798	Carpenters	Halifax
1813	Miscellaneous mechanics	Saint John
1815	Tailors	Halifax
1816	Miscellaneous mechanics	Nova Scotia
1827	Printers	Quebec
1827	Shoemakers	Hamilton
1827	Miscellaneous mechanics	Newfoundland
1830	Tailors	Montreal
1830	Shoemakers	Montreal
1831	Bricklayers, masons, plasterers	Toronto
1832	Printers	Toronto
1832	Carpenters	Hamilton
1833	Printers	Montreal
1833	Carpenters	Toronto
1833	Carpenters	Montreal
1834	Bakers	Montreal
1834	Miscellaneous mechanics	Montreal
1834	Firemen	Montreal
1834	Carpenters	Yarmouth
1835	Sawyers	Saint John
1837	Carpenters	Saint John
1837	Printers	Nova Scotia
1830s	Coopers	Upper Canada
1840	Blacksmiths	Saint John
1840	Founders	Saint John
1840	Hammermen	Saint John
1840	Horlogers	Saint John
1840	Tailors	Saint John
1840	Painters	Saint John
1840	Bakers	Saint John
1840	Shoemakers	Saint John
1840	Cabinetmakers	Saint John
1840	Riggers	Saint John
1840	Coopers	Saint John
1840	Ship carpenters	Quebec
1840	Carpenters	Chatham, N.B.
1841	Painters	Quebec
1842	Foundry workers	Hamilton
1844	Stonecutters	Montreal
1845	Sealers	Newfoundland
1845	Tailors	Toronto
1847	Milkmen	Montreal
1848	Shipwrights	Kingston
1849	Longshoremen	Saint John
1849	Shipwrights	Saint John

NOTE: Unions lapsed and formed again within a decade are counted only once.
The above list encompasses purely local unions, and where a union lapsed and reformed within a decade there has been no double-counting. Dating is related to the first mention of a union, and does not necessarily indicate formation. The major source consulted in drawing up this listing was Eugene Forsey, *Trade Unions in Canada, 1812*–1902 (Toronto: University of Toronto Press, 1982), but it has been supplemented by material drawn from other secondary sources and original newspaper references.

lives of youthful workers. But as apprentices grew to journeymen and as some attained the status of craftsmen, individualism was replaced with collectivity, and the rebelliousness of debauchery was overtaken by a sense of the rights of an eminently respectable social group. And the hallmark of respectability, in the years prior to 1850, was the journeyman's capacity to initiate, even to sustain, trade unionism in an age that prohibited "Meetings and Combinations endeavouring to regulate the rate of wages, and to effectuate illegal purposes." Under the auspices of benevolent and charitable societies, early Canadian mechanics followed principles of mutual aid and craft autonomy. From Table 1.4 it can be seen that some unions and trade associations were established early in the century, and that their numbers increased in the 1830s and 1840s.

Skilled craftsmen were an important component of the urban population in the first half of the century: they made up approximately 7 percent of the population of Quebec in 1805 and 1831, 12 percent of the population of Montreal between 1790 and 1830, and 10 percent of the population of York-Toronto in 1833 and 1851. Twenty-nine percent of the heads of households in Halifax in 1838 came from the ranks of artisan tradesmen and their journeymen. The latter led the way in forming a number of significant, if short-lived, unions of skilled workers. Starting with Halifax building tradesmen and shipwrights in 1798, and led by printers and carpenters, workingmen formed at least 45 unions in the years before 1850, establishing major centres of skilled labour in Saint John, Quebec, Montreal, and Toronto. Many of these organizational efforts took place in the early 1830s, and the resulting unions usually failed to survive the depressed economic years and troubled political climate of 1837–39. The next decade saw a revival of local unionism. But even in the face of failure, and among skilled craftsmen who formed no stable institutions of their own, a collective sense of craft was deeply embedded. By the 1840s, the phrase "Once a printer, always a printer" had appeared, a reminder that respectability built upon a foundation of craft pride that entailed shared, rather than individualized, experience.

Nowhere was this more apparent than in Saint John, New Brunswick, where building tradesmen and waterfront workers led the way in the creation of a local labour movement that, by the 1840s, was unrivalled in Canada. As Richard Rice has shown, mechanics' meetings and parades in Saint John in 1840 could draw from 1,200 to 2,000 workers, including blacksmiths, founders, hammermen, horlogers, carpenters, tailors, painters, bakers, riggers, coopers, shipwrights, coachmen, cartmen, and draymen. One local newspaper described the first of these "trade union" processions (something of a misnomer since not all the trades marching were unionized): "We have travelled . . . seen some splendid "turn outs," in New York and other places, but never saw anything that surpassed what we witnessed on Wednesday . . . whether we refer to the respectability of appearance, the appropriate devices on the banners, the badges which were worn. . . ." A second workingmen's parade, organized to welcome the Governor General in July 1840, once more elicited laudatory comment on the "splendour of the display of the Trades, and the truly British feeling evinced."

Mechanics like those who marched to honour the Governor General in 1840 also participated in a wide range of self-help activities, joining temperance societies and fraternal lodges, or patronizing mechanics' festivals where "habits of steadiness and perseverance" were praised. Most of these craft workers offered their support to the early mechanics' institutes, desiring educational advancement and considering themselves to be the manufacturers' partners, contributing to the country's industrial progress. Indeed, the first Saint John's trade procession had been called to celebrate the laying of the cornerstone of the local Institute, and similar halls were established in Montreal (1828), Quebec (1830), York (1831), Halifax (1832), London (1835), Brantford (1836), Hamilton (1839), and a multitude of other Canadian communities in the 1840s. While leading citizens played prominent roles and often acted as patrons, early institutes stipulated that working mechanics were to head the boards of directors, and in Kingston a "large majority" of the 350 members were "mechanics and apprentices" who enjoyed attending lectures and having access to the technical and popular literature in the reading room. Such endeavours cultivated a sense of respectability, which some have interpreted as a repudiation of working-class interests and an attachment to the aristocratic cultural norms established in the interests of stable social relations and the status quo.

A sense of respectability did link the skilled worker to nonworking class elements, establishing a cross-class cultural alliance in many of these institutions, cultivating a shared world view, and encouraging a chauvinism that could manifest itself in craft exclusiveness or a narrow attachment to national or even local priorities. Certainly, the continuity of the paternalist order resulted partly from the desire of workers, as well as employees, to maintain certain norms. However, the respectability attributed to employers was not always embraced by workers. Evidence of this emerged in the aftermath of the Saint John parade as an employer commented that "the Mechanics of St. John had more wages than Mechanics at other places, and that in consequence, their wives were dressed in furs and silks, and that they looked more like ------ than decent women." This condemnation, which at least one mechanic thought libellous, drew a quick response in the local newspaper: "The respectability of our mechanics, though it may be maligned by the ignorant," claimed the *Morning News*, "is too well understood by the intelligent ever to be misconstrued." But this voice of support cracked slightly, its condescension and worry seeping into its defence of the workingmen: "We hope that our friends know themselves too well, ever to suppose that the breath of one individual can do their respectability any mischief; or that they will descend to vulgar means to maintain their rights, while we have the best laws in the world for our protection. Indeed we have too high a respect for mechanics, generally, to suppose that they will."

This commentary on Saint John labour depicts well the contradictory place of respectability in the emerging class relations of the period. Among workers and employers, respectability came to be perceived differently. The very attachment to self-help and self-advancement that led workers to denounce drink and illiteracy or proclaim their loyalties to the Empire, could also motivate them to take collective action and to unionize in order to preserve what they saw as the *rights* of respectability. Employers pleased with the forms of respectable behaviour adopted by the skilled found little to applaud in this realization on the part of craft workers that, as citizens, they had specific privileges. As those privileges came under attack or were threatened, Canadian mechanics were capable of viewing self-advancement in terms of mutual, rather than individual, effort. Many saw the need to associate and unite with their fellows for "mutual support and protection [of] their trade."

Class conflicts revealed this thinking most obviously. In a partial listing of Canadian strikes prior to 1850, skilled craftsmen led 28 of the 57 confrontations, with carpenters, tailors, and miners in Pictou County and the far west being particularly active. (See Appendix I.) Among the most significant of these early struggles were a June 1815 hatters' attempt to resist the encroachments of specialization encouraged by two Quebec masters, William Hall and the Bernard brothers James and Isaac; a York shoemakers' protest in 1830 against "scanty wages . . . beds of straw . . . tyrannical oppression"; and an 1833/34 Montreal carpenters' and joiners' effort to secure the ten-hour day.

It was in Toronto that the craft worker's sense of respectability would lead most openly to conflict. The York Typographical Society had been formed in 1832 "to maintain that honourable station and respectability that belongs to the profession." Its first anniversary banquet was addressed by William Lyon Mackenzie, who praised its efforts to "secure respectability to journeymen without interfering with the prerogative of the employers." Like other mechanics, Mackenzie noted, the York printers were possessed of a "free, manly independent spirit, . . . always on the side of justice, always for fair play." (Respectability was thus equated with independence and manhood, and was related implicitly to the craftsman's capacity to earn enough to support his family, thereby overcoming the stigma of dependence upon charity or the socially superior.)

But three years later Mackenzie had changed his opinion: "If all the journeymen were editors, and each had a press of his own," he wrote [in a statement that left no ambiguity as to his assessment of property's place in the relations between master and man], "a more resolute, determined, I had almost added *obstinate* body, would not be found on this continent." Mackenzie's printers had had the temerity to strike his and other Toronto establishments demanding higher wages, parity with New York piece rates, and the limitation of the number of apprentices hired per shop. Independent-spirited workers, defining their manhood in terms of their ability to support families in a respectable manner and preserve craft traditions, ran headlong into the wall of employer obstinance. Respectability, once praised by the reform-editor, had, in his eyes, given way to "divisions and animosities in society," arraying "classes against each other who could otherwise be united by a common interest." The printers' strike of 1836, in Mackenzie's words, was an ungrateful, ill-informed attempt to "split up the community into so many selfish and mischievious monopolies."

Hatters, shoemakers, carpenters, and printers were only some of the skilled workers who took steps to preserve their respectability by fighting against specialization, unlimited apprentices and hours, and wages that they judged to be inadequate compensation for their skills as well as insufficient for their needs. Perhaps one of the most illuminating testimonies of the skilled worker's self-image emerged from a meeting of mechanics employed on the Cornwall canal held on 14 April 1835. "Though not gifted with patrician hauteur, nor Hereditary greatness . . . a very numerous and respectable assembly of Masons and Stonecutters" convened at Carnerous' Inn to condemn "the mean chickanery, the unhallowed traffick, and the deep-laid and combined plans for the reduction of prices [wages]," characteristic of "a few designing, speculating contractors." After paying homage to their distinguished forerunners, from Archimedes to Benjamin Franklin, the mechanics condemned the peonage that kept men "destitute of capital" silent in the face of injustice. Resolving "not to sit tranquil while their dearest rights [were] invaded," the masons and stonecutters noted that only two of the men employed by the offending contractors had chosen to absent themselves from the meeting. Their unanimity and their talents, they felt, entitled "them to a voice in the body political of this our adopted Country."

This sense of labour's worth, and of the necessity of preserving it from debasement, extended beyond productive relations. It was, of course, intimately connected to craft pride, but might reveal itself in strange quarters. Thus, in a July 1830 action that suggests a level of organization previously unexplored by historians, journeymen tailors rioted in opposition to a circus play, "Billy Button," convinced that it undermined their respectable status. The play met with two nights of rioting in Montreal, in spite of appeals from the master tailors for quiet, and when it moved to Quebec City, it encountered similar violence, necessitating the calling out of the magistrates and constables, as well as the termination of the satirical performance. This collective act coincided with the first unionization of Montreal tailors, a body organized from 1830 to 1834. Its members were said to be bound by a masonic-like oath reinforced by threats that all defectors who failed to support their colleagues' efforts to win wage increases would have their thumbs cut off.

Attempts to extend craft consciousness and the conception of skilled labour's respectability to the ranks of all labour were rare until the 1830s. The erection of a penitentiary in Kingston in 1833–36 united local mechanics in a movement to oppose training convicts in craftsmen's skills. Fearful that products would be "dumped" on their market and wary of prisoners "apprenticing" in a state institution, Kingston's producers gained support across the Canadas.

With the establishment of newspapers explicitly devoted to the producing classes, an all-encompassing view of skilled and unskilled labour gained ground. Dr. O'Callahan's *The Vindicator* (Montreal) championed "the classes whose labor is the real source of wealth" throughout the 1830s, pillorying Canada as "the Ireland of America." An obscure Quebec journal, *The People's Magazine and Workingmen's Friend*, appeared in 1842, condemning the political and social inequalities separating rich and poor. In Saint John, Patrick "Paddy" Bennett led the crusade for respectability and rights from his experience as an Irish immigrant. Bennett played a pivotal role in the organization of the waterfront unions and perhaps contributed to the disproportionate role played by unskilled labourers in militant actions and organizational efforts in Saint John. He imparted to his brethren on the docks a hatred of injustice and petty, arbitrary tyranny, leading the ship labourers to a condemnation of incompetent foremen in 1849. In the pages of his *True Liberator* he exposed the suffering of the quarantined famine Irish, isolated on Partridge Island. But Bennett himself eventually fell victim to destitution. His last days were spent in the Alms House. Bennett's fall was a sharp reminder that respectability, as a way of life embraced by a segment of the producing classes, was perched on a thin edge. When wage rates were cut, jobs lost, injuries sustained, or the economy depressed, the respectable found the gulf separating them from the rough narrowed considerably.

The Rough

Within every trade, of course, there were those who defied the social conventions of respectability. Some trades — coopering, shoemaking, tailoring — were known to harbour a disproportionate number of dissolute workers, and in the Kingston dockyards (1813–15) or the

Marmora iron works (1823) skilled workmen drove their masters to persistent complaint because of their "vile and disorderly conducts," a euphemism for drunkenness and absenteeism. But most craftsmen of this epoch would defend their good names against the vilifications of those who would cite particular cases of dishonourable behaviour to besmirch an entire calling. When one newspaper editor charged that compositors were generally a drunken lot, a Montreal printer was quick to condemn the editor's "insult [to] a whole class for the sake of venting . . . malignity against one or two of its members." This self-proclaimed "sober setter of type" linked the editor's discontent, not to his intemperate hands, but to the employer's anger at "the better class of compositors [who] will not work for him on the conditions . . . his hands are forced to submit." In the printing trades, as in all respectable crafts, "certain little necessary forms or customs [were] regularly observed," and editors who arbitrarily neglected them faced the workingman's hostility. But there were those among the producing classes who toiled without such necessary forms and customs. Devoid of skill, earning marginal wages on casual and seasonal work that allowed only bare subsistence, these workmen were the roughs upon whom the respectable stratum of workers often looked with condescension, pity, or contempt.

At the centre of the rough subculture were the Irish labourers who had thronged to Halifax, Quebec, and Montreal in the years after 1817. In cities like Montreal and Halifax they found employment on the docks, at construction sites, and in the homes of the rich: one-half of the adult Irish males in Halifax in 1838 were labourers, servants, and truckmen. But it was outside the cities that the rough most commonly worked. With pick, shovel, and axe they combined and competed with unskilled French Canadian labour to construct canals like the Shubenacadie, Lachine, Rideau, Williamsburg, and Welland, or to bring the timber of the Ottawa and the Mirimachi to the export ports. Predominantly Ulster Protestants in the 1820s (a group that would eventually secure a measure of upward mobility), the Irish labouring poor were increasingly Munster and Connaught Catholic in the 1830s and 1840s, even before the massive influx of the famine years, and on the canals there were large numbers of Irishmen who crossed the border into Canada after working on construction sites in the United States. Of the 1,200 Irish attracted to the Welland Canal in 1842, for instance, two-thirds were from Ohio, Illinois, and Indiana, while one-third were recently arrived immigrants.

Such canal construction sites were among the first operations to provide mass employment of labour in the Canadas, prefacing, in their impersonality and sheer size, the factory experience of later years. Commencing with the construction of the Lachine Canal in 1821, hundreds, then thousands, of canallers huddled near work sites in shantytowns composed of single men and migrant families. By the

1840s, these congregations of ill-used labour had become gigantic: 3,000, at least, worked on the Lachine and Beauharnois Canals in 1843, while 10,000 gathered the next year along the Welland Canal between Broad Creek and St. Catharines, although only 3,000 of the 5,000 males were actually employed. These canal navvies faced intolerable conditions: gruelling work and long hours; depressed wages; inflated charges for makeshift lodging; the ravages of diseases (cholera and "fevers" being most common); seasonal unemployment; the violent animosity of the resident "country folk"; wages paid monthly and often in script redeemable only at the contractor-controlled "pluck-me" store, where an uncontested monopolistic power over the distribution of provisions "gouged" the captive market; and contractors who absconded without settling their wage accounts with the work force.

Like the skilled, whose treatment at the worst of times was infinitely better, the Irish canallers rebelled at this harsh treatment, and thus fashioned a conception of their own respectability. John Cox, "an obedient and humble servant," addressed the *Montreal Transcript* in the midst of an 1843 strike, and "for Self and Fellow Laborers" vindicated "the poor self-expatriated Irish . . . from calumny and misrepresentation of the worst kind" by explaining the grievances and intentions of the Lachine canallers:

> They did not anticipate . . . cruelty or treatment and disrespect from foremen, which subsequently we experienced at their hands, and which was connived at and sanctioned by the Contractors or those who represented them, . . . incompetent foremen who were as ignorant of a man's labour in canalling as they were of astronomy or navigation. . . . we wrought from dark to dark, without being allowed the usual hour for breakfast. . . . The informant . . . is fearing that the city would be flooded with applicants for charity. We beg to state in reply thereto, that . . . our earning and industry for the last few years, together with the moral precepts of the Very Rev. T. Mathew, has rendered us independent of charity . . . notwithstanding the hopes entertained by our enemies, we are all fully determined to steer clear of any infraction of the law.

Cox no doubt wrote sincerely, but the history of the canallers' response to the oppression and exploitation of the 1821–46 period is one in which "steering clear of the law" was not a dominant tendency.

To begin with, the Irish canallers struck work sites with some regularity, violating the spirit if not the letter of English law as it was then stipulated in the Combination Acts of 1799–1800. A partial listing of Canadian strikes in this period indicates that on *at least* 20 separate occasions (and this is likely a gross undercount), Irish canal labourers conducted formal and easily recognizable strikes, which means that this ethnic-occupational stratum of the producing classes was involved in approximately one-third of the strikes of the pre-1850 years. (See Appendix I.) But riots, more than strikes, provided Irish canallers with a special form of collective bargaining and political negotiation, as well as a means of preserving control over jobs and asserting their cultural distinctiveness, even among themselves.

An incomplete tally of Canadian riots in the pre-1850 period, which is once again only a rough gauge of this most pervasive form of collective behaviour, lists at least 204 such crowd actions. (See Appendix II.) Although this list omits figures for whole regions like the timbering community of the Mirimachi, it does suggest the important place of the Irish canaller in the history of early Canadian riot: almost one-third of the riots identified (64) involved Irish labourers on the canals. Most common were work-related protests or clashes with constituted authority (constables, election candidates the canallers opposed, or those who threatened the labourers with the disciplinary action of the courts). Thirty-seven riots stemmed from such causes. Nineteen eruptions resulted from the longstanding feud between Munster and Connaught men. Smaller numbers of riots grew out of the explicit effort to secure canal labour as the special preserve of the Irish by driving French Canadians off, or from religious or ethnocultural conflict within the Irish community, as in the case of Catholic canallers battling Orangemen or militant Protestants.

When their jobs appeared to be threatened by other workers or by machines, Irish canallers reacted with dispatch. They rioted against the French-speaking labourers at Lachine and Beauharnois (1843); threatened to destroy an excavating machine at Queenston (1843); dumped 52 wheelbarrows into the St. Lawrence (1845); and attacked and set fire to a steam dredge at Port Dalhousie (1848). Against authority the canallers were even more resolute in their stand. A state of virtual civil war existed along the Welland Canal in the summer and fall of 1842, with canallers ("Midnight Legislators") gathering in bodies of 400 to 500, under the cover of darkness, marching brazenly through the streets of nearby towns demanding "Work or Bread." One authority noted that "the labourers are hourly becoming more audacious," while another expressed his conviction of the existence of the "illegal combination which bring these people together," and concluded by condemning "the organized system for Evil purposes established amongst them." By 1844, the authorities demanded a solemn certification from each labourer, signed by Priest and Magistrate, that he did not possess firearms or other offensive weapons and that he would keep the peace. But even this proved ineffective, and the summer months saw the region under seige once more. One newspaper concluded that "no government on earth but this of Canada would congregate large bodies of men in its employment and suffer them to arm themselves, to the terror and annoyance, and often worse, of its peaceable subjects." The rough put up a formidable opposition.

If this was clear on the canals, it was perhaps even more explicit along the Ottawa River, where Irish Catholic raftsmen employed in the timber trade defied respectable society and its law in a reign of terror that stretched from the late 1820s into the 1840s. The struggle for supremacy on the river began as a French-Irish confrontation over control of jobs, and developed into the Shiners' Wars of the 1830s, a battle between the rough timber workers led by Peter Aylen, and the Protestant authorities of Bytown. The details of this war, explored by Michael Cross, reveal a subculture of brazen hostility toward social betters mediated by the patrician control of the ethnic paternalist Aylen. Like Francis Hincks, who moved "Potash" Brennan's Griffintown mob to such effect in the Montreal elections in the 1840s, Aylen was an opportunist who had discovered that the rough raftsmen, shunned by respectable society, could be manipulated to his own financial ends. Never as socially significant as the canallers (they numbered, at most, a few hundred), the Shiners were the roughest of the rough and they aspired to a place in the social order. Their success was partial. They were often victorious in their crusade to define rafting as an Irish preserve, but won little in their attempts to challenge the authority of the Bytown gentry. Their weak position was also reflected in their dependence upon Aylen. When he saw that the "wars" were not going well, he departed from the Ottawa Valley, leaving the Shiners leaderless and directionless. Their strength had lain in a weakly developed collectivity, superimposed by Aylen, rather than cultivated among the workers themselves. It disintegrated in the 1840s.

Both canaller and raftsman, then, raised the threat of disorder in the early history of the Canadas. Given to violent rejection of authority and riotous challenge, they took on the threatening posture of dissolute behaviour, defiance, and indiscipline. Unlike the respectable, whose union activity might be curtailed by enforcement of the Combination Acts, the rough seemed immune to the law.

Crime, Anticrime, and Class

The paternal order rested upon the law, a force of majesty, justice, and mercy that drew its ultimate authority from the fear that it could inspire. To counter "the opaque and discordant traces of a corrupt nature . . . to regulate the enjoyment of property, and to prevent personal hostility," Tory judges advocated "terrible examples" to prove that "justice *dares* array herself in terrors when it is deemed necessary." If people committed crimes because they were "unsubdued in temper, and strangers to the restraints of discipline," the public execution would remind all of "the majesty of the law." It was in this ideological context that early Tory paternalist use of the law affected the plebeian world of the early Canadas. Hangings became the conjuncture where all sectors of society met. Thousands attended executions, where cakes, gingerbreads, and confessional tracts were hawked beneath the gallows.

Mercy was occasionally shown, the condemned being pardoned; the rule of law was publicly reinforced, paternalism's benevolent cheek turning favourably to the criminal and the crowd which often cheered him. But the other cheek could also turn. One 1827 Montreal hanging had been preceded by a parade through town, a regiment of soldiers accompanying three would-be victims of the hangman, who marched behind carts carrying their own coffins. Two of this trio would be saved from the noose at the last minute by official decree, but the third would swing, indeed swing twice, for the rope broke on the first attempt. The law had been well-served: mercy, justice, and majesty surrounded an act of *terror*, in which the ritualistic but deadly earnest punishment of the offender proved an effective tool against individual infringement of the law.

If, as Chief Justice John Beverley Robinson or Justice of the Court of King's Bench James Buchanan Macaulay believed, crime was a consequence of individualized failings, "uncongenial qualities" and "brutal passions," this paternal and ritualistic use of the law could function reasonably effectively. But criminal behaviour often extended beyond the individual and became something of a social malaise. It became associated with whole sectors of the producing classes, going beyond the "rough", and invading the territory of the "respectable". This, it is clear, is part of the history of workers from 1820 to 1850, as rough canallers and raftsmen were joined, on the margins of society, by impoverished refugees from the respectable producing classes.

As Upper Canada entered into its own agricultural crisis and access to the land tightened in the 1840s, crime in the country escalated. "We hear of horse thieves, of forgers, and of burglars of every description, prowling about the country in organized gangs, and the peaceable inhabitants have to guard themselves and their properties against the nocturnal depredations of these banditts," noted the *British Colonist* in 1846, concluding that "the crimes which are daily committed . . . show what a remarkable change has taken place, as the settlement of the country has progressively advanced." The Markham gang, brought to trial in 1846, was a product of this period, and according to one report used travelling tailors to ascertain the wealth and susceptibility of prospective victims. In the Newcastle District near Peterborough, a "regularly organized" gang known variously as Captain Blazer's Party or the Cavan Blasers terrorized the community. Incendiary acts (one local mill was burned) and animal maimings were but two of their noted activities. With their faces painted or otherwise disfigured, these "Organized Banditti" blocked the roads, cut the tails and ears off horses, and attempted "to create a monopoly" to coerce their foes and plunder their opponent's property. From a slightly later period, William Townsend, "the Dick Turpin of the Niagara Peninsula," left a marginal coopering shop in Dunnville to become a highwayman. These and other developments helped to transform the conception of just how law would be used, and as early as the 1820s the need for reform was recognized.

Symbolic of the emerging dependence upon institutional, rather than ritualistic, curbs on criminality, was the new Kingston Penitentiary. Built in the 1830s, it stood as a reminder of waning Tory paternalism. By the 1840s it was becoming all too clear that crime was no longer usually an individual act of malevolence; rather, it was symptomatic of deeper social evils, including the emergence of class cleavages. To counteract these new trends, laws were made more comprehensive and enforceable. The Master and Servant Act, passed in 1847, was an attempt "to regulate the duties between Masters and Servants or Labourers in that part of the Province formerly called Upper Canada." As Paul Craven has argued, the new legislation was a complex if calculating blend of paternalist persistence, as the very name of the act makes clear, and concession to the impersonality of the wage nexus. For apprentices, craftsmen, labourers, and servants, the law now institutionalized punishment for "abandoning" the employer. Such formal sanctions, aimed at curbing desertion, also reinforced managerial authority in the workplace. Pressed into being by worker recalcitrance and the structural imperatives of a labour market not yet glutted, where bottlenecks giving rise to labour shortages could still occur, the Master and Servant Act was not unlike workers' legislation in Great Britain, the Canadas, Nova Scotia, and New Brunswick at mid-century. Such legal innovations were designed to curb sailors' desertions, which averaged between 1,800 and 3,500 a season in Canadian ports between 1845 and 1857. By mid-century the law had shed some of its ritualistic paternalism, much of its mercy, and not a little of its majesty. The terror it could induce was decreased considerably. But its range, especially pertaining to class, had been extended.

Rough Justice

The law circumscribed plebeian experience; it did not define it. Indeed, there were moments when the producing classes stepped outside the law to defy constituted authority by imposing their own alternatives to legalistic norms, measuring out a moral authority of their own. The strike, in the productive sphere, was often an expression of this conscious attempt to recreate conceptions of appropriate social relations. Beyond work, as well, within the community and in everyday life, the producing classes used ritualistic forms of behaviour to lend force to their views of right and wrong. In a period when law itself was being transformed from a highly ritualized to an increasingly impersonal and distant authority, the producing classes, especially their rougher elements, resorted to custom and ritualized behaviour to sanction what law could or would not.

Many customary and ritualized practices could be discussed here: when marriages broke down and recourse to divorce was unavailable to the poor, a "sale" might be arranged, which, if properly conducted, would unite "illicit" lovers in a matrimonial ceremony regarded as legal and binding; convicted prostitutes might be paraded in a cart by the hangman, the taunts and jeers of the crowd expressive of plebeian hostility; journeymen whose wages had been cut could react by "daubing" their employer's entire house with excrement; soldiers were known to initiate their own "drumming out" ceremonies for those of their ranks who consistently violated the trust of their fellows; and workmen "razed" brothels that offended community sensibilities. These and other practices were part of a wide-ranging rough justice that defied the liberalized institutionalization of law. As such, they connect with a ritualistic practice that illuminates an unfolding contest within the plebeian culture in the years prior to 1850, a contest between law as it was imposed and law as it was conceived.

The charivari, a pervasive ritualistic practice with historical roots stretching back to the medieval period, was common in early Canada. Like all rituals, it followed a specific pattern, and through persistent repetition and a stylized or patterned form, it became, in public consciousness, a readily understood and recognized feature of local experience and community life. Persons who violated certain standards, norms, and accepted modes of behaviour were subjected to the charivari. A crowd would gather at the house of the offender, usually masked or in disguise or under the cover of darkness, treating the object of their displeasure to all manner of discordant sounds: muskets were shot in the air, fish horns were blown, and ribald songs were sung, while tin drums, broken fiddles, kettles, and pots were all "played" to produce a screeching din that let all neighbours or villagers know that an individual had been ostracized. Often the charivari party demanded money to treat itself to drinks at the tavern, but more common, especially among French Canadians, were requests to provide for the poor. Occasionally, in cases of much bitterness, the offender would be seized, put on a donkey or on a wooden beam and ridden about town or along a country road to the screams of abuse and mock derision of the crowd. Physical beatings, tarrings and featherings, even killings were not unheard of, and an escalating pattern of violence across the Canadas in the 1820s, 1830s, and 1840s led to a series of local by-laws outlawing the charivari as an outrageous act of barbarism. But it continued unabated: hundreds of such ritualized confrontations took place over the course of the nineteenth century.

Three types of charivaris emerged. The first was directed against a series of what were judged to be domestic infelicities. Particularly prominent were charivaris in opposition to "unnatural marriage" (a widow or widower marrying a younger person), although wifebeaters, husbandbeaters, cuckolds, adulterers, and parents who mistreated their children or step-children might also be paid a visit by the charivari party. In a society based on the land and the hereditary acquisition of skill, these charivaris were something more than irrational acts of intolerance. They protected the family as an essential vehicle in the transmission of craft training and property, and stood in firm opposition to the deterioration of the interests of the children of the first marriage.

Charivaris could also be waged against social offenders who violated the racial, ethnic, or religious values of a sector of the community. Finally, charivaris could also be enacted as a form of economic or political protest, and in the rebellions of 1837/38, they were used to express disapproval of the perceived inequities of the social order. Along the Welland Canal, Irish navvies often prefaced their riots with actions typical of a charivari, and one contractor claimed that "the firing of Guns and blowing of horns throughout the night . . . is the sure presage of trouble." While by no means the exclusive terrain of the producing classes, then, the charivari reveals much about the class relations of the paternal order. Occasionally led by the patrician élite, and therefore indicative of the organic connection linking the top and bottom of the social order, the charivari also points to social cleavages separating the plebeian masses of producers from their "social superiors."

One charivari of particular note took place in Quebec City in 1804. Arising out of a domestic "impropriety," it was described by an English gentleman in a letter to the press:

> Sir, I am a stranger in this Province, and many things appear new and curious to me, which perhaps, are not so in themselves. The other night . . . I observed hundreds of dim and glimmering lights dancing, as it were, towards me full speed. Presently I began to distinguish a multitude of glittering and gaudy figures. . . . They were all in disguise, even to one another; and enjoyed liberty and equality to a very great extent. . . . One of the figures, that was in the character of a female, approached a young girl of genteel appearance who, like myself, was looking on, and in a *rampant* humour began stroking her — cheeks; by degrees lowering his caressing motions to her — petticoats, *bupe*, off he flees like a vision, screaming out loud, *Charivari! Charivari!* A young gentleman who seemed to be the young lady's friend stepped forward. . . . Thousands of hideous figures instantly crowded around him. . . . One in particular, who was dressed in a buffalo hide and brandished a *huge* pair of horns on his head, came balancing along all giving way before him and with a twirl of his *panache* gave [the gentleman] a hoist and left him sprawling, head over heels in the mud. . . . Horns! and Charivari! resounded from all quarters. The place seemed in a riotous uproar; and women in *certain* situations were greatly alarmed.

Without glorifying the assault on the young bourgeois woman, it is important to see past this act to recognize the "liberty and equality" of the crowd, which proceeds outside of any usual constraints. Costumes, masks, the man dressed as a woman: all gave the charivari party a certain licence to defy conventional forms of social interaction. Deference is rejected, and a young gentleman's attempt to intervene physically is rebuffed; sexual licence in the stroking of the young woman overcomes previous inhibitions but does so, curiously, because of the female appearance of the man engaged in the act. Finally, there is no hint of any actual possibility of turning the crowd back. It does what it wants. Charivari here was a world turned upside down, a carnival atmosphere of disguise, producing the possibility of overthrowing the social relations of a paternalistic order.

Socially motivated charivaris were even more threatening to public order, while the much rarer political charivaris were used both to challenge and legitimate Tory rule. In the village of St. Pie in Canada East, an 1843 series of charivaris was employed by Catholics against a group of French Protestants described as "cobblers and journeymen . . . of the lowest and most ignorant class," themselves well-known as practitioners of "rough music." These debased artisans drew the antagonism of their neighbours by attempting to interpret the scriptures to them, and in the words of *La Minerve* made "a trade and merchandize of religion." Angered at such blasphemous behaviour, the Catholics led a charivari that culminated in torching the house of the leader of the sect. These kinds of ritualistic protest at the social level could rise to political purpose. Moreover, in an age in which paternalism was losing its grip on social order, charivaris could be used by those defending the status quo as well as those opposed to it.

A Swiss-born missionary, Madame Feller, noted the role of the charivari in the outbreak of the rebellion in Lower Canada in 1837:

> The movements of the rebels always took place at night. They met in companies of one hundred, two hundred, and sometimes more. They were all masked, and were furnished with instruments of every kind imagineable, to get up a *charivari*. They went from house to house mingling with their infernal music shouts and imprecations still more infernal. Those who did not come out immediately and join them were pelted with stones and threatened with fire. Some houses were entirely destroyed. . . . I could hardly believe they were men.

A year later, after the suppression of the revolt, Tories used charivaris and effigy burnings to show their displeasure with the reform sympathies of the colonial office.

The class composition of these ritualized public gatherings remains obscure, although the evidence suggests the predominance of rough elements in the more noteworthy domestic charivaris. The *Montreal Gazette*, for instance, described charivaris as "a motley assemblage of the rabble of all quarters." In social charivaris, however, all sectors of the producing classes were more likely to be found. Finally, in the more politicized variants of rough music, both patrician and plebeian elements were active. It should be clear, then, that no easily discernable class grouping stood behind the ritual: in the paternal order, it was embraced by many, if not all, social strata and it would be used in strikingly different ways appropriate to varying levels of social station.

Prior to 1850, then, the charivari was a constant reminder that rough elements of the producing classes would challenge the rule of law, justice, and the courts by asserting, through ritual, their own conception of right and wrong. Custom provided an order, an authority, that was, in contradiction to the law (in either its paternalistic or increasingly bourgeois forms), spontaneous, immediate, personal, commonly known, and relatively unchanging. The charivari, practised in defiance of authority by plebeian crowds in some cases, led and licensed by paternalistic patrician elements in others, and used to displace law by rowdy elements of the local élite in others yet, underscores the significance of rough justice in these years of the transformation of the paternalist order.

To see the society in this way is to see the cultures of the labouring classes prior to 1850 growing out of a context in which the rich and the propertied established certain rules and allegiances, but proved incapable of ensuring that such rules and allegiances would be conceived and lived *only* in their interests. Rough justice revealed all of this, buttressing the paternal order at the same time that it exacerbated essential tensions and contradictions. In its essentially apolitical cast, it held only the most limited capacity to challenge and confront authority. Yet, for all of their ambiguities and ambivalences, charivaris and the rough justice of which they were a part, could function subversively, leading toward the autonomous activity of the producing classes. "That the assembling of a crowd for a Charivari may also be used as a pretence by evil disposed persons, to effect purposes of a very different nature, or more dangerous to the public security," commented one judge in a shrewd assessment in the 1820s, was grounds enough "to be hoped that by the vigilance and exertion of those charged with the administration and execution of the laws, such disturbances will be suppressed, and never permitted to recur in any shape, nor under any pretence." When popular initiatives stepped out of their proper sphere, it was feared, they flirted with the insurrectionary moment: the terror of authority then faced the terror of resistance.

The Insurrectionary Moment

The paternal order confronted crisis in the years from 1800 to 1850. Economic dislocation, tension on the land, oligarchic rule, and resistance bred of class formation and the recalcitrance of the popular culture rocked the social stability of Canadian life. This process of political turmoil was constant throughout the period. In Upper Canada, it stretches forward from the moment of settlement, the predominance of Americans serving as an irksome reminder to the official compact that their rule was a precarious one. The Gourlay agitation (1817–19), the debate around the alien question in the early 1820s, and the growth of the reform movement after 1824, culminating in armed insurrection in 1837/38 and the struggle for "responsible" government in the 1840s are sufficient reminders of the extent to which Tories were placed on the defensive in these years. In this battle to secure a way of life, or to challenge it, class was by no means the central issue, and the producing classes did not play the most important role. But neither were they totally hidden from view. At the insurrectionary moment they would be seen and heard, although other shouts and the din of much-studied voices has tended to drown them out in our historiography. To hear them we must listen attentively to voices often ignored; to see them we must look, not necessarily at the main actors of the age, but at a set of moments of defiance enshrined in symbolism and a counter-theatre of resistance and egalitarian politics.

As early as the turn of the century, the indications of discontent and disaffection within the producing classes were plentiful. Early petitioners proclaimed their loyalty to the Crown but protested "that His Majesty Has Sent Officers to Rule over us, which Officers Disobey the King and Rule as they please," and closed by asserting that the populace "Cannot live under such tyranny and oppression." Whole districts were said to be "poisoned against the officers of the government," while even the militias were not exempt from complaint, one lieutenant declaring that he was a Republican and "despised a monarchal government and that the British government had lived by Robing and Plundering for this ten years past." In 1804 there were reports "of a Revolt which is about to take place against his Majesty's Government in Upper and Lower Canada." Cattle and horses were being sold in American markets, the proceeds diverted to arms procurement. "Arms are to be prepared during this winter," wrote one informant, "and conveyed down the River on Rafts to Lower Canada for the use of the Insurgents." A ship to convey the arms to Lower Canada was apparently to be outfitted in France and manned with rebellious Irishmen. The source of this information was a former Canadian resident, Mathew Wing, described as "a very ordinary man." A series of 1807 depositions confirmed the existence of this or another plot, identifying one leading figure as "as great a Jacobine as any of that Character either in England or in this country," while another disgruntled yeoman was said to have claimed that "he would wade up to his knees in blood for the cause," that his Majesty's garrisons were to be blown up, and "nothing was then in wanting for that purpose but the match."

Such clandestine efforts prefaced the more open Upper Canadian challenge of Robert Thorpe, Joseph Willcocks, and William Weekes, a patrician trio moved toward dissidence and the people by their own frustrated ambitions. Led by Thorpe, a Wilkes-like figure who drew upon his Irish heritage and position of authority as a judge to mount a popular opposition to the "servile reptiles" and "Scotch peddlers" who surrounded the official compact at York, this group posed the first challenge to a segment of the early Canadian state in the years 1805–12. Lieutenant-Governor Gore attested to Thorpe's appeal: "If this Province becomes à bed of Thorns it can only be from the Principles that Mr. Thorpe is so industrious in disseminating. He indeed is very busy . . . in sowing the seeds of Ingratitude and Disloyalty . . . *I the People*, though not the actual language is in reality a Characteristic motto of Mr. Thorpe and every other factious Demagogue."

As J.B. Walton has noted, Thorpe's appeal rested upon the imagery and symbolism of the United Irishmen, and he took to the electoral hustings under the "seditious emblem" of a Harp without a Crown (displayed by the Irish Republicans at Vinegar Hill in 1792). In the words of the Reverend John Strachan, Thorpe's 1807 candidacy "equaled Westminster" (an unambiguous reference to the Wilkite agitations of the eighteenth century) and with badges inscribed "Thorpe and the Constitution," he and his followers moved toward radical republicanism, communicating with English Jacobins in self-exile in the United States, one of whom was the executor of Tom Paine's will. Such "abuse and disaffection" drew stiff rebuke, especially the tarnishing of "the solemnity of the judicature," which Thorpe disgraced by "blending with it the rant of theatre." An attack in the *York Gazette* of 1807 summarized the paternalist order's grievance against Thorpe, as well as stating its intention:

> You have endeavored, while preaching and pratting upon harmony and union, to fill one class of subjects with enmities towards another, to fill them with foul suspicions of every man in office but yourself and to destroy that original confidence so necessary to the existence of civil society. You endeavoured to violate the peace of the public . . . upon the altar of your indistinguishing malice and ambition. What can have been your aim, is an insoluable enigma. May heaven protect the country from your designs and disgorge you from its soil.

Thorpe was actually driven from the province shortly after this harangue, and although Willcocks remained long enough to establish the first antigovernment press in the colony, *The Upper Canadian Guardian or Freeman's Journal* (1807–12), he too would take his leave, joining the American forces in the War of 1812.

This early agitation, scuttled by an overt state opposition in the form of mail openings and other illegal acts, was not necessarily based on class conflict. But, rhetorically and symbolically, it hinted at the role that American republicanism and Irish nationalism would play in future reform contests in Upper Canada. Moreover, with the influx of Irish after 1817, this appeal was grounded in the masses. By the late 1820s, rumours were in the air of an Irish conspiracy led by supporters of the radical nationalist Daniel O'Connell. He was well known among rough and respectable alike by the mid-1830s, with stonecutters, printers, and canallers rallying to the name of "the Great O'Connell." As in Ireland, O'Connell's authority was rivalled only by that of the priest. In 1843, with a number of strikes breaking out on the canals of Upper and Lower Canada, it was claimed that "thousands of Irishmen in Canada [were] wedded to the principles of O'Connell."

By the time of the coming of the Irish, a consciousness of class distinction was also beginning to enter into the political arena. "Old Country" and "Yankee Radicals" exacerbated tensions, "haranguing the People" in the manner of Thorpe, and by the 1820s a reform movement had come into being. This was the reform movement in which William Lyon Mackenzie was to figure prominently and which culminated in the rebellion of 1837/38. Politicians affiliated with the movement were usually not members of the producing classes and were often as paternalistic as candidates linked to the Tory culture, but they did realize the need for political change, and promised to democratize the institutions and procedures of early government. Men like Captain Mathews of the Talbot District exemplified the new breed of politician. He regarded himself as "an *Honest Independant Man* . . . who while he sincerely regards the rights of the Crown, will never consent to vote away the rights of the Subject, nor to tax the Poor to add increased wealth to the already opulent office-holder." Reform supporters, by the early 1830s, were described by disgruntled Tories as "runaway negroes and people who have neither habitation nor property in the country," and as "Methodists and social levellers." In Brockville, Matthew Howard stood for the Reform party, his 1830 electoral effort pilloried by Jonas Jones' Tory newspaper in a bitter condemnation of the intrusion of class considerations into the polite workings of a politics long orchestrated by gentlemen:

> a great noise was heard at the doors of the Committee, when lo in walked *Matthew Mushroom Howard*, Esq., carrying *"a millstone round his neck"* and supported on the right and the left by the Most Reverend Fathers William Hallock and James Cameron his tail and other habillments upheld by an innumerable host of "Saddle Boys." . . . Gentlemen slaves! Mr. (M.M.) Mulberry Mushroom Howard is a Miller, a grist Miller, A Farmer, a Trader, a straw hat maker, a pumpkin pie dresser, an onion sauce stewer and . . . a mighty, mighty clever man and what more do you want for the good of the country.

Beyond the satirical dig of the élite it is possible to glimpse a counter-theatre of democratic forms that reformers placed in opposition to the theatre of the official Tory culture, with its pomp, ceremony, and élitism. Obviously, the rules of Tory procedure were beginning to be questioned, and politics was no longer the restricted domain of a chosen few.

This counter-theatre escalates in the popular discontent of the 1830s as a shift to the symbolism of republicanism attests to the growing preoccupation with insurrection. Marching in the town of Preston in 1832, the reformers promised an "awful commotion if concessions are not made to suffering people." One of their number bore a flag inscribed, "He that hath no sword let him sell his garment and buy one, for taxation without representation is Robbery!" At Stouffville, postmaster W. Doyle introduced William Lyon Mackenzie at a reform rally, "brought out a rifle tied upon a pole, and placed it over Mr. Mackenzie's head, and said he wished the Governor and the damned Tories were there to see it; and they would know by looking there at what they had to depend on before the lapse of many months." After the Bond Head election of 1836 convinced many radicals of the futility of electoral reform, this symbolism of insurrection became commonplace. Across the province there were reports of "revolutionary parties," of "nests of radicals," and of "disaffected persons who would at once join the standard of rebellion were it raised in the province." In July 1836 Mackenzie's *The Constitution* (first published on the 4th of July) announced:

> The first sign of revolt has been observed in this city in the shape of a Liberty Pole set up on the roof of the Governor's dwelling house, right in the centre over his Head. Some of the old ladies are terribly frightened, more especially as the house has just been painted a pale orange, chimnies and all. — We rather think there is no great apprehension, "the Old Man" having probably intended it as a gibbet on which some of his Sheriffs might hang a radical now and then.

Such caricatures of physical artifacts were lent substance by appeal to physical force: "There must be an ARMY as well as a CONGRESS. There must be PIKES and RIFLES as well as men and tongues."

Meetings in August 1837 attested to the use of symbol, rhetoric, and theatre in widening the appeal of this call to arms. At "the Second Great Northern Meeting" at Lloydtown there was the usual talk of erecting a Liberty pole, and flags flew "proudly in the breeze," their bearers "conscious of the principle they indicated." The American eagle was prominent, as was support for Papineau, Bidwell, Perry, and Rolph. One banner depicted "a large star, surrounded with six minor lustres — in the centre, a Death's Head, with the inscription of 'Liberty or Death.'" Other flags bore, in huge letters, "Daniel O'Connell" and "Liberty," and the colours of the Irish were prominent. Lines of verse told of the rebel purpose, the needs of the hour, and the constituency addressed:

> Ireland will sound her harp and wave,
> Her pure green banner for your right,
> Canadians never will be slaves!
> "Up sons of Liberty to the Fight!"
> By Liberty's eternal name,
> Our country's proudest glory. Arm!
> Sweep from our shore's oppression's shame,
> Canadians! cleanse the locust swarm.

The republican sentiments of "Lloydtown" were paraded by a boy, hoisting a placard with a picture of a young girl over which was pencilled:

> Of Monarchs tender, Monarchs tough,
> We thank our stars we've had enough.

At this and other meetings, plenty of pikes, swords, trumpets, cannons, and muskets adorned the banners and flags, "by way of relief to the eye," and target practice was directed toward a loaf covered with butter, perhaps a symbolic representation of the appropriated affluence of the oligarchy.

At such gatherings, resolutions were passed in profusion, and the crowds were in agreement that "much could be done without blood." But the drift of political feeling was most emphatically toward a revolutionary stand. As "Reform" urged in the pages of the *Cobourg Star*:

> Take this piece of advice from an *ignorant elf*:
> *Let each ipso facto Reform one himself*
> And then my dear Roger, you'll see in conclusion,
> A glorious — a grand — and a great REVOLUTION.

Small wonder that Mackenzie, clandestinely referred to in communications passed among the rebels as "the editor," drew sharp and bitter attack from defenders of the status quo:

> Wha do ye think on a mission was sent,
> The breedin' o' Johnny's bull-dogs to prevent,
> Because they made havoc on Jonathon's hens see?
> Wha but the white-liver't mawkin McKenzie!
> Painche-awimet, sheep shanket, cow-rin' McKenzie;
> Midden-bred, filthy-jakes-scourin' McKenzie.

There was more than a little theatre here, on both sides of the political fence.

Awareness of class differences helped to push this symbolic discontent and counter-theatre toward the insurrectionary moment. Of the 855 radical democrats arrested in the aftermath of the Upper Canadian revolt, 375 were yeomen, 345 labourers, 80 carpenters, foundrymen, and other tradesmen, and the remaining 85 professionals, merchants, and innkeepers. These figures gesture toward the social forces behind the parades, rallies, marches, military drills, and local organizational efforts that consumed much of the year 1837. Dutcher's foundrymen and Armstrong's axemakers (indicative of the producing classes bound by the paternalism of the small shop) were the men that Mackenzie judged could be counted upon at Toronto. An anonymous letter to the tavernkeeper Montgomery, seized by the authorities, made cryptic reference to plans to send arms to "the carpenter beyond Thornhill." In Merrickville, the leading radical reformer was one John Graff, a tailor "in low circumstances and not very respectable," described as "a full-blooded Papanau man," and an activist shrewd enough to destroy the list of members of the local Reform Society at the outbreak of rebellion. From Ingersoll came the report that, "A Yankee rascal by the name of N.P. Hogue . . . has . . . threatened that if any rising took place that the whole of Ingersoll's buildings and property should be burned; this fellow is a wagon maker — has no stake in the country, but is a perfect firebrand."

Even Bond Head recognized that the rebels' awareness of class differences contributed to their revolutionary fervour. Glorying in the repression of this force in the Tory political victory of 1836, he proclaimed in December of that year:

> In place of blacksmiths and carpenters reeling from daily labour with no
> farther knowledge than that which appertained to their calling, and with
> obstinacy and perverseness proportionate to their ignorance and vulgarity;
> we have for the most part GENTLEMEN of an intelligence, information,
> and talent, capable of discussing the measures which they are called upon
> to deliberate and decide.

One of these denigrated "blacksmiths and carpenters" was Middlesex's representative Parke, supported by "pedlars and strollers," a political thorn in the side of Talbot's Tory machine. Parke would be one of the few reformers to retain his seat in the 1836 election, and Mackenzie noted that he was taunted in London "because he was a tradesman." His 1832 victory drew attack from the defeated candidate, who claimed that he had been overthrown by "the despised mechanic and the derided farmer," a typical Tory assessment of the urban and rural wings of the producing classes. As Graeme Patterson notes in a study of Middlesex politics in this period, "Considerations of economic interest, as was so often the case in the Canadas, seemed to be outweighing ideological commitment. Considerations of 'class' seemed to be outweighing those of 'nation.' "

Representative of this increasing place of class in the politics of dissent was another of Bond Head's despised mechanics, the blacksmith Samuel Lount, a Pennsylvanian who arrived in Upper Canada in 1811. First elected in Simcoe County in 1834, and defeated in 1836 by the usual combination of bribery, intimidation, and land grants, Lount was a committed revolutionary by the fall of 1837. He led one of the earliest explicitly insurrectionary meetings on 18 November 1837 at Newmarket, firing volleys, cheering Papineau, and groaning Head. Before 100 to 120 supporters, he defied the local magistrate to report on their treasonous activities: "You may find it out if you can and make the most of it. It is the voice of the people, which is power, and that, the Forces will find out to their cost before three months were passed." Bent over his forge, engaged in the wholesale manufacture of pikes aimed at the Compact's collective throat, Lount was the expression of what Bond Head could not fathom, and Rolph and Bidwell could not stomach: the possibility of insurrection. An 1838 charge of a jury detailed his crimes against the early Canadian state:

> Not having the fear of God in his heart nor weighing the duty of his allegiance but being moved and seduced by the devil . . . devising and intending to disturb the peace and public tranquility of this Province [with about 500 people] armed and arranged in a warlike manner that is to say with colours flying and with Guns, Rifles, Swords, Pistols, Pikes, Clubs and other weapons as well offensive as defensive being then and there unlawfully maliciously and traitorously assembled and gathered together against our . . . present soverign Lady the Queen.

On 12 April 1838, Lount and another rebel, Peter Mathews, were hanged for high treason. Petitions had flooded the offices of the provincial secretary, begging for mercy; one of these petitions had over 3,500 signatures, and another, more than 6,000. But at the moment of insurrection it was terror, not the mercy of the law, that was paramount.

The recourse to repression during the events of 1837/38 indicate that the reform movement was taken as a serious threat. Nevertheless, the Tories emerged victorious in 1838/39, and a restrained but well-placed public use of the gallows and of transportation was used to eradicate the "peculiar *Popular* offence to that class of people impatient of restraint; to whom the Laws of Society, or for the protection of property, are oppressive." But the symbolic and theatrical component of opposition established a continuity in the aftermath of Lord Durham's report of 1839, in which the reform cause was vindicated. Durham meetings were called in support of "Radical Jack's" endorsement of reform, while the appeal to arms and insurrection survived in a series of "Patriot" invasions led by rebels and American supporters. Although suppressed, reform sympathies were by no means eliminated in the immediate aftermath of the rebellion. One fierce loyalist in Kingston, well known for his prominent role in the repression of December 1837 found a favoured dog shot dead on his door, a note posted on his gate: "God damn colonel Hill and all his crew shall die so God help me, if I have strength to kill the old beggar, let the curse of God await him. He had better have stayed at home." A postmaster, upon hearing that the rebels had been defeated at Toronto, offered a public threat to another loyalist:

> You d----d Tory your Dye is Cast your doom is sealed Your person and property is Consigned to a Conflagration and I shall rejoice to see it. You

may escape one week and the longest two weeks and then you will come as a supplicant to me and what judgement will I meet out to you; then we will have the Laws of Liberty established here, we will not be ruled by Tyranny and Oppression any longer.

These and other developments help to explain official correspondence from communities like Chippewa. At that place, Colonel Cameron informed the Provincial Secretary that "very many, among them some who carry arms in our Ranks, would not hesitate to rise again if there were an opportunity or chance of success."

Lacking such opportunities and potential successes, the producing classes expressed their resentments only obliquely. In 1839, three carpenters, described as "possessing no property, principles, or influence" (an appropriate paternalist trilogy of denigration), erected a mock gallows on the banks of the Humber River, and there hung effigies of John Beverley Robinson, Francis Bond Head, and Christopher Hagerman. From the likenesses of these three pillars of Tory rule they suspended signs reading: "I will condemn right or wrong; we must have a rebellion; and I will prosecute unto death."

In Lower Canada, the insurrectionary moment was more protracted, encompassing two distinct rebellions that galvanized not hundreds willing to risk their lives in armed confrontation, as in Upper Canada, but as many as 10,000. Complicated by the question of national oppression and led by a more entrenched and mature petty bourgeoisie, with its economic roots embedded in the commerce of the cities, and by the landed relations of the seigneurial system, the *patriote* agitations drew upon a similar counter-theatre of protest, in which the banners and rhetoric of rebellion were cast in terms of *indépendence*.

After the 1834 adoption of the "92 Resolutions," an extensive listing of the grievances of *les canadiens* endorsed by 80,000 signatures (over one-quarter of the adult population), Lord Russell drafted a set of imperial counter-resolutions in 1837 that attempted to suppress French reform initiative. These "coercive" resolutions were condemned by the London Workingmen's Association and in Lower Canada were greeted with the Phrygian cap of republicanism and a Canadian flag of green, red, and white, replete with beaver, maple leaf, and maskinonge. The American eagle was Canadianized, a maple branch in its beak. Nor were the Tories without their theatrical thrust, advertising a "Canadian" shooting match, "a plaster figure representing a certain great agitator, to serve as bull's-eye," members of "the British Legion or the Doric Club" being requested to "hold themselves in readiness."

Active before the Upper Canadian rebels, the *patriotes* early declared, "Better a bloody but just and honourable fight than cowardly submission to a corrupt power." Papineau was their leader, the Daniel O'Connell of the French Canadians, and a man who could unite the worst of both nationalism and radicalism. The shock troops were distressed *habitants*, driven to the brink of dispossession of their land and destitution by years of agricultural crisis, and day labourers in Montreal. There the *Fils de la Liberté*, an organization set up by students and young professionals, soon gathered hundreds of journeymen, apprentices, and unskilled and unemployed workmen, not a few of whom were Irish, following the resolute O'Callaghan. A military camp at St. Eustache attracted the discontented with its ribald irreverence: "Come with us; we're all armed, we have fun; it's like a wedding; we drink; eat, play fiddles, dance, we're free, we do what we want. . . . It's our right, we poke fun at the King, the Queen, and the Clergy." Here was one grand charivari of revolt.

Perhaps 700 to 800 tradesmen and labourers were drawn to insurrection by the *Fils de la Liberté*, and north and south of Montreal the rural districts provided between 4,000 to 7,000 recruits, most of whom were *habitants* who possessed less land than the statistical average. A number of landless labourers and country artisans also gravitated to the movement. Quebec City and other districts in the lower province provided only insignificant numbers. The 108 court-martialled after the first rebellion in 1837 included 66 poor farmers, while 25 were unmistakably of the bourgeois or petty bourgeois class, and only 15 belonged to trade groupings or the labouring poor. Among a dozen *patriotes* executed, seven were professionals and five farmers. There were no counterparts to the Upper Canadian Samuel Lount, although the second uprising at the end of 1838 carried a more radical tinge, as noted by Fernand Ouellet: "Nelson's declarations of independence in February and November of 1838 proclaimed abolition of the old social régime and also universal suffrage, appealing directly to the urban and rural proletariat." In the aftermath of defeat, this orientation brought the radical minority of workingmen to the cause of francophone nationalism. At Quebec City, for instance, in October 1839, a company of journeymen printers employed at *Le Canadien* staged a theatrical performance of *La mort de César* by Voltaire, a tragedy depicting a struggle between father and son in which the offspring kills his parent "for the love of liberty." In the words of the English Tory press, the play "was replete with the most extravagant republican declamations and expressions of hatred of Kings," and the disaffected journeymen were determined "to get up an excitement among the people connected with the fatal source of the misfortunes of the Province, national origin, which they will endeavour to turn to *any* advantage that may offer." Within this working-class group of advocates of *indépendence* we see those processes that colour the entire epoch stretching from 1800 to 1850: collective action and mediation. These advocates of *indépendence* were typical of the more radical workers, who actively set out to convince their peers of the value of collective action and the need for protest. Other workers took a more conciliatory stance toward their "social betters." Both approaches were adopted during the first half of the century and gave rise to worker/employer relationships fraught with contradiction.

Mutuality and Mediation

Evidence of collective defiance of the paternalist order existed in the producing classes as early as 1809, when carpenters employed at the Kingston dockyard proved a stubborn and troublesome group, their overseer requesting "authority to employ a Lawyer to bind them down to their agreement as they are a set of men who require it very much." Among early Canadian ironworkers a similar history of recalcitrance unfolds, albeit obscurely. A restricted supply of skilled men in the trade meant that, according to John Mason of Potter's Creek, ironworkers were "the very worst sort of men to manage." In 1817 he claimed that "not one of a hundred of them will take every advantage of his master in his power." At Marmora's works the establishment of the iron-making facilities was delayed in 1822, in the words of Charles Hayes, because of "some wicked combinations among my work people — whom I have had no power to control." These reports, attentive as they are to "sets" of men and "combinations" point out that the paternalist order was not always capable of undercutting embryonic forms of class solidarity.

But counterposed to these instances of mutuality were the processes of mediation. At the Kingston dockyards, for instance, the employers had recourse to the law at the same time that they made material concessions. Pushed by their labouring people, the masters eventually retreated into a brutal militarization of labour, and also utilized seasonal dismissals and layoffs to temper workers' demands. In 1816 it was suggested that the barracks-like living arrangements of the dockyard mechanics bred a dangerous mutuality in which "there is no distinguishing the good from the bad and that which is the duty of the whole collectively to perform becomes finally the duty of none individually." To counteract this drift to a threatening impersonality, it was suggested that the establishment of a church and individual homes for workmen would lend "improvement to our whole political fabric", blending "safely and happily" civil life with "a military control." Indeed, after the threatening demonstration in the dockyards in 1813, workers were forced into acquiescence by the military, their "mutinous spirit" crushed.

Collective action and mediation, while often posed in the course of conflict, also emerged as part of the organic connections of community life. Thus, in 1822, Kingston's master and journeyman shoemakers came together to protest the conviction of one of their number for "assault, battery, and Riot." John McMullin was sentenced to be "imprisoned two months and to be publickly whipped twenty-five lashes," for his part in "riding upon a rail a certain man for having abused his wife." The 13 shoemakers — substantial tradesmen and lowly, propertyless journeymen — who petitioned for mercy attested to their knowledge of the offender as "a workman and a shopmate," and expressed their conviction that "so far as he was concerned it was no more than a frolic, unjustifiable and illegal indeed, but not resulting from any malicious or mischevious design." Such a petition for pardon is evidence of an emerging sense of collectivity among shoemakers as a craft group, and also points to the mediating influence of status, respectability, and property within the trade.

Throughout the 1800–1850 years, these processes of mutuality and mediation were at work within the social relations of the epoch. While mediation operated at many levels, rooted in the particular paternalist experiences of the small shop, landed property, political authority, and ethnic or religious attachments, the emerging mutuality of the producing classes was of three types. First, it brought together workers in specific trade or work sectors, a limited unity that embraced only the particular calling, from tailors and shoemakers to raftsmen and navvies. Second, a sense of mutuality helped overcome some (never all) of the isolation and sectionalism of craft experience, uniting labour across the trades. Third, mutuality began the process of uniting workers across the Canadas, revealing commonalities of experience and linking workers of one city to those of others. The rise of Mechanics' Associations in Kingston, Toronto, and Montreal in the early-to-mid 1830s demonstrated all three levels of mutuality, while the Saint John, New Brunswick, labour parades of the 1840s attested to at least the first two types of mutuality. All three levels, moreover, were reinforced in the face of a set of common, if not necessarily commonly conceived, grievances. Rising numbers of desertions among apprentices, soldiers, sailors, militarily conscripted labour, and others attested to this, as did riotous clashes with the authorities and strikes across the spectrum of the skilled trades.

Even if the producing classes were a fragmented, vertically ordered body when examined from within the confines of their own experience, they were often perceived by the élite as a unified group. While mutuality never superseded economic, social, political, and cultural divisions within the producing classes, it was sufficiently well developed, especially in moments of challenge, to cause producers to be viewed from above as a threatening contingent. To counteract this threat, the ruling order offered many innovations, as has been shown, in law, and in other realms. Educational reform, as Alison Prentice has suggested, was one of these realms of innovation, and at least a part of the school promoter's purpose was to reduce emerging class antagonisms, inculcating discipline among all labourers, integrating them into the structures established by developing capitalist authority. In this contest for hegemony, schools became a counterpart of the prison, and by mid-century one chief superintendent's report described the educational system of Upper Canada as "a branch of the national police," aiming to "occupy a large part of the population" and "support and restrain many of the grown up population." But like so much of the cultural experience, education was two-edged. More than a simple imposition of authority, it produced a discipline and an awareness that could be used to resist at the same time that it was marshalled in the interests of submission.

Class relations in the 1840s were largely a reflection of the delicate balance between resistance and submission, between collective defiance and mediation. Workers throughout Upper Canada, for instance, petitioned the Provincial Secretary throughout the 1840s. They voiced their protests in a language and style that articulated the producing classes' self-conception of the unity of interests binding them to their "betters" and the governing élite. They raised their discontents as part of a general alliance of manufacturers and mechanics that often relied upon a state which assumed ultimate authority in charting progress and stimulating prosperity. For their troubles, these mechanics often received curt lessons in political economy, classical style. "The Governor General has no power to prevent erection of machinery," the Kingston mechanics were informed in 1842, "and were it otherwise, His Excellency is of the opinion that by lessening the cost, and increasing the facility of building, machinery greatly tends to induce an influx of Inhabitants, an increase in the number of houses and the growth and general prosperity of Kingston and consequently instead of being prejudicial to that highly useful class of Tradesmen interested in building, it is likely to tend greatly to their advantage."

Such homilies correspond poorly with an 1852 statement made by Etienne Parent, editor of *Le Canadien*, before a working-class audience in Quebec City's St. Roch district. In his words, "The Providence of the poor is the state, which must not leave them at the mercy of the masters, who are too often pitiless." Faith in state authority died hard, although the basis for a distancing of the popular classes from the state had, in fact, been laid by Parent earlier, in the reform debate of the 1840s. "The government may keep us in a state of political inferiority, it may rob us, it may oppress us," he wrote. "It has the support of an army and of the whole power of the empire to enable it to do so. But never will we ourselves give it our support in its attempt to enslave and degrade us."

The 1840s saw other kinds of implicit and explicit defiance of the power and authority of the state. When two miners at the Albion Mines in Pictou County, Nova Scotia, threatened to desert their fellows (200 strong) in the midst of a 12-week strike in 1841/42, they "had their effigies burned, and were effectively deterred from entering the pits." After their successful resistance of a wage cut, one investigator claimed that, "There is no business with which I am acquainted that could sustain itself against the influence of such a monopoly as this [group of workers]." In Quebec City in 1843 sailors struck and threatened "a strict look out, night and day, for such offenders" as would defy their publicly proclaimed objectives. Carpenters in a Montreal strike of 1845, described as "sound constitutionalists," nevertheless practised a disciplined intimidation of those outside their ranks and threatened to desert the city if they were not offered protection "from oppression," while four years earlier seamen demonstrated in groups of 200 to 300 to demand increased wages.

Such events suggest labour's emerging sense of class identity, while the bulk of the petitions of the 1840s reveal that the ultimate political paternal authority to which many workers looked was still strong. If the hold of the landed élite was obviously weakening, other remnants of paternalistic power continued. A decade of contradiction and ambiguity, the 1840s was a fitting moment of reprieve for the old paternal order of the Canadas. The conception of the "one and indivisible" reciprocity of master and man was proclaimed enthusiastically by the Toronto Typographical Society at its 1849 anniversary dinner, where employer and employed sat down to feast and toast the "better understanding between two parties, who are sometimes carried away with the erroneous idea that their interests are antagonistical instead of being, as they in reality are, mutual and reciprocal."

But by the end of the 1840s, the signs of an old order on the verge of collapse were visible. Some hailed this, others mourned, but few denied that the old Tory paternalism was disintegrating. Indeed, the demise of paternalism had been irreversible since the rebellions of the 1830s, when Tory rulers had retained their offices but not their authority. Charley Corncobb, "poet laureate" of reform, put the message of discontent to verse:

> Toryism's sun is set
> 'Tis down, 'tis gone forever
> Some say that it will start up yet,
> But will it? Nonsense, never.

Years later this message reached the patrician reform element, which began to comprehend just what had been lost. Robert Baldwin, moderate advocate of change since the 1820s, would, ironically, come to mourn the passing of an order that he had helped to bury. In 1851 he readied himself for the worst: "If the sober mind of the Country is not prepared to protect our Institutions it can't be helped." For Baldwin a "reckless disregard of first principles" was about to lead to "widespread social disorganization with all its fearful consequences." At the same time, John Macaulay, a member of the old élite, observed: "The most alarming symptom . . . in the country is the decay of old-fashioned loyalty, and a general want of respect for authority and station which once prevailed among us . . . when, whatever were the failings of the much abused 'Family Compact', we had a Government of Gentlemen." In the years from 1850 to 1880 these prophecies and complaints would, in large measure, be borne out as the Canadas entered into an unmistakable age of industrial capitalism and consequent class cleavage; there would be far less mediated mutuality after the middle of the nineteenth century, and far more openly antagonistic collectivity.

Chapter 2

The Emergence of Class Antagonism 1850–1880

> They may know well enough how to drive spikes or frame the timbers of a ship; whilst at the same time be thoroughly incompetent to frame a motion for the good of society . . . . They have taken the liberty to be born and they expect and demand to be fed. It is a mistake. The world does not want them and can get on perfectly well without trade unions and trade unionists.
>
> I.B. Taylor (government printer),
> *Ottawa Citizen* (1869)

The Social Formation

The 1840s, more than the 1830s, was a decade of profound change in Canada. Replacing the bluster of an insurrectionary moment aborted almost before it was conceived, were the vast transformations in economic and political life of 1846 and 1848: the dismantling of the colonial mercantilist tariffs and the attainment of "Home Rule" were the first changes to set Canada on the route to greater independence. A whole way of life, and the patrician paternalists who had stood as guardians of its official Tory culture, was replaced with a more materialist orientation. The state, once little more than a style of rule, was created to address substantive questions of national development and political consolidation. Mercantile capital and an unmistakable agrarian dominance gave way to a more pervasive industrial capitalism; urban centres grew; and an impersonal labour market, stocked by the famine Irish, broke down some of the barriers to productive capital. Economic growth was facilitated by reciprocity with the United States (1854–66), and by the external demand for both manufactured goods and the old staples that resulted from the growth of the home market, the Crimean War, and the American Civil War. Technological advances (the introduction of machines in key sectors such as tailoring and shoemaking) and the innovations in banking throughout the 1850s and 1860s, culminating in the first Bank Act of 1870, added to economic growth. New men of power rose out of this context — railway promoters like Allan Napier MacNab and Francis Hincks and lawyer-businessman-politicians like Georges Etienne Carter and John A. Macdonald — while the Talbots and the Baldwins receded from view. In the years from 1850 to 1880, the foundations of a modern industrial-capitalist state were laid. While these years did not totally overcome the entire range of contradictions and ambiguities so deeply embedded in the pre-1850 social formation, they nevertheless stand as the point of entry into Canada's Industrial Revolution.

Railways symbolized the new age. From a mere 72 miles of railway track in Canada in 1850, mileage expanded to over 2,000 in 1865. Early railways radiated from Montreal and, secondarily, from Toronto. The resulting concentration of industry in these two centres reflected the regional character of future economic growth. The end of the age of wood, wind, and sail, and the arrival of the age of iron and fire left much of British North America to plot its own indigenous path to industrialization, a process sure to leave the Maritimes, parts of rural Quebec, and the far west locked into the subordinate economic place of uneven development. The construction of a transcontinental railway (the Canadian Pacific) in the 1870s and 1880s, and the completion, in 1876, of the Intercolonial Railway linking the Maritimes and central Canada were ironic mechanisms by which these relations of inequality were perpetuated at a time when railway mileage tripled and the movement of goods and staples was facilitated.

As Gustavus Myers noted long ago, great fortunes were made in railway construction, and they were accumulated through wheeling and dealing that produced not only political scandal, but also a peculiarly Canadian social formation, in which capitalism and the state went hand in hand. A colony but recently removed from the clutches of imperial markets was, as Pentland noted, able to absorb its own empire after 1867, when Confederation consolidated an "unequal union" that replicated, in politics, the economically privileged position of central Canada. Subsidized by this early Canadian state, railway contractors provided the material foundations upon which this political capitalism proceeded. Capital imports from Britain leapt up from the moderate level of $10 to $15 million in the canal era to $100 million during the railway boom of the 1850s, and while the government had built the canals, private corporations (buttressed by grants and guarantees) created the railways, often in a zealous and competitive fashion that led to overproduction. American contractors like Samuel Zimmerman, reputed manipulator of Canadian politics and leading figure of the Great Western Railway, mastered tactics of collusion and corruption, while Casimir Gzowski and his associates on the Grand Trunk followed suit. In the process, politicians' pockets were lined, but much capital was also generated and fed into productive outlets. Gzowski and others established the Toronto Rolling Mills in the 1850s, and by 1866 this imposing edifice employed over 300 men in rerolling old rails or puddling iron for new ones. A proliferation of metal-producing speciality shops and foundries emerged in the 1850s to cater to the needs of the railway age, while huge shops like those of the Grand Trunk in Montreal (employing 3,000) and of the Great Western in Hamilton (employing 500 to 600) provided additional stimulus to economic development. D.C. Masters commented appropriately that by 1860 "the increasing prominence and activity of the rising capitalist class" was evident in Toronto. Indeed, recent scholarship had been unambiguous in demonstrating the truth in the *People's Journal*'s 1871 assessment of the 1860s as a decade that "set agoing an industrial revolution."

Much study remains to be done on work environments of this period, but, as in the Philadelphia studies of Bruce Laurie and Mark Schmitz, production took place in at least five unevenly developed environments. Factories were just emerging in this period, and can be defined arbitrarily as any industrial shop employing 50 or more workers, and driven by waterwheel or steam-engine power. In the nineteenth century factories were often called manufactories, although they might be either mechanized or nonmechanized. Usually such work settings employed no fewer than 25 workers, and in the shoemaking and clothing industries, advancing technological change and the occasional use of steam power transformed the work process, introducing a previously unprecedented degree of impersonality and division of labour. Unmechanized firms employing from 6 to 25 workers were like sweatshops, in which labour was driven to excess, exploited viciously to cut costs and to meet contractual obligations. Some contractors avoided the sweatshop grind by relying on outwork, a labour process especially suited to the garment trades and prone to reliance upon women workers and the desperately poor. Artisan shops, traditional enclaves of skilled craftsmen, also survived into this period, and usually employed small numbers, although labour forces of 30 were not unknown. Beyond the factories and shops, of course, lay work on the docks and railways, where such classifications had little meaning.

A view of Hamilton, Toronto, and Montreal in the years from 1850 to 1870 reveals the overwhelming changes that occurred during that period. The industrial workforces of these cities comprised 16.7 percent, 16.8 percent, and 19.7 percent of their respective populations by the latter date. Whereas 24 percent of the workforce of Hamilton had laboured in shops employing ten or more people in 1851, this percentage had risen to 83 in 1871. Machinists, sons of the industrial revolution, increased in numbers by 800 percent in Hamilton between 1850 and 1870. As Katz, Doucet, and Stern have noted, Hamilton contained a number of large employers by 1871, and almost 53 percent of the city's 4,450 employed worked in settings of 50 or more labourers. Gregory S.

Kealey presents a similar picture of Toronto, which produced about double the industrial output of Hamilton, and with a labour force of 9,400, employed almost twice as many workers. In 1871, 57 percent of those employed in Toronto worked in factory-like settings employing 50 or more workers, and the rise of the clothing industry, where almost three-quarters of the workforce was female, attested to the introduction of women into wage work on a mass scale. (The Globe, in 1868, estimated that 3,800 women laboured in shops or in their homes on outwork). As in Hamilton, however, the increasing predominance of the large, impersonal work setting did not necessarily indicate the elimination of the small shop: in Toronto's boot and shoe industry mechanized (but not necessarily steam-powered) factories accounted for 90 percent of the workers, 86 percent of value added, and 20 percent of employers. These factories competed with smaller, more traditional, shops that made up the balance.

As important as boots and shoes were in Toronto, they were even more vital to Montreal, where, in 1871, 117 producers (more than twice as many as in Toronto) employed 5,175 workers (more than three times as many as in Toronto). Indeed, Montreal was the premier manufacturing city in the Canadas, and its growth since mid-century had been spectacular. Out of 44 firms listed in an 1856 booster publication, 24 had been established between 1850 and 1855, while in the important industrial district of St. Anne's Ward, Alan Conter showed remarkable rates of expansion between 1851 and 1857. Geared towards export production, with a captive home market, Montreal firms expanded markedly in the years from 1850 to 1870 and benefitted from the low wage structure of the city. As John McCallum argues, Montreal's industry was far more capital intensive than its largely Ontario-based rivals, and outstripped other Canadian manufacturing centres in productivity. In its leading sectors of boots and shoes, furs and hats, and tobacco, Montreal's firms exceeded competitors in value added per worker by 19, 87, and 81 percent respectively. A Montreal employer described his 700- to 1,000-employee factory in 1874, attesting to the advanced methods of production and their impact on labour: "We use a good deal of machinery; and we therefore do with a great deal less labor than those who do not; for instance, we have a 15 horse power engine running three machines having 50 needles each, with a knife which cuts the cloth by steam, so that four cutters will do the work of from twelve to fifteen." One commentator estimated that Montreal's diversified and advanced manufacturing sector accounted for 75 percent of the total production of Canada in 1875. If productivity did not stand the city in good competitive stead, a lock on the market might: Redpath Sugar, established in 1855 and employing more than 100 workers, was the only producer in Canada and supplied seven-eighths of the domestic demand for white sugar throughout the late 1850s.

Other metropolitan centres may not have kept pace with Hamilton,

Toronto, and Montreal, although the years from 1850 to 1870 often saw parallel developments. In Halifax, for instance, boot and shoe production also led the way in manufacturing, and 29 establishments employed 371 adult and child labourers. As in Toronto, the clothing industry was also a strong local producer, employing 238 people. Although the Maritimes remained oriented toward the old staples in these years, and in spite of the tight grip that commercial capital retained on economic activity, metropolitan centres like Halifax necessarily supported a manufacturing population. Smaller centres, especially in Ontario, also produced for local, regional, even national markets, so that by the 1870s domestic production was extensive. Jacob Spelt has demonstrated the importance of this production in south-central Canada, and an unpublished study of railways and their relation to labour, capital, and the state addresses the issue squarely for the years from 1850 to 1879. J.V. Barkans estimates that by 1870 domestic production supplied large percentages of the consumption of agricultural implements (95 percent), boots and shoes (99 percent), furniture (97 percent), machines (93 percent), woollens (85 percent), paper (82 percent), and foundry products (79 percent). Increasing attention to manufacturing output necessarily stimulated interest in innovation, as indicated by the rising numbers of patent applications, which grew from insignificant numbers in the 1850s to 1,124 in 1873. Concern with protection for native Canadian industry also arose and was formally implemented in the 1858/59 Galt–Cayley tariff and expanded in the 1860s. Such processes, and the brief description of manufacturing above, indicate just how far the economy of British North America had progressed since the days of colonial commercial dominance, staple trade, and agricultural production of the pre-1850 years.

Also stimulating production was the expansion of the home market, evident in the urban growth of these years. Between 1850 and 1880 the urban population of the provinces of Ontario and Quebec increased from 14 and 15 percent to 27 and 24 percent. Montreal led the way, with a population soaring from 90,000 in 1861 to 140,247 in 1881. In the same years, Toronto grew from 45,000 to 86,500, while Quebec City expanded from 42,000 to 62,500. Smaller centres often stagnated as they became absorbed into metropolitan hinterlands, but overall growth was impressive. For Ontario as a whole, urbanization was most pronounced, city populations expanding considerably. In 1851 the urban population had been 133,463; 30 years later it stood at 375,848.

It would, of course, be wrong to imply that this economic development and urbanization represented steady progress. For the advancing pace of production and population explosion concealed the beginnings of a downward turn in the economic cycle, and continual poverty if not deteriorating conditions of life. Two major depressions cut *depression*

into the economic buoyancy of these years, curtailing urban growth and severely disrupting life in Canada in the 1857–60 years and, again, from 1873 to 1879. Both depressions would take their toll on the petty producers and merchant princes, thereby furthering the relative interests of industrial capital and concentrating economic power. Out of these developments would come the highwater mark of competitive capitalism in the 1880s.

The 1857 crash brought to an end the easy continuity of handicraft production and the unquestioned hegemony of mercantile capital. Indeed, the depression struck both simultaneously. As the price of wheat plummeted, dropping from $1.92 to 85¢ a bushel in Toronto over the course of ten months in 1857/58, the leading merchant houses drew in their belts, withdrawing the credit they had liberally extended to many artisan producers. Petty capital and merchant capital nosedived as the commercial boom of the early 1850s gave way to a devastating crash. By 1858, this crash was most noticeable in the public "bursting of the railway bubble," as the speculative and corrupt juggling of public monies diverted to questionable projects came to light before a specially struck Select Standing Committee of Public Accounts. Hundreds of thousands of pounds had been siphoned off to the Grand Trunk and other railway lines. For those who were able to draw upon assets to survive the crash, the later 1850s ushered in a new age of optimism. Three major Montreal fortunes were consolidated in these years, as the Redpaths, Ogilvies, and Hugh Allan captured large shares of the sugar refining, milling, and steamship businesses. But for small men of limited means, as Michael Katz shows for what he calls "the entrepreneurial class" of Hamilton, this was an extremely difficult time, in which failure, bankruptcy, and turmoil were the lot of the producer. Between 1851 and 1861, 27 percent of Hamilton's master craftsmen/manufacturers moved down into the ranks of skilled labour, and in the next decade this trend accelerated, 43 percent of the petty producers experiencing proletarianization.

The impact of depression is also evident in the downturn of 1873–79. Like the earlier crash of the 1850s, the crisis of the mid-to-late 1870s was a world-wide phenomenon, following on the heels of a speculative frenzy culminating in European stock market crashes and American railway bankruptcies. Ontario's economy, still geared to the export of staples and imports of capital, was especially hard hit. But there would be some who would profit: between 1871 and 1881 the number of agricultural implements works in Ontario decreased by 32, while the workers employed increased by 1,050. One hundred fewer sawmills were manned by 3,000 more hands, while the number of tanneries decreased by 110 at the same time as the number of workers employed remained stable. Out of the troubled times of the 1870s emerged the drift toward monopoly in cotton production, and in factories producing railway cars and locomotives a modest rise in the number of firms was paralleled by a thirtyfold expansion of the workforce. Depression, in the years from 1850 to 1880, was a process spurring the concentration and centralization of capital, as well as a destructive force producing destitution and misery.

By the 1870s, then, Canada had gone through a period of state building, urbanization, and increasing expansion of the manufacturing sector. To be sure, the economy was still dominantly agricultural, but it was no longer overwhelmingly so. As O.J. Firestone has pointed out, value added by manufacturing in 1870 was 19 percent of gross national product, compared with 34 percent for agriculture; manufacturing provided 13 percent of the total jobs, while agriculture remained the key work sector, with 50 percent of total employment. Manufacturing activity was heavily concentrated in the Toronto-Hamilton and Montreal regions, which, according to Chambers and Bertram, accounted for a hefty percentage of all value added in manufacturing in central Canada. Although the large shop was beginning to overshadow the smaller concern, traditional work settings remained. As late as 1871, the average firm in Hamilton employed only 17 workers (compared to 5 in 1851), while in Toronto 88 percent of industrial establishments still employed fewer than 30 workers in 1871, although this large majority of establishments hired only 33 percent of the workforce. An industrial revolution, while in the making, was not yet consummated.

Class differences in these years widened, but consciousness of such disparity remained somewhat inhibited and constrained. Particularly in the 1870s, with the onslaught of a general price deflation that would continue through to the end of the century, competitive capitalists attempted to widen their share of the market by reducing costs. When directed at labour, this took the form of the wage cut and, taken in conjunction with the severe dislocations of depression, put labour on the defensive. Depression thus stimulated economic concentration, as well as alerting employers to the necessity of keeping their workers' wages relatively low. Throughout the years 1850–80, labour took advantage of prosperity and capital's productive needs to attempt to gain tangible wage increases, improve job conditions, and combat the expanding capitalist authority in the workplace that grew out of the accumulation of assets. But as labour reared its head in moments of upsurge, both its strengths and weaknesses would be revealed. Like the economy itself, workers were constrained by the business cycle, subject to the greater power of employers and politicians whose fortunes fluctuated with it. Thus, the first stirrings of a Canadian labour movement were stilled in the economic crises of the 1850s and 1870s.

An Insurrection of Labour

After a difficult period of adjustment to the revisions of the Corn Laws in the late 1840s, British North America experienced a pronounced commercial boom. Prices rose approximately two percent annually between 1850 and 1870, with the years from 1850 to 1854 marked by a particularly sharp rise in commodity prices that plateaued in 1854–57, dipped in the depression of the late 1850s, and, only in the mid-1860s, settled back to its 1852 level. To counteract the adverse effects of this pre-1855 inflationary surge, workers early resorted to the strike.

Railway labourers on the Quebec-Richmond, St. Lawrence and Atlantic, St. Lambert, St. Andrews (near Saint John, New Brunswick) and Great Western lines launced their demands in a series of riotous strikes between 1850 and 1853. Largely Irish (81 percent of the railway navvies in the Sherbrooke region in 1852 were Irishmen, only four percent French Canadian), workers on these construction sites reenacted the scenes of violence and disorder produced in the 1830s and 1840s by the canallers.

Skilled craftsmen were another group who suffered from the escalating prices of prosperity. But a more serious issue to craftsmen was the introduction of machines, which threatened the very basis of their respectable status and skill. In Montreal, shoemakers first encountered "Labor-Saving machinery" in 1849, when they formed a "Journeymen Shoemakers' Society" and declared a strike against the leading manufacturer, Brown & Childs. Toronto's tailors led the struggle against mechanization, reviving in 1852 the moribund society that had been established in the 1840s and dictating a new price list to their employers. One of the merchant tailor firms, Hutchinson & Walker, then introduced the first sewing machine into a Canada West manufactory, bringing a woman operative with the device from New York. The "knights of the needle" responded with a strike, and upon Hutchinson's capitulation celebrated their victory on King Street. Parading about the town, they ridiculed the detested machine, and symbolically buried it, hoisting it high in the air, carrying it on their shoulders after "the fashion of a corpse on its way to the burial grounds." The woman seamstress returned to the United States. Hutchinson & Walker sought to mollify their tailors, and provided a dinner for them; the men replied in kind, presenting their masters with "a silver crouching lion, the emblem of their establishment." But the employer's paternalist authority had been substantially assaulted, and he was to be plagued with "labour problems" again. Two years later the modernizing merchant charged that the organized journeymen had terrorized his workplace, and backed up his charges with legal action culminating in one of the best-publicized conspiracy trials of the decade. (George Brown's 1854 crusade against his printers was similarly publicized.) Hamilton tailors followed in their Toronto brothers' footsteps in 1854, protesting the introduction of machinery into their craft. "The fiend that has come amongst them," declared the *Hamilton Spectator*, "is none other than the steam engine with his sewing machine and other implements of evil, threatening the whole craft. It is no wonder, therefore, that they have come out and separated themselves from the evil, and have left the monster alone in his glory with his gussets and seams and shirts." The site of this confrontation was Lawson's tailoring establishment, "the largest in Canada," which employed 100 men in 1853, and boasted two sewing machines. In 1861 the number of machines had risen to ten, the number of male tailors employed had dropped to 29, and 69 female seamstresses had been introduced. For the craftsmen, the machine had taken its toll.

These conflicts seemed remarkably similar to earlier confrontations. The presence of symbolism and theatre, the localized nature of the struggles, the trade consciousness, and obvious concern with preservation of craft status recall the struggles of the 1830s, while the rough methods of the Irish are easily traceable to earlier upheavals. Strikes among early British Columbia miners in Fort Rupert (1849/50) and Nanaimo (1855) seem reminiscent of actions taken in previous decades by similarly isolated and "obnoxious" workmen and drew a like response from authority:

> It is moreover highly desirable that there should be a resident magistrate at Fort Rupert, as the miners and labourers there have shown a marked disposition to riot, which if not checked may lead to serious consequences, the Indian population being numerous, savage, and treacherous; and the distance from Victoria and the total want of means of communication between the two places increases the inconveniences.

But in fact, strikes of the early 1850s represented a preface to a dramatic shift in class relations, rather than a throwback to the past. As conflict between master and man continued, polarization occurred. Especially pronounced among the respectable trades workers, this emerging class cleavage widened a breach that had seemed minor and was mediated relatively easily in the pre-1850 years. The result was an 1853/54 strike wave that was "looked upon by the press and the public as the beginning of an insurrection of labour." (See Appendix III.) Commencing in the spring and summer of 1853, when craft workers took advantage of apparent labour shortages and expansive productive activity to initiate six struggles in Toronto, Hamilton, and Kingston, the insurrection of labour escalated, as Paul Appleton's unpublished Masters thesis demonstrates, to an unprecedented level of confrontation in May–June 1854, sweeping across south-central Canada in a labour upsurge that encompassed at least 22 strikes. In two months skilled craftsmen waged almost as many struggles as they had in the 50 years prior to 1850. While employers reacted with a grudging acceptance of craft workers' assertiveness in 1853, by 1854 a new truculence was evident in an invigorated stance of opposition that pushed worker and employer into open battle.

Accompanying many of these struggles were tactics of intimidation and the intransigence of employers willing to resort to the Combination Acts or the Master and Servant Act. A sense of grievance and class distinction was also growing. As a Toronto correspondent in the *Montreal Chronicle* reported "a general cessation of labour [in May 1854] . . . extending to almost every mechanic trade," the stonecutters responded to George Brown's attack on their attempt to secure shorter hours:" Are rational and intelligent beings, under the banner of freedom to be trampled under the feet of despotic, dollar hunting railway contractors? Are canals, *etc.*, instead of stone, to be built on the skulls and marrow of men? Freedom says no! Common sense and public opinion echo no!" In a situation in which "every shop and store is thronged; manufacturers and mechanics are working double time, and labourers cannot be had for love or money," the stonecutters' determination had a certain appeal and strength, and in 1853/54, workers often won their demands.

Unskilled labourers were noticeably absent from this insurrection that was described as "all but universal," an indication of the gulf still separating skilled and unskilled. Labour shortages in 1853/54 undoubtedly ensured that the unskilled had satisfactory wages, especially on the railway projects, and strikes may have been unnecessary. Ship labourers in Quebec were apparently able to double their wage rate from $1.50 to $3.00 daily between 1853 and 1854, without recourse to a strike. Of the 28 strikes known to have taken place in 1854, for instance, only six involved labourers, and the bulk of these were unskilled workers in the cities, with ties to craft workers or holding positions on municipal projects. But a strike of railway navvies working on a Welland Canal bridge near Port Colborne at the end of October 1854 introduced the unskilled, once more, into the fray. Striking for payment of back wages, these labourers, unlike the skilled, adopted the strike in a stance of defence, rather than in an aggressive effort to establish mechanisms of shop control, thwart machines, or reappropriate a slice of labour value extracted from their skill.

By the autumn of 1854, and certainly by 1855, the economy was dipping toward the crash of 1857. In this context of economic recession the skilled backed away from confrontation while the unskilled were increasingly forced into it. When Montreal stonecutters struck in November 1857, the newspaper response was a curt, "Are these men mad?" Between 1855 and 1859 only 14 strikes and riotous worker confrontations are known to have occurred, and of these more than half were mass strikes of relatively unskilled labour: Quebec ship labourers, Grand Trunk workers at Point St. Charles, labourers on western Ontario or Nova Scotia railway lines. Often spontaneous, these uprisings of the unskilled often led to pitched battles, as in the Ridgeway Riot on the Buffalo, Brantford, and Goderich Railway in 1855, an eventful occurrence that precipitated an American contractor's invasion of Canada to quiet his workmen with a force that the Canadian state could not provide. At St. Mary's, navvies sacked a church, beat overseers, and attempted to drive off newly imported workers. In April and May of 1855, Grand Trunk workers in Point St. Charles struck for better wages and shorter hours, destroyed 11 labour-saving derricks, and managed to spread their strike movement to other Griffintown shops, especially the foundries and Redpath's refinery. One senses neighbourhood and kinship ties at work here, emboldening the strikers to proceed to a number of industrial establishments "with a perfect sense of impunity," thus securing a limited victory.

The only comparable action among the skilled was a large strike of workmen in the Great Western Railway shops in London and Hamilton in November–December 1856, when mass action secured the reinstatement of a shopmate dismissed arbitrarily. Other struggles of the skilled were minor affairs: printers, woodworkers, and shoemakers were all involved in small-scale conflicts in the years of the later 1850s, but they often proved unsuccessful. More noteworthy was a massive demonstration of the unemployed in Quebec City in late November 1857, led by the ship carpenters. Congregated at City Hall, over 3,000 workingmen petitioned the Mayor for relief, demanding "work at any price." Speakers mounted the roof of the municipal building to address the throng in French and English, urging "the maintenance of law and order." After proceeding through the principal streets of Lowertown to the St. Roch district, the assembled drafted a public statement demanding action: "Winter is approaching and will find us in the midst of a severe pressure. What is to become of our labouring population? The hopes held out of a resumption of the ship building trade, which employs so many industrious hands at this season of the year may be fallacious. No time is to be lost, some arrangement should be made to aid the poorer classes in their struggles with poverty and distress."

This meeting provides a fitting statement on the close of the decade, a reflection of the devastating impact of the 1857 crash upon the beginnings of a Canadian labour movement. Silenced by the close of the 1850s, workers had nevertheless waged more than 65 strikes between 1850 and 1859. In the flush of solidarity of 1853/54, they had mounted a labour campaign that aimed beyond the sectional interests of craft, and hinted at a broad-ranging collectivity that might well have included the unskilled. Retreating into whatever security they could find in the post-1857 collapse, the skilled sought "work at any price" and recession likely conditioned an exclusivist stance of detachment. Nativism seemed on the rise within the society itself, and this served to divide many workers. Both the strengths and weaknesses of labour at this turning point lay in workers' organizations, in a local and international unionism that was forged in the 1850s and carried through to the next period of boom and bust — the 1870s.

Unionism: Local and International

The strikes of the 1850s, and particularly the insurrection of labour, had been sustained by workers' societies, associations, and unions, almost all of them composed of skilled labourers rooted in particular local settings. Centred in Saint John, Montreal, Quebec, Toronto, Hamilton, and London, there were dozens of isolated trade societies that flourished after mid-century, and organization even spread to the far west, a bakers' society forming in Victoria in January 1859. Eugene Forsey's exhaustive researches on the early Canadian labour movement suggest that there were two-thirds as many local unions in existence in the 1850s (about 30) as there had been in the entire first half of the nineteenth century. Seal skinners in Newfoundland were organized in 1855 and in Saint John, New Brunswick, an early centre of labour activism, Richard Rice's study of workers' organization reveals the existence of seven societies. Led by carpenters, tailors, printers, and shoemakers, these early unions were as interested in social and benevolent activities as they were in defending labour's economistic or workplace interests. Particularly notable, inasmuch as it grew out of the distressed context of 1857, was the Quebec Ship Labourer's Benevolent Society, led by a small contingent of Irishmen known as authentic " 'Little' Champlain Street harps." Organized on street corners on summer nights, the body eventually formalized its meetings (gathering regularly in the Temperance Hall) and its dealings with shipmasters and the stevedore middlemen, becoming one of the most formidable associations in Quebec City.

In its heydey in the years 1860–73, which corresponded with the last prosperous phase in the trade in square timber, the Ship Labourers' Society embraced five locals and 2,000 members, 95 percent of whom were Irish. Brought to public attention by its involvement in a mass strike in 1866, the Society outraged Quebec's leading merchants, increasingly resentful of the "decidedly and undeniably illegal" actions of the labourers, who refused to countenance either "scabs" (and actually invaded the sacred precincts of the naval dockyard to do battle with strikebreakers) or steam-driven machinery on the docks. By the late 1870s the Ship Labourers' Society was in decline. The collapse of shipbuilding in Quebec, traditionally a preserve of French-Canadian labour, pushed Québécois workers into longshoring, and they formed their own body, *L'Union Canadienne*. Riotous clashes between French and Irish took place in 1878/79, signalling the termination of the Irish "reign" in the ship labouring trade. Eventually this rift was healed, French and Irish uniting in the 1880s under the auspices of the Knights of Labor, but it marked the end of an epoch of local unionism in Quebec City.

Over the course of the 1860s and 1870s local unionism thrived, especially in Ontario, where as many as 80 societies existed. In the Maritimes between 1860 and 1875 there were at least 13 labour bodies in Halifax, one in Pictou, nine in Saint John, one in Chatham, and one in Charlottetown. Montreal was, similarly, a centre of activity, while in Britsh Columbia the shipwrights, typographers, and miners boasted organizations. Such figures may reveal only trends in the process of local unionism, for much more local research and study is required before we can grasp with any certainty the character and structural dimensions of working-class experience in this period.

As with the institutional context, there is a lack of precise figures on the extent of conflict between these shadowy local unions (as well as unorganized workers) and employers, although, once more, the trends seem reasonably clear. Ian McKay notes the existence of 15 strikes in Halifax between 1850 and 1874, an indication that eastern port cities may have been caught up in some of the same developments that were rocking central Canada and leading to the insurrection of labour. Combining Forsey's discussion of strikes in Quebec with material compiled in Jean Hamelin's, Paul Larocque's, and Jacques Rouillard's *Répertoire des Grèves dans la Province de Québec au XIXᵉ Siècle* and ongoing research in Montreal newspapers, it is evident that more than 30 strikes were waged in Montreal and Quebec between 1861 and 1869, the bulk of them occurring after 1867. Many of these conflicts proceeded in the absence of worker organization, but others, like the Montreal carters' strikes of 1863/64, studied by Margaret Heap, undoubtedly had some form of association behind them. As Heap points out, such struggles reflected the growing awareness of class, the increasingly impersonal nature of work under unambiguously capitalist conditions creating fissures and antagonisms that led to battle. The number of carters in Montreal had grown from 201 in 1825 to almost 1,200 in 1861, while the Grand Trunk Railway assumed a monopolistic hold over the vitally important transportation sector. As one carter noted, the strike of 1864 turned on the resentments engendered by this process: "There [are] at this moment six hundred men, formerly as happy as kings, some with their single horse and cart, who [are] now mere drivers for the Grand Trunk."

Some general patterns of conflict can be discerned, which distinguish the experiences of the skilled crafts from those of the day labourers. The latter, for the most part, struck to secure wages and to gain an immediate and tangible end. Victory or defeat tended to depend upon local conditions and the availability of surplus labourers willing to fill the positions vacated. Unless backed by large organizations, like the ship labourers of Quebec or Saint John, labourers' strikes were usually short affairs of one or two days' duration. Labourers engaged in the construction of Montreal's street railway, for instance, struck work in 1861 and 1864; both conflicts were resolved in a day or two. Workers with a skill to bargain with, however, were more likely to use the strike to achieve a variety of ends: to gain wage increases, to resist wage cuts (especially in the 1870s), and to secure a measure of autonomy or mundane workers' control at their work sites. In the last case, workers often struck to limit the hiring of apprentices, thereby preserving the character of skill and limiting the supply of labour, or to restrict output or maintain the standard wage rate, both of which stood as badges of respectability and craft pride. For the skilled, an appropriate demeanour toward the boss was essential in maintaining craft dignity. An 1864 stonecutters' dispute supports this point. Refusing to abridge their own time and be called to work prematurely, they wrote to explain their position: "We say, we will not answer roll call at a quarter before seven and a quarter before one. The contractor can adopt a method to obviate that necessity. He may have roll called (for stonecutters only we speak) at seven o'clock and one. *We will have one hour for dinner.*"

This kind of insistence understandably drew opposition, and as early as 1861 the *Montreal Gazette* reported that "strikes were becoming epidemic among skilled mechanics." In 1867 Montreal's Médéric Lanctôt, a local journalist drawn to the workers' cause, claimed that strikes had occurred yearly over the course of the previous three decades. Local unions provided one vehicle in which early Canadian workers could ride out their resentments, and they stood behind many conflicts. By the 1860s, however, while still important, they were less significant than the growth of internationally connected organizations of labour, bodies that sought to create wider solidarities within trade sectors and that linked workers of one locale to those of another. To combat the emergence of national, indeed international, labour markets and combinations of capital in these years, workers quickly gravitated to similarly conceived bodies of labour. At the beginning of 1859, British North America contained only one internationally connected union, affiliates of the British-based Amalgamated Society of Engineers having small branches in Hamilton (14 members) and Toronto (11 members). Thirty years later, there were two British internationals (the Engineers were joined by the Amalgamated Society of Carpenters and Joiners) with 11 branches and 11 American craft unions with 43 locals. These figures, moreover, understate the impact of internationalism, for a number of unions, such as the Coopers International Union, had been strong in the late 1860s and early 1870s, only to succumb to changes in the work process that eroded skills. As their trade was mechanized, coopers found themselves redundant, employers no longer hired them, and their craft union lost members month by month until there were no longer sufficient supporters to keep the organization going. All unions also suffered setbacks in the depression of 1873–79.

Entirely restricted to the skilled, international craft unionism was centred in the Iron Molders International Union (18 locals from Halifax to London, 1859–80), the International Typographical Union (11 locals in Ontario and Quebec, 1865–72), the Coopers International Union (which organized 24 locals in the first two years of its existence in the early 1870s), and associations of engineers, carpenters and joiners, locomotive engineers (who would wage the first major railway strike in 1876/77) and firemen, and cigarmakers. The short-lived Knights of St. Crispin galvanized early Canadian shoemakers in the late 1860s and early 1870s, and there were possibly as many as 26 Crispin lodges from Saint John in the east to Petrolia in the west. They had all but disappeared by the end of the depression of the 1870s, victims of economic downturn, employer hostility, and skill dilution.

Like the local unions, internationally affiliated bodies were drawn into conflict situations. Violently opposed by individual employers as well as international associations of capitalists such as the Troy-based Founders' Association, craft unions led a number of Canadian strikes and were often subjected to lockouts. Moulders led the way, engaging in at least 19 strikes and lockouts in the 1860s and 1870s, while cigarmakers with eight, coopers with four, and the Knights of St. Crispin with 13 strikes between 1869 and 1873 were also prominent. Among such workers the desire to govern everyday apsects of their working lives was of special importance, and these strikes often turned on the question of such control. The Coopers International Union pledged that all barrelmakers should "allow no one to teach a new hand" in order "to control the supply of help." In strikes fought to gain this and other similar ends, however, financial support from international headquarters was crucial. One unsuccessful cigarmakers' battle in Toronto in 1873 was sustained by $1,675 in aid, while the Canadian moulders, whose locals averaged approximately 25 members each in the late 1860s, received over $5,000 in support from the United States in 1874/75. This represented nearly one-third of the union's total expenditure on strikes and lockouts, and Hamilton's local, no. 26, benefitted from an immense donation of $3,480, which made it the best-funded union in North America in its moment of adversity. Generous aid of this sort lent material meaning to the I.M.I.U. seal, which bore impressions of both the American coat of arms and the royal crown, across which stretched the clasped hands emblematic of the international solidarity of labour.

By 1873, on the eve of the nineteenth century's greatest depression, there was a total of at least 123 unions (local and international) in Canada. Far more than mere bodies of economic protection, these unions were social institutions as well. They had their own rituals and often publicly paraded in ceremonial procession. As centres of benevolence and fraternity, they encouraged a unified working-class experience outside the workplace and the realm of conflict. Leisure, politics, and education became points of collective concern, and at union meetings, workers debated temperance and Confederation, as well as the standard wage rate.

The social and cultural place of early workers' organizations can be determined partly by examining attendance at public parades. One of the earliest of these took place in Saint John, as an 1853 procession honoured the European and North American Railway. Five thousand marched, among them 40 house carpenters and joiners, workers from 16 shipyards, tool manufacturers, printers, 200 farriers, 300 founders, 50 painters, 100 stonecutters and masons, 80 bakers, 250 shoemakers led by King Crispin and Queen Crispiana, 150 tailors, 12 millers, 100 riggers and sailmakers, 90 cabinetmakers, and 1,100 millmen. Each group sported banners, uniforms, and emblems, and many paraded alongside wagons bearing representations of their labour. A printing press drawn by four grey horses was emblazoned with the message, "Knowledge is Power," and was attended by the ubiquitous "printer's devil," supported by likenesses of Franklin, Guttenberg, and other notable figures. A song composed by a local printer came off the press to be distributed along the parade route. A concluding stanza proclaimed the worth of the printers' craft:

> Worthy strangers while we pay
>   Honor to this happy day;
> While we honor you no less,
>   Let us not forget the press:
> High as is the power of Steam;
>   Great as is the Railway scheme;
> High above Electric wires,
>   Still the glorious Press aspires.

Craft banners articulated pride in artisan skills and the dignity and essential place of productive labour: the blacksmiths and founders walked under banners depicting a woman hanging from an anchor reading, "By hammer in hand, all arts do stand"; tool makers let onlookers know that, "Tis by our aid all work is done"; "For the good of all," read the bakers' banner, adorned with sheaves of corn and men in working dress; the cabinetmakers followed a wagon laden with furniture with a simple message, "Love and Unity," superimposed on a placard depicting clasped hands, its obverse carrying a figure of justice. The moulders spoke for the entire procession with their motto, "Industry and Benevolence unite in Friendship" (a carryover from 1840 blacksmiths' badges), while the tailors, outfitted in matching suits and scarves and preceeded by Adam, Eve, and a Golden Lamb, exemplified the tradition of the erudite artisan with a Latin inscription, "Concordia Pariae res Crescunt."

Such celebrations of respectability and craftsmanship were not the sole prerogative of the skilled, although in Saint John the powerful Irish Ship Labourers had not marched. In Quebec City, ship labourers were at the centre of the public procession, and marched each 23 July to commemorate the founding of their Society. Winding their way through Lower Town, the marchers circled Upper Town "four abreast" and, after an eight-mile parade in which "serenades" were offered their supporters, returned to the dock area. Discipline was rigorous: fines were levied on those who did not take part, and there was no indulgence allowed, a visit to the tavern meriting expulsion from the ranks. Bands, flags, and placards accompanied the labourers, and a huge banner depicted a ship being loaded and carried the motto, "We support our infirm; we bury our dead." Such public displays reinforced the worker's self-image, and thus held great personal value for many members of the working class. At the same time, public processions could be directed against class enemies. Saint John labourers, in the midst of an 1875 upheaval attempting to secure control of longshoremen's jobs for members of the Labourers Benevolent Association, turned out to march in the funeral procession of one of their number, a common practice for all unions in this period. The *Telegraph* expressed its unequivocal disapproval, reading into the event a menacing purpose:

> And if the strike does not have the desired effect, there are other means behind it. . . . On the occasion of a death of a member other members are obliged to suspend work and attend the funeral, and the mourning portion of the programme — the long procession, walking two and two — is so carried out as to assure the public in reference to the large number of persons who are thus bound together. It is probable that these displays are not intended to be acts of intimidation: there is no denying, however, that they have this effect and that the society derives quite as much benefit of its kind, from their lengthened processions as they ever obtained from attacks on "outsiders" engaged in their occupation.

The funeral, like the public parade, provided an opportunity to demonstrate self-worth and the power of solidarity.

By the late 1860s these parades had come to occupy an important place in the world of the Canadian worker. In 1867 Médéric Lanctôt formed the Grand Association of Canadian Workingmen (also known as the Association of Industrial and Mechanical Classes of Canada). Claiming 8,000 members, the new association promised to avert the strike, and endorsed cooperation. The bakers quickly made a mockery of such attempts to stifle militancy through organization, and struck work under the auspices of the association. On 10 June 1867 the Association held a torchlit procession. Although chastised in the press as "very badly managed and a complete failure," the parade nevertheless displayed the usual banners and symbolic representations. From the coopers' blunt statement, "We work well when well paid" to the cabinetmakers' reminder that "Equal justice only will insure permanent peace," the mottoes reflected labour's emerging pragmatism as well as its humanistic concerns. Early support for Canadian national feeling, especially the economic nationalism of a protective tariff, was also demonstrated by workingmen in public parades. Hamilton's workers, for instance, marched in a grand "Celebration Day" procession on 1 July 1867 accompanied by the usual craft displays, regalia, and banners.

Not all the workers in such parades were unionists, of course, but many were. Nor were those involved in the increasingly common class conflicts of the years from 1850 to 1880 all organized. Much of the rough culture of the earlier years remained, and might be used by workers who lacked access to organization or traditions of conflict. Dry goods clerks in Ottawa who engaged in an early closing agitation in April 1865 outraged respectable society, "daubing over with filth" the front of one mercantile store holding out against the attempt to close all retail outlets at 7:00 P.M. In the Red River Valley, Thomas Scott, later to be executed by Riel, led an 1869 strike to secure payment of travelling expenses for a road-construction crew. Upon winning their demand, Scott and others seized the contractor, threatened to duck him in the Seine River, and extorted the wages they would have received had they not been out on their two-day work stoppage. The contractor acquiesced, but later filed a civil suit for aggravated assault.

Such actions were far from rare in the third quarter of the nineteenth century, and were complemented by the beginnings of political activity among the urban working class, which will be explored shortly. This emerging class presence drew stiff rebuke from some quarters, the Halifax *Evening Express* proclaiming in 1874:

> No burning questions of capital and labour divide our people and distress our rulers. Strikes are infrequent, there is not much enforced idleness, there is no tyranny over the workman that he should rise against, there are no laws which oppress him, there is no tariff that he objects to being unfair . . . . We protest against . . . the beginnings of that dangerous species of combination among workmen which gives so much distress to the authorities and inflicts so much ultimate evil on the workingman himself.

This portrayal of Canadian society may well have been more wishful thinking than social analysis, but the anger, indeed fear, evident in such an excerpt was real enough. It had, in part, grown out of increasing class antagonisms, rooted in a social formation that, for the first time in Canadian history, was unmistakably industrial and capitalistic. While the escalating rate of unionization, in both its local and its international forms, and the growing numbers of strikes were all a part of working-class experience, they were by no means the only expression of late nineteenth-century working-class culture.

Associational Life

One of the most significant features of the Victorian cultural landscape was the proliferation of associations, clubs, societies, and lodges in the years from 1850 to 1880. It was during this period that fraternal societies, sporting clubs, and other forms of associational life began to supplement the institutions of self-help (mechanics' institutes) and community protection (fire companies) that had their roots in an earlier age. The magnitude of this associational network was quite striking, and in a period predating mass culture and highly commercialized forms of recreation, it formed a vital part of everyday life. More than one-third of the Orange Lodges that existed in the nineteenth century were established during the 1850s, when approximately 550 were formed. Claiming a membership of 200,000 in 1864, the Canadian Orange Order no doubt exaggerated its strength, but it was nevertheless a critical component of late nineteenth-century society, and by 1900 there were about 1,450 active lodges with approximately 40 members each. And this was just one fraternal order: there were societies associated with people's national origins, like the Sons of England, as well as the Masons, Oddfellows, Knights of Pythias, Independent Order of Foresters, and others. By 1880 there were apparently 100 lodges of the Ancient Order of United Workmen in Ontario alone, enrolling over 3,000 members. There were also large numbers of sporting clubs in urban centres, drawing baseball, lacrosse, snowshoeing, rowing, or fishing enthusiasts to their ranks. Almost every city had a series of volunteer fire companies which gradually gave way to professional brigades by the close of the century. While by no means the sole territory of the working class, this matrix of lodges, associations, and volunteer groups was not without its plebeian component. With histories extending into the 1880s and 1890s, indeed well into the twentieth century, these forums of cross-class social interaction were of special attraction to labouring people in the third quarter of the nineteenth century.

There was much, for instance, to draw the worker to the fraternal lodge or secret order. This was especially true of the skilled worker, whose respectability was being threatened by the introduction of machines and by a society that was beginning to place ever more value on profit than on craft worth. Friendly societies offered death benefits and the promise of a proper burial, a badge of status in an age of insecurity. Beyond this, the very language of the fraternal lodge was often borrowed from the crafts, appealing to a sense of dignity and pride of workmanship well understood by the mechanic. The comforts of shared sympathies and impressions must have drawn wandering emigrants, on "tramps" of unnatural severity. Many skilled Scots were attracted to the St. Andrew's Society, just as Irish Catholics joined the St. Patrick's Society. Moreover, the elaborate ritual and solemnity of the secret societies undoubtedly cultivated a sense of fraternity cherished by men of the trades. Many nineteenth-century workers might also have been attracted to the charitable protection provided by both voluntary and secret societies, as a means of transcending economic constraints.

It is not surprising, then, to find so many workers flocking to various associations in the latter half of the nineteenth century. In three Toronto lodges of the Orange Order studied by Gregory S. Kealey, membership in the 1870s was between 49 and 83 percent working class, while in Hamilton the 63 occupationally classifiable officials of the various lodges of the Orange Order in the years from 1863 to 1878 were 85 percent working class. Labour leaders often occupied key posts in societies, and it is not unlikely that prominent figures in local unions might have belonged to three or four other associations, as well as fulfilling their responsibilities within their craft organization. Outside the Orange Order, where urban lodge membership was overwhelmingly plebeian, workers were seldom dominant. But in societies like the Masons or Oddfellows, they could comprise a solid one-third of the membership. By the 1880s one working-class figure would pronounce with confidence that nine-tenths of the fraternal orders' membership was working class. This was an overstatement, but it did emphasize the importance of these societies in the cultural experience of the working class.

It has become something of a reigning conventional wisdom that this participation in societies that leaned toward the chauvinistic, the sectarian, or the exclusivist was itself a repudiation of class. In friendly societies where journeyman, master, manufacturer, and merchant "prince" might rub shoulders, it has been argued that workers came to see their society in pluralistic terms, lost any measure of class consciousness, and began to harbour disdain for those workers whose life-styles did not conform to the fraternal order's image of respectability. There is some truth in such a perspective, but it obscures as much of the actual situation as it clarifies. For in the friendly society, the workingman learned the value of mutuality, of fraternity, of cooperation, and of equality. As class awareness came increasingly to the fore in the 1880s, these lessons could translate into a conception and practice of solidarity.

Beyond the fraternal order, workingmen also met in mechanics' institutes, the fire companies, and the sporting clubs. Small towns like Napanee, Goderich, Woodstock, and Paris, as well as larger centres like Halifax, Montreal, Hamilton, and Toronto all supported institutes in these years. According to Foster Vernon, there were 67 institutes in Ontario by 1858 with a membership of about 7,600, and by 1879, despite some failures, the number had risen to 72, and those enrolled in institutes had climbed over 9,000. Although often controlled by upper-class elements, these local institutions offered workers a wide range of scientific and pleasurable reading material, providing an environment in which workers could relax and the more industrious could educate themselves.

In fire companies, workingmen had the experience of participating in community service and in convivial gatherings of peers over beer and conversation, as well as the company of their fellows at picnics, parades, or oyster suppers. Often created, led, and staffed by workingmen, the fire companies of manufacturing centres such as Brockville or industrial cities such as Hamilton were an expression of the Victorian working-class penchant for associational life.

Companies like Hamilton's Great Western Railway had their own fire brigades, manned by their workers, and such enterprises also gave rise to sporting associations. Team sports emerged in the latter half of the century as a significant feature of working-class associational life. Hamilton's workers were avid baseball players, and printers, cigarmakers, moulders, and shoemakers all spent many early evenings and Saturday afternoons on the diamond. In Montreal, sporting clubs gained working-class support among the machinists and mechanics of the industrialized wards of St. Anne's and St. Mary's, where the Lachine Canal and Canadian Pacific Railway sheds concentrated workers, providing meeting areas. At Point St. Charles, the Grand Trunk Railway shops gave rise to numerous workingmen's clubs, while the city's internationally prominent lacrosse club, the Shamrocks, although financed by well-to-do Irish Canadians, was dominated by Irish Catholic mechanic players.

Associational life was therefore a realm apart from the troubled conflicts of the workplace in the years from 1850 to 1880. Overriding class barriers at certain times, it was also an experience that could serve to reinforce notions of class difference. Morgan O'Connell, captain of the Montreal Shamrocks, reacted to some adverse criticism of his club in 1874 with the words, "I hope this is not because we are only mechanics, and Irish Catholics at that." Moreover, regardless of how much it conditioned in workers a social perspective that denied class, associational life stimulated attachments to benevolence, mutuality, and fraternity that would lead to the working-class movement's later commitment to collectivity. But for all these egalitarian notions, associational life was dominated by men. In fraternal society, secret order, fire company, or sporting club, it was workingmen, not women, who participated. By mid-century, with the advent of machines diluting the acquired skills necessary to craft work, women had begun to join the ranks of a burgeoning workforce. Occupying unskilled rungs on the hierarchy of occupation, and confined by proscriptions against women's involvement in public life, their role in working-class associational life was limited. But as the fraternal order's stress upon mutual aid and proper burial suggests, associational life, however much it was a male sphere, was often related to the survival and preservation of another realm, in which women figured prominently. In the family, which embraced working-class experience, as well as extending beyond it, young workers were born and socialized to their class position in the social order. And here, too, as in the lodges and clubs of respectable workingmen, the practice of mutuality was rooted deeply.

Families

In spite of its central importance in the history of the working class, the family remains virtually unstudied. Only with the recent attempts of quantitative historians to probe accessible manuscript census material have we come to some tentative and suggestive assessments of the ways in which working-class families responded to the emergence of industrial capitalism's beginnings in the years after mid-centruy. Here lies an essential research priority, in which a great deal of exploration must proceed if we are to uncover a history buried in inarticulate experience.

The importance of the family in nineteenth-century working-class life emerges out of many developments. Ritualistic practices like the charivari, which was used to punish violators of domestic norms, proclaimed a general attachment to the family itself, and pointed to the need to sustain it. In the outports of Newfoundland, as Gerald Sider suggests, work was organized along family lines, and yearly ritualized gatherings such as Christmas mumming provided a structured but relatively informal way of reforming work relationships, recognizing the link between domestic and labouring life. Regardless of where we look — at the land of an increasingly market-oriented, wage-supported agriculture, at the coastal villages of the Maritimes, where the harvests of the sea defined much of economic life, or at urban centres dominated by industrial-capitalist growth — the family appears as a social foundation defended by working people. In spite of a series of hardships and forces working to disrupt family life, it remained an institution around which the labouring class developed work-related strategies of survival as well as cultural standards that, if influenced by material considerations, were not primarily economic. It is possible to discern family patterns that divide workers from nonworkers, including different structures of fertility and class-based variations in the meaning of "childhood" and "domesticity."

Economic threats to the family, of course, were often at the root of working-class grievances, and precipitated many a social conflict, especially between skilled mechanics and their employers. "There can be no doubt that the dollar would go farther in a family twenty years ago than double that sum can be made to supply at the present day," explained a discontented workingman in the midst of an 1864 Halifax house joiners' strike. "Under the circumstances, therefore," he continued, "the workmen are justified in looking out for themselves and the dear ones dependent on them for their daily bread." Outside this kind of common defence, particular strategies pursued by workers within familial relations often related to work and economic possibilities. Normand Séguin and Chad Gaffield have shown that for the Saguenay and Ottawa timber districts, seasonal labour in the lumber industry could sustain entire families on landed holdings that were marginal at best, underwriting a precarious but persistent process of family formation.

Workplace conditions also affected the structural features of the family, and heightened the class distinctions between working-class and nonworking-class families. Central here was the expanding employment of women and children, ushered into the workplace by expansions in plant size, mechanization of trades, and dilution of skill. While these years were dominated by uneven development in which routinized factory production coexisted with small handicraft manufactories and artisanal work, the influx of unskilled labourers who were often under the age of 16 or female was considerable. Moulds invented in the early 1860s transformed the cigarmaking trade and stimulated an influx of women and children; textile production expanded employment opportunities for working women and the young considerably; and the introduction of sewing machines in the clothing industry and the McKay stitcher in shoemaking in the 1860s undermined the position of male workers.

The proportion of women and children in Montreal's shoemaking and clothing industires increased 50 and 80 percent, respectively, between 1861 and 1871. One in three workers in Ontario's three leading boot and shoe production centres in 1871 was a woman; one in seven was under 16 years of age. As bakeries expanded from manufactories to factories, the employment of women and children increased. In Halifax this process was especially notable in the 1870s, as the percentage of children increased from roughly 9 to 22 percent of the labour force in baking; the percentage of women jumped from 11 to 16 percent. Tobacco works in Ontario employed 371 male hands, 91 women, and 245 children in 1871. In Hamilton's four sewing-machine factories, children comprised one-third of the labour force in the early 1870s. Across the country, more women and children worked in tobacco manufactories than men in 1881; they they made up 42 percent of the industrial workforce in Montreal in 1871 and 33 percent in Toronto; and in the former city approximately one in every four boys aged 11 to 15 was employed in wage labour. Such figures provide the starting point for an understanding of working-class family life in the years from 1850 to 1880.

In these years, as work by Bettina Bradbury (Montreal) and Michael Katz and his associates (Hamilton) suggests, working-class life unfolded within a family, rather than individual, economy. The family of labouring persons subsisted, not on an individual wage, but on the combined earnings and unpaid contributions of men, women, and children. Katz notes, for instance, that in Hamilton between 1851 and 1871, fertility rates among the business class (composed of professionals, agents, clerks, merchants, manufacturers, and employing master craftsmen) decreased strikingly. Desiring more consumption for their families and more education for their children, the bourgeois and petty bourgeois limited the number of children they conceived in order to appropriate rationally the optimum in material goods and social benefits. In contrast, fertility rates among skilled workers increased over the same period, while the numbers of children born to labourers increased even more dramatically, at twice the rate of the skilled. This cresting fertility was thus one expression of class need: those social classes most constrained by economic necessity responded positively to the opportunities of an expanding teenage labour market, which could be exploited to help provide sustenance for the family. By the 1880s there is evidence of entire families being recruited to particular work settings, especially the cotton mills. There family discipline functioned in the interests of capital, but could also mount a challenge to attempts to fragment the family wage. "Why did you dismiss my daughters?" asked one irate mother, "I have need of their assistance to live."

Indeed, those families whose children had not reached the age of 11 were at an economic disadvantage, for married women were not likely to work for wages in the traditional sense. Employed in their younger years as servants, seamstresses, or milliners, women often left the workforce upon marriage. By the 1870s, with increasing employment opportunities in factory work, some married women drifted into this type of wage labour, but their numbers were not large. Bradbury's study of two Montreal wards in 1871 notes only 2.5 percent of wives resident with their husbands reporting an occupation. If a woman was widowed, of course, the likelihood of her engaging in wage labour would be much higher, but even here it was more common for women to have recourse to the "putting-out" system, whereby they did consignment work in their homes at reduced pay rates. And it was here that most women found employment, structured into the confines of an age-old rationalization that saw "secondary" earners as deserving of only the most meagre payment. A Montreal clothier explained that he hired a number of women who worked in their own homes for "very cheap . . . to buy finery . . . which they would not be able to buy but for this industry." In fact, however, such women worked out of sheer necessity, and were a part of a process of family survival. Sometimes survival meant sharing a household with another family. Although Katz has found 80 percent of the households in Hamilton to be nuclear, Bradbury's examination of working-class wards suggests a lower figure of from 56 to 63 percent, although this difference may be rooted culturally in French Canadian society. Other means of family subsistence included sending children into wage work and retaining links with relatives in the country. These were all elementary steps in keeping the family unit together through unemployment, recession, seasonal curtailment of work, and sickness.

There were many times when such efforts failed, when death, disaster, or personal failings (manifesting thenselves most often in intemperance or desertion) struck a blow at the family. Two thousand children under the age of 16 were housed in the Montreal prison in 1869, while Protestant and Catholic orphanages in the same years sheltered abandoned babies and children who could no longer be adequately cared for by their natural parents. Over 1,000 girls passed through one such institution, the St. Alexis Orphanage run by the Sisters of Providence, in the years from 1860 to 1890. Only one percent of these children had definitely lost both of their parents, testimony to the harsh blows struck against the working-class family by poverty, sickness, and death. The loss of a mother, for instance, even though it may not have meant the loss of a wage, shook the family to its very foundations, and might well have forced reluctant fathers into hasty remarriage or the "boarding out" of children they could not care for adequately. Widows who lost husbands faced even more pronounced material anguish, for they were often left without a source of income or the skill to provide cash in sufficient quantity to continue child rearing. As Bradbury notes, fragmenting the family for a short period, placing children in charitable institutions until they could be reclaimed at an age when they could be put to work, was one means by which the Victorian working class attempted to secure its long-term survival.

It was thus in families both fragile and resilient that the working class reproduced itself over the course of the nineteenth century, families in which cultural attachments and visions, ideals and a measure of autonomy were circumscribed by material realities and the pervasive influence of work. As such, the working-class family was a force that embraced the related currents of conscious human agency and structured social necessity. Partly created by working people, it was also, in part, moulded and shaped by the largely impersonal developments of the age of nascent industrial capitalism. Men and women walked to the altar, conceived children within the context of intimate emotional and physical ties, but behind their backs events unfolded which limited the range of their choices, structuring behaviour along appropriate paths. Aspects of working-class culture waged an incoherent resistance against this process, striking out sometimes in blind, unconscious rage at this ordering of life. For some, drink was an avenue of defiance, the tavern an alternative to or escape from the family.

Tavern Life: The World of Joe Beef's Canteen

Working-class culture was always a many-faceted historical presence, and there were aspects of the experience of the labouring poor that remained untouched by the confinements of respectability or the family. The tavern was one such realm, and one with a long history. Innkeepers in Upper Canada were known for their "independence" and republican sentiments, which, ironically, gave them "no zeal to oblige"; their premises were often centres of political discussion and agitation. By the 1840s the proliferation of drinking establishments in urban centres was regarded as a serious social problem, and in towns like Kingston, one house in seven sold spirits to the public. Politicians, of both Reform and Tory schools, cultivated votes through licensing these establishments. As social polarization increased in the years after 1850, the tavern, like many institutions, reflected class distinctions. Fine hotels catered to those with aristocratic pedigree or pretension, while other houses attracted moderate artisans or city swills and dandies. Then, too, there were "the Great Houses of the Vulgar People," and there were hundreds of these "low rum holes" among the over 1,200 licensed premises in Victorian Montreal. Historians have long known the importance of this tavern "underworld" haunted by the "undeserving poor." But it has remained an obscure realm, dimly lit by the rare pieces of evidence that have survived the passage of time. An exceptional study by Peter de Lottinville describes the Montreal waterfront establishment of Joe Beef's Canteen, a meeting place for canallers, longshoremen, sailors, and ex-soldiers ("unkempt, unshaven, fierce-looking specimens of humanity").

Joe Beef's was established by Charles McKiernan, an Irish Protestant ex-soldier of republican attachments. Patronized by day labourers, his canteen was an environment for the crude and the rude: it was furnished with rough tables and chairs, had a sawdust-covered floor, was adorned with skeletons, bottles of preserving fluid containing mementos of interest, and housed a fantastic menagerie of monkeys, parrots, wild cats, and bears. Beer was sold for five cents, and some of the bears were known to consume 20 pints of beer daily. Their lack of sobriety, as well as the client's rowdiness, made Joe Beef's Canteen an object of attack by crusading reformers, newspaper editors, and temperance advocates. As part of a criminal subculture that existed on the margins of working-class life, it was a well-known rendez-vous for the "sun fish and wharf rats" of the harbour, and was much frequented by youth gangs. In his *Autobiography of a Super Tramp* W.H. Davies claimed that, "not a tramp throughout the length and breadth of the

North American continent . . . had not heard of [Joe Beef's Canteen] and a goodly number had at one time or another patronized his establishment."

McKiernan's tavern attracted casual labourers, the unemployed, and the transient for three reasons. First, he offered them sustenance with their drink, and at one end of the bar huge piles of bread, cheese, and beef were there for the taking by those indulging in a brew. Dollar bills and notes of credit were deposited with McKiernan, tucked into an engraving above the beer taps, drawn upon as regular customers found themselves out of work or behind bars. The tavern even functioned as an informal hiring hall, and McKiernan was known to lend out shovels and picks to the unskilled. Joe Beef's also served as a cheap boarding house, and for 10 cents "guests" were provided with a blanket, access to a tub and barber, "medical" advice and "cures," and accommodations for the evening. As many as 200 men could be crowded into the sleeping quarters on any given night; newspaper boys aged 12 to 14 comprised three-quarters of McKiernan's boarders, and for 20 cents a day they received food and lodging. Second, Joe Beef provided an escape from the cares and troubles of the world in an atmosphere of reckless abandon and hilarity. Any given night might see McKiernan engaged in a game of billiards with one of his bears, or the dogs set upon this very same animal. Musicians were commonly employed, in spite of legal prohibitions, and Joe Beef himself was prone to harangue the crowd in rhyming couplets, drawing from local newspapers and Irish journals from the United States ammunition fired out in an endless stream of debate.

Out of this came the final attraction of Joe Beef's Canteen, its unmistakable role as a defender of the poor, an institution with a direct ideological message of the equality of men and the worth of the supposed worthless. Utilizing newspapers to advertise his establishment, McKiernan promoted Joe Beef's Canteen as a house in which social outcasts could find a niche uncrowded by the condescension and deference that "Beaver Hall Bogus Aristocrats" practised and demanded:

> Citizens, we eat and drink in moderation;
> Our head, our toes, and our nose are our own,
> All we want is to be left alone!
> We eat and drink what we like,
> and let alone what we dislike.

Joe Beef's lent this rhetorical flourish substance by offering food and lodging to the poor free of charge if they were destitute, and, although supported mainly by the Protestant and English-speaking, refusing to cater to the prejudices of the age:

JOE BEEF OF MONTREAL
Who will feed a Poorman, if [he] is hungry
Cure him if he is sick — He does not give a damn
Whether he is an Indian, a Nigger, a Cripple, a
Billy or a Mick — He never let a poorman die on
The floor and never went back on the Poor.

Adept at bridging the contradiction, McKiernan could challenge the arbitrary and class-bound nature of the law at the same time that he provided information to local police, vilify the British Empire while ruling his own "den of robbers and wild beasts" with "infernal majesty in loyal style," or satirize the crass commercialism of the age and the tyranny of the "lousy dollar" at the same time proclaiming that "all Joe wants is the Coin." "Son of the people," Joe Beef cared not for "Pope, Priest, Parson or King William of the Boyne." Thoroughly materialist, he provided the poor with what they needed to survive — food, lodging, and pride — and denigrated the empty promises and salvations offered by "Churches, Chapels, Ranters, Preachers, Beechers and [other] such stuff [of which] Montreal has already got enough."

Although a notorious partisan of the Conservative cause, who would enlist his ranks in that time-honoured practice of electioneering by riot, McKiernan could also turn his activities toward the unfolding class struggles of his age. The most explicit demonstration of this came in the midst of an 1877/78 strike of labourers on the Lachine Canal. Over 1,000 French and Irish workers on the canal enlargement project dropped pick and shovel to resist a wage cut and protest "truck" payment. Joe Beef's provided the strikers with wagon-delivered daily rations of 300 loaves of bread, 36 gallons of tea, and a like quantity of soup. The Canteen housed the out-of-work labourers, 300 finding shelter under its roof. As the private charities closed their doors to the striking workmen and their families, Montreal's working class was provided with a stark reminder of the essential difference between the undependable charity of the upper classes and the mutual assistance of members of their own class. McKiernan also offered the canallers an elementary lesson in political economy, complementing the bread, soup, and lodging freely donated to the cause:

My friends, I have come here tonight to address you on "the Almighty Dollar." The very door bells of Montreal seem to ring with "the Almighty Dollar." The wooden-headed bobbies nail you, and you have to sleep on the hard floor provided by the City Fathers, and the next morning the fat Recorder tells you: "Give me the 'Almighty Dollar,' or down you go for eight days." The big-bugs all have their eyes on the "Almighty Dollar," from the Bishop down, and if you die in the hospital, they want the almighty dollar to shave you and keep you from the students. No can can blame you for demanding the "Almighty Dollar" a day. The man who promises 90¢ a day and pays only 80¢ is no man at all. The labourer has his rights . . . Now I won't ask you to cheer for prince, bishop, or any one, but for the canal laborers.

The "Loud Cheering" that followed this speech helped to prompt one contractor to overstate McKiernan's role in the labour dispute: "All of the trouble which we have had on the canal this winter has been caused mostly by men that have never worked a day on the canal," he claimed, adding that the conflict was "started in a low Brothel kept by one Joe Beef who seems to be at the head of it all." In the end Joe Beef's role was not an insignificant one, and in popularizing the grievances of the men and helping them carry out their work stoppage, he contributed to the canallers' eventual victory.

McKiernan's strike support was but a part of a more wide-ranging commitment to that "liberty tree" with which he adorned his wife's grave in 1871. His libertarian stand often vented itself in satirical rage, directed especially at zealous pietists and temperance advocates. He was known to set his bears on those foolish or naive enough to enter his rooms. By the late 1870s such forces of morality and social order were on the ascent, and Joe Beef's began to face competition from the YMCA recently estalished in the waterfront area. When a regular Canteen customer died of overconsumption of drink in 1879, the public attack on McKiernan was stepped up and the next years saw the erosion of Joe Beef's reputation as patron of the poor. As workers gravitated toward more explicit forms of class action, centred in the rising Knights of Labor or the challenge of workingmen's politics, tavern life at Joe Beef's became less and less associated with the class positions, defences, and stands taken in the 1870s. The atmosphere of the Canteen, according to a report of 1887, was no longer one of jocular conviviality, but of sombre, dull, and vacant silence, expressive not of the old combativity, but rather of resignation.

Charles McKeirnan must have found this changed context of the 1880s difficult to adjust to, and his displacement from the centre of the rough waterfront world must have proved a hard and bitter pill to swallow. He died on 15 January 1889. "Always the poor man's friend," McKeirnan's body was accompanied to its grave by representatives of 50 Montreal labour societies. Not all mourned his passing, however, and one virtuous bourgeois editor scoffed at the accomplishments of Joe Beef's "talented proprietor," who had operated a "resort of the most degraded of men . . . actively at work . . . for the brutalization of youth." An advocate of Christian philanthropy, this editor's uncharitable caricature of Joe Beef revealed the limitations of a reformism that could not comprehend the labouring poor any more than it could appease them. Joe Beef, the product of an age of transition in which class perspectives were coalescing, had attempted to provide something else for the unemployed, the casual labourer, the tramp. While perhaps an atypical tavern, Joe Beef's Canteen bridged the gulf separating rough and respectable, all the while refusing concession to the hypocrisies of the consolidating bourgeois ethos. A pioneer who linked the physical, social, and cultural needs of the poor with a system of social welfare that could be perceived as self-generated, Joe Beef's place in working-class experience was about to be taken over by other pioneers.

The Nine-Hour Pioneers

In the 1860s, the industrial-capitalist Anglo-American world was rocked by struggles to shorten the length of the working day. Originating with the London building trades in 1859, the demand for the nine-hour day captured the sympathies of engineers in Newcastle, England, and led to agitation in the United States for the eight-hour day, from 1866 into the early 1870s. George McNeill, prominent American labour reformer, recalled this movement in the 1890s, and explained: "Men who are compelled to sell their labour, very naturally desire to sell the smallest portion of their time for the largest possible price. They are merchants of their time. It is their only available capital."

In Canada the working-class effort to secure shorter working hours occurred during the first six months of 1872, coming in the wake of the commercial prosperity and post-Confederation exuberance of the early 1870s. Treatment of the Canadian nine-hour movement has generally focussed on the struggle of the Toronto printers, an episodic clash involving mass mobilization of working-class elements, fierce employer resistance led by George Brown of the *Globe*, and the arrest of the 24-member Typographical Union's Vigilance Committee. But as John Battye has noted, the Toronto printers' strike of 25 March 1872 was, in essence, a breach of a much more significant labour effort, a movement that stretched across central Canada in an effort to secure fundamental social reform and a shift in the nature of productive relations. As a defiant refusal to subordinate particularistic craft interests to a coordinated orchestration of struggle, the printers of Toronto, lacking an organized nine-hour league, fought valiantly but in isolation. Their unwillingness to make common cause with Canadian labour as a whole prefaced the future disintegration of the movement. But this is to anticipate, for in the spring months of 1872 the nine-hour day became the major issue in a series of labour-capital conflicts across the Dominion.

As an organized movement, the nine-hour agitation of 1872, like the labour insurrection almost two decades before, originated in Hamilton. Dan Black's Tavern and the Mechanic's Institute were the sites of early meetings of blacksmiths, machinists, and carpenters, and by late January 1872, the Iron Molders International Union no. 26 had lent its support to the struggle for the shorter workday. James Ryan, a Great

Western Railway machinist described as "a Communist missionar-ee,/An immigrant, late from the Old Count-eree,/Sent out by the great International band/To enlighten the darkness of this savage land," quickly emerged as the movement's spokesman, a man dedicated to establishing the nine-hour day "throughout the Dominion." Bringing together union and nonunion men, Ryan helped to stimulate the formation of nine-hour leagues across central Canada, especially in cities like Hamilton and Montreal, where large railway shops provided an organizational centre. In Toronto, the *Ontario Workman* emerged as the voice of labour's upheaval, a paper founded on the cooperative principles that many nine-hour advocates must have endorsed. Throughout February, March, and April the movement initiated a series of meetings and minor confrontations, in which newly arrived British craftsmen, likely affiliated with the Amalgamated Society of Engineers and the Amalgamated Society of Carpenters and Joiners, figured prominently. Ryan travelled to Montreal to address delegates from the 2,000-strong English-speaking league, led by James Black, and he proposed strike dates of 15 May in Hamilton and 1 June in Toronto. In return for financial support from the Montreal League, he argued that Montreal workingmen would undoubtedly secure the much sought-after shorter workday, claiming that Montreal employers would succumb to their workers' demands "without driving you to resistance." Ryan had thus devised a workable plan, in which the highly organized and militant workers of Hamilton were to be materially supported by the larger industrial centres of Montreal and Toronto. He contended that a first strike would provide a show of strength and educate employers in the folly of opposition. But as Ryan told the Montreal delegates, the success of the venture rested upon solidarity and support. "Resistance without funds," he said, "is useless." Thus, when Toronto printers refused to support Ryan's plan, leading a premature attack on George Brown and the other leading employers in the trade, they won their strike but abandoned the nine-hour pioneers in Hamilton.

The scheduled strike, billed as a celebration of labour's victory, nevertheless took place in Hamilton on 15 May. A giant procession wound its way through city streets as 1,500 men marched four abreast. Wagons exhibited the mechanics' wares while banners proclaimed their beliefs, purposes and sense of worth: "Wisdom is Better than Wealth"; "United we Stand, Divided we Fall"; "Art is Long, Life is Short"; "Nine Hours and No Surrender." As 3,000 onlookers cheered them on, the workers circled the city, one of their wagons bearing a monument inscribed, "Died 15th of May, 1872, the ten hour system." At a mass meeting and dance at the Palace Grounds, Ryan told the assembled throng that the eyes of the Dominion were upon them, and promised that "it was beyond the power of any capitalist to put the movement down." However, the spontaneous exuberance of the moment was not enough to win these workers the reduction in hours of labour that they sought. Ryan's assessment of the inevitability of victory gave way to impassioned pleas to "hold on, all depends on Hamilton." The following days were ones of agonizing defeat.

By June, the striking Hamilton workers were back at their employment; most returned without gaining the reduction in hours, while in those cases where the nine-hour day was won it represented only a minor concession to the highly skilled. Craftsmen in Toronto, Hamilton, and Galt were forced to flee the cities of their work to take up jobs in the United States. In Montreal, the movement was finally crushed in August 1872. How had the pioneers of labour come to this end? An explanation of the failure of 1872 lies partly in the fact that the 1870s represented a period of transition in labour organization, one in which a certain ambivalence on the part of workers had not yet been overcome. While the nine-hour pioneers looked forward in their vision of solidarity, the localized, fragmented experience of working life remained a powerful barrier to success, as did the inhibitions of political paternalism. Out of a social formation promising capitalist development, developed a labour movement that could only promise collectivity. If it did not fulfill this promise, it nevertheless presaged developments of labour's upsurge in the 1880s.

The 1870s: Beginnings and an End

By the 1870s, it appeared that Canadian labour had left behind much of the narrow, trade-oriented provincialism of its past. Unionism was advancing, and workers in specific crafts were enlisting in the common cause, not only in the nine-hour leagues of 1872, but also in trade associations and assemblies formed in Hamilton, Toronto, Montreal, Ottawa, and St. Catharines. Out of James Ryan's Canadian Labor Protective and Mutual Improvement Association (CLPMIA), formed 3 May 1872 in the midst of the nine-hour agitation, would emerge a political voice for labour. It was created by workers from Hamilton, Toronto, Brantford, and Dundas (Montreal would affiliate later), received endorsement from Sarnia, London, Oshawa, Guelph, St. Catharines, and Ingersoll, and there was reason to believe that labour in Stratford, Brockville, Kingston, and Sherbrooke was also sympathetic. The CLPMIA proved the forerunner of the first so-called national central labour body, the Canadian Labor Union (CLU), organized in 1873. Around this labour centre would gravitate the emerging working-class leadership of the 1870s, a contingent of reform-minded skilled mechanics concerned with political representation, immigration, prison labour, the legal position of unions, apprenticeship, child labour, a mechanics' lien law, the hours of labour, the tariff, cooperation, and extension of the franchise. Exhilarated by the prospects of intervention in the political process, workingmen elected their first candidates to federal and provincial office in these years, sending Hamilton's Henry Buckingham Witton to the Dominion parliament in 1872 and Daniel J. O'Donoghue to the Ontario legislature as Ottawa's member in 1874. With the *Ontario Workman* and Montreal's *Northern Journal* championing the cause of labour, workers now had access to a press of their own, an important advance over previous years, during which labour newspapers had been established but never sustained for any significant length of time. Militancy, too, seemed to peak. Kealey notes that in 1870–74 Toronto workers fought 27 strikes, or more than have been recorded for that city in the entire period from 1800 to 1860.

These changes seem to indicate the beginning of labour's public presence as a class, with concerns, institutions, and politics reflective of labour's unique social position and economic needs. But while beginnings were made in the 1870s, the period was as much the end of an old order as it was the launching of a new one. The nine-hour movement had failed, and the early organization of the 1870s had foundered on some old inhibitions. The worlds of skilled and unskilled remained distinct, and solidarity, even among craft workers, proved a fragile entity. Within politics, it was the sway of labour's paternalistic superiors that won the first battle in the war between capital and labour. The Canadian working class entered the 1870s riding the crest of a wave of workplace militancy and political agitation, but by the end of the decade it was in a trough of economic recession, stifled militancy, and Tory hegemony.

In the aftermath of the nine-hour struggle there was a revival of the paternalistic mediation of workplace antagonisms. A part of this was imposed, none too benevolently, from above, with employers forcing workers to agree to "pledges" and "documents," eliciting promises to desist from agitation, or establishing shop rules that curtailed efforts to reduce the hours of labour. This was but one part of a collective response on the part of capital, a relentless opposition to the nine-hour leagues that must not be underestimated in the demise of the movement. But labour, itself, seemed to slip rather easily back into the "cordiality" of respectable relations between master and servant. J.N. Tarbox, manager of the Wanzer Sewing Machine works in Hamilton, which was bitterly contested ground in the short history of the 1872 battle, was presented with a gift from the establishment's workers upon his retirement in September. Brief months after he had helped to quell the nine-hour rebellion, Tarbox was the recipient of a gracious tribute: "We also regret that near the close of your stewardship there should have anything happened to mar the good feeling always existed between master and man. That little incident is now passed, and we desire to remember your former kindness and the gentlemanly manner in which you have invariably treated your men." Wanzer's mechanics may well have regretted these words in the months to follow, as a new price list cut back wages 35 to 50 percent on piece work, and militants were driven from the shop. As one dissident argued, "This was very like a new years gift for those men who in the largeness of their hearts went back upon the short time movement and accepted the gilded bait held out to them last summer." A "social revolution," imminent in April and May 1872, had indeed been reduced to a "little incident" by January 1873. At root here, was a willingness to abandon workplace militancy and organization and to rely upon other forms of activity and nonworking-class "support."

This process was perhaps most apparent in the political sphere, where Macdonald and the Tories successfully manipulated working-class voters. Outrage at George Brown's efforts to silence Toronto's printers with conspiracy charges was easily translated into working-class opposition to Brown's party, the Grits, and the Tories were the obvious beneficiaries. They assured themselves of the workers' allegiance, with the passage of the Trades Union Bill in April 1872, legislation that provided the illusion of trade union legality. (The empty promise of the Trades Union Bill was, however, rather fuller than it may appear, for it was the spirit of enactment, rather than its letter that was lived up to.) In Hamilton, Macdonald's allies stood behind the election of Canada's first "bona fide" worker to the federal parliament. H.B. Witton, Tory mechanic, would prove a sorry representative for Hamilton's nine-hour pioneers. Lady Dufferin captured his transformation in a terse line: "We had met him soon after his election, when he dined in a rough coat, but now he wears evening clothes." Witton failed in his effort to secure reelection in 1874, a year in which the Tories suffered because of the Pacific Scandal, and in the 1880s he would be remembered with contempt. "The first situation that was offered him he took," recalled one labour reformer with venom, "and went to Vienna on some government exhibition business."

In Toronto the post-1872 election months saw an even more unambiguous drift towards Tory hegemony, as the *Ontario Workman* was purchased by a triumvirate of Conservative workingmen secretly financed by John A. Macdonald. While the *Workman* remained a working-class organ, advocating a range of reforms and promoting the interests of labour, it avoided direct assault on Tory political rule, narrowing the nature of its social critique. Around this organ, the Toronto Trades Assembly (TTA) and the Canadian Labor Union (formed in 1873) consolidated what Gregory S. Kealey has appropriately dubbed a Toronto "junta" led by J.S. Williams and prominent nine-hour agitator John Hewitt. Committed Tories, the "junta" members dominated the developing Canadian labour movement in the 1870s, lending it a thoroughly Conservative cast. When the CLU met in Toronto in September 1873, 26 of the 45 delegates were from Toronto, and the new labour centre became little more than an extension of the Toronto clique. Championing labour's cause in the political arena, this inner ring, speaking from the rostrums of the TTA or the CLU, did much to consolidate labour's emerging electoral power, but it did so in a voice muffled by its acquiescence to the party of Macdonald.

Even among labourers far removed from the Tory influence in Hamilton and Toronto, the 1870s proved to be a decade during which potential labour power was restricted by the workers' inability to express themselves unambiguously as a class. Thus, the election of the supposedly "independent" workers' candidate, Ottawa's D.J. O'Donaghue, in the provincial election of 1874, was something less than a victory for autonomous working-class politics. As Debi Wells shows in an unpublished study of the Ottawa working class in the 1870s, the surprising election of O'Donoghue, while indicative of the increasing importance of the workingman, owed as much to religious and ethnic controversies in the deeply divided Ottawa constituency as to any clearly defined working-class agitation. Supported by Conservatives who saw the need to elect a Catholic in the dominantly Irish and French seat, O'Donoghue would champion independence, but was neverthe-less loosely allied with Mowat's Reform Grit government. Like Witton, he was a relatively subdued advocate of the working class. By 1875, seeking reelection, he declared himself "a Reformer . . . [and] re-pudiated the idea that he represented a class of citizens, but [promised to do] his utmost in the interests of all classes." Toronto's Alf Jury noted in 1877 that labour had only one man in the Ontario legislature, "and they had only half of him."

Workingmen might well have moved beyond these limitations to embrace a more definitive independence and class stance in the later 1870s, but just as they had entered partisan politics, an economic depression occurred. Unemployment, short time, and the voracious demands of deflationary capital for wage cuts, put workers into a position where they had to fight for basic survival; other battles were postponed. Few were the unions that weathered this storm, fewer still the individual workers that emerged from it unscathed. Central Canadian workers looked to political representation as a means of remedying the problems of class conflict in a period of prosperity. However, politics had no solutions for labour's difficulties within the context of depression. Essential institutions — unions and central labour bodies — and rudimentary class perspectives had not yet been consolidated to the point that they could provide a foundation upon which greater militancy could develop. The price exacted by the depression of the 1870s cannot yet be understood fully, for basic data (such as the extent of unemployment) is lacking. But it is known that labour suffered greatly and that employers used the economic depression to attempt to destroy powerful unionized adversaries.

Moulders were often forced into disastrous conflicts, and in other trades the depressed economic climate led to deteriorating conditions and workplace defeats.

But workers who participated in defeated strikes were actually more fortunate than many others, whose jobs disappeared as firms failed or strikes were broken by "scabs." There are said to have been over 500 heads of families unemployed in the nation's capital in 1879/80, in spite of indications of a business revival; deputations of unemployed waited upon the prime minister, but obtained little by way of relief. James Pitsula has studied admissions to the Toronto House of Industry in the years 1879–82, where over 2,000 unemployed applicants sought charity. In Montreal, the changing character of working-class protest followed a logic of escalating demand. December of 1875 saw a series of demonstrations in which labourers pleaded for work or bread. Originally peaceful, these actions drew more than 1,000 workingmen and culminated in a confrontation with police and an attack on bakers' sleighs. The municipality eventually hired hundreds of destitute labourers to work on public roads at wages of 60 cents a day, "just enough to keep a man and family from starving." One year later, the Montreal unemployed were still seeking work, but no longer were their grievances couched in the language of polite request: they demanded "bread or blood." Circumstances such as these placed severe limitations on sophisticated organization and political activity within the working class.

In this period of catastrophic downturn, however, three developments served to guide labour out of the confusion of the 1870s. First, working-class political involvement toward the end of the decade remained dominated by Tory attachments, but the formation of Tory front groups such as the Workingmen's Liberal–Conservative Associations of Ottawa and Toronto unwittingly contributed to limited forms of independence for workers in politics. In the capital, a Workingmen's Association championed working-class aspirations regardless of party affiliation. Second, even among the trades most sympathetic to the nonworking classes, the severity of the 1870s depression precipitated a stance of defiance, expressed in the Brotherhood of Locomotive Engineers' 1876/77 assault on the Grand Trunk Railway. At Stratford, Belleville, and Brockville, labour's supporters attacked strikebreakers and helped the engineers to win a major victory. Third, and finally, as all labouring people confronted the spectre of unemployment, workers across trade and skill lines began to come together in deputations to protest the lack of jobs. The growth of independence within labour politics, the involvement of the previously nonparticipating engineers, and the common confrontation with distress all mark the end of an epoch in which labour was subordinate and the beginnings of a period of consolidation of working-class culture.

Chapter 3

The Consolidation of Working-Class Culture 1880–1895

> Thus, albeit in some new as well as some continuing forms, a socialist cultural revolution has still to be rooted in potential majorities which can, by their own organization and activity, become effective majorities. . . . In this assertion of possibility, against all the learned habits of resignation and scepticism, it is already a definition of practical hope. . . . there will be certain decisive confrontations. . . . But what will get us through such confrontations, and in some important cases into them, is not only association and organization; it will be also what we can call . . . the "material force of the idea": the production and practice of possibility.
>
> Raymond Williams, "Beyond Actually Existing Socialism," *New Left Review* (1980)

The Social Formation

During the 1880s, competitive capitalism consolidated in Canada, building upon past accomplishments and going beyond them. The rate of manufacturing output attained annual growth rates in the 1880s surpassing those of both the 1870s and 1890s, rates that would not be exceeded until the boom years of monopoly capitalism in 1900–1910 and 1926–29. Indeed, it is the growth of manufacturing facilities in many industries during the cresting fortunes of the National Policy (1880–84) that is most striking. Between 1880 and 1890, for instance, the value of cotton cloth output rose by 125 percent, but even this dramatic increase understated the gains of the decade's first five years: the number of mills, spindles, looms, and capital invested tripled in that half decade. Urban markets for the rising production of the late nineteenth century expanded considerably in the 1880s, with the percentage of population living in cities growing significantly in the years 1870–1900. The percentage of Quebec's urban population swelled from 20 to 36 percent in this period, while Ontario's actually doubled, rising from 20 to 40 percent. Across Canada the figures climbed from 18 to 35 percent. Much of this urban growth was concentrated in expansion of the industrial sector, as in Ontario where the number of employees in manufacturing rose from 87,000 to 166,000 between 1871 and 1891. Railway mileage expanded as well, shooting up from 3,000 in 1873 to over 16,000 in 1896, but it was the construction of the transcontinental railway that epitomized the attainments of the age. Facilitating the movement of goods and people, the Canadian Pacific Railway stimulated economic growth and expansion and contributed to a political consolidation that, for the first time in the country's history, began to overcome regional diversities, however tentatively.

Expansion was most pronounced in the metropolitan centres. In Toronto the protective tariff of the National Policy helped to stimulate the local economy, and between 1878 and 1884, 36 new major factories came into being. The number of hands employed in these large work settings more than doubled, while capital invested and the value of the annual product soared accordingly. Between 1881 and 1891, the total number of productive establishments in Toronto more than tripled, the number of workers doubled, the capital invested increased roughly 265 percent, the annual product, 220 percent, and the value added, 215 percent. This diversified expansion was accompanied by increasing concentration and specialization of particular productive sectors, and Toronto established itself as a leading centre of printing and publishing, chemical and secondary wood production, and the clothing industry. Canada's other leading industrial centre, Montreal–Hochelaga, also experienced considerable expansion in the 1880s, and climbed into a position of dominance in the food and beverage industry (almost 40 percent of the total production in this sector was located in Montreal–Hochelaga) and in the production of transportation equipment (almost 40 percent of the national output, with thousands of workers).

In the Maritimes, industrial expansion was also quite dramatic, and indeed Nova Scotia's output increased 66 percent over the course of the 1880s, outstripping Ontario and Quebec, which had 51 percent increases. Wholesale shippers, lumber and ship manufacturers, and petty producers attempted to adapt the old staple economy to the new imperatives of the National Policy, basing their optimistic vision of the future upon iron and steel (fuelled by the region's coal reserves) and textiles. While regional interests would be thwarted in the 1890s, Maritime capital experienced its years of boom in the 1880s: coal production, centred in Pictou and Cape Breton, doubled between 1880 and 1890, with 2,100,000 tons of coal mined. The relative increase in industrial capital, average wages, and output in Saint John, New Brunswick, surpassed that of Hamilton, Ontario; ventures like the St. Croix Cotton Manufacturing Company drew upon American and

Canadian capital to turn once-peaceful villages into "hives of industry." Out of the foundries of Amherst, the rolling mills of New Glasgow, and the sugar refineries of Halifax flowed the products of competitive capital's brief decade of expansion. Far to the west, in Winnipeg, the faint beginnings of a similar process were unfolding. As late as 1870 the region was still described as "a Great Lone Land treked by Indians and Traders." But massive railway construction in the late 1870s and early 1880s secured Winnipeg the status of "entrepot of a great agricultural and commercial economy" that was coming into being in the Northwest.

As T.W. Acheson has shown, this expanding manufacturing sector was led by a few hundred entrepreneurs, predominantly manufacturers of immigrant origin (first- or second-generation Canadians). Concentrated in the central Canada of the Lake Peninsula and the St. Lawrence Valley, the members of this rising class of capitalists were, in Acheson's words, "the proletarians of the business community," men of small means who had captured a large share of local markets and moved into national prominence. Competitive, grasping at each opportunity to secure an advantageous market position, these new men of industrial might were often rooted in the small community (over 50 percent of the manufacturing of Ontario in the 1880s took place in communities where populations never exceeded 10,000). They rose to power and authority out of the depression of the 1870s and the buoyancy of the early years of tariff protection, and their collective histories intersect with times of deflation, which, according to one early economist, saw the ratio of commodity prices plummet from roughly 100 in 1873 to about 75 in 1886. We know little about the social impact of this secular decline of prices in Canada, but if the experience of the United States is at all representative, it might well be speculated that although real wages no doubt rose, employers responded to deflation with increased application of technology, intensification of labour, and, most importantly, wage cuts. The latter would have been most prominent in the troughs that a number of economic historians have located around the years 1879/80, 1885, and 1888. For the wage cut was the most useful mechanism by which competitive capitalists could recapture some of the losses resulting from deflation. Engaged in an anarchic, individualistic, and ruthless quest for the spoils of production, the first true generation of Canadian capitalists soon learned that the way to secure advantage over business rivals was to heighten the extraction of surplus from labour by cutting back wages, thus allowing larger amounts of capital to be sunk back into production.

This brief sketch of the economic situation in the 1880s gives a partial indication of why, for the first time in Canadian history, a mass movement of working-class resistance developed. That organizational upsurge had critically important social, cultural, and political consequences and checked consolidated capitalism's unrestrained attempts to bring production under its own control. For the 1880s was a decade of unprecedented working-class militancy and cultural cohesion, centred in the emergence of an organization called the Noble and Holy Order of the Knights of Labor. The strength of the Knights of Labor may have helped to create a situation in which the working class kept wage rates at least partially intact, inhibiting capital's assault, resisting employer efforts to implement reductions, or lessening the severity of such wage cuts. If this was the case, then the Order would have played an important role in depressing the rate of profit and curbing the process of capital accumulation; the social cost of labour would have been relatively high, compared to the Laurier boom years of the twentieth century, and the process of appropriation curtailed. Finally, breaking the back of the intransigent labour movement would have been a political, social, and economic imperative for an industrial capitalism moving away from the stage of anarchic competition towards monopoly. The Knights of Labor, in conjunction with the craft unions, may thus have helped to rally the individualistic and once-divided capitalists that Michael Bliss has depicted as in quest of "a living profit" to employer combines that led out of the nineteenth-century context of competitive entrepreneurship and into the age of monopoly. And, in Canada, where the state always had a hand in economic endeavours, they may have helped to consolidate a particularly political form of capitalism, in which intervention in "labour relations" was to be particularly acute in the years 1900–1920. In this sense, the moment of cultural self-affirmation of the working class (as demonstrated by the strength of the Knights of Labor) and the structural development of the political economy were part of a complex relationship, a relationship that will be examined in more detail in the closing section of this chapter. Now let us turn to the working-class experience itself, looking at the varied dimensions of a unique moment in the self-activity of the Canadian workers.

Knights and Workmen

The most vibrant institutional development in the history of nineteenth-century North American workers began in Philadelphia in 1869, as a small group of garment workers came together under the leadership of Uriah Stephens. They created a secret society, bound by oaths, elaborate ritual, and a commitment to the unity of all workers. More than a trade union, the resulting body, which they dubbed the Noble and Holy Order of the Knights of Labor, was to combine aspects of a religious brotherhood, a political reform society, a fraternal order, and a pure and simple unionism. Expanding into Pennsylvania coal mines, Pittsburgh shops, and New York factories, the Noble and Holy Order grew slowly in the 1870s, and Stephens was succeeded by Terence V. Powderly, uncharitably described by one historian as a vain and disingenuous rabble rouser. But under Powderly the Order threw off the cloak of secrecy and, in the 1880s, captured the support of the American working man and woman as had no other labour-reform organization.

The Knights drew workers into their ranks through a relatively simple procedure and institutional apparatus. Individual members joined Local Assemblies, either in mixed assemblies (according to diverse occupational affiliations) or trade assemblies (adhering more rigidly to specific craft categories). For a local assembly to be formally organized, a minimum of ten members was required, and once established, LAs were known to swell in membership to over 1,000. Initiation fees were set by the local, but the minimum fee was $1.00 for men and 50¢ for women. Local dues, again, were controlled by individual assemblies, but they were to be not less than 10¢ per month. Members were also expected to contribute to the cooperative fund, the monthly fees being 10¢ for men and 5¢ for women. The cost of organizing such an assembly was approximately $20.00, which included a charter, supplies, and a seal, as well as a $10.00 fee that went to the organizer (in the case of a woman's assembly this fee was $5.00). If a specific geographical region or trade contained five or more assemblies, a District Assembly could be formed. The Order, then, was a highly centralized body, with a well-defined hierarchy and structure; yet it was also egalitarian, and the local assemblies had a large measure of autonomy, with their own courts to prosecute those who transgressed the disciplines and regulations of knighthood.

To determine what kinds of workers were involved in this early form of labour organization and to understand their potential impact on capitalist production, certain questions must be answered. How many of these local assemblies were there, where were they located, and what type of assembly prevailed in specific locales? Let us explore these questions at length for Ontario, and conclude with some brief comments on other regional experiences.

Although strongest in rapidly expanding industrial cities such as Toronto and Hamilton, the Knights also penetrated the province's towns, villages, and tiny hamlets. In its approximately 30-year lifespan (1875–1907), the Order organized locals in 83 towns from Amherstburg in the west to Cornwall in the east, and from Port Colborne in the south to Sudbury in the north. These 83 towns contained a total of at least 252 local assemblies, which, in turn, formed ten district assemblies. Toronto, Hamilton, and Ottawa led the way with 58, 30, and 12 LAs, respectively, but the Knights were also active in eight communities of less than 1,000 people, and there were 31 LAs in places with populations of under 3,000. Ontario's five largest cities in the 1880s (Toronto, Hamilton, Ottawa, London, and Kingston) contained 46 percent of all Knights of Labor assemblies, but it is the range and dispersal of the Order that is

FIGURE 3.1. Concentrations of Knights of Labor local assemblies in Southern Ontario, 1880–1902

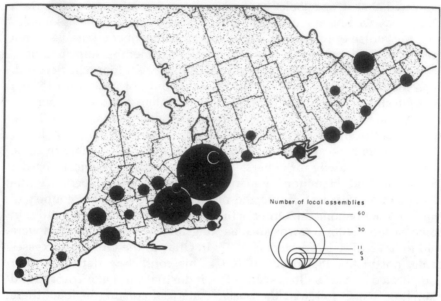

SOURCE: Gregory S. Kealey and Bryan D. Palmer, "The Bonds of Unity: The Knights of Labor in Ontario, 1880–1900," *Histoire Sociale/Social History* 14 (November 1981), 386.

perhaps most significant: of the 47 Ontario towns with a population of at least 3,000 in the 1880s, fully 38, or 81 percent, witnessed the formation of a local assembly. In the 34 railway centres in Ontario in the 1880s, only two were not known to have a formally established LA. (See Figure 3.1.)

There was an almost even division between Ontario's trade and mixed locals, but if we consider the size of the town where the assembly was situated, a discernible pattern emerges. Mixed assemblies were far more popular in smaller places, while trade assemblies were most often found in the cities. Thus, in towns of under 5,000 people, the mixed assembly was dominant with 58 percent of all LAs, while trade assemblies and and locals of unknown character each provided 21 percent of all LAs. Cities with a population in excess of 30,000, however, were more likely to house trade assemblies: 57 percent of all LAs were of this type, and 30 percent were mixed, with 13 percent of unknown character.

How many members were drawn into the ranks of the Knights of Labor? This is difficult to determine. In the United States, the Knights were said to have enrolled, at their peak, between 700,000 and 1,000,000 members, but this is a static count taken in the spring months of 1886, the highwater mark of membership. The data are always questionable, and tend to underestimate the membership. Moreover, the central problem is the timing of influx into the Order, for membership peaked at different moments in different regions. Thus, Jonathan Garlock has estimated that if one looks beyond peak membership, the American Order may well have enrolled over 3,000,000 workers in its assemblies over the course of its history. There are problems of comparable, if not greater, magnitude in the case of Ontario, for membership data after 1885 are incomplete at best, and official estimates seldom reliable. And, as in the United States, the Ontario Knights did not peak until 1886, a year which saw the founding of 99 local assemblies, and even then the dating of the upsurge varied from region to region within Ontario. Thus, across south-central Ontario, membership in the Knights of Labor climbed to its highest point in 1886 and then declined, rapidly in some locales, more slowly in others. Towns near the American border (Brockville and Hamilton, for instance) seemed to experience the Order's impact earliest. But in the northwest, in the timber country of the Muskoka region, the Order achieved prominence later, as it did in some eastern Ontario towns such as Kingston, where the Knights were said to have 1,500 supporters in 1887. In Ottawa, the Order's successes came, not in the 1880s, but in 1891. This conflicting data is further complicated by the fact that even *within* industrial cities like Toronto and Hamilton, which followed the classic pattern of cresting in 1886, there were some working-class sectors — letter carriers, longshoremen, and the unskilled — that joined the ranks of the Knights even after the Order was in obvious retreat. Thus, any attempt to address the numerical significance of the Order will founder if it is reduced to a count of peak membership at any given point in time.

Nor do available data on official membership figures allow us to make any firm calculations as to the percentage of the workforce organized by the Order. The tendency is always to underrepresent the strength, and the volatility of the rank-and-file compounds this problem of under-counting. However, if total peak memberships across the province (at specific points in time with no account taken of volatility) are added together it becomes obvious that over the course of their history, the Knights organized a minimum of 21,800 members. (A figure double, perhaps even triple, this might not overstate the numbers actually enrolled.) This represented 18.4 percent of the hands employed in manufacturing in 1881 and 13.1 percent of those so employed in 1891, although it must be recognized that the Order also attracted adherents in nonmanufacturing sectors of the economy. The trade unions, however, also expanded considerably in this decade, and numbers of organized craftsmen did not join the Knights of Labor. If we add together all the workers affiliated with unions and local assemblies, it is apparent that the 1880s saw impressive percentages of the workforce organized, however cautiously we estimate the figures and whatever recognition is given to problems of classification (manufacturing employees being the smallest category, nonagricultural or total workforce figures being larger). Certainly, the organizational boom of the 1880s outstripped all previous nineteenth-century developments.

At the local level, conservative estimates by Gregory S. Kealey and myself based on available data suggest that the Knights of Labor drew 20 to 40 percent of the hands employed in cities like London, Hamilton, Brockville, Toronto, Stratford, Woodstock, and Oshawa to their ranks, and even higher percentages in railroad towns such as St. Thomas or manufacturing centres such as Gananoque or Merritton. Such figures, whether taken in the province-wide context or in city or town settings, must be compared to the bleak picture of labour organization before World War I: at no other time was more than ten percent of the total nonagricultural workforce organized, and not until the post-World War II organization upsurge and the unionization of the public sector did national figures for the percentage of organized workers climb to 35 percent and beyond. The Knights of Labor therefore represented a peak in the organizational history of Ontario's nineteenth-century workers.

Research has not yet proceeded far enough for other regions to be examined even in the tentative manner in which the Ontario experience of the Knights of Labor has been discussed. But it is nevertheless clear that some of the regional barriers separating the histories of particular geographically rooted working-class sectors were breaking down in the 1880s, for the Knights of Labor influenced the development of labour in provinces other than Ontario. Although hardly as significant as it was in English-speaking central Canada, for instance, the Order played its part in the Quebec of the 1880s, where it was known as Les Chevaliers du Travail, as well as touching workers in the developing prairie cities and on the west and east coasts.

In Quebec, the organizational centre of the movement was in Montreal, where 64 local assemblies were formed between 1882 and 1902. Unlike the case in Ontario's metropolitan centres, Montreal's upsurge of the Knights continued throughout the 1890s, with a period of significant expansion in 1893/94. Approximately 2,500 workers were enrolled in the Order in 1887, and local assemblies in 1886 averaged 193 members. A secondary district was that of Quebec City, where at least a dozen LAs were formed, and surrounding towns (Sillery, Cap Rouge and Pointe-Lévis) were also Knights of Labor strongholds. In Hull, Buckingham, Valleyfield, Sherbrooke, and Upper Bedford, as well as in other manufacturing towns, the Knights were also known to exist, and across the province of Quebec the Order established over 100 local assemblies, bringing French- and English-speaking workers together in the industrial cities and providing the first workers' organization for many *canadiens* in smaller towns.

To the west, the Knights of Labor quickly established themselves in the expanding railway and industrial towns of the prairie provinces.

Telegraph operatives, railway workers, tailors, and carpenters led the way in Winnipeg, where as many as six local assemblies were probably established by 1887. Organization drifted west with migrant workers, and in Calgary, LA 9787 was set up by itinerants from Owen Sound and Winnipeg. But it was in British Columbia, where labour would emerge as a forceful and radical presence in the opening decades of the twentieth century, that the Knights of Labor found their most receptive western Canadian audience.

Wellington-based miners had battled Robert Dunsmuir's coal empire throughout the 1870s, facing a stern Scot who tolerated no unionist assault upon his arrogant and uncompromising rule. Politically and economically omnipotent, Dunsmuir drove his workers to clandestine organization, and they created a Miners' Mutual Protective Association that surfaced in periodic clashes between capital and labour in the years 1877–83. Other British Columbia workers reacted sharply to Dunsmuir's efforts to crush worker resistance by importing Oriental labourers as strikebreakers, and in Victoria, they formed the Workmen's Protective Association in 1878 to combat "the great influx of Chinese." Building on such precedents, the Knights of Labor entered British Columbia in 1883, establishing six local assemblies in Vancouver, two in Wellington, and one in each of Nanaimo, New Westminster, Victoria, Yale, Kamloops, and Rossland. These local assemblies gained prominence in the mid-1880s, and rallied the west coast's white workers in opposition to the Chinese, recently thrust into the labour market with the termination of their exploitation in the construction gangs of the Canadian Pacific Railway. In Victoria, the Knights of Labor upheaval coincided with the emergence of John Duval's *Industrial News* and the rise of the Anti-Chinese Union. But the exclusion of Orientals, however nefarious, was far from the only cause promoted by the Order: shorter hours, antagonism to monopolies, condemnation of political corruption, the call for reform, as well as organization and resistance at the workplace, were all critically important, if unstudied, aspects of the Order's presence in British Columbia.

On the east coast, the Knights of Labor also secured a foothold, albeit a weak one. Local assemblies existed in Moncton, Saint John, Halifax, Amherst, North Sydney, New Glasgow, Campbellton, and Truro, although they never extended into the working class in any significant way, being almost entirely restricted to the telegraph operatives whose defeat in a momentous 1883 international conflict seemed to seal the fate of the Order in the Maritime provinces. A number of LAs emerged in the late 1890s among the coal miners of Cape Breton, organized in District Assembly 35 at Glace Bay, but this minor organizational growth was but a pale reflection of the east coast's more entrenched and previously established regional labour movement, based in a body that opposed the Knights of Labor at the same time that it seemed strikingly similar.

As workers in central Canada flocked to the Knights of Labor in the 1880s, east coast labourers in the mines, on the docks, and in the shops cast their lot with Robert Drummond's Provincial Workmen's Associa-/ tion (PWA). Originally formed in the woods adjacent to the Springhill Mining Company, the PWA established its pioneer lodge in late August 1879, and first bore the name of the Provincial Miners' Association (PMA). But like the Noble and Holy Order of the Knights of Labor (also formed by workers of a particular craft), it soon extended its organizational focus as well as its name, and took as its slogan the words, "Strength lies in unity." Led by the miners of Springhill, Stellarton, Westville, and Thorburn, the Provincial Miners' Association organized loaders, check weightmen, trappers, labourers, and miners in the mainland coal fields of Nova Scotia, and by October 1879 had enrolled 646 workers in its cause. Wharfmen at Granton, engaged in loading coal on the ships, formed a lodge soon afterwards, and following the October 1880 meeting of the PMA in Truro, the five-lodge body changed its name to the Provincial Workmen's Association and encouraged Drummond to bring the Cape Breton miners, previously unorganized, into the ranks of the new body. Nine lodges were soon established, and the PWA claimed a membership of 1,200 in Cape Breton (probably an exaggeration since there were only 1,725 miners on the island, and they did not attain closed-shop status during this period). Glass and foundry workers in New Glasgow and Pictou county also joined, and throughout the 1880s the PWA expanded; in 1884 it had 1,860 members in good standing. In Amherst, boot and shoeworkers once associated with the Knights of Labor (LA 2209) founded Concord Lodge of the PWA in 1891 after their employer fired a number of the Order's activists.

By 1897 the PWA claimed to be "the strongest single labour organization in Canada," but it was already on the verge of an internal crisis, its leader Robert Drummond following an increasingly conciliatory policy of refusing to oppose the "pluck-me" stores of the Dominon Coal Company in return for the company's willingness to collect union dues regularly. This collaboration angered Drummond's members, who were increasingly won over to the more militant tactics of the Knights of Labor in the years after 1898. By 1899, the number of PWA lodges had declined from 16 to 3, and membership had dropped from 1,400 to 1,000. Surviving into the twentieth century (and outlasting the Knights), the PWA, abandoned by Drummond, would continue to follow a moderate stance in its dealings with employers and would be used later as a force to keep the United Mine Workers of America (UMWA) out of the region's mines. Its powerlessness apparent by 1904, the Provincial Workmen's Association eventually succumbed to the larger international union: where the Knights of Labor failed, the United Mine Workers would succeed, and in 1918, 98 percent of the PWA's membership voted to affiliate with District 26 of the UMWA. Ultimately liquidated by its own rank and file, the early PWA was nevertheless, as Sharon Reilly has recently argued and as an 1886 statement claimed, "a response to the wishes of men who had been subjected to indignities, who had suffered loss, who were well trodden down, and yet who had in them a sturdy spirit of independence." Like the Knights of Labor (which it resembled in its attachment to ritual and fraternity, as well as in its message of solidarity), the Provincial Workmen's Association was an initial announcement of the consolidation of the working class that was developing throughout Canada in the 1880s.

Knights and Workmen, in the organizational upsurge of this decade, dramatically expanded the institutions of the workers' movement. The preceding discussion has provided a cursory introduction to that process, a brief listing of some quantitative achievements. But these developments constitute only a small portion of the history of the years 1880–95. As Terence V. Powderly pointed out, the great upheaval of the 1880s represented much more than a quantitative breakthrough for North American workers: it also marked a crucial qualitative shift in the orientation of the working class. Because Powderly sensed that the historian would prove incapable of appreciating that shift, he dismissed attempts to apply "logic and scientific research" to the history of labour in the 1880s. Such a history would, he felt, divide "the emotions, the passions, and the feelings" of the working class from the history "of the day in which it moved and did its work." For this reason he warned that, "It does not do, therefore, to take the historian too seriously; at best he weaves the warp of fancy into the woof of fact and gives us the web called history." Powderly's words are worth taking seriously, and if we are to avoid the consequences that he feared would proceed from a history based on mere numbers, we must look to the people themselves, to their wants and needs and strivings. It was here that the experience of the 1880s attained its greatest accomplishments as the ambiguous, fragmented, and unfocussed raw material of working-class life was moulded into a movement culture of opposition and alternative.

A Movement Culture

This movement culture was most visible in the Ontario experience of the Knights of Labor, where ritual and procession, symbolism and soiree, combined to proclaim the unity of all labour, a cultural undertaking of opposition and challenge that distinguished the 1880s from previous decades of labouring people's experience. The working-class culture that predated the rise of the Knights of Labor, for instance, reflected many continuities with older, established modes of behaviour. We can recognize, for theoretical purposes, the distinction between this residual, class culture, marking off worker from employer, directing us toward two very different ways of life, and the emergent movement culture, represented by the Knights of Labor that united previously divided segments of the working class, proclaiming the potential of a new social order. But it is problematical, if not impossible, to isolate these two strands, separating here a residual aspect, there an emergent development, for surviving evidence is almost entirely coloured by the movement's presence, by its ideology, leadership, and the challenge it presented to bourgeois stability. In fact, the Order's effectiveness stemmed from the dialectical relationship between the residual *and* the emergent, between the mundane class distinctions of daily life *and* the rise of a movement that attempted to unite all workers to oppose the oppression and exploitation that they lived through both off and on the job. On the one hand, the Knights of Labor developed out of the class culture while, on the other hand, they pushed that culture forward, posing alternatives, striking a posture of opposition. To view the experience of the Ontario worker in this way is to capture much of the significance of the Knights of Labor in the closing decades of the nineteenth century, and to understand the milieu in which the "labour question" became a public concern as it never had before.

These men and women of the new movement entered their local assembly halls with deeply held convictions. In the symbolism and richly suggestive ritual of the Noble and Holy Order of the Knights of Labor, both the strengths of the past and the purposes of the present were revealed, introducing us, as well, to the class values upon which the Knights constructed their alternative vision, and the movement culture which sought to transform the very nature of the society in which workers of the 1880s found themselves.

Indeed, each Knight of Labor entered the Order through a ritualistic procedure that cemented him or her in these traditions, pledging eternal secrecy, strict obedience, and scrupulous charity toward new brothers and sisters. Every initiate vowed to defend the interest and reputation of all true members of the Order, be they employed or unemployed, fortunate or distressed, and was instructed that "to rescue the toiler from the grasp of the selfish is a work worthy of the noblest and best of our race." Upon admittance, the recently christened Knight was informed that "open and public associations have failed, after a struggle of centuries, to protect or advance the interest of labor," and that the Knights of Labor merely imitated "the example of capital," endeavouring "to secure the just rewards of our toil" and to prevent the trampling of "poor humanity in the dust." Secret signs, oaths, passwords, and grips further consolidated the attachment to collective principles and protected labouring people from the hostile opposition of anti-Knights of Labor employers. Reverberating throughout this ritualistic and symbolic content of the Knights of Labor was the centrality of class pride, the awareness of the worth of the working man and woman. It was this, above all else, that drew adherents to the cause. By the 1880s, Canadian workers and employers stood divided, as years of experience had produced divergent ways of life and conflicting values. The symbolism and ritual of the Knights of Labor revolved around this essential development, infusing old forms with new purpose and passion, and in the process creating a culture of collectivity in which labour unity, mutual aid, and solidarity were visible manifestations.

Festivals, dinners, and workers' balls lent this developing culture force, "cementing together the bonds of unity," as one early labour newspaper reported in 1873. Picnics and dinners came to assume an importance beyond mere recreation, uniting workers and making them more "competent to fight the Monster (Capital)." Across central Canada in the 1880s — in Hamilton, Toronto, London, Montreal, Oshawa, Gananoque, Belleville, and Ingersoll — workers affiliated with the Knights of Labor mounted "monster" labour parades and demonstrations drawing thousands to a movement of labour reform. French and English came together in a series of labour demonstrations, picnics, and excursions in Montreal that took place throughout the 1880s and culminated in a grand Labour Day parade held in September 1891. Such events, like the earlier trades' processions in Saint John, New Brunswick, were visible reminders of labour's strength. But unlike the community-based events of 1840 and 1853 in Saint John, the parades of the 1880s linked one labour-reform centre to another, and were as common in the small towns as in the burgeoning cities. If the district assemblies of Toronto and Montreal drew 8,000 to 15,000 people to gala picnics and celebrations, no less impressive were the thousands the Order could attract to manufacturing hamlets like Ingersoll or Gananoque.

Whole segments of the dominant culture were challenged by such public displays of workers' unity, forced to adapt to the new realities of industrial-capitalist society polarized along class lines. Established religion, for instance, suffered setbacks in this era, and there is evidence that in many communities the Knights of Labor usurped the traditional role of the church, community members gathering on evenings to hear a labour "sermon." Montreal labour activist William Darlington claimed: "The Knights of Labor preach more Christianity than the churches." Throughout the period church sources bemoaned "the gradual falling away of those whom the respectability of the middle classes does not see and the dignity of the rich . . . ignores," as well as expressing distress at the "lapsed masses." Hamilton's "Vox Populi" voiced what must have been a widespread critique in labour circles of city pastors and their houses of worship: "You love Jesus Christ, you love to preach about him and do his will, I too with my Br. Knights love his doctrine, and strive to carry out his will, also to obey his command, love one another . . . it is not Christ I find fault with, but the inconsistent doctrines taught in or favored by the church."

"Unity", an anonymous writer of the time, commented on "the growing disposition of the working classes not to attend Church," attributing it to "the fact that many of our places of worship have become simply Sunday Clubs or open halls, intended to attract rich congregations." As G. Levine's researches in the *Journal of the Synod of Ontario* suggest, the Church of England was itself aware of the replication of class distinctions within religious institutions severing "the artisan from the man of business." If a minister wanted a working-class congregation, "Unity" suggested that he say a few words from the pulpit on "usury, land grabbing, and the oppression exercised by capital." One "Well Wisher," writing to the *Palladium of Labor*, echoed what appeared to some working-class activists as religious indifference to the plight of labouring men and women:

> I could tell you how for years I attended church regularly, but for want of that brotherly society and sympathy fell away, and how becoming a K of L my soul rekindled with that human love, with that desire to help my brother man, and it grieves me to say that when I go to church instead of having more fuel placed to that fire it becomes quenched and smothered by the cold and intensely refined religious atmosphere which pervades the churches, and I would fair cry out with thousands of my fellow churchmen, O for a warm, kindly, Christ-like church, a common place where we could all meet on an equality, and be brothers in Christ in this world, even as we hope to be in the next.

Such a church, this writer knew, would address "questions concerning the welfare of the working classes . . . for in these questions rest to a large extent the growth and prosperity of that church whose foundation lies in the humble Nazarene, Jesus Christ himself a carpenter and a workingman."

Among Methodists and Presbyterians, especially, these words found a hearing with condemnation of "selfish capitalists" and the admission that, "upon our land lies a dark reproach. By those in high places the poor are repressed." Aware of a "world of iniquity . . . untouched by their influence," the late nineteenth-century Protestant churches remained committed to the status quo, but some were moved to a recognition of the class distinctions of the age. At Kingston one minister proclaimed that, "Labor was squeezed and enslaved by monopolies . . . because of this enslavement production was slackened just as land was shackled also, the same effect was produced." Such words appealed to advocates of Henry George's Single Tax and, like an 1899 statement by future social gospel leader, Salem Bland, who endorsed unions as being "Christlike" and as an expression of "brotherliness," did much to overcome the early association of the church with capital.

Many labour activists took this association from the *Christian Guardian*'s much-publicized attack on the workers' movement in 1887. Religion, then, was challenged by labour's upsurge and forced to adopt a stance and a language of appeasement. This probably had only minimal effect during the years of strength of the Knights of Labor, when an alternative "brotherliness" thrived, displacing that of the churches to a certain extent. Later, in the 1890s, with the Knights disbanded, workers may have returned to the churches. Few had lost their particular class-rooted conceptions of Christian behaviour. Workers' brotherliness had not so much been defeated by religious institutions, however, as Christian practice had been modified in the face of it.

Even in Catholic-dominated Quebec, for instance, where Church opposition to the Knights of Labor in particular and labour militancy in general far exceeded that found elsewhere, circular letters from Archbishop Taschereau (2 February 1885) and all bishops (20 June 1886) prohibiting membership in this "cosmopolitan" "occult-led" secret society failed to drive the Order from the province. Although the membership did indeed decline after this antagonistic intervention, the Vatican overrode Taschereau, and Richard J. Kerrigan, a Montreal workers' advocate, recalled "the dynamic year of 1886" as one in which the Knights defended themselves against the Archbishop's attack:

> The Knights of Labor grew to alarming proportions in the country, and the Province of Quebec, always the political storm centre of Canada, had to get drastic treatment if it were to be kept safe and sane for law and order. Bishop Taschereau of Quebec launched his famous excommunication decree against the Knights of Labor . . . This did not hurt the Knights much . . . This high-handed action of this over-officious servant of God had the effect of driving the bulk of the intelligent French-speaking proletariat away from the "faith of their fathers" and when the edict was spoken of among the French militant Knights of Labor it was agreed that, "De cela on n'en meurt pas" . . . "Of this we will not die."

Across Canada, the bishops' opposition produced only the most minor problems, and even in Montreal, where one would expect the edicts to have their most far-reaching consequences, 23 new local assemblies were organized in 1886. While the ecclesiastical hysteria may have led to the disappearance of some Montreal assemblies and of a few others at Richmond and Upper Bedford, those throughout the rest of the province survived, and by 1887 the Order in Quebec was approaching its peak strength. The religious institutions supported by the upper classes and so often regarded as a force inhibiting working-class solidarity seemed incapable of stifling the movement culture of the 1880s. Where religion retained its force, it accommodated labour reform rather than opposing it.

Other aspects of the dominant culture also seem to have undergone change, in response to the rise of the Knights of Labor. Temperance, an early plank in industrial-capitalist work discipline, became a mark of working-class independence, a cause for all Knights of Labor to champion vocally and practically. Instead of reading dime novels or popular religious tracts, many workingmen and women began to pick up works of social criticism: George McNeill's *The Labor Movement; the Problem of Today* and the works of Henry George. The cumulative effect of these, and other, developments altered the nature of social relationships in hundreds of Canadian communities, where more than 400 local assemblies of the Knights of Labor were established, and pushed workers toward a new understanding of their place in the larger social order.

The most vital contribution of this movement culture was the message of labour solidarity. Overcoming divisions that had historically separated the skilled from the unskilled, the male from the female, the Protestant from the Catholic, the Irish from the English, the Knights of Labor did much to create a national working class committed to the internationalism of the labour movement. Albert Cross of Hamilton's LA 2481 revealed how thoroughly this notion of labour solidarity permeated the ranks when he wrote to Powderly in 1887:

> When we entered the Order we were taught that in the home of labor there would be no distinctions of Country, Creed & Color because all were of the Earth and with equal rights to Earth, when we understood this great truth that all men are brothers we rejoiced, and we solemnly resolved that we would do all in our power to strengthen the bonds of unity between the workers of the world and we are still steadfast to our principles. . . .

This promise of working-class unity was realized in the integration of Irish workers into the labour movement in the 1880s, the Knights of Labor taking great steps in burying "the bloody shirt" of religious sectarianism and national chauvinism that had long divided Canadian workers into particularistic camps. During the 1880s, these subgroupings overcame past resentments and formed a radical alliance that was one part support for Irish nationalism and another part endorsement of labour reform. The Knights of Labor hailed efforts to unite the Orange and Green, declaring that "Sectarian bigotry is now the only weapon that capital has to wield, and . . . [the Order] is rendering it more and more harmless every day." Gordon Bishop, a Gananoque steel worker, recalled in the 1940s that the Knights were led "principally by members of the Irish race who fled the slavery of peonage in their own lands and who hated as fiercely the economic slavery of the New World."

Symbolic and ritualistic practice, coupled with public display and assaults upon previously divisive forces therefore stood at the centre of the movement culture's experience throughout the 1880s. As the Knights of Labor swept across Canada, they forged a unity among labourers previously unanticipated. It found some of its strongest backers among working-class intellectuals and activists, and achieved new organizational strength by including women, uniting the particular oppression of sex with the cause of the exploited workingman.

Brainworkers

In April of 1886, J.L. Blain of Galt wrote to T.V. Powderly, describing himself as a well-educated "rat from the sinking ship of aristocracy." He told of his efforts in the cause of labour reform, of the lectures he had given on "Capital and Labor," where he proposed remedies for the "present unjust state of society in which 50 percent of the products are absorbed by nonproducers." Blain was one of literally hundreds of intellectuals (called "brainworkers"), activists, editors, lecturers, people's poets and organizers who "spread the light" during the 1880s and 1890s. As both products and producers of labour's upsurge, these working-class advocates emerged from the local assemblies of the Knights of Labor and the trade unions, mounted platforms in labour demonstrations where their talents as speakers were exploited to the full, and penned social criticism that attacked the inequities of the age.

The labour-reform newspaper was their most obvious vehicle for activism. In the pages of well-known Hamilton–Toronto journals, such as the *Labor Union, Palladium of Labor, Wage Worker, Trade Union Advocate, Canadian Labor Reformer, Labor Record,* and *Labor Advocate,* the movement culture of the 1880s and 1890s was at its most vibrant and visible. The existence of other organs, from the Victoria-based *Industrial News* to *Butler's Journal* in Fredericton demonstrated the scope of the working-class and reform presence in these years. Throughout the 1880s, short-lived labour newspapers furthered the cause and advocated a broadly based resistance. In St. Thomas, George Wrigley, future socialist and farmers' advocate, published the *Canada Labor Courier,* while in nearby London, the *Evening News* was established by striking printers in the midst of an 1884 battle with their employer. Eastern Ontario organs included the Brockville *Equalizer* and Ottawa's *Free Lance* and *Capital Siftings.* Other papers published were Winnipeg's *People's Voice,* Quebec's *Le Travail,* and Montreal's *Ouvrier* and *Saturday Times.*

Always balanced delicately on the brink of financial ruin, such newspapers kept afloat during these years only by dint of extraordinary effort, personal perseverance, and occasional support from a long-established trade union. Dependent on advertising revenue, limited by their subscribers' inability to contribute financially, with circulation often hovering around the 1,000 mark, seldom over 5,000, these papers occupied an unenviable position in the often gloomy world of the nineteenth-century press. In spite of their difficulties, reform editors attempted to move the late nineteenth-century working class beyond economism, striving "to take a broader and more comprehensive view of the entire subject of Labor Reform than is embodied in mere unionism, and to grasp and apply those great underlying principles of equity and justice between men which alone can permanently and satisfactorily solve the issues between Labor and Capital." This was an important component of what Frank Watt has referred to as the "freely germinating radicalism" of the 1880s, a phenomenon encouraged by, though not solely the creation of, the Knights of Labor.

In their efforts to challenge workers to envision a more egalitarian order, the reform editors may well have been aided by popular evening dailies like the *Toronto News*. Even established Grit organs such as the *London Advertiser* and the *Globe* courted a working-class readership, running columns like "The Knights of Labor Corner," and providing a haven for dissident journalists. Men like these took a stand against what they referred to as "intellectual prostitution" and attacked peers who failed to sympathize with labour's plight. It was in this environment that Canada's most significant late nineteenth-century labour reformer eventually came of age as a radical social critic.

In the early 1860s, while working for the *St. Catharines Post*, Phillips Thompson started the intellectual odyssey that would take him from the humour columns of the daily press through the Knights of Labor to the post-1900 Socialist Party. By the 1880s, his writings consistently sought to elevate people's conception of their own sense of self, striking at deeply rooted feelings of inadequacy. For Thompson, as for so many other "brainworkers" in labour's cause, the industrial struggle was waged, not just in the factories, mines, and shops, but also in the realm of ideas. In his major work, *The Politics of Labor*, Thompson alerted Canadian workers to new ways of viewing history, political economy, and literature, launching a trenchant critique of bourgeois culture. Always suitable for mass consumption, his message was nevertheless unique in that it sustained a high level of intellectual integrity. Representing the "high" side of the movement culture, this sophisticated and radical scrutiny of developing capitalism attacked monopoly in the economic sphere and the privileged snobbery of the "uppertendom" in the areas of social relations or the arts. Quietly assimilated if not loudly endorsed by local reformers, Thompson's arguments found an echo in the "low" realms of the movement culture, appearing in anonymous lines of verse that chronicled class grievances:

> Oh! ye toilers have ye felt cold and hunger,
> And been warned with poverty's breath?
> Have your hearts been soaked with your sorrow?
> Have you slept in the shadow of death?

or offered words of encouragement:

'Tis the foremost thing to do—
    Spread the Light!
Till the world is made anew—
    Spread the Light!
It is darkness that enslaves,
Those who dwell in dens and caves,
    Knowledge strengthens — knowledge saves—
    Spread the Light!

This kind of exhortation to activism was at the centre of the recruiting drive that brought the Knights of Labor to prominence and that pushed the ideas and activities of labour reform across Canada.

Those cities in which Thompson figured centrally — Toronto and Hamilton — produced labour spokesmen whose impact would be felt across the province: D.J. O'Donoghue, A.W. Wright, Alfred Jury, Charles March, William H. Rowe, George Collis, William Vale, Thomas Towers, and Edward Williams. In Montreal, activists like A.T. Lépine and future socialists William Darlington and Richard Kerrigan were prominent, while in the Maritimes Robert Drummond of the Provincial Workmen's Association, and Martin Butler of Fredericton championed the workers' cause in the 1880s and 1890s. The latter was an exemplar of nineteenth-century radicalism, proclaiming his religion as "universal brotherhood" and determining, by 1893/94, to "abolish the false economic system that makes one man rich out of the blood and sweat of a thousand of his fellow men." By the close of the century, this one-armed printer (who had lost his limb to a bolting machine while working in an American tannery at the age of 18, thereafter pursuing his living as a pedlar, journalist, and poet), saw his *Butler's Journal* fade as the eclectic radicalism of the 1880s and 1890s died. "The democratic tree has been pulled up by the roots and the ground seeded down with the seeds of imperialism and aristocracy," he noted in 1900. Like Thompson, he left behind the nineteenth century to turn to the twentieth century where, he told his readers, "One star only shines on the horizon, and that is Socialism, the doctrine that all men are brothers, have the same rights to opportunity, education and enjoyment and the product of their hands, wrung from the bountiful mother earth, created by the Father of all for the equal use of his children." Thompson and Butler thus followed the trajectory of those ideological "fading beams of the nineteenth century" that Gene Homel has noted experienced a revitalization in the 1890s through contact with a tougher and more thoroughly class-conscious socialism.

What was therefore unique about the 1880s was that it produced a stratum of bona fide working-class leaders, some drawn from the ranks of labour, others attracted from the outside. These "brainworkers" served, as G.H. Allaby has argued in a study of New Brunswick labour reformers at the turn of the century, as "prophets of radicalism." In the 1860s there had been only a handful of these men, often embracing activities and rhetoric that were thoroughly compromised; by the 1870s a few more had come into being, but their words, however valuable, turned, for the most part, toward economic gains in the workplace or party politics. By the 1880s, however, working-class intellectuals and activists were a significant social stratum, a dispersed collection of dissidents with a movement at their back and institutions and vehicles at hand to help propagate their ideas. They helped to cultivate, in Phillips Thompson's words, a vision of an alternative society, in which universal democracy and cooperation could triumph over war and monopoly. The brainworker's "beautiful ideal" of social reorganization was born in the 1880s, when for the first time, Labor Reform was recognized as

> a much wider and more comprehensive question than the mere matter of wages or hours — that it includes everything relating to the mental, moral, and physical advancement of the worker, and implies a war to the death against every influence which tends to depress the condition of Labor. Just let us think for a while what the effect upon government and society would be supposing the great majority of workingmen everywhere were thoroughly educated in the principles of Labor Reform, and determined at any sacrifice to carry them into effect. Let us picture to ourselves the social condition that would result were our ideals realized by the resolute determination of the masses in all civilized lands to use their power for the good of the whole people, instead of letting the selfish few play upon their prejudices and passions, and rule them for the benefit of the upper class.

This ability to dream of what might be "if the world's workers were only educated and organized" was deepened and complemented by significant achievements in drawing an important and previously excluded segment of the working class into the movement culture of the 1880s.

Women

Women had become a vital component of the labour force across North America by the 1880s, representing approximately 15 percent of the gainfully employed, and numbering almost 3,000,000. Shunned by most labour associations, women were even excluded from the Knights of Labor until, in 1881, Mary Stirling and her coworkers in Philadelphia's Mundell & Company's shoe works defied their employer in a strike and spontaneously organized the Garfield Assembly, named in honour of the recently assassinated president. With the aid of some male Knights, Stirling and her sisters persuaded delegates at the 1881 General Assembly to open the Order's doors officially to women. From that point on, women became a force in the Knights of Labor, and by 1886 almost 200 women's local assemblies had been organized in the United States.

In Canada, especially in the Ontario stronghold of the Order, women welcomed the opportunity to participate. By 1891, one wage labourer in eight was a woman, and female workers comprised a low-paid stratum that the Royal Commission on the Relations of Labor and Capital in Canada (1889) reported could be "counted on to work for small wages, to submit to exasperating exactions, and to work uncomplainingly for long hours." Concentrated in cotton textiles, shoe factories, and domestic service (by far the largest category) women also worked in the sweated trades of garment production, the tobacco industry, and were scattered across a wide array of other employments. (See Table 3.1.) Their wages, on average, were approximately one-third that of their male counterparts: in 1884, for instance, the Ontario Bureau of Industries reported that the average male wage for a 59-hour week was almost $400.00 annually, compared to $133.00 annually for women; male and female cigarmakers' weekly wages were $9.45 and $3.72, while in white-collar occupations such as bookkeeping or teaching the wage differential was less marked, but still significant.

TABLE 3.1 Leading occupations for women, 1891

Servant	77,644
Dressmaker	22,686
Teacher	14,803
Farmer	11,590
Seamstress	10,239
Tailoress	7,834
Saleswoman	4,409
Housekeeper	4,035
Laundress	3,679
Milliner	3,277

SOURCE: Julie White, *Women and Unions* (Ottawa: Canadian Advisory Council on the Status of Women, 1980), 4.

These material divergences had long formed the basis of a profound separation between male and female workers, and the introduction of women into the mass struggles and organizational upsurge of the 1880s began to overcome decades of complacency. While the Order as a whole failed to penetrate to the root of the particular oppression of sex, often inhibited by a confining adherence to the consensual norms of Victorian morality, it nevertheless raised the question of the role of women within working-class circles for the first time. In examining the fragmentary historical evidence of the Knights of Labor's relationship to female workers, it becomes obvious once again that the Order contributed to an alternative vision of social relations, edging working-class culture toward an emergent sense of opposition to the status quo and laying stress upon the need for a unified class perspective. For if the Knights of Labor remained inhibited by the cultural norms of a society that circumscribed the woman's role and established the usual "proper sphere," it did defy the same norms in its attempts to build a movement encompassing all workers, male and female.

Hamilton's *Palladium of Labor* reflected the Order's refusal to ignore the plight of the woman worker at the same time that it echoed the confinements of the age. It argued, on the one hand, that women came into the Knights of Labor as the peers of men, equal to them and deserving of the same pay in the workplace and the same recognition in the political and social spheres. There was apparently no position within the movement that a woman could not hold, and women such as Leonora M. Barry became organizers, while others, such as Amherstburg's Rose Le May became District Master Workmen. This practice of equality, however, was often tarnished by a retreat into the domestic ideology of the age and a chivalrous deference of feminity: "Upon motherhood we base brotherhood, and in our family circle we pledge ourselves to defend the fair name and reputation of an innocent sister even with our lives," declared this organ of labour reform. "If there is any preeminence given either sex in our order," closed the *Palladium*, "it is given to women." The Order thus defied convention by opening assembly halls to female workers at the same time that it extended this invitation to organize in a most traditional manner. When Canadian women were won to the cause, it was seldom through the strike, the mass campaign, the boycott, or the demonstration. Rather, for the "fair sex," the ticket into the Knights of Labor was often stamped at the soiree, the hop, or the social, and it was possible for Knights of Labor editors like Hamilton's William H. Rowe to contrast the "pining and wasp-waisted, doll-dressed, consumption-mortgaged, music murdering, novel-devouring, daughters of fashion and idleness" to the "real lady" who could "darn a stocking and mend her own dress . . . a girl that young men are in quest of for a wife."

Rowe's crude moralizing and limited view of women's place did not deter workers like Katie McVicar, Hamilton's pioneer woman organizer, from posing the issue of central concern to working women in a more realistic manner: "Our employers are organized for the purpose of keeping the selling prices up and the manufacturing prices down, and we ought certainly to accept the assistance and invitation of our gentlemen Knights and organize; remain no longer strangers to each other, but combine and protect ourselves to some purpose." In the years after 1884, McVicar's line of argument would be pursued by others, albeit often anonymously. But women also came out openly for reform, and a few, like the Belleville poet Marie Joussaye or the Picton, Ontario, social critic and reform-writer Elizabeth Johnson, joined the ranks of central Canadian "brainworkers." These developments helped to instill a sense of sisterhood among working women, but one that was class bound. An open letter to the "working girls" of Canada in 1885 closed on the note that female workers must not look to the law, the church, or "the high-born sister women" for help. "Sisters," concluded this address, "by our dignity, co-operation, and organization, we must protect ourselves." As the movement grew and more women became attached to the cause of labour, gains were made, gains in understanding that went part of the way toward raising an assault against the restrictions of women's place.

Out of this emerged demands for women's suffrage, a recognition of the vitally important place of unpaid domestic labour, attempts to organize previously unorganized women workers, and calls for equal pay for equal work. It was the act of drawing women into the labour movement — women who had before been isolated on the margins of trade union, political, or workplace struggles — that was of lasting significance in a number of Canadian communities. Over the course of the 1880s, approximately 10 percent, or 25 out of 250, of the Ontario local assemblies contained women. Penetrating previously untouched work sectors, the Knights of Labor secured most of their female advocates among workers employed in the cotton mills, shoe factories, and the garment industry, while the more isolated individual female clerks and domestic servants were less responsive to the appeal to solidarity. Throughout this effort, it was the Order's defence of "the right of women to be regarded in all matters of citizenship and all relations between the government and the people as the equal of men" that was paramount. This, according to Phillips Thompson, could "hardly be denied by any clear-sighted and consistent Labor Reformer." Henry George put the matter in a similar light when he argued before a Hamilton audience that "The women have a right to come into your organizations. . . . The women are the best men we have."

In late nineteenth-century Knights of Labor strongholds like Belleville, Brantford, Hamilton, Montreal, Stratford, Thorold, and Toronto, then, women joined the Order in assemblies named "Hope" and "Advance," with the intention of realizing the possibility of women's emancipation. From today's standpoint, attendance at musical and literary entertainments as "Goddesses of Liberty" or membership in an LA named "Excelsior," which expressed elevated status, might point less to liberation than to an innately sexist idolization of feminity. Yet in the challenge of the 1880s, such honorifics were, in fact, an articulation of dignity and worth felt to be the birthright of all individuals, including labouring women. To acknowledge the place of working women within the general human condition represented a great advance over the past practice, and played a not inconsiderable role in changing male workers' view of women and female workers' view of themselves. The possibility, in the end, was far from realized; but it nevertheless existed. The Order had begun the process whereby the questions of class and sex could be considered as one.

Politics

The movement culture of the 1880s shifted the existing terms of class experience, drawing unskilled workers, women, and the Irish from the periphery into the very centre of late nineteenth-century labour-reform agitation. In this developing solidarity, workers glimpsed the potential of working-class unity that could change the world in which they lived. As Raymond Williams has argued, this process of wanting and actively struggling to convince others that a new human order is seriously possible is central to any attempt to create alternatives. It is part of a long history of resistance "where intention and consequence, desire and necessity, possibility and practice, have . . . bloodily interacted." In attempting to accelerate this process, the movement culture of the 1880s posed an alternative hegemony to the dominant hegemony of bourgeois rule. It found itself, inevitably, in the political arena.

Leaders of the Knights of Labor knew that party attachments were strong among workingmen (women, too, had their loyalties, but they could not vote) and particular leaders were often committed to one of the established parties, Grit or Tory. By this time, the reformers of the 1830s had disappeared completely, although the Grits often went under the name "Reform." Then, too, politics seemed to attract the manipulators, con-men, and opportunists like no other reform activity, for there was money and influence to be had from the conventional parties. Workers in the 1880s attempted to overcome these barriers to their political activity in varied ways. Some opted for pressuring the established parties to advocate labour reform, but the more unique and lasting accomplishment of the decade was the initiation of independent working-class political action. Lewis Allchin, an Oshawa iron moulder active in his international union and in the Knights of Labor, was one workingman whose views were representative of advanced political feeling in the 1880s. In 1884, he wrote to Powderly that he was "waiting for the as yet unformed Independent Party to rise phoenix-like from the ashes of corrupt officialdom and sluggish Whiggery." Until that happened, however, he considered that he could not place his ballot aside, and he voted "in the interests of the working class be the candidates Reform or Conservative." In cities such as Toronto and Ottawa, where partyism and corruption were strong, such compromises would often serve the long-established parties well, but even given the victories of the dominant culture, the politics of the 1880s increasingly turned toward class issues. John A. Macdonald, leader of the federally entrenched Tories, worried by the mid-1880s that his party was not "in a flourishing state." The "rocks ahead" which threatened the Conservative ship were "Riel, Home Rule, the Knights of Labor and the Scott Act."

From the moment of its entrance into Canada, the Order engaged in politics actively. December 1882 saw the first stirrings of political involvement as Hamilton workers helped to elect two prolabour aldermen, and the Toronto labour council played a prominent role in defeating a candidate particularly hostile to working-class interests. The initial successes propelled labour reformers in both cities into independent campaigns in the 1883 Ontario provincial election. Both Toronto and Hamilton workers' efforts in these political contests saw disgruntled Tory workingmen accuse the Grits of double dealing, and this would be a constant impediment to future reform struggles in the political realm. Hamilton's Knights of Labor and trade unionists took the lead in combatting such divisive complaint by forming the Hamilton Labor Political Association, encouraging the move toward an independent working-class political party. Subsequent municipal elections in 1883/84 were marked by the Association's presence, and, led by shoemaker Robert Coulter and coppersmith George Collis, the Knights of Labor managed to secure the election of a number of their supporters to alderman's posts. The best-known of these newly arrived political figures was the Irish carter Thomas Brick, who was a colourful and bombastic spokesman for Hamilton workers.

Excelsior Assembly provided a leadership core of labour reformers in Toronto, where Daniel O'Donoghue, Alfred Jury, and Charles March engineered the Knights of Labor into a position of dominance in the Trades and Labor Congress of Canada (TLC) which first met in 1883 and in the Toronto Trades and Labor Council (TTLC). Once entrenched there, they proceeded to use both bodies to launch lobbying efforts, especially against the federal Tories. By 1885 the concerted action of this group fed into a general discontent with the Tory's monopoly on the mayor's office, and a sweeping reform victory placed W.H. Howland in the city's leading political chair. Supported by the Toronto Trades and Labor Council and the Knights of Labor, Howland's success brought the political power of labour to the attention of the federal Tories, who could no longer afford to dismiss the reality of the working class as an electoral force. Soon after the Toronto mayoralty contest, and on the eve of a federal election, John A. Macdonald orchestrated a series of concessions to discontented workingmen, urging settlement of a strike at the Tory-controlled newspaper, the Toronto *Mail*, and setting up a royal commission to investigate the relations between labour and capital.

Aimed at a vocal and politicized working class, these Tory concessions did little to placate labour. Both the December 1886 provincial election and the February 1887 federal election saw unprecedented working-class action. In the provincial contest, seven working-class candidates took the field. One ran for the Grits (Reform/Liberal) and two ran for the Tories (Conservative), but their labour affiliations were made more important than those of previous working-class candidates in that they billed themselves "Liberal-Labour" and "Labour-Conservative," respectively. Four candidates ran as independents. St. Thomas brakeman and leading Knight of Labor Andy Ingram, won the West Elgin seat for the Tories, while in Lincoln–St. Catharines, Lib–Lab candidate William Garson was elected. A.W. Wright, on a Labour-Conservative ticket in Lambton, lost, as did all the independents, an indication of just how strong the resistance to independence could be. But those who ran outside the confines of the traditional parties often took a major share of the old guard's vote. London's Samuel Peddle, a Knight who campaigned with temperance support, gave Tory opposition leader W.R. Meredith significant opposition before going down to a narrow defeat. In the previous election, Meredith had gained his seat by acclamation. The February federal election saw similar results, although labour won no victories.

Ontario's workers had thus made a tentative entry into politics, aware of both the necessity of action and the obstacles to success. Their ventures did little to convince them that politics was anything more than a necessary evil, especially in the apparently removed realms of provincial and federal legislative halls, where representatives of labour often retained close ties to traditional parties. The very presence of prolabour members of parliament did, however, increase their lobbying power, supplemented in the late 1880s by the creation of a Canadian Knights of Labor Legislative Committee. Nevertheless, throughout the late 1880s, the most accessible political lever was still that of the municipal council, and combined Knights of Labor-trade union forces won a number of impressive political battles in this area: Brantford, Chatham, Brockville, and Ottawa were all sites of municipal victories.

In Quebec, labour's political voice was heard most clearly in the Knights of Labor stronghold of Montreal. Described in detail by Fernand Harvey and in unpublished studies by Victor Chan and Robert Cox, labour became especially active in politics in Montreal in 1886, when the Order supported three candidates in the provincial election. Another workers' candidate, Charles Champagne, campaigned in the industrial district of Hochelaga. All were backed by the working-class community, all were affiliated with the Knights of Labor, and all would refuse to compromise their independence by running for the established Grit and Tory parties, which were now more commonly known under their modern designations of "Liberal" and "Conservative." However, none of these labour candidates would gain election.

Least successful was the Scots saddler William W. Robertson from Montreal West. An autodidactic artisan, his electoral appeal was diminished by his pro-*canadien* stand against vaccination during the 1885 smallpox epidemic. Montreal's English-speaking population tended to attribute the outbreak of the disease to the so-called "innate slovenliness" of the French Canadian labouring population and demanded a massive inoculation campaign. Robertson's refusal to accept such views undoubtedly cost him the votes of many anglophones. The other workers' candidates, William Keys, an Irish machinist who had worked as a foreman in various Griffintown shops, and a French printer, Adélard Gravel, who worked for the company that published *La Presse*, fared better. Both were key figures in the city's labour movement. In Gravel the Knights found an ideal candidate. He had long been associated with the workers through his presidency of the French-speaking wing of the Montreal Typographical Union, was fluent in French and English, cosmopolitan (he had tramped the United States from New York to Chicago to Raleigh, North Carolina), and uncompromising in his political integrity. When the Liberal–Mercier camp tried to woo him on nationalist grounds, he refused the bait. "I will not put the labour question in second place," he promised. "I will vote with Mr. Mercier in all the political questions, but the workingmen will claim my first attention." Keys and Gravel would win strong support in working-class ridings, Keys winning St. Anne's ward in Montreal centre, Gravel capturing St. Mary's ward in Montreal East. Although defeated, the labour trio gained 6,000 of the 18,000 votes cast in the three Montreal districts.

Their program called for amendments to contractual relations between masters and apprentices, protection for child and female labour, arbitration in the case of industrial disputes, equality before the law, endorsement of public libraries and institutions of working-class instruction, restrictions on state-aided immigration, suppression of the liquor traffic, revision of the municipal tax system, the establishment of bureaus of labour statistics, amelioration of abuses of wage payment (including truck and infrequent or irregular paydays), passage of factory acts, and a forceful attack on the Statute of Labor Tax which, it was claimed, deprived over 18,000 workers of the vote in municipal elections. Typical of political platforms raised across the country, this program was defended vigorously by Robertson, Keys, and Gravel in a number of mass meetings and intimate gatherings. "Make the labour candidates custodians of the country's morality and integrity," shouted Robertson at one audience, raising the movement culture's banner of an alternative to partyism and corruption. Keys spoke for workers and their class when he offered his assessment of the campaign: "Although defeated I consider my candidature to be a triumph as it has shown the wealthier classes what workingmen can do."

Two Liberals and a Conservative would thus sit for Montreal in the Quebec legislature after this contest, but in future political struggles the established parties would pay more attention to the working class, attempting to mend some of the fences that had been broken as labour took to the electoral field in 1886. For the Conservatives, especially, this policy paid dividends, although workers were also beneficiaries. Campaigning in the 1887 federal election, Knights and unionists again failed to secure a representative. But one year later, in an 1888 federal contest, A.T. Lépine, a Tory workingman affiliated with the Montcalm Assembly of the Knights of Labor, founder of the *Trait d'Union*, and secretary of the central labour council, emerged victorious over his liberal opponent in Montreal East. Although activists like Gravel would not have chosen any such party affiliation, Lépine's connection with the Tories led to a victory that publicized the importance of the working class in the political arena, a sphere in which Montreal workers would continue to wage battle well into the 1890s. As in Ontario, the most important victories may well have taken place at the municipal level, where the Order elected an alderman and a councillor in Quebec City in 1892, and the mayor and 9 of 12 aldermen in Hull in 1894.

Miners on the east and west coasts also took their first strides into the political field in these years. The *Trades Journal*, voice of the Nova Scotia-based Provincial Workmen's Association, declared in 1885:

> The time has come when the workingmen of Nova Scotia . . . must rally behind their forces and demand . . . representation in our Legislatures. Too long have the interests of the working classes been over-looked . . . trampled upon and treated with contempt . . . by both political parties . . . . Our interests must be guarded well by representatives of our own choosing . . . . [The] ballot must be the means to secure our just desires, maintain our rights, put good men in power, and hurl tyrants from the position . . . . Let us go forward, fearing no man. Let there be one aim — advancement, "Organize, AGITATE."

Originally confining their activities to lobbying and supporting reform-minded candidates from the traditional parties, the PWA, like the Knights of Labor, took its stand on independent politics at the local level. The Cameron Lodge of Westville formed a Workingmen's Political Club and Cape Breton municipal elections in the early 1880s saw independent candidates seek office. Political activism peaked in 1886, when James Wilson of Pioneer Lodge ran in Cumberland County on an independent labour ticket, and Robert Drummond stood for Pictou as a Lib–Lab candidate. But defeat was the outcome of such efforts and only in 1888 did a PWA candidate secure victory, capturing a municipal office in Cape Breton.

In the west, workers raised their objections to the importation of Chinese labour and the land-grant system that gave concentrated economic authority to the coal baron Robert Dunsmuir. Although not solely the creation of the Knights of Labor, west-coast political action was greatly influenced by the Order. As Paul Phillips notes, the four workers' candidates nominated in 1886 were unmistakably linked with the cause of the Knights of Labor. In Victoria, one candidate, John Duval, was a reform-editor whose newspaper, the *Industrial News*, was endorsed by the province's Knights of Labor, while a Nanaimo candidate, S.H. Myers, was a coalminer member of the Order who would later die in a mine disaster. The platform of the Workingmen's Party called for mine safety laws, land reform, and exclusion of the Chinese. Like the New Westminster Reform Party established to contest the 1887 federal election, it signalled the first political expression in British Columbia of "a basic divergence of interest between the 'toiling masses' and the 'wealthier part of the community.' " Municipal politics also became a focus of activity in Vancouver, while in Winnipeg, political action seemed restricted to the provincial election of 1886.

Peaking in the provincial-federal political activities of 1886/87, these diverse and uncoordinated labour efforts stand as evidence of the underlying similarity in working-class experience that bred a movement culture of workers' resistance in the 1880s, a movement building on common class experiences and advanced by Knights and Workmen. All such efforts marked the first concerted attempts to decrease workers' dependence upon old-line political parties and often led to a sense of political independence within the working class. While few independent labour candidates won seats, the move toward independence was itself something of a victory. The movement culture did not succeed in overcoming all the tensions within the working-class world of the 1880s, and partisan attachments remained a strong inhibition to independent working-class political activity. Yet on the local level, tangible gains were being made: early closing, union wages and jobs in corporation work, just assessment rates, opposition to bonusing capital's consolidation, and responsible public transit were just a few of the issues that were, on occasion, resolved in favour of labour. In the national sphere, significant concessions were won as both Liberals and Conservatives courted a growing working-class constituency increasingly aware of its own potential as a "spoiler" in electoral battles. Oliver Mowat, premier of Ontario, and, to a lesser degree, Macdonald in Ottawa, responded to this new development of the 1880s with factory acts, bureaus of labour statistics, arbitration measures, suffrage extension, employers' liability acts and improved mechanics' lien laws. Hence, the political struggles of this period cannot be dismissed as failures. But independent labour politics was still far from a realization in the 1880s and early 1890s. The established political parties proved sophisticated opponents of this drift toward autonomy, and through patronage and concession, managed to contain much of the working-class opposition of the 1880s. But in the workplace, where class relations often unfolded in their sharpest, least mediated manner, a growing divergence of labour and capital was becoming apparent.

Strikes

One expression of the rift between labour and capital that emerged in the 1880s was the rising number of strikes. This willingness to resort to the strike pointed to an increase in working-class grievances that grew out of the movement culture, indicating that labour was beginning to see alternatives to accommodation. To be sure, many of the conflicts of the 1880s were mundane confrontations over wages, the size of the slice of the economic pie that labour was to receive, but workers also made attempts to retain control over work processes that seemed to be drifting into others' hands as capital consolidated its authority.

The increase in strike activity in this period is indisputable, and this alone accounts for a good deal of the public recognition of a working-class presence in politics, in the pages of the daily newspapers, or between the covers of late nineteenth-century popular novels such as Albert Carman's *The Preparation of Ryerson Embury* and Agnes Maule Machar's *Roland Graeme: Knight*. In Hamelin's, Larocque's and Rouillard's *Répertoire des Grèves dans la Province de Québec* (a useful source that nevertheless understates significantly the number of strikes) there are references to 102 strikes between 1880 and 1895, compared to a mere 61 conflicts in the entire period from 1843 to 1879. Kealey's *Toronto Workers Respond to Industrial Capitalism, 1867–1892* indicates that 112, or over 70 percent, of the 156 strikes fought in Ontario's largest city in the post-Confederation period occurred in the years after 1880. More than 430 labour-capital conflicts erupted across Canada over the course of the 1880s. Compared to the 1870s this represented a rough doubling of the number of strikes and lockouts; if the 1880s are set against earlier decades–the 1850s or 1860s–such figures indicate a sixfold increase in conflict. Individual craft unions led the majority of these struggles, but relations between unionists and Knights of Labor were so close (especially prior to 1886) that it is often difficult to distinguish the role of the trade unions from that of the local assemblies. Knights were of course involved heavily in a number of Montreal conflicts; in Toronto they waged at least 20 strikes between 1883 and 1889, and in Hamilton in the mid-1880s they led approximately half of the work stoppages (nine in total). In Ontario, iron moulders affiliated with both their international union and the Knights of Labor fought at least 25 strikes between 1880 and 1893, as well as at least three others in Quebec. This represents an increase over the number of moulders' strikes that occurred in the 1860s and 1870s, difficult years in which the Iron Molders International Union established itself in Canada.

Even where craftsmen and Knights were weak or virtually nonexistent, as in Halifax, there are indications that the 1880s marked a new period of class conflict. An unpublished study by Ian McKay contends that there were as many strikes conducted in Halifax in the 1880s (15) as there were in the preceding two decades, while communities previously uninterrupted by the upheavals of class conflict, like Milltown, New Brunswick, first witnessed strikes and labour organization (the formation of a Knights of Labor local assembly) in 1886. The 1880s, then, was a decade of heightened workplace militancy, symbolized by the Halifax Carpenters' Union, which marched on Labour Day in 1888. It displayed the Stars and Stripes indicative of the internationalism of labour, and for the first time brought before the public a handsome silk craft banner, made in London in 1864 at a cost of $250. Bearing a Latin inscription, "By diligence and perseverance we overcome all things," the carpenters' 1888 unveiling of their union's motto did indeed indicate that finally, after a quarter of a century, their craft pride and organization had moved beyond fear of hostile reception. But lest others miss this message, the carpenters of the 1880s introduced yet another symbolic piece, expressive of the new social climate of the 1880s: an enormous mallet that they claimed would be employed to level scabs. As McKay notes, in the conjuncture of the symbols of old and new, workmanship and militancy, lay a part of the meaning of the 1880s and labour's perception of itself.

The Knights of Labor epitomized this new self-perception. In fact, in the Order's earliest years in Canada, it grew because it was willing to organize class forces larger than itself, marshalling numerous trade sectors or industrial groupings for a particular struggle. Thus, in Toronto the Knights of Labor contributed to the formation of a coalition of forces knit together by experienced labour reformers and trade union militants who all found common cause in the need to support striking women boot and shoe operatives in the spring of 1882. This was apparent again in the summer of 1883 when District Assembly 45 (Brotherhood of Telegraphers) engaged in a continent-wide strike against the monopolistic telegraph companies that united operatives in Canada from Sydney in the east to Winnipeg in the west. Although DA 45 had done little preparatory work within the Order before their epic struggle began, as a bitter Powderly would argue again and again, it established enough local contacts across North America for organized labour, and especially the Knights of Labor, to rally to its cause. Out of this momentous international struggle would come not only the Order's first major defeat in Canada, but also union contributions to the strike fund and a wave of benefit concerts, lectures, and theatricals. The first series of massive labour festivals and holidays, unsanctioned but worker-proclaimed "Labour Days," were organized by the Knights of Labor in the midst of the telegraphers' strike, as labour forces in Hamilton, Toronto, and Oshawa united in support of the men and women who proclaimed:

> We're bound to fight,
> Our cause is right,
> Monopoly is sore.
> We have left our keys
> To take our ease,
> Let Jay Gould walk the floor.

The ultimate failure of the telegraphers' strike, and its bitter aftermath, which saw DA 45 withdraw from the Knights of Labor, appeared less important, in 1883, than the solidarity expressed in its course. Workers had struggled to obtain abolition of Sunday work, the eight-hour day and the seven-hour night, equal pay for members of both sexes, and a universal wage increase of 15 percent. They posed the moral authority of what the Knights liked to call "modern chivalry" against the "tyranny and unjust treatment of a soulless corporation." And when they lost this battle it was not defeat they remembered, but the importance of solidarity, and the necessity of continuing the struggle. "The telegraphers' strike is over," declared Hamilton's *Palladium of Labor*, "The People's Strike is now in Order."

"The People's Strike" took many forms in the years to come. At its most dramatic it involved mass strikes that crippled whole industries or polarized entire communities. Examples of struggles of this magnitude included the two Toronto street railway strikes of the spring and summer of 1886, cotton mill strikes in Merritton in 1886 and 1889, in Cornwall (1887, 1888, 1889), and in Milltown in 1886. The great lumber workers' strikes in Gravenhurst in 1888 and in Ottawa-Hull in 1891 were also part of this wave. Each of these strikes unified working communities, increased the level of class struggle to previously unmatched heights, and involved workers long excluded from labour action in a wide-reaching solidarity that linked men and women, skilled and unskilled, French- and English-speaking in a bond of unity. For the most part these labour upheavals that were waged to secure organizational recognition, humane conditions, and better wages, had few parallels in the history of labour before 1880. The only previous strikes comparable in sheer numbers were the early canallers strikes, which lacked the level of solidarity achieved in the strikes after 1880, and the ship labourers' conflicts in Saint John and Quebec City, which failed to draw other workers to the cause with the same force.

Beyond these epic battles, Knights of Labor often formed alliances with long-established craft unions to mount smaller struggles aimed at the preservation of particular forms of worker autonomy or control. The Order provided an institutional backing for literally thousands of workers who sought to maintain wage standards in the face of prosperity's inflation and the wage cuts of more depressed years. In 1885, for instance, Montreal coopers associated with the Knights of Labor went on strike against a new system of payment, in 1886, 150 leather workers organized by the Knights of Labor battled against mechanization of their craft, and in 1889, 100 shoeworker Knights went on strike to protest the behaviour of a foreman. One of the most massive confrontations occurred in January 1887, when more than 1,000 primary metalworkers led by the Knights of Labor walked out of the Montreal

Rolling Mills and two other companies in opposition to a 10 percent wage reduction.

Among Canadian moulders, perhaps the most conflict-ridden trade in the 1880s and early 1890s, Knights and unionists fought classic battles that turned on the issue of workers' autonomy and managerial prerogatives. Organized throughout Ontario and Quebec and to some extent in the Maritimes, moulders were concentrated in agricultural implements shops and stove foundries. Employer opposition to unions, workers' rejection of wage cuts, moulder demands for limited numbers of apprentices, union attacks on employer use of helpers, known as "berkshires" or "bucks," revisions in the standard wage rate or "shop book" prices, and antagonism to arbitrary authority led to a series of worker-employer clashes throughout the 1880s.

But to discuss only strikes is undoubtedly to distort much of the character of productive relations, however much such conflicts contribute to our understanding of employer-worker relations in these years. For the labour-capital relationship was a symbiotic one, based on give and take, in which workers appropriated some of the power of decision making at the workplace, establishing procedures and controlling limited aspects of the production process. This is revealed dramatically in an exciting study of workers' control among the Springhill miners by Ian McKay. Basing his study on rare papers and minutes of the Pioneer Lodge of the Provincial Workmen's Association, McKay argues that between 1882 and 1886 miners and proprietors existed within a structure of "organic control," in which pit democracy, workers' autonomy, and a culture and ideology of independence thrived within the mining community. Workers enjoyed extensive powers over production, although long-term decisions regarding entrepreneurial strategy rested in the hands of the company. Collective bargaining evolved within this structure of organic control and resembled a situation in which proprietors (one the owner of capital, the other, of labour) struck a bargain within well-defined relations of reciprocity.

The importance of McKay's study, aside from its larger purpose of clarifying the nature and significance of workers' control, lies in its demonstration of just how influential a sense of working-class autonomy was in the mines of the 1880s (which seem rather similar to the craft shops of the industrial cities). The minutes record 137 attempts to resolve particular worker grievances through lodge action in the years 1882–86. Almost 20 percent of the cases involved discussion of the possibility of a strike, although the lodge actually undertook only four recognized work stoppages in these years. Dominated by wage-related concerns (52 percent), the Springhill miners' minute books also included discussions of hiring (13 percent), discharges (5.8 percent), mine management (19 percent), and assorted other issues. While solidarity in the mines was a difficult process of creation, McKay's study indicates that miners debated and detailed their working lives with great care, demonstrating "their profound intention of placing their stamp on the mine and of retaining their own history, written in their own way and for their own use." Different data exists for the craft shops of the industrial cities, but here, too, a similar relationship between employer and worker had developed, suggesting that the sense of worker autonomy expressed in the Springhill miners' records cut across lines of trade and region.

Throughout the 1880s and early 1890s, then, a sense of working-class autonomy, often resulting in conflict, was never far from the surface of class relations. Whether it emerged visibly in a walkout of 2,000 and more lumber workers in Ottawa–Hull, in a riot against Toronto's street railway magnate, Frank Smith, or in a defeated struggle to control the nature of production in a Brockville foundry, or whether it was the subject of deliberate debate in the lodge room of Springhill's PWA, the strike was a forceful feature of social relations and everyday life. An elementary lesson had been learned in these years, as a movement culture heightened workers' awareness, bringing together the unskilled and the skilled.

The Close of a Century

The modern Canadian labour movement, prefaced by the short-lived, Tory-linked Canadian Labour Union of the 1870s (which succumbed to the strains of the 1873–79 depression) emerged in the 1880s. More than a dozen cities and towns had managed to establish Trades and Labor councils by the end of the decade, with strong city centrals thriving in Toronto by 1881, Montreal by 1886, and Vancouver by 1889. Often led by Knights of Labor activists (the Toronto triumvirate of O'Donoghue, Jury, and March was especially significant), these bodies provided a forum for interaction between Knights and unionists as well as a focus for the labour movement's economic and political work. They also provided local foundations for the creation of the Trades and Labor Congress of Canada, which first met in Toronto in 1883. Forty-eight delegates attended this original gathering (only 11 from outside of Toronto), but in the years to come, the TLC would grow to embrace a wider constituency. In 1886, 109 delegates were in attendance, and the TLC's conventions would continue into the 1950s. By the 1890s, however, it was clear that labour's ship was battling stormy seas, and in 1893 only 70 delegates appeared at the Trades and Labor Congress meeting; two years later the number had declined to 39. The movement culture was in trouble.

Part of that weakening was caused by the breakdown of solidarity in the years after 1886, as Knights and craft unionists began to disagree on more and more issues. Major rifts had erupted across North America between the Knights of Labor, who advocated united concern for all workers, and the international trade unions, which were, by definition, oriented toward more exclusive interests. This division was most acute in the Cigarmakers' trade, with the International Union endorsing the blue union label and Knights of Labor LA members advocating their own white label. This intraclass rivalry played a large role in the collapse of a unified labour movement, and affected major centres such as London, Hamilton, and Toronto. Historians have traditionally viewed this parting of the ways in the late 1880s as an inevitable separation, in which the utopian and "backward-looking" Knights of Labor lost out to the more pragmatic, less reform-oriented, strictly "bread and butter" unionism of the international associations of craft workers. Such an analysis, generally proposed by scholars with little attachment to the Order's humanistic commitment to alternatives to capitalist authority, has only recently come into question in Canada and the United States. But this reigning interpretive orthodoxy has contributed to some distortion of working-class organization at the close of the century.

To lay stress upon the craft unions' "victory" over the Knights of Labor and to argue that a committed and intellectually aware stratum of North American labour leaders consciously chose the narrow path of trade unionism over the politically oriented, reformist purpose of unifying all workers, is to mistake historical outcome for strategic direction. And surely it is also to misread the histories of the trade union pioneers, who, in Canada, as in the United States, were often simultaneously Knights and unionists. D.J. O'Donoghue, often depicted as the aristocratic father of the Canadian labour movement, was a labour activist dedicated to the Knights of Labor well into its years of decline in the 1890s and eclipse in the early twentieth century. There were many others like him, and in 1893, four out of every seven delegates attending the Trades and Labor Congress were still affiliated with the Noble and Holy Order of the Knights of Labor.

It will therefore be difficult to understand fully the decline of the movement culture of the 1880s if it is attributed only to the inevitable rise of a "superior" trade unionism. A full comprehension of this decline necessitates an examination of the social and political structures within which the movement culture came to prominence in the 1880s. This analysis will reveal the character of productive relations, the nature of the state, and the limitations that these forces imposed upon the movement culture, leading toward the failure of the cross-Canada organizational efforts of the Knights of Labor and the Provincial Workmen's Association to sustain themselves into the twentieth century.

The 1880s represented the culmination of an age of competitive capitalism and political localism, and the movement culture developed as a working-class challenge to those structures. Consolidating a working-class that had long been fragmented, proponents of this movement struggled to unite French and English in Quebec, miner and shopworker in the Maritimes, and Irish and English, man and woman, skilled and unskilled in Ontario's industrial heartland. As Norman Ware argued almost 40 years ago: "The fact is that the Knights of Labor more fully represented the wage-earners as a whole than any general labor organization either before or after its peak year, 1886." The bonds of unity did not grow out of economic need alone, but were rooted in ritual, a sense of brotherhood and sisterhood, and an activism informed by working-class intellectuals who saw reform as the only hope in an age of degradation. For the first time, Canadian workers struggled for the same political, economic, and cultural improvements in spite of great differences in region, culture, and workplace. Across the country, the movement culture was motivated by what American historian David Montgomery has called a "moral universality," and both Knights and Workmen seemed engaged in a "crusade" to "impose economic order" on an individualistic and acquisitive capitalism. In the process, it became a prophetic, if eclectic, voice of radical dissidence.

But in all of this, the movement culture was, ironically, raising grievances that were even more prophetic than they were real. While the movement culture of the 1880s saw the writing on the wall, it had no conception of just how large the letters would eventually come to be written. For at precisely the moment that the labour upheaval of the 1880s erupted, the context that had ushered it into being was on the brink of transformation. Opposing monopoly, Knights and Workmen battled a capitalism that was actually dominated by entrepreneurial competition. Attacking the misuse of political power, they themselves endorsed the politics of independent working-class activity in an age that understood little of the eventual authority of the interventionist state. It is thus perplexing that history should judge this essentially forward-looking movement as reactionary and backward. The problem was less the movement culture's backwardness than it was its understandable limitations: aware of the awesome change being effected throughout North American society, working-class leaders and their followers in the 1880s had only their past experiences to draw upon in forging their collective response. And those experiences inhibited the extent to which they could effectively respond to changes that were taking place, but which would not, in fact, leave their full imprint upon the social order until well into the twentieth century. The movement culture was thus forward-looking in its realization of capital's potential destructiveness and in its strategic call for labour unity, at the same time that its tactics, learned in the school of the actual experiences of the past, were limited and failed to meet the needs of the new hour.

This ambiguity, of a prophetic and visionary stance inhibited by the limitations of specific realities, lies at the heart of labour's failures in the

1880s. An eclectic radical critique, capable of uniting the working class around the perceived threats of a rising economic and political oligarchy, would eventually see its worst fears confirmed in the late 1880s and 1890s. As monopoly began to develop and as political power in a nation born only 20 years earlier grew more centralized and more sophisticated, the tactics of the past proved ineffective. Change was proceeding at such a quickening pace and the older social relations were being superseded so dramatically that working-class bodies like the Knights of Labor and the Provincial Workmen's Association were thrown into a state of confused agitation. What they needed most was time to adapt; this is what they never had. For the whole process of forging a collective response had to be begun anew. What had appeared as adequate in the movement culture's euphoric rise in the early 1880s, came to be seen as inadequate in the troubled years of post-1886 breakdown. The "moral universality" fostered by the movement culture started to disintegrate. In the 1890s the search for solutions to labour's dilemmas would be renewed in the rise of socialism and the drift toward a more dominant pragmatic unionism. But by then, the damage had been done, and the movement culture of the 1880s was in a shambles.

All of this explains the supposed failures of the movement culture. Economically, the Knights of Labor have often been criticized for their ambivalent practice at the workplace, and their hesitancy in strike situations is well known. The enthusiastic reception accorded arbitration and cooperation is often read as a naïve and uninformed attempt to create social relations of production in an age of industrial capital similar to those that prevailed during some "golden age" of the artisan producer. Yet, in essence, such orientations and commitments were by no means irrelevant to all that the Knights of Labor leaders and rank-and-file had experienced in an age of competitive capital, when small-scale production and community formed the background of much of economic and social life. That this was in the process of changing just as the movement culture raised these solutions, is both understandable and tragic, for it meant that the movement culture lacked an economic strategy at precisely the moment it needed it most, drawing on an experience that was about to be suspended. In fact, capital had begun to resist workers and consolidate its own power in the late 1880s, which led to more employer-worker conflicts and more losses on the part of the workers. Trade unionists began to see that their interests might be better served in a more disciplined and restricted body, such as the union devoted to their particular craft. Employer hostility, as much as any clear-cut philosophical disagreement over the direction of the labour movement, caused the division between knights and unionists in the very last years of the century. It was a separation that broke the back of solidarity, with skilled workers retreating in the face of capital's power, which by the 1890s seemed to grow more awesome day by day. Women and the unskilled, perhaps the major beneficiaries of the movement culture of the 1880s, slipped back into a state of unorganized dependence upon capital's mercy and the politician's benevolence, a far from enviable situation. It should not be possible to regard this as a product of skilled workers' reactionary exclusivism, given much of the craft community's support for socialism or syndicalism in the years before World War I, and the Knights of Labor's longevity in certain Canadian circles, especially in French Canada, discredits this view. Rather, we can see the trade union retreat, not as the agency of an aristocratic abandonment, but as part of a necessity imposed by capital's late nineteenth-century surge toward monopoly. That capital itself understood the necessity of breaking the back of the movement culture, and knew well that bodies like the Knights of Labor lent to trade unionism a perniciousness that could not be tolerated, is evident from this 1891 statement in the *Journal of Commerce*: "The spirit of trades unionism," declared this pious organ of one of the copartners of a future monopoly capital, "is strangling honest endeavour, and the hard-working, fearless, thorough artisan of ten years ago is degenerating into the shiftless, lazy, half-hearted fellow who, with unconscious irony, styles himself a Knight of Labor."

Labour's political failures in the 1880s and early 1890s may also be understood within this context of transformation. For in the 1880s the state could not be seen as we know it to exist today: born only in 1867, the Canadian state was actually obscured throughout the 1880s by its essential unfamiliarity, and the workers' movement struggled to devise strategic directions to take toward politics. Given the history of incorporation that preceded the 1880s, the record of achievement should not be understated. As early as the 1850s and 1860s, workers had entered into an economic-political alliance with manufacturers and far-seeing mercantile elements, forming a common front based on a vision of the Canadian nation as one dominated by producers. This "producer commonwealth," from Confederation on, came to be associated with the pragmatic economic nationalism of Macdonald's Conservative party. Committed to high tariffs, railroad building, industrial growth, and westward expansion, Tory policy promised employment for workers caught in an age of insecurities, and abated the nine-hour opposition of 1872 by introducing a Trades Union Bill. A Tory–worker alliance was thus at the centre of working-class politics until at least the 1878 election, which, as Gregory S. Kealey shows in his study of Toronto labour politics, saw a movement towards a more independent stand for labour. It was in the 1880s, under the impact of the movement culture, that political autonomy became an actual demand among a developing stratum of Canadian workers.

Skeptics will of course point to the failure of the movement culture to elect independent candidates to parliament, and no doubt partyism continued to exercise its sway. But this is to miss the mark and to direct attention away from those spheres that should be considered of vital importance in our understanding of this late nineteenth-century context. For the dominant experience within which labour reformers emerged in the 1880s was not national politics, or even provincial campaigns, although these are the most visible and studied realms of past political experience. Even when successful in incorporating labour in an early national policy that promised to speak for a wide amalgam of class interests, the Canadian state was often perceived through working-class eyes that focussed, not on the national state as an emerging institutional force, but rather on local individuals who concretized a distant, mystical state in particular community settings and neighbourhoods, championing state policies as their own, promising specific benefits to their constituencies. In this personalized context, the movement culture of the 1880s looked neither to the state nor to its traditional individualistic representatives, but rather to a self-organized society. And such a social order was to be created out of the immediate, rather than distant, context: local politics were the neutral ground upon which contending forces battled for political direction.

A pessimistic appraisal of the failures of the political campaigns of 1886/87, therefore, misses much of the point of labour-reform politics in the 1880s. The real failure was that just as the Knights of Labor and Provincial Workmen's Association mounted their seemingly spontaneous and localized political campaigns of the 1880s and 1890s (which nevertheless contained within their collective histories a larger logic), running candidates for mayor, alderman, and councillor far more often than they contested the federal and provincial elections, a new political age was in the process of formation, an age in which the presence of national political concerns gained prominence over local ones. Like its critique of monopoly, the movement culture's political efforts fell short of a mark that demanded a new strategic direction, one in which the state was conceived as a powerful, indeed autonomous, force supporting the status quo. Lacking such an orientation, the movement culture concentrated on the locale, flirted with a larger political reality in the 1886/87 campaigns, and, unaware of the potency of processes of incorporation, slipped back into the party fold as the defeats mounted in the post-1886 years. The cause of labour reform went into its tailspin. Eclectic radicalism had not been enough.

These economic and political changes understandably altered the ideological direction of countless brainworkers, and the eclectic radicalism of the 1880s, once something of a broad and fraternal coming together of dissident minds and thoughts, splintered. Working-class activists once loosely associated in the cause of reform now gravitated to diverse camps: socialism, syndicalism, the Independent Labor Party. Divisions previously unknown became paramount as those who had once thought the single tax, theosophy, Irish nationalism, and currency reform compatible became more uncompromisingly convinced that such panaceas were but facades obscuring more precise and programmatic conceptions of change.

And it was on this note that the century ended. With the Knights of Labor in a shambles, with the Provincial Workmen's Association barely hanging on to its members, with the craft unions drawn inward, with brainworkers now moving in more forceful but occasionally opposed directions, the working class was not the unified cultural entity that it had been in that year of upheaval, 1886. The consolidation that had appeared so unambiguous in that year of challenge was now in the throes of dissolution, and in the post-1895 social formation there would be much to cause further disruption. But the strength and legacy of the movement culture of the 1880s was considerable, the continuity of personnel, ideals, and forms of resistance sufficient to ensure that in the changed context (which bred its own oppositional strivings) of 1895 to 1919, some remnants of a consolidated working class lived through an Indian Summer, before the forces of repression and fragmentation overtook workers' experience in the 1920s.

Chapter 4

The Indian Summer of Working-Class Culture, 1895–1919

> The bourgeoisie cannot exist without constantly
> revolutionizing the instruments of production,
> and thereby the relations of production, and
> with them the whole relations of society. . . .All
> fixed, fast frozen relations, with their train of
> ancient and venerable prejudices and opinions,
> are swept away, all new-formed ones become
> antiquated before they can ossify.
>
> Karl Marx and Friedrich Engels,
> *The Communist Manifesto* (1848)

The Social Formation

As the economy became noticeably depressed in 1893, ushering in a period of hard times that would last until 1896, the political scene also began to change. One casualty of the depression was Tory hegemony, as the political hold of the Macdonald Conservatives weakened with a series of crises in the late 1880s and early 1890s. The Jesuits Estates Act, the Manitoba Schools Question, and the death of Macdonald himself all contributed to the Tories' loss of favour, and when the failure of the economy was attributed openly to the shortcomings of the National Policy, the party was ousted from government. Thus ended the Tories' "right" to embrace economic nationalism as their particular political property. Wilfrid Laurier and the Liberals, the lessons of their 1891 defeat fresh in their minds, avoided the temptation to raise, once again, the banner of free trade with the United States. They quietly condoned tariff policies more suitable to business magnates, and won an 1896 electoral victory settled in the industrial heartland of Ontario and Quebec. The new prime minister's claim that the twentieth century would "belong to Canada" was based on a conception of the classless society. Such a view may have appeared tenable at the turn of the century, as labour was far from a forceful presence on the political scene, and in the 1890s, at least, there was more political dissidence among farmers than among workers. But in the aftermath of the economic retreat of the 1890s, the presence of labour as a class, felt so strongly in the 1880s, would be evident once more, if only for a brief period. However, the working class existed in a changed context, for the century promised to all of Canada's citizens, belonged, more correctly, to monopoly capital.

This had tremendous ramifications, and caused a radical restructuring of the working class and consequent changes in its perception of itself and the place to which it was assigned by nonworkers. In the workplace, managerial innovations, technological change, and newly developing industrial sectors diluted many skills, created a new hierarchy of job classifications, and increased the need for unskilled workers. This last development, which grew upon the foundation of the increasing concentration and expansion of productive forces, provided the "pull" required to attract a multitude of immigrants from the fields and factories of eastern, western, and southern Europe. The consequence was a labour market and a labour force that was fragmented ethnoculturally and structurally. Gains made in the 1880s, as skilled and unskilled workers came together, were outstripped by the complexities of new labour markets that made such primitive distinctions obsolete. The cultural cohesion of that decade, moreover, disintegrated as the working class was no longer overwhelmingly Anglo-American in origin.

In spite of these changes, however, the working-class remained a distinct entity, with a culture marked off from that of its rulers. This was especially true in new settings like the recently developed industrial-capitalist west. The labour "problem," for all of capital's conquests, still existed. This led to an acute crisis for the industrial order, necessitating the intervention of the progressive state in the social relations of production. In fact, the development of Liberal hegemony largely resulted from the recognition of class as a political issue of vital and continuing importance. It was obvious that workers had to be considered as a class with a unified voice and that the *ad hoc* manner in which they had been treated in the late nineteenth century was no longer applicable. William Lyon Mackenzie King, a youthful 22 in 1896, was in some respects a product of the interpenetration of politics and class relations, as demonstrated by the positions he held in the years 1895–1920: labour "expert" and journalist, editor of the *Labour Gazette*, Deputy Minister of Labour, member of parliament, Minister of Labour, architect of labour legislation, freelance labour conciliator, "humanitarian" author, and federal leader of the Liberal party. In 1921, "Willie" King, the industrial relations authority, occupied the prime minister's office, a position he would hold for most of his remaining years. This period, then, consolidated the Liberal party as well as the contemporary Canadian state, a pyramid of finance, business, the judiciary, and the civil service that drew a good part of its early sustenance from the need to respond to class antagonism.

To see the social formation of the early twentieth century in this way is thus to focus on three discrete areas, separable for the purposes of analysis. Economic concentration and the transformation of the workplace were the key factors that led to changes in the social composition of the workforce and the rise of the interventionist state.

The period was marked by great economic change, establishing the years 1900–1914 as those of the most rapid growth in the history of post-Confederation Canada. At the root of the accelerating pace of economic life was the increasing concentration of productive power: while enclaves of entrepreneurial capitalism of course survived in many sectors — in Alberta's coal mines, Ontario's garment industry, or in the realms of resource-processing manufacturing dispersed throughout the country — the drift was toward monopoly, a far from accidental development that was, in reality, orchestrated by finance capital in the metropolitan centres of Toronto and Montreal. Combines and concentration had developed, as the Knights of Labor had perceived even during the 1880s, and that decade witnessed the first movements toward oligopoly in textiles (culminating in the formation of the Canadian Coloured Cotton Company in 1892) and agricultural implements (epitomized by the creation of Massey-Harris in 1891). This process reached new heights in the years after 1900. As Tom Naylor has argued recently, the Great War ushered in a new age characterized by increasing government involvement in economic life, refinements in fiscal policy conducive to capital accumulation, and shifts in income streams favourable to the propertied. This was the age of business writ very large indeed. Corporate mergers thus became a hallmark of the new age, with joint-stock companies emerging as the most typical industrial form, displacing the family dynasty and allocating to boards of directors the power that was once wielded through patriarchy and individual autonomy. Fifty-six major industrial consolidations occurred in the years 1900–1912, leading to the formation of a number of overcapitalized corporate giants.

Behind such consolidations stood a new breed of industrial financier, professional promoters like Max Aitken and Rodolphe Forget. Aitken, the future Lord Beaverbrook, engineered the takeover of Nova Scotia's regional banks and no doubt applauded the gentleman's agreement establishing close ties between the Royal Bank, whose sphere of influence extended from the Maritimes to the Caribbean, and the Bank of Montreal, which dominated the central Canadian financial scene. More regionally based, Forget, along with his brother Louis, Sir Hugh Allan, Senator Robert Mackay, and Sir Herbert Holt, orchestrated the creation of the Montreal Light, Heat, and Power Company, an infamous gas monopoly known as "the Octopus." Managing such overblown affairs became big business and gave rise to specialist managerial magnates like Frank Jones and Joseph Flavelle of the Davies Packing Company.

The merger movement, then, linked finance and industrial capital, concentrated production, and gave rise to new strata within the capitalist class. It changed the very nature of production: 63 percent of value added in manufacturing in 1890 was produced by almost 2,900 plants, while three decades later, a similar percentage of the value added was generated by fewer than 950 concerns. Between 1900 and 1920, almost 200 consolidations had absorbed approximately 440 firms. Such a trend had a dramatic effect on the quantitative dimensions of industrial output. Production soared. In traditional spheres such as boot- and shoemaking and textile, tobacco, and iron production, the net value of goods increased three- to fivefold, allowing manufacturing to outpace agriculture as the leading economic sector (44 percent of the value of production in 1919).

The patterns of growth were, of course, coloured by regional economic differences. British Columbia depended upon extracted resources of coal, fish, lumber, and nonferrous metals. On the prairies, wheat was the prime resource, stimulating new demands for central Canadian manufactured goods, agricultural implements, and processed products, although Winnipeg was itself a manufacturing centre of importance, ranking fourth in the nation. Regional economies, like those of the Crow's Nest Pass and Cape Breton, turned on coal. Production in Alberta climbed to a pre-1945 high of 6,909,000 tons in 1920. Quebec's economic well-being was centred in Montreal's financial district and in the explosive development of the pulp-and-paper industry in the hinterland. Indeed, pulp and paper, along with the automobile industry (as well as related production in rubber, parts, and machinery) and the production of hydro-electric power and electrical apparatus, were among the most dynamic sectors, helping to lend credence to Ontario's vision of its central role in the new industrialism. Automobile production was negligible at the turn of the century, but grew markedly in the years 1910–23, the value of production increasing 18 times. Chemicals, chemical products, and electric light and power saw even more dramatic increases in the value of products from 1900 to 1923: chemical-related goods rose in value by a factor of 14, while electric light and power produced in 1923 was 34 times more valuable than that generated in 1900. Between 1910 and 1920 these newly established industries displaced older manufactures, laying the groundwork for an industrial structure that survives to this day. The business of Canada was central Canadian business, and social and political practice would turn on this essential recognition.

The increasing concentration of Canadian industry, coupled with the expansion of output and tariff protection, attracted American investment, and the dependent status of Canadian capital was established during this period. As Marshall, Southard, and Taylor noted in 1936, the years 1900–1905 saw the most rapid rate of growth of American-owned firms in Canada, when the number of these enterprises more than doubled. Between 1900 and 1914, American investment in Canada increased five times, and doubled again, to approximately $1,630 million, in the World War I years. The number of American firms entering Canada rose from an average of 12 a year in the 1900–1905 period to over 33 yearly from 1915 to 1920. Concentrated in the Toronto–Hamilton–Niagara region and in Montreal, the branch-plant economy was embedded in the centre of industrial-capitalist Canada, although similar dependent economic structures also reached into British Columbia railways and smelters, Alberta coalfields, and eastern Canadian steel production. International Harvester, General Electric, Westinghouse, American Locomotive, Swift, Singer, American Asbestos, Standard Oil, National Cash Register, Sherwin-Williams, Du Pont, Ford, and Goodyear were among the scores of Canadian branch plants established in the opening decades of the twentieth century. They brought advanced technology and helped to introduce new methods of managing labour that fell upon the receptive ears of indigenous Canadian capital.

It was in these years, for instance, that efficiency experts came on to the shop floor armed with stop watches and slide rules, with the intention of standardizing tasks, minimizing workers' autonomy, and, thus, increasing output. This was an age of "scientific management," ceremoniously announced by the "principles" of an idiosyncratic but determined American engineer, Frederick Winslow Taylor. It was also a period of the professionalization of management, of stricter cost accountancy in business, industrial betterment (which often translated into profit sharing, improvements in working conditions and company facilities, or factory beautification schemes), and closer attention to the hiring procedure and maintenance of stable personnel relations. "System" was the buzzword of the new century; order, the ultimate aim. While far from universal in its impact, the managerial revolution had its most pronounced successes in the highly concentrated and advanced sectors of textiles, high-technology manufacturing (especially precision-production and railway supplies), and the new industrial staples, notably smelting and pulp-and-paper production. It was notoriously difficult, if not impossible, to manage scientifically a mine, the docks, or the lumber camp, nor was it likely that agricultural labour, the building trades, or relatively small, specialty shops, where social relations retained much of their handicraft character, would fall to the reorganization of the experts. The transformation of the workplace was thus concentrated in central Canadian corporate enterprises where mass production, technological innovation, and expanding markets were all increasingly important. Advocates of the new science of production, however, undoubtedly had an ideological impact extending well beyond the actual implementation of various schemes and plans, making efficient use of labour a prime concern of most employers.

Case studies of the implementation of managerial innovations detail the diversity of particular forms, as well as the underlying motivations of reduction of labour costs and heightened productivity. Taylor's hand-picked disciple, Henry Gantt, reorganized the CPR's locomotive repair facilities in Montreal's Angus Shops, while in the Grand Trunk freight yards in Toronto, a newly developed system of "intensive" management prevented "Chaos." Management journals such as *Industrial Canada* popularized new supervisory methods, and employers used royal commissions to lobby the government to encourage awareness of systems developed in pace-setting American firms like General Electric and the Baldwin Locomotive Works. H.L.C. Hall of the International Accountants' Society restructured working life at Hamilton's B. Greening Wire Company, transferring authority from skilled workmen to foremen, standardizing tasks, eliminating all lost time and motion, tabulating the minutes required to perform each job and the materials and tools employed, and adopting piece rates and premium plans. At the Lumen Bearing Company of Toronto a similar regime increased production from 28 castings a day to 65. "It is the story of economy of time and energy," boasted one advocate, "of making the head serve the hand; the story of developing more efficient workmen." Like most such efforts the intention was, "First, to induce economy by the elimination of waste and second to induce economy by intensifying production."

Such developments — the increasing concentration and expansion of economic power and the reorganization of work — were not received passively by the working class. Those workers who retained a measure of skill and saw their workplace authority whittled away during this period reacted most vigorously. But one part of capital's capacity to effect such growth and change was the structural alteration in the working class itself. During this period, mass immigration inundated the Canadian labour market.

Because many of the new immigrants lacked industrial skills, they provided suitable material upon which the productive and managerial imperatives of capital could work. They had the raw muscle and sheer numbers to work the mines, railway construction projects, and mass-production industries of post-1900 Canada. Other immigrants found themselves in the semiskilled positions of entirely new economic sectors, which lacked traditions of labour resistance and organization. Many thousands spoke no English, their workplace communication restricted to acceptance of the wage, which came to them in pay envelopes catalogued with an impersonal number rather than a name (one immigrant worker in Hamilton had been dead for hours before anyone could ascertain who he actually was). Off the job, they relied upon their ethnic community, rather than class allegiances, retreating into their own cultures, often conditioned by English-speaking workers' open contempt for their way of life and their role as a wage-depressing reserve of labour.

While immigrant arrivals in the years 1852–1902 had averaged 418,000 per decade, a startling 2,206,342 new citizens reached Canada's shores in the period from 1903 to 1912. Even given the barriers blocking immigration in the World War I years, the immigrant flow continued, numbering over 1,100,000 in 1913–22. The bulk of these were British, although hundreds of thousands came from various corners of continental Europe. Once sojourners attached to their homelands, these new immigrants quickly became permanent settlers, establishing communities across Canada. By 1921, the Italian population of Montreal had grown to almost 14,000. One in ten male workers in Hamilton was European-born by the 1920s, and in 1918 it was reported that "foreigners" did "practically the whole of the heavy and laborious work" in the iron, steel, and metalworking shops and factories. Almost every major industrial centre had similar ethnic enclaves, and in the west most members of the working class had just arrived in Canada. In the coalfields of Alberta in 1911, nine out of ten miners were said to be immigrants, the list of nationalities numbering 15 to 20 separate ethnic groups, including Bohemians, Finns, Poles, Ukrainians, Slovaks, and Swedes. It is not surprising that real growth in population leapt forward by 65 percent in the first two decades of the twentieth century.

This quantitative transformation could not but affect the nature and position of class forces in Canadian society. With the city replacing the country as the centre of social and economic life, the voice of the working class should have acquired authority. With the percentage of workers gainfully employed in nonagricultural pursuits expanding from 54 in 1891 to 67 in 1921, class discontents should have moved more unambiguously into the social and political arena. In fact, they did. But because class unity was impeded by language barriers and because grievances varied so markedly from sector to sector and region to region, the potential for class solidarity was mediated by processes of fragmentation and division. Nevertheless, there would be instances of solidarity all the more remarkable because they developed in the very face of cultural diversities and labour-market segmentations that capital was always ready to exploit to the full. When this occurred, however, the working class faced yet another hurdle: the increasing authority and power of the state.

Explored most recently by Paul Craven, the evolution of William Lyon Mackenzie King's particular conciliatory form of industrial relations paralleled the rise of the Liberal state in the years 1900–1911. In his astute recognition of the need to draw community, capital, and labour together, King attempted to mediate class antagonism by bringing both labour and capital under the jurisdiction of established political authority, creating state bodies that were to act as disinterested voices of the community. The conflicting interests of workers and employers were to be subjected to the scrutiny of the "impartial umpire" of the state. The creation of a Labour Department and the passage of the Industrial Disputes Investigation Act of 1907 were part of the new strategy. Although the progressive, interventionist state claimed impartiality, it more often worked to ends that fulfilled capital's needs and aspirations. The IDIA, for instance, cultivated a measure of industrial peace through its advocacy of compulsory conciliation, the endorsement of a "cooling off" period necessary to "reasonable" bargaining between capital and labour, establishing tripartite boards of arbitration, and recognizing the need for special treatment of "public interest" disputes. Designed only for utilities, railroads, and coal mines, the Act nevertheless set the tone for labour-relations policy in the early twentieth century, indeed, well into the 1940s. Between 1907 and 1911, 101 disputes were in fact "handled" under the IDIA, and in nine cases out of ten, strikes were averted. Why did labour participate in such a system, which gave no protection to unions, stripped organized workers of the ability to exploit the timing of a dispute, and provided no guarantees that workers would not be dismissed before or after the process of negotiation? Such a law had the support of the working people largely because they had every desire to uphold universal principles of law and order, and were encouraged by their unions, families, and communities to follow legal channels that seemed reasonable and productive of social harmony. Organized labour would often oppose the IDIA, especially after 1911, but King's orchestration of class antagonisms was accepted as the only pragmatic solution by many Canadian workers who saw little hope in waging an all-out war with capital, which they recognized as an increasingly well-armed foe.

However, capital and the government did not hesitate to take extreme measures. Refusal to comply with an investigation of a dispute or to postpone a strike in accordance with the Act could be penalized by imprisonment. If working people entered somewhat willingly into King's theatre of reconciliation, then, they were also coerced into compliance: during the opening decades of the twentieth century when the Act itself was passed, military intervention in class struggles was on the rise. Of the 33 strike-related instances of "aid to the civil power" in the years 1867–1914, discussed by Desmond Morton, the rate of intervention increased appreciably in the post-1895 years. Well over two-thirds of the total number of militia involvements in strike situations after Confederation took place in this 1895–1914 period. Among the most bloody battles were those that pitched Cape Breton, Springhill, and Vancouver Island miners against their employers and the armed force of the state. When one considers that monopoly capital began to arm itself ever more effectively in this epoch, drawing upon detective agencies, employer associations, spies, blacklists, and open-shop campaigns, it is clear that the working class was indeed a "community under seige." "Whatever King's impenetrable doctrines of conciliation amounted to," observes Ian McKay, "they barely concealed the crucial new fact that, in defence of capitalism, the state was prepared to kill."

Worker organization, of course, was often the stimulus to such violence, threatened and actual, just as it was one obvious response to concentration of industry and managerial attempts to impose a more rigorous discipline at the workplace. In an age of big business backed by interventionist government, it was hardly surprising that large unions found a receptive audience among Canadian workers, who discovered in the years 1895–1920 just how little of the century was actually theirs.

Material Life

Recent studies of real incomes, job security, working-class housing, and health standards in the urban centres of Montreal, Toronto, and Vancouver in the years 1900–1921 establish the existence of a labour force struggling unsuccessfully to keep pace with rampant inflation. R.H. Coats' 1915 observation that wage levels did not rise comparably with increases in productivity in the first 15 years of the century has been substantiated by the arguments of Terry Copp, Michael Piva, and Eleanor A. Bartlett. As prices soared, the wholesale commodity index skyrocketing from a 1900 base level of 100 to a 1920 high of 287.5, wage rates rose and fell between 1900 and 1915, then inched imperceptibly upwards. Major wage hikes were recorded during World War I, when labour shortages allowed unskilled labour and a variety of skilled trades to extract concessions from employers; hourly earnings increased 20 percent and more. But the cost of living between 1915 and 1918 soared, perhaps as much as 40 percent, wiping out all gains at the workplace by forcing real incomes down.

Working-class incomes were also highly differentiated. Segmented labour markets emerged and consolidated; various "grades" of labour were marked off by a hierarchical wage scale expressive not only of skill, age, and gender, but also of status and "race." Highest paid were the skilled males who, in the opening years of the century, might draw $2.75 to $3.00 daily. Labourers would earn less than $1.75, especially if they were Italian, Ukrainian, or members of other non-Anglo-Saxon immigrant groups. Messenger boys might count on 80¢ to $1.00 per day, while other male child workers, aged 10 to 14 years, might fare slightly better. Women, working at piece rates in the garment industry or as waitresses or domestics (where food and lodging might be incorporated into the wage), experienced diverse scales of payments. But $4.00 to $5.00 per week was not uncommon. While a minority of skilled female workers, such as stenographers and nurses, might command as much as $20.00 weekly, there were instances in sweated or outwork situations of women earning 53 cents a week (in 1895) or the equivalent of 2 cents an hour (in 1901). In general, women's wages were roughly 40 to 60 percent of men's wages, although for the rare women who broke into the crafts, wages were almost equal. Such meagre economic prospects for working women made prostitution an attractive alternative to wage labour. However, the most important effect of low wages was to discourage women from entering the labour market at all. With the man as the primary wage earner, family incomes varied between $550.00 per year for unskilled labour in Montreal in 1914 and $1,135.00 for skilled labour in Toronto in 1921. In order to support the family, the wage earner had to work six days a week, 52 weeks a year, without sickness, unemployment, or vacations, spend nothing on drink, furniture, education, or savings, and, with luck, have an employable wife, teenage son, or daughter to "put out" into domestic service.

In an epoch that predated basic welfare measures, however, such working-class good fortune was seldom, if ever, realized. Self-discipline, moreover, was no safeguard against the ravages of unemployment, which occurred with alarming frequency. Periodic recessions (one study identifies seven complete business cycles between the years 1896 and 1921, with major downturns in 1904, 1908, 1915, and 1919), coupled with seasonal fluctuations that disrupted many trades and unskilled callings, affected all workers, cutting earnings and forcing working-class families into poverty. Even in good times, and "in season," if the workforce expanded faster than the number of jobs available (through a combination of natural increase and immigration), the existence of a labour surplus would keep many workers unemployed. Houses of industry, piecemeal public works projects, and the meagre sums expended on relief (roughly $35,000 yearly in Toronto from 1901 to 1921) achieved little in alleviating the plight of the jobless, while religious societies, the cornerstone of Catholic Montreal's welfare structure, were no more successful. "The fear of unemployment," declared Toronto District Labour Council Secretary William J. Hevey in 1919, "is one of the most dreadful things in the life of the workman."

Conditions of life were no better. At the workplace, hours were long (44 to 60 a week, and if subcontracting or "sweating" prevailed, they might be considerably more), ventilation poor, safety minimal, and the production rates increasing because of the reorganization of work. Factory acts protecting workers were vague and ineffectual, and not until 1909 in Quebec and 1914 in Ontario did workmen's compensation reform overcome some of the deficiencies of the old employer-liability legislation of the 1880s, which workers found increasingly unsatisfactory as an effective guard against disabilities incurred through rising numbers of industrial accidents. In the dangerous extractive industries of the west, or in railway construction work, high accident rates actually imposed structural impediments for capital to overcome, creating labour shortages. While improvements were made, they were generally in the interests of capital and had little to do with recognition of the socio-political grievances of the workers. "Benevolent" employers were convinced that reform would increase productivity, curtail absenteeism, and forestall unionism. In 1920, it was still possible for one labour spokesman to claim with justification that workers were "left to the mercies of their employers who . . . have in many industries required them to work under conditions that are constantly jeopardizing their lives and their health."

If the shop floor was a far from ideal environment, neither was the working-class home. In Montreal, 80 percent of the population rented accommodations, and housing shortages created the opportunity for landlords to gouge tenants, charging $10 to $12 monthly for basement rooms. This might represent 25 percent of an unskilled worker's wage at that time. Rents increased 50 percent in the pre-World War I years, making it necessary for families to share accommodation. When the Board of Health examined Montreal's housing in 1918, it found almost 2,000 dwellings damp, overcrowded, or dirty. A similar survey in Toronto claimed that in one sample of 235 houses, half were occupied by more than one family, and one-fifth to one-third were without basic sanitary facilities. A larger investigation, also undertaken in 1918, established that of 13,000 domiciles inspected, 8,000 were overcrowded, a product once more, of landlords attempting to secure whatever the market would bear. One zealous entrepreneur took two $11-a-month cottages, divided them into four units, and almost doubled his intake, charging rent totalling $42. Ameliorative efforts, such as the Toronto Housing Company's proposal to build low-cost housing for rent rather than for sale, and Quebec legislative reforms, made only a modest impact on the problem in the pre-1920 years. If the native Canadian working class experienced privation in this realm, the immigrant worker fared even worse. Ethnic slums drew the early ire of J.S. Woodsworth, who quoted a mission worker's report to convey the character of one Winnipeg immigrant household: "John Klenbyel and wife and six children, and from fifteen to twenty boarders live in four rented rooms. The place is "beastly" dirty. The boarders bring home kegs of beer nearly every day. Two of the older girls are "working out." One of them told our visitor the other day that she cannot stay at home; she is happier away." "Comment is hardly necessary," snorted Woodsworth.

Such living arrangements, exacerbated by inadequate sewage systems, a primitive notion of how to combat disease, low nutritional intake, and often contaminated food and milk, bred poor standards of public health. One in three Montreal infants died before reaching the age of 12 months in the years 1897–1911, with gastro-intestinal diseases taking a particularly heavy toll. In Toronto, infants fared better, but in the first two decades of the twentieth century more than one in ten died young. Those who survived might face the ravages of tuberculosis, diphtheria, or typhoid, illnesses contributing to high death rates in industrial cities. At the root of persistent health problems was nothing less than inadequate working-class incomes, one doctor reducing the issue to its lowest common denominator: "The destruction of the poor is their poverty."

However one looks at the experience of material life, then, there was little in the first two decades of Canada's century to excite the working class. If anything, standards of life were deteriorating, just as real wages declined. Workers who saw affluence increase around them, were locked into alienating jobs, depressing living conditions, and a life cycle of insecurity and ill health. Some workers responded to this situation with resignation; others, with resistance.

Internationalism

Material difficulties constrained all workers, and if the crafts and their unskilled brothers and sisters remained distinctive status groupings, all were reminded of the harsh commonalities of class experience. In the face of what were perceived as deteriorating conditions, many workers, especially those with a remnant of skill to be undercut, turned to the most powerful proponent of labour's interests. The Canadian history of international craft unionism, as we have seen, commenced in the 1850s. Although they played a secondary role to that of the Knights of Labor in the 1880s, the craft unions, not the Noble and Holy Order, survived into the twentieth century. All unions avoided confrontation in the depression-ridden years of the mid-1890s, and some internationals, like the Molders', suffered serious setbacks in the face of a virulent capitalist offensive in 1890–92. But even in defeat, organized workers were still poised for action, and the cause of the internationals was given a boost by the aristocratic railway conductors and trainmen, whose Orders and Brotherhoods won a critical victory against the CPR and William Van Horne in 1892. But the lesson of the 1890s was clear, and in the words of the Toronto *Globe*, no union could expect recognition "until it [was] strong enough to force it." That strength flowed, not only from the internal state of the crafts, but also from the external conditions of economic life. As the clouds of hard times lifted in the late 1890s, craft unions reasserted themselves, and their collective fortunes over the course of the next two decades, like the pattern of strike activity, followed the crests and troughs in the business cycle. Organization boomed in the 1897–1904 upswing, settled into a holding pattern until

1915, when the war brought the country out of a major recession, and exploded thereafter, union membership expanding from 166,000 in 1914 to 378,000 in 1919.

In the post-1896 labour upsurge, the craft unions established their supremacy within the Canadian labour movement, capturing the one-time stronghold of the Knights of Labor: the Trades and Labor Congress of Canada. As late as 1893, the Knights dominated this institutional centre of organized labour, but at the historic Berlin Congress in 1902, all who opposed supremacy of the powerful international craft unions were banished. Driven from the ranks of officially organized labour, the Knights and other "dual" unionists formed their own "national" labour centre, the National Trades and Labor Congress, which gave way to the Canadian Federation of Labor in 1908. But these were only a minor threat to the TLC. Internationalism was the central tendency within the Canadian labour movement in these years, a trend that Robert Babcock has dubbed American labour continentalism. Samuel Gompers, craft union boss of the American Federation of Labor, one-time socialist cigarmaker in the 1880s, but by the turn of the century a committed pragmatist given to demanding nothing but "more, more, more" for his membership, cast his shadow into Canada.

His influence spread across the country with the efforts of men like Hamilton's John A. Flett, a carpenter and former Knight appointed the AFL's first full-time general organizer in Canada at the turn of the century. Volunteer advocates like Montreal's George Warren, Harry Corcoran of Prince Edward Island, and printer–activist J.W. Patterson in Ottawa soon became officially recognized and commissioned agents of the Federation. These men, and many others, bore much of the credit for the 250 percent increase in the number of chartered international unions in Canada in the years 1897–1902. By 1902, well over 1,000 AFL-affiliated unions existed across the country. Fifty-nine percent of these were in Ontario, 13 percent in British Columbia, 11 percent in Quebec, 9 percent in the Maritimes, and 7 percent on the prairies. Urban centres like Toronto, Montreal, Hamilton, Winnipeg, and Vancouver had the highest concentrations, with from 35 to 105 union locals each. By 1914, the number of Canadian locals had risen to 1,775, with an average membership of 75 each. (See Table 4.1.)

Some scholars claim that international craft unionism had the effect of quelling the resistance of Canadian labour, acting as an agent of incorporation and quiescence. The Canadian labour movement in this period has been viewed as ideologically confined by American pragmatic but bureaucratic unionism, or "Gompersism," as it came to be called. There is some truth in this, and no doubt the exclusive "bread-and-butter" unionism of Gompers left less room for the unskilled, the woman, and the class conscious than had organizations

TABLE 4.1   Canadian membership in international unions as percentage of total union membership, 1911–78

Year	Total union membership (× 1000)	Canadian membership in international unions (× 1000)	Percentage of total membership in international unions
1911	133.1	119.4	89.7
1915	143.3	113.1	78.9
1920	373.8	267.2	71.4
1925	271.1	199.8	73.7
1930	322.4	230.9	71.6
1935	280.6	143.6	51.2
1940	362.2	227.0	62.7
1945	711.1	471.0	66.2
1951	1028.5	726.6	70.5
1955	1268.2	893.8	70.5
1960	1459.2	1052.0	72.1
1965	1588.8	1124.7	70.8
1970	2173.1	1359.3	62.5
1975	2875.5	1478.6	51.4
1978	3277.9	1553.5	47.4

SOURCE: J. Smucker, *Industrialization in Canada* (Department of Labour, 1980), 205.

such as the Knights of Labor. But craft unionists played a fundamental role in socialist reform politics and battled at the workplace, where they confronted a determined resistance to any notion of unionism. The lessons of the 1880s were still remembered by some. Gompers' assertions that Canadian and American workers were "one and the same in spirit, in fact, in union, with one common polity and policy; with identical principles, hopes and aspirations," rang true in many workers' ears. "There is no 49th parallel of latitude in Unionism," declared one British Columbia miner. "The Canadian and American workingmen have joined hands across the Boundary line for a common cause against a common enemy." Internationalism still meant something noble and necessary to workers, in spite of the fact that Gompers' exclusivism tarnished its reputation. If the international unions failed to provide all the answers for all workers, they nevertheless offered tangible solutions to some immediate problems. It was the first step toward organizational revitalization. Only time and 20 years of change and conflict at the workplace and in the realm of politics would reveal the fatal flaw in craft unionism's Pyrrhic victories during the years 1897–1902.

Workplace Confrontation

Strikes, as we have seen, were not unusual in the nineteenth century; between 1901 and 1914, however, they became something of the norm, rather than the exception, in the social relations of production. Two recent studies explore patterns of strike activity in the three Maritime provinces and in the structural core of capitalist Canada, south-central

Ontario. Both point to the pervasiveness of conflict, the important place of regional peculiarities, and the influence of the character of the workplace in conditioning the nature of class struggle. Finally, each study looks beyond the obvious battle over the wage, envisioning the strike as an essential confrontation over power.

In an unpublished examination of the strike in Nova Scotia, New Brunswick, and Prince Edward Island, Ian McKay raises most of the empirical and analytical issues at the centre of an understanding of workplace confrontation. Across the region, 324 strikes were fought in the period 1901–14, with the tempo of class conflict following closely the fluctuations of the business cycle. Strikes tended to be fought in the "good times" of 1904–5 or 1909–11, rather than in the years of recession associated with 1908 or the pre-World War I downturn that was well underway by 1914. But the particular character of specific Maritime groups, as McKay points out, loomed large in strike activity. Unskilled labour fought a large percentage of these battles (37 percent), the skilled crafts were involved in 28 percent of the confrontations, and miners led confrontations in 18.5 percent of the cases. Factory workers, classified as semiskilled, engaged in 13.6 percent of the strikes, and fishermen and other workers, not easily classified, were a group of minor importance in the history of the strike (approximately 3 percent of the strikes were waged by members of such occupations). Less skilled workers responded almost immediately to changes in the economic climate, and the predepression year of 1907 represented the highwater mark in the number of labourers' strikes. Craft workers had more diverse reasons for striking, but the building boom associated with the construction of the steel works at Sydney in the first years of the century created a tight labour market and rising prices that provided the structural inducements to strike. Miners, something of a community apart, tended to follow a unique pattern, and the years 1909–11 overshadow all others in the history of class conflict in this period. Labour's discontents extended well beyond the coalfields of Cape Breton (56 percent of the strikes in these years took place in the ports of Saint John and Halifax), but these miners accounted for 76 percent of the days lost to strikes. Most dramatic were the massive confrontations in the coal communities of Glace Bay and Springhill, where battles were fought and lost over recognition of the United Mine Workers of America. Involving over 1,300,000 striker-days, the coal conflicts of these three years were among the most protracted and vehement battles in the country. In the region itself, they were of unquestionable significance in the twentieth century prewar years, making up over 80 percent of days lost to strikes in the coalfields and over 60 percent of all days lost in the Maritime provinces.

Such strikes often turned on the wage, which existed in a particularly stunted form in the Maritimes, and which workers perceived to be losing ground to inflation. Sixty-five percent of Maritime strikes in these years, by one method of classifying issues involved in industrial conflicts, were related to wage-increase demands or opposition to reductions. But there were other issues as well, including union recognition, control of apprenticeship, objections to forms of payment or new work systems, and opposition to supervisory personnel. Broadly conceived, these and other discontents relate to workers' attempts to secure or retain some hold on a measure of autonomy at the workplace.

The strike was thus a privileged moment in which, to employ Tawney's phrase, "autocracy [was] checked by insurgence." There was a sense in which workers grasped intuitively that monopoly capital was about more than the appropriation of their labour power; it was also very much about the appropriation of dignity. Indeed, a voracious capital seemed to want to devour both with equal dispatch. As a consequence, the history of workplace confrontation turns, not only on the reappropriation of the value of the wage, but also on various attempts to reclaim the pride and dignity that workers sensed they were losing. In the mines, this related quite directly to matters of life and death, for the workers themselves saw that their own standards and ethics would ensure safety, whereas management's flirted with disaster. If Maritime workers did not use the strike to oppose mechanization (no strikes were fought on this issue alone) and the "scientific" reorganization of work (only seven conflicts might have related to this problem), this "quiescence" relates more to the economic context than to worker passivity: both grievances were of only minor significance in the prewar history of port workers or coal miners, the dominant regional economic sectors. Labour, however, was quick to walk out in protest against tyranny on the job, be it a blunt dismissal by a foreman or the recalcitrance of an employer. A Springhill miners' spokesman summed up this working-class demand for respect in his 1907 attack on a boss: "The manager in charge at Springhill cannot appreciate that a man working in his mines at Springhill IS STILL A MAN, and after 18 years of experience has not yet learned that the miners are rational, intelligent, human beings, with more than an ordinary amount of general information, and education, and while they are amenable to reason, will not be dogged or driven." Such views fed directly into the upheavals of 1909, when one miner declared: "[A] time comes in the life of nations, it comes in the life of communities, and in the life of organizations when THEY CANNOT ENDURE ANY LONGER THE IMPOSITIONS FORCED ON THEM BY AN AUTOCRATIC AND OVERBEARING SPIRIT." From the employer's point of view this appeared to be an alarming drift toward coercion.

Strikes in the Maritimes thus follow complex patterns resulting from national developments, regional peculiarities, and diverse experiences within the working class. From the dramatic challenge to capital expressed in the coal confrontations of 1909–11 to the frustrated defeats of women, immigrants, and the unskilled, through the ambiguous job actions of craftsmen, who might strike to retain the exclusive status of their trade (a losing battle, in the long run), industrial conflict ran the gamut from the heroic to the tragic, from the limited victory to the defeat that nevertheless signalled the beginnings of a class stance. Employers imported strikebreakers by the thousands, stood fast against unionism, drew upon the state and the law, and, in the end, constructed an elaborate hegemony that would carry them through the war years and into the period of the regional economy's ultimate collapse. They had won the battle, but would lose the war. It is more difficult to determine the extent to which labour was victorious.

At a superficial glance, the history of Maritime strikes in the years 1901–14 is one weighted down with defeat. But in the midst of labour's crushing losses in these years emerged solidarities and organizational forms, strategies and understandings, that would resurface in the class conflicts of the 1920s. It was in 1903 that a Springhill miner articulated the class resolve associated with that period of the miners' revolt, declaring in the midst of a strike: "We are prepared to stay out fifteen

TABLE 4.2   Comparison of strike issues in the Maritimes and south-central Ontario, 1901–14

	Maritimes	Ontario
Category I		
For higher earnings	190	212
Against wage reductions	21	28
Category II		
For recognition of union	7	32
For shorter hours	40	58
Defence of trade unionism	24	73
Sympathy	4	14
Apprenticeship control	2	12
Objection to new system of work	14	20
Change in conditions of work	21	22
Objection to employment of particular persons	22	18
Adjustment of procedures of wage payment	20	8
Other	—	17

NOTE Category II includes those struggles considered to turn, broadly, on the question of control. Since strikes often involve two or more issues, some strikes are "double counted" in order to show all the issues involved. The total number of strike issues therefore exceeds the total number of strikes (324 in Maritimes and 421 in Ontario).

SOURCES: Craig Heron and Bryan D. Palmer, "Through the Prism of the Strike: Industrial Conflict in Southern Ontario, 1901–1914," *Canadian Historical Review* 58 (December 1977), 423–458; Ian McKay, "Strikes in the Maritimes, 1901–1914," (unpublished manuscript, Halifax, Dalhousie University, 1980), forthcoming *Acadiensis*. Note that McKay's paper centres on all strikes in the Maritimes, while the Heron-Palmer article covers only conflicts in ten southern Ontario cities. McKay's data are currently being revised slightly for publication.

years. . . . No, we will not tolerate the interference of politicians or any one else this time. We are running the affair and will settle it to suit ourselves." Words like these would be rare in central Canada, but if they were spoken they would come, not from a miner, but from skilled craftsmen, concentrated in the metal trades, where managerial revolution and technological change provided the incentive for workplace protest.

Craig Heron and I have argued that strikes in ten south-central Ontario cities were also numerous in these years, and at least 421 struggles were waged. As in the Maritimes, strikes were commonly resorted to in times of prosperity (1901–4, 1906/7, 1910–13), when concessions were more easily wrung from employers. Strikes occurred less frequently in the recession years of 1908 and 1913/14. Locale also played a role, with the large urban centres of Toronto and Hamilton experiencing 47 percent and 22 percent of the strikes, involving over 50,000 workers, or an overwhelming 89 percent of the strikers. But unlike industrial conflict on the east coast, the strike was the particular weapon of the skilled, and was less likely to precipitate a mass upheaval. More common were smaller, shorter confrontations, an ongoing theatre of conflict. Workers in the building and metal trades led fully half of all of these strikes, and unskilled labour participated in less than six percent of the conflicts. The diversity of the economy of south-central Ontario and the range of manufacturing pursuits explain some of this, as does the rise of the branch plant and the implementation of various efficiency schemes and managerial innovations. Whereas labour in the mines and on the docks dominated the Maritime workforce, in the cities of south-central Ontario, from London in the west to Peterborough in the east, moulders, machinists, garment workers, carpenters, painters, and bricklayers made up a greater part of the workforce.

They struck, of course, against wage cuts and for supplements to the wage payment. But they also engaged in battles for control: over apprenticeship, against arbitrary foremen, in opposition to new systems of payment and management. As efficiency-conscious employers restructured the nature of work, subdividing tasks, accelerating the pace of work, and intensifying operations, workers fought back. In 1907, female operators at Toronto's Bell Telephone struck unsuccessfully against a particularly unreasonable managerial dictate that would have cut hourly wage rates at the same time that it extended the workday, which was rigidly monitored, from five hours to eight. Electricians, female knitting-mill workers, carpet weavers, and garment workers waged similar struggles against the modernization of the labour process, but often to similarly unsuccessful ends. More often victorious were the skilled tradesmen, who might extract concessions *before* recourse to the strike, or adopt workplace strategies of resistance that flowed from their unique knowledge of the technical and human components of production. But regardless of their situation within the workforce, all workers came to resent the incursions of zealous innovators, whose purpose was to engineer men and women as they did the symbols of the new age, machines. "The 'one man two machines,' the 'Taylor,' 'Scientific,' 'Premium,' 'piece work,' and other systems introduced into the metal shops are making of men what men are supposed to make of metals," declared one labour journal. An anonymous poet expressed a generalized class sentiment when he addressed these lines to an "Efficiency Expert in Hell":

Your times and motions I've studied well
    As you hustle the sinners in
And I find you have here but a third-rate hell
    And the way it is run is a sin.

In the face of the relentless erosion of their skills and autonomy, workers in central Canada, and especially in south-central Ontario, came to use the strike as a weapon in a war fought over who would retain authority in the workplace. Against the working-class attempts to wrestle a small amount of power from the employers or to curb the excesses of tyranny and arbitrary authority, their adversaries took drastic antilabour initiatives.

In central Canada these included employers' associations (more than 60 in Ontario alone) such as the National Founders' Association and the National Metal Trades Association, which joined their American counterparts in a crusade against unionism. Capital also looked to the courts, where it secured legal victories prohibiting picketing, and boycotting (the systematic use of the injunction dated from a Toronto metal trades dispute in 1902), blocking the legalization of the union label, deflecting legislation establishing the eight-hour day, and amending the Alien Labour Bill to allow employers a free hand in importing workers. Flooding the labour market with British workers and European immigrants, of course, undercut the viability of any working-class resistance. Supplemented by increased supervisory rigour, paternalistic policies, and welfare capitalist measures, as well as the armed intervention of the state and the conciliation of the IDIA, these tactics helped employers carry out their strategy of subordinating labour by driving unionism from the country.

Opposition of this order stimulated class conflict across Canada. In Quebec, according to Stuart Jamieson's review of the strikes enumerated in the *Labour Gazette*, the centre of the storm was in the labour-intensive sector of the "light" industries — textiles, boot- and shoemaking, clothing — that figured prominently in the provincial economy. Aside from various struggles on the railways, where the Industrial Disputes Investigation Act was invoked in the post-1907 years, these sectors were most often the scene of conflict. A 1908 royal commission investigating conditions in the cotton textile industry cited wage cuts, long hours, and evasion of laws regulating child labour as critical areas of working-class grievance in Quebec. A classic confrontation erupted in October 1900 at the Montreal Cotton Company's Valleyfield plant, a centre of conflict throughout this period (strikes took place in 1901, 1907, and again in 1908). Precipitated by unskilled labourers engaged in doing excavations for the company, the strike expanded to include many of the 3,000 textile workers, who were outraged when the company summoned the militia from Montreal. Federal mediation was required to bring the workers back to their jobs.

To the west, the years from 1900 to 1914 saw an unprecedented escalation of conflict. In burgeoning cities like Winnipeg and Calgary a wide range of urban workers embraced the strike: railway shop workers, street railwaymen, saddlers, machinists, and carpenters. "The great lesson which organized labour learned here in 1903," declared Calgary's *Bond of Brotherhood*, "was the fact of the class war existing here as naked and unashamed as in the older cities most of us have recently left." The dominant forces within the western class struggle, however, were the coal miner and the railway worker. These years represented the heroic years of international unionism in the coalfields of western Canada, the United Mine Workers of America battling for the rights of a membership employers were dedicated to blocking. Organization strikes, like that of the massive two-year confrontation between 7,000 Vancouver Island miners associated with the UMWA and Canadian Collieries Limited, led to the importation of Chinese and occidental strikebreakers, riots, and military intervention. After outlays of $16,000 weekly, totalling $1,500,000, the international was forced to concede defeat, and after 1914, the union was driven decisively from the island, just as it had been after an earlier confrontation. The power of the Dunsmuir coal interests, and their successors, the Canadian Collieries Ltd., proved more than the union could bear.

Equally powerful was the Canadian Pacific Railway, symbol of monopoly and its intimate connection with the state. As an industrial crisis deepened in 1903, the United Brotherhood of Railway Employees challenged the CPR, opposing the "secret warfare" of monopoly capital's attempt to break the union through intimidation, dismissal, and use of labour spies. Wedded to the organization of all railway workers, rather than subdivided craft bodies, the UBRE battled from Revelstoke to Winnipeg, "to perpetuate their union, nothing else." Initiated in February 1903, the strike continued into March, when sailors from Victoria, Vancouver longshoremen, and Calgary teamsters stopped work in sympathetic job refusals to handle "scab" freight. Winnipeg's Trades and Labor Council declared the CPR "unfair" across the west, and other city centrals took up the same stance of opposition. Public outcry developed as strikers were jailed and one militant socialist, Frank

Rogers, was shot dead by company thugs while picketing the CPR tracks in Vancouver. But the craft brotherhoods, condemned for their "scabherding" policies and "reprehensible and traitorous conduct," refused their support, and with their aid and the availability of strikebreakers, the CPR was able to break the strike. The UBRE suffered defeat, its major accomplishment being the creation of a royal commission whose findings simply heightened class tensions and elicited indignation from British Columbia workers.

In the southeastern British Columbia and Alberta coalfields of the Crow's Nest Pass, the workers and their union, the UMWA, fared better. Unlike the immensely powerful and authoritative CPR, or the Vancouver Island mining companies, the Pass was characterized by small employers, all scrambling to make ends meet. Over 300 mines were in operation by 1918. Pitted against weaker employers than had been confronted in either the east or the west, unionists gained a foothold here early in the twentieth century. From the outset, radicalism was associated with organization, the Western Federation of Miners (later to associate with the Industrial Workers of the World) pioneering unionism in the mines. In British Columbia, Fernie, Coal Creek, Michel, and Morrissey were early centres of strength, and strikes were fought in 1903, when Frank, Alberta, also came under the WFM's sway. But effective unionism dated from the UMWA breakthroughs in 1905/6, and the first major instance of class war, the Lethbridge, Alberta, strike of 1906. Although far from a union victory, the Lethbridge confrontation won wage increases, other concessions, and the company's promise of nondiscrimination against union members. It thus secured the UMWA a foothold in the region, known as District 18, and was a landmark in the history of western miners. As Allen Seager and William Baker have shown, in separate unpublished studies, it was won as much by Mackenzie King as it was by the miners and their families. The miners, who fought for almost nine months, responded to the Alberta Railway and Irrigation Company's employment of scabs and refusal to arbitrate the dispute by ritually abusing nonunionists, rioting, engaging in disciplined militancy, and class voting at the polls. Scabs were escorted to their homes with charivaris by strikers, and strike leaders condemned both Liberal and Conservative parties as "merely committees of the capitalist class," refusing the intervention of state agents "at any price." This, and the resulting "coal famine" in large parts of Alberta and Saskatchewan, of course, simply heightened the need for the presence of an objective mediator, and King's manoeuvres eventually proved successful. As in most cases, King's involvement managed to produce a settlement that, in the words of the *Frank Paper*, had "the look of being a decided victory for the men." But compared to other union agreements in District 18, it was a setback, and the majority of the miners' original demands were quietly forgotten or fundamentally altered in the final compromise.

The Lethbridge strike was therefore a fitting introduction to the contradictory developments of this period. It proved the mettle of miners' unionism in the pre-World War I years. It and another strike in 1911, of the ten major Alberta work stoppages waged by the miners between 1905 and 1945, remained the only conflicts to be supported by significant financing from international union headquarters. At the same time, however, it introduced into the coalfields an undependable third party in the form of the state. Indeed, the 1906 confrontation laid the foundations for the Industrial Disputes Investigation Act. In the years when the act was in force, miners in the Crow's Nest Pass would be forced to take up the strike again in 1907, 1909, and 1911. While some workers' interests were incorporated in the act, the IDIA permitted the establishment of the open shop, "limited" recognition of the union being all that the miners could now legally wrestle from the employers. In the coalfields of Alberta and southeastern British Columbia, the "impartial" umpire of the state assumed the same series of roles fulfilled in south-central Ontario by scientific management, employer associations, and the selected use of injunctions.

The history of workplace confrontation in the years 1900–1914 hints at the vast changes that swept over working-class experience in these years, and serves notice of the resilience of class forms of resistance, attachments to respectability and autonomy, and of the potency of new organizational efforts. While the period was one of harsh defeats, it also witnessed moments of working-class initiative and solidarity all the more impressive because of the range and diversity of monopoly capital's opposition. Economic change, the transformation of the labour process in specific sectors, the rise of the interventionist state (in both its military and conciliatory dress), and the flooding of the labour market with new workers, forced Canadian labour to fight back as never before. In the process, it reminded capital that it was not resigned to the lot that had been cast for it, a position of challenge also evident in the political sphere.

The Politics of Dissent

The tendency within the craft unions was to support electoral candidates who endorsed specific reforms associated with working-class demands or those who, in addition to their commitment to the movement's aims, also came from the ranks of the toilers. Centred in the Trades and Labor Congress of Canada, this political orientation was never more than a tendency, and the period actually opened with the Socialist Labor Party's admission to the TLC. One year later, the SLP was removed from the Congress, the 1895/96 conventions serving notice of socialism's presence within trade union circles as well as its controversial status. Over the course of the years 1895–1919, working-class politics were pushed beyond a Gompersite policy of rewarding labour's friends and punishing its enemies by the emergence of two strands of dissent: labourism and socialism.

Labourism's platform was codified as early as 1898, although its impact in the political realm would not be felt until a few years later. Always severely compromised by its affinity with the Laurier liberals, labourism nevertheless played a vital role in moving the working class beyond accommodation and toward the stand of political independence. Its origins lay in the first political stirrings of labour in the 1870s and 1880s and in British experience; its most explicit statement was that of the 16 points and preoccupations laid out at the 1898 meeting of the Trades and Labor Congress. A compilation of progressive demands that could be endorsed by most Anglo-Saxon organized workers, labour's program included free compulsory education, the eight-hour day, a minimum wage, public ownership of railways and telegraphs, tax reform, abolition of the senate, extension of the franchise, abolition of child labour, and prohibition of prison and contract labour. Supplemented by the demand for equal suffrage for men and women, appended in 1917, these and other demands formed the backbone of labourism's attempt to inject democracy and humanitarianism into the body politic. However, also included among labourist political planks was an assault on Chinese immigration. Anti-Orientalism continued to highlight the exclusivism of labour's parliamentary program.

Originally stimulated by western labour reformers, labourism experienced some setbacks before it spread throughout the land. Two Liberal-backed labour candidates, Arthur W. Puttee, editor of the Winnipeg labour paper, *The Voice*, and Nanaimo, British Columbia's Ralph Smith, miners' leader and one-time president of the TLC, won federal seats in 1900. Such victories stimulated discussion of an independent labour party, although the practice of Smith and Puttee was, as A.R. McCormack and others have pointed out, always subordinate to the interests of the Liberal party. Concessions were won, to be sure, but they were not so much demanded and extracted from authority as they were begged and bargained for in yearly meetings between the labour representatives and Laurier and his cabinet.

Although working-class candidates secured victories in provincial elections in British Columbia, by 1904/5 labourism appeared to be on the wane. Puttee was defeated in 1904, Smith defected to the Grits, and the president-elect of the TLC, Alphonse Verville, suffered a setback in his attempt to gain election in Quebec City. Puttee had been abandoned by the Liberals, who were attempting to capture the growing East European immigrant vote in Winnipeg. The Liberals had healed a number of party rifts that had kept them divided, and hence were no longer as dependent upon labour for votes as they had been in the earlier 1900 contest. In 1904, Puttee's campaign was fought on class lines. Unlike the case in 1900, when he had presented himself as the reform candidate of all classes, in 1904 he ran as the advocate of "Mr. Workingman." Labourism defeated nevertheless represented the beginnings of labourism as a legitimate expression of class interest. Similarly, in Quebec, Verville's defeat induced a Montreal delegate to the 1905 convention of the TLC to urge labour bodies in Quebec to unite in the formation of an independent labour party. Such calls for action received increased support from organized workers in the TLC who, by 1906, had elected Verville to the House of Commons in a sweeping Montreal victory, passed a resolution endorsing "independent political action," and made moves to establish the Canadian (Independent) Labor Party. Much of this political ferment was of course related to workplace confrontations, which conditioned a climate of class antagonism. As Ralph Smith noted in a letter to his political master, Wilfrid Laurier, society appeared on the verge of breaking into two armed camps, "just as Marx had predicted." Some would look upon such a development with fear and loathing; others could applaud it. Eugene Debs, central figure in American socialism and symbol of working-class repudiation of Gompersism, visited Toronto in 1906 and found the Canadian labour movement in a "more healthy condition" than that of the trade unions to the south.

The CLP/ILP proposed in 1906 was slow to emerge, and when it did develop, it took many forms. Blocked by socialist strength in British Columbia, the creation of a labourite party proceeded in Manitoba where a similar body had existed as early as 1895. Puttee and other "old country" reformers founded the Winnipeg Independent Labor Party in 1906, a year of confrontation on the street railway and public appearances by British labour advocate Ramsay Macdonald. Active in municipal politics, the Winnipeg ILP was to be hampered by divisions created out of a debate over collective ownership of the means of production, a stand advocated by the popular British labour leader, Keir Hardie. Middle-class single-tax advocate, Fred Dixon, captured some of the ILP supporters in the post-1910 years and, through alliances with Liberals, sustained victories on the "Independent" ticket. Labourism, increasingly moderate, won political stature but lost its role as the sole exponent of the working class.

In Ontario, the CLP/ILP seemed more vibrant. Six hundred delegates convened to establish the party in 1907, representing the major industrial and manufacturing centres of the province. Heartened by the provincial election of labourite Allan Studholme in Hamilton in 1906, the Ontario CLP/ILP seemed the centre of labourism by 1907. Studholme himself would carry the banner through the war years until his death in

1919, securing his seat in the Ontario legislature at repeated elections. Hamilton East's "little Labor Man" had ridden to victory on the back of class solidarities cultivated in the 1880s and consolidated around the struggles of street railway employees in an epic 1906 clash with their employer, city authorities, and the militia. Other ILP supporters from Hamilton stood at the centre of labourism — Samuel Landers and Walter Rollo — and, along with James (Jimmy) Simpson, helped to orchestrate the movement's revitalization in the war years, after a post-1908 decline in its fortunes. By 1917, a host of local labour parties was united under the auspices of the newly created Hamilton-based Ontario Labor Party. Farmer-labour cooperation swept the Conservatives from office in the October 1919 provincial election, the United Farmers of Ontario electing 45 candidates and the ILP winning an unprecedented 11 seats, with particularly impressive showings in Hamilton and London. Two labourites would serve as cabinet ministers in the UFO-ILP government.

Nowhere else did labourism gain such victories. In Quebec, the Labor party exerted its limited strength in Montreal where Gustav Francq and Verville promoted the cause of independent labour representation, the latter winning election in 1908 and 1911. These years also witnessed the rise of the labour town in the coalfields of Vancouver Island, the Crow's Nest Pass, and the east. Two socialist aldermen were elected in Nanaimo in 1914, while in Fernie, British Columbia, Tom Uphill of the United Mine Workers of America was first elected mayor in 1915; he would hold this civic post for much of the next 40 years. Among Alberta's miners, socialism, rather than labourism, prevailed, but the ILP drew some support, especially among those of British descent. In industrial Cape Breton, labourite candidates ran for federal office as early as 1904. By 1918, the ILP was well established, tending to dominate town politics in coal centres like Glace Bay. A coal miner was elected mayor in 1918, and the ILP ran candidates for town councillor in five of the six wards. Campaigning under the slogan "Corporations vs. The Masses," all five labourite candidates were victorious. After another election in 1919, Glace Bay's town council took on the appearance of a working-class body. Joining a manager, an engineer, and a contractor were two machinists and seven coal miners. Besides Glace Bay, workers won control in New Waterford and Dominion, as well as securing minority representation in Sydney, Sydney Mines, and on the county council. As David Frank has argued, these early labour victories reflected a shifting balance of power in the Cape Breton coal towns, and were not without their material ramifications: the coal companies were challenged, the use of the police in strike situations curtailed, and the assessment of taxes revised.

Here, in the understudied realm of local politics, lay the ILP's greatest contribution. For the rise of labourism itself was but the political expression of the various forms of limited, semiautonomous working-class organization and initiative that had been developing across Canada since the 1880s. As the annual report on labour organization in Canada pointed out in 1921, fully 271 working-class candidates ran for office in 44 municipalities in 1920: 111 were elected, including mayors in Westville, Moncton, Sault Ste. Marie, Port Arthur, and Fort William. These political campaigns had their origins in the rise of labourism in the years 1900–1920, as well as in the emergence of its staunchest foe. For within the politics of labour the orientation of independent representation was challenged, not only by partyism and the employers, but by socialism as well.

In central Canada, socialism was pervasive. If far from effective — *Cotton's Weekly* estimated that the socialist vote across the country totalled a mere 3,500 in 1903 and an improved, but still disappointing, 17,000 in 1913 — socialists were ubiquitous in the manufacturing belt that stretched from London in the west to Montreal in the east.

With the vast changes wrought by the full-scale impact of industrial capital and the emergence of monopoly, the moral universality of the labour-reform critique of the 1880s had died, its eclecticism lacking substance and strategic direction. While the essential solidarity and working-class character of this presocialist radicalism of the 1880s was a moment of great achievement, as we have seen, its disintegration in the 1880s was simultaneously a loss and an advance. The emerging socialist movement, while divided and never capable of drawing masses of workers to its ranks, did indeed encourage the spread of a socialist ideology and experienced some organizational breakthroughs. Major socialist organizations appeared, for the first time, in the 1890s: followers of the American Marxist, Daniel DeLeon, recipient of a rare commendation from Lenin, formed the first Ontario branch of the Socialist Labor Party (SLP) in 1894, while the more mass-oriented Canadian Socialist League (CSL) was initiated by George Wrigley, former Knights of Labor and farmers' advocate, by editor Phillips Thompson, and others, in 1899. If the Socialist Labor Party was doctrinaire and opposed to moderation and reformism, the Canadian Socialist League presented a mild Christian socialism premised on the need for democracy and public ownership.

An Ontario Provincial Socialist League was formed in 1901 and, after contesting the 1902 election, changed its name to the Ontario Socialist Party. Organizers spread the socialist word to the west, cultivating support in Winnipeg, and the Socialist League gained adherents in the east, with Fredericton a centre of activity from 1902. But the real foundation of Canadian socialism lay in British Columbia, where allies of the Canadian Socialist League led the way, miners associated with the Western Federation of Miners, workers affiliated with the Vancouver Trades and Labor Council, and Christian cooperators being especially active in the new politics.

It was on the west coast, in fact, that the DeLeonite and reformist wings of Canadian socialism joined. Prior to 1904, these two factions had battled for labour's allegiance, and both often lost to the labourites. The Socialist Labor Party's insistence upon a critical stance toward the unions, which it often considered a barrier to the attainment of true class consciousness, won it few friends among the Ontario and Nova Scotia communities where it was active in the opening years of the twentieth century. But in British Columbia, by 1903, a combination of factors merged ideological and ethical differences within the socialist camp, forging a unified group that would result in a rejuvenated Canadian socialist movement.

DeLeonite socialism on the west coast had a stormy history that encompassed the formation of an SLP local in Vancouver in 1898 and the creation of the party's trade union arm, the Socialist Trades and Labor Alliance, which was dedicated to waging relentless war on the collaborationist AFL and craft unions in 1899. Subsequently, part of the organization split from the mainstream to form a socialist club that became the United Socialist Labor Party in 1900. More conciliatory toward the unions, the new party soon became the leading socialist body in the region, enrolling 250 members and running a respectable electoral campaign. As class struggle escalated in these years, especially in the coal mines and on the railways, and as American socialist literature and organizers filtered across the border, the validity of the socialist attack on capital appeared to be confirmed and recruits to the revolutionary movement became commonplace. By 1901, attempts to unify the restructured DeLeonites and the Christian socialists led to the drafting of a socialist platform and the creation of a provincial organization, the Socialist Party of British Columbia (SPBC). The more revolutionary wing of the movement, Nanaimo's miners, feared for the loss of socialist principle, and imported a propagandist from California. E.T. Kingsley was a former state organizer for the SLP, a man converted to socialism on his hospital bed, where he had read Marx while recovering from an industrial accident that took both of his legs. He was not one to soften socialist doctrine with faith in capitalism's capacity to effect reform. He would leave his mark on British Columbia's movement and, in the process, stamp the pre-World War I socialism of Canada with a particularly vehement advocacy of class struggle in the political arena.

Kingsley's successes mounted in 1902/3, as employer hostility to unionism and a series of defeated strikes left the miners "ripe for socialism." Organizers claimed the province was reaching "the beginning of the final stage of capitalism," and socialist candidates were occasionally polling an unprecedented 40 percent of the vote. New converts to socialism were made every day; one authority estimated that one-half of the new SPBC's membership had been drawn to socialism in the years 1902/3. A Cumberland, B.C., miner testified to the transformation in workers' consciousness when he appeared before the 1903 royal commission on industrial disputes in the province. When asked, "What is socialism?" he was quick to reply:

> It is the scientific analysis of human society and capitalist production. . . .
> It is the emancipation of the working class. . . the working class will control the machinery of wealth and production. . . . by capturing the reins of government. It means that the people will be the government, and all natural resources will be controlled by the people. . . . if you want to obtain the scientific analysis of the situation, you could procure a copy of Karl Marx's *Capital* . . . that is the groundwork of modern socialism . . . the scientific analysis of capitalist production.

Confronted with words like these, the royal commission was quick to condemn unions as political bodies, claiming the existence of "a class of so-called union men developing rapidly in Western America, which is really not a trade union at all, but a secret political organization whose members are bound by an oath. . . . The primary object and common end of this class of organization is to seize the political power of the state for the purpose of confiscating all franchises and natural resources without compensation."

In April of 1902, 60 representatives of socialist and labour organizations met in Kamloops to establish the Provincial Progressive Party (PPP). Had the socialists been victorious, this body would have in fact fulfilled the worst fears of the royal commissioners. As it was, reformers carried the day, signalling the beginnings of a contest between labourism and socialism in British Columbia. The gradualist labourites had won the first battle, but the ultimate victory would go to Kingsley and the revolutionary socialists. While the socialist movement would never descend to the pre-1900 DeLeonite assault on trade unions, a series of developments reinforced the socialist rejection of reformism and also eased the labourites from power in British Columbia. Crucial successes came in the 1903 provincial election, when the uncompromising platform of the SPBC shattered the reformers' arguments that mass support would never go to such doctrinaire radicals. Socialist candidates won election in Nanaimo, Newcastle, and Slocan, while in Vancouver, socialists averaged over 1,100 votes each. This gave Kingsley and his supporters all the evidence they needed. Orthodoxy became the key issue, and prominent printer-agitator R. Parmeter Pettipiece articulated the new self-conception prominent in B.C. socialist circles: "fate has decreed this position in the world's history to use and we should prove to the workers of the world that we can rise to the occasion; let us stand firm; keep our organization iron-clad, aye 'narrow' and see that we shy clear of the rocks of danger that have wrecked so many well-meaning movements." By the end of 1903, the labourite-dominated PPP was disbanded, revolutionary socialists controlled the provincial executive of the SPBC, and Kingsley sat in the editorial chair of the *Western Clarion*, regional voice of socialism. Revolution, rather than reform, was now on the agenda.

These advances served to encourage eastern Canadian socialists, who gained a new respect for the effectiveness of the "uncompromising principles of revolutionary socialism." Kingsley and his allies were seen as the new vanguard, pacing developments, not only in Canada, but in the socialist world. Negotiations with socialists in Winnipeg and Ontario led to the founding of the Socialist Party of Canada (SPC) late in 1904. The SPC proclaimed that capitalism could not be reformed, that trade unions could not benefit workers in the long run, and that class-conscious political action designed to seize the state in the interests of the proletariat was the only way to destroy the wage system and further the interests of all labour. The SPC regarded itself as the most revolutionary socialist body in the world and rejected affiliation with the "reformist" Second International. It should be noted, however, that in practice local party members were less dogmatic about the ineffectiveness of trade unions; 40 to 60 percent of SPC members also belonged to the unions. Between 1905 and 1910 the new party functioned across the country, with 15 locals in the Maritimes and a number in Ontario and Quebec. But its real strength lay in the west, where Keir Hardie's admonition "none but socialists need apply" seemed to hold true. In the Crow's Nest Pass, the miner leader Frank Sherman was active in SPC work in District 18. Between 1909 and 1913, the Rocky Mountain Coal Communities elected socialist candidates with regularity; in some communities they captured over 65 percent of the vote. Allen Seager notes that one such socialist, Charles M. O'Brien, combined the rhetoric of the Wobblies, the imagery of Jack London, and the prestige of Eugene Debs. He was described in 1911 as "broad enough to be friends with everybody and everything except the capitalist system . . . a ripened and mature revolutionist, a sturdy rebel." The fact that he was regarded as the UMWA's representative in the legislature, gives further evidence that the SPC's antiunion stand was far from uniformly carried out in practice. Among Vancouver Island coal miners the party was equally popular. They regularly sent socialist candidates to the B.C. Legislature, where they made a mockery of parliamentary decorum.

With a total Canadian membership of approximately 3,000, the Socialist Party of Canada managed to exert an influence within the working class far out of proportion to its small membership. In British Columbia, for instance, it increased its share of the provincial vote in contested constituencies from 10 percent in 1907 to 22 percent in 1909, winning 11,000 votes and returning two candidates. Narrowly defeated in other ridings, the socialists claimed to have wiped out "the Liberal Party [and] cleared the field for a struggle to the death between the two extremes of capitalist society; capital on the one hand, dominant, aggressive and brutal; on the other, labour awakening from the lethargy of ages and determined to conquer its freedom from class rule and exploitation."

Among immigrant workers, the SPC also made early gains, breaking down the Anglo-American stranglehold on Canadian socialism. By 1908, Ukrainian branches of the party existed in Winnipeg, Portage La Prairie, and Nanaimo; Ukrainians were active in at least four other locales, the newspaper *Chervony Prapor* declaring itself the voice of the SPC, "serving that section of the proletariat that spoke the Ukrainian language." Other ethnic groups such as the Finns, Italians, Germans, and Slavs also made common cause with the SPC. Such alliances tended to disintegrate over time and the party's ultimate inability to transform itself into something more than an exclusive contingent of British migrants manifested itself in the exodus of many of its ethnic supporters. But it would be wrong to underestimate the importance of this brief moment of class solidarity, which secured tangible victories and symbolized the internationalism the party proclaimed.

In spite of these accomplishments, the SPC lost support in the 1910–17 years, wracked by internal dissension, revolts among its Ontario and foreign-language sections, and the pressure of the rising tide of labourism, which it failed to stem. Moderate British socialists and East European immigrants revolted against the increasingly sectarian practice and theoretical orientation of the SPC and gravitated toward the Social Democratic Party (SDP), founded in 1910. Confronted with this new opposition, the SPC failed to revitalize itself. By 1912, Kingsley admitted that locals were "either semi-defunct or in a state of philosophical dry rot." The vanguard had lost its power to lead.

Labourism and socialism thus contended for the labour movement's political votes in the pre-World War I years. James Simpson and R.P. Pettipiece of the International Typographical Union and Frank Sherman of the United Mine Workers failed to convince the Trades and Labor Congress that the Socialist Party of Canada should be recognized as the legitimate political voice of labour in British Columbia and Alberta. From this point on, labourites and socialists clashed repeatedly. The socialists, to be sure, often worked closely with the trade unions and struggled for those reforms their propaganda and press so curtly dismissed, and many labourites undoubtedly voted the SPC ticket, especially where no ILP advocates stood for election. In fact, the two constituencies were never completely disparate in practice, and District 18 of the UMWA offered the SPC its official endorsement after 1914. But schisms and differences existed within the ranks of labour. On one side were the pure socialists, readers of Marx, Engels, and August Bebel, such as Hamilton's leading radical authority H.P. Bonny and the western socialists Kingsley and O'Brien. On the other were labourites like Winnipeg's F.J. Dixon and S.J. Farmer, who had been influenced by Fabian tracts, social gospel texts, and copies of *Merrie England* or *Poverty and Progress*. The beleaguered miners of British Columbia and Alberta, labour intellectuals, and European immigrants affiliated themselves with the first group, while the second was more likely to attract urban craftsmen of British descent. Had these been the only two political streams within the working class, the politics of dissent may have developed and flourished. But the loyal ties of many workers still lay elsewhere. The casually employed, the unskilled, and the tradesmen who refused the independence offered by labourites and socialists tended to resign themselves to voting Grit and Tory, as their fathers had. If denied the franchise, they might eschew political action altogether. In Winnipeg, in 1906, for instance only 7,784 persons out of a population of more than 100,000 were listed as municipal voters. Either alienated by the recognition of their political impotence or unwilling to venture beyond partyism, many Canadian workers did not gravitate toward the politics of dissent. In one region, however, labour radicalism went beyond political action in its traditional sense.

Regionalism and Radicalism

While by no means a major tendency within the Canadian working class, radicalism was a force to contend with. In industrial cities like Hamilton, workers encountered intellectuals and petty proprietors in the Marx Club. Critically important revolutionary leaders, such as industrial Cape Breton's J.B. McLachlan, gained widespread popularity in this period and enclaves of radicals could be found in many trades. In Toronto, metal polishers wrote to their craft journal under the pennames "K. Marx" and "Sansculotte," while 146 of their 157 members endorsed independent labour political action; patternmakers declared themselves unhesitatingly for the abolition of the wage system. A May Day parade in Montreal in 1906 was headed by the "Red Flag" and drew 5,000. Newfoundlanders elected Fisherman's Union Party candidate George Grimes, lay preacher and self-proclaimed socialist, to the legislature in 1912. But it was in the west that radicalism was especially widespread, stimulating a regional consciousness of wage slavery and its oppressions. Aside from the political action that has already been described, efforts were made by radical leaders to reformulate the very conception of political practice as one which began in the labourer's experience at the workplace. While the SPC and ILP battled for workers' votes, other groups portrayed the struggle at the point of production as the supreme political act.

The Industrial Workers of the World, for instance, as A.R. McCormack and David Bercuson have argued or implied, made few inroads into eastern Canadian industrial communities, but their impact in the west was great. The IWW, known also as the "Wobblies," was a group of itinerants who could be found anywhere across Canada — among the unemployed of Hamilton in 1914 or in the coalfields of Cape Breton, where the famous Wobbly, "Big Bill" Haywood, lectured in 1909. But the west was their favoured terrain. In the mines of the Kootenays, where the IWW had five functioning locals by 1907, or among the western blanket-stiffs who migrated from the head of Lake Superior to Vancouver Island to find work in the logging camps and harvest fields or on railway construction sites and docks, the Wobbly's message fell on receptive ears. It was a simple but effective message of self-worth, directed at workers who toiled incessantly for low wages, under intolerable conditions, without the hope of security. Told that they were the basis of the economy and that they had it within their means to stop the wheels of production if only they were organized into one united contingent, western workers began to see the potential power they wielded. By 1912, according to McCormack, approximately 5,000 had become associated with the IWW, joining a dozen large locals stretching from Victoria to Winnipeg. (One IWW source claims a membership of double this by 1911.) Among workers who built the CNR and the Grand Trunk Pacific, the industrial unionism of the Wobblies was particularly prominent: 40 percent of railway construction workers in the region belonged to the IWW. Ethnically heterogeneous, the IWW advocated the organization of all workers, even the Orientals so long opposed by the labour movement. "Wops" and "Bohunks" comprised a large component of its constituency, just as they provided the bulk of unskilled labour at many job sites. Foreign-language locals thrived, and the Vancouver longshoremen and lumberers who fought the first IWW strike on the west coast were drawn from 18 different nationalities.

Egalitarian to a fault (any Wobbly could act as a full-time organizer as he travelled from job to job), the IWW charged low fees and transferred membership cards without inhibition. Camaraderie was cultivated, and Wobbly halls served as dormitories, mail drops, and employment agencies. For the alien worker without a vote or the unskilled and illiterate, the Wobblies' brand of radicalism was perhaps the only one that offered adequate solutions. The only training required of members was that of working-class life itself, the only classics demanding attention, those that came from the oppression and exploitation of labouring experience. "Everything is founded upon the job," explained one British Columbia Wobbly, "everything comes from conditions on the job which is the environment and life of the toiling slaves. The job is the source of civilization." And "the job" would be the basis of change. The IWW considered every strike a "miniature revolution," and saw social transformation being attained through a general strike that would leave the workers in control of production.

With the economic recession of 1913/14, the collapse of the railway boom, and the scattering of its Wobbly labour force, the forces of the IWW were weakened. Canada's entry into World War I provided a context in which employer hostility to the Wobblies would be supplemented by increased state repression: IWW organizer Dick Higgins was tried under the War Measures Act in Vancouver, and late in 1918, Diamond City mine union leader, Tom Shannon, was imprisoned for possessing "IWW literature." Always closely tied to the larger American-based movement, Canada's Wobblies also suffered organizational disarray because of the American repression of 1917, which saw 110 Wobblies arrested on conspiracy charges laid in Chicago. By 1918, the IWW in Canada was nearly nonexistent. But its vision, its hope, and, in many ways, a part of its strategic orientation to the working masses, would be taken up with renewed vigour in another movement of western radicalism, the more distinctively Canadian challenge of the One Big Union.

If the IWW was no longer a force to be reckoned with as the war neared its conclusion, conditions in the mines and shops of the west and the agitations of socialists like the SPC and social democrats like the SDP had nevertheless conditioned a particular stance of defiance within the western working class. Rampant wartime inflation forced large numbers of western workers into strike actions and set off sympathetic strikes among other trade groups. The railway machinists' bulletin noted that, the "ability of individual trade unions to enforce their economic demands is becoming less as the master class unite." Militancy crested in this period, pushing aside many moderate labour leaders like Winnipeg's Arthur W. Puttee, whose failure to support a 1918 sympathetic strike wave in Winnipeg earned him the scorn of many workers associated with the increasingly radical Metal Trades Council. Among such western workers, opposition to capital grew. Resentments against employers would soon be translated partially into antagonism to a cautious, eastern-dominated craft unionism. A split within the Canadian labour movement was in the making.

At the Quebec City convention of the Trades and Labor Congress, in September 1918, the split occurred. Westerners, with the support of some eastern radicals, launched a direct attack on the Congress leadership. However, the west had sent only 45 delegates to the convention (or less than one-tenth of the total), and its voice of opposition went unheard. Convinced that TLC conventions discriminated against western labour as they were often held in the east and therefore had more eastern delegates, the radicals from the west decided to hold their own conference before the TLC convened in 1919. Before this occurred, there was much debate, an escalation of state repression against wartime radicals, and considerable international development, notably the rise of the One Big Union movement in Australia and the armistice of 11 November 1918. It was in the midst of such developments that the Western Labor Conference convened in Calgary in March 1919. Orchestrated by radicals committed to socialism and industrial unionism, the gathering, originally conceived as an attempt to plan a radical comeback within the TLC, quickly took on a secessionist hue. Before the opening speech was made, the *Western Labor News* proclaimed, "The more effete East is burdensome to the West and the slavish subservience of parliament to the interests of vested wealth has filled the cup of the West to overflowing." And it was the "radical core" that led the convention. Vancouver trades council secretary and SPC member Victor Midgley had astutely arranged for the radical British Columbia Federation of Labor to hold its annual convention in Calgary just prior to the Western Labor Conference, thereby assuring the presence of his radical followers. In the words of Desmond Morton, they "completely managed" the convention, and "railroaded" moderate delegates. Resolutions passed quickly. They denounced censorship, made common cause with the Bolshevik Revolution, eschewed traditional political action, raised high the banner of the general strike, and advocated the foundation of a new labour organization unencumbered by the exclusivist trappings of the craft unionism of the American Federation of Labor. In the weeks to follow, "Midgley & Company" (historian David Bercuson's characterization), led the way in the formation of this body, the One Big Union.

Historians like Bercuson and Morton consider the OBU little more than the expressiosn of "chiliastic faith," "designed by the maneuverings and machinations of a small handful of millenarians while the tens of thousands of western workers ready to revolt against capitalism and craft unionism had no chance to determine what the vehicle of their discontent would be like." But the events of March–June 1919, and the background of the previous two years, call into question this kind of interpretation. Miners in District 18 had adhered to revolutionary demands for workers' control since 1918, and the 5,100 members of the UMWA were staunch industrial unionists. Trades councils in Victoria, Vancouver, and Winnipeg (where 75 percent of the city's organized workers embraced the new militancy) were overwhelming in their support for the OBU, while 5,500 organized loggers lined up behind W.A. Pritchard by a ratio of nine to one. To be sure, there were centres of opposition, especially among urban craftsmen in Alberta, where Calgary was a TLC stronghold, and Saskatchewan. But as A.R. McCormack points out, the anti-OBU forces were far from effective, and in the turmoil of the spring of 1919, militant industrial unionism won a mass base in the west.

Radicalism was thus something more than a matter of faith. If it lacked precise programmatic direction, it was nevertheless rooted in working-class experience and discontent. The manoeuverings and machinations, the conspiratorial intrigues of "sterile" and "fuzzy" socialist thinkers were, in fact, less important in its creation than other conspiracies and machinations. Miners who had tasted the autocractic authority of the

Dunsmuir interests for decades and railway workers who knew the antilabour practice of the CPR, were not about to oppose those who held out the hand of solidarity as the salvation of the class. Those who remembered the shooting of British Columbia labour leader, Ginger Goodwin, or who had heard the story of Vic Midgley being forced into the street to kneel and kiss the Union Jack, had other conspiracies and manoeuvers on their minds. Almost 90,000 "enemy aliens" were forced to register in Canada during World War I, and over 2,200 were interned. The 64,000 Russian subjects present in Canada at the time of the Bolshevik Revolution bore the brunt of a particularly hostile nativism. Violence directed at these immigrants, many of whom were socialists and workers, as well as attacks on ethnic clubs, called into question moderate reform thought and action, just as the perceived complacency of labour statesmen in the east provoked western workers to split with the labourites. In eastern industrial cities, too, in immigrant quarters as well as among the skilled, there were signs of radicalism. A Montreal organizer expressed his astonishment that "the Soviet idea was so rampant . . . among the foreign-speaking iron and steel workers" of Hamilton. And if this was the background to labour radicalism that conditioned a climate in which an admittedly poorly conceived organizational strategy would emerge, and the OBU would be founded, the fortunes of radicalism were and would be determined, in large measure, by the contexts of war and class struggle, by the relentless opposition of capital and the state.

The War for Democracy

World War I proved to be a watershed in the development of radicalism in the west. It brought the country decisively out of the 1913–15 recession: in those years trade union membership had fallen 20 percent and the number of strikes had declined to a twentieth-century low. But with the new demands for production, especially in wartime industries such as coal mining or munitions, the post-1915 years revitalized labour's bargaining position. By 1917, the country's employers faced a shortage of 100,000 workers, and this tight labour market increased the chance of success in a strike, enhanced the likelihood of union recognition, and created a new structure of demands that radicals were able to exploit. With unemployment no longer a great threat, and with wages sometimes increasing at rates higher than inflation, the labour movement appeared to be regaining lost ground. Between 1914 and 1918, approximately 150 strikes were fought yearly.

For the first time in the new century, Alberta's miners' wages increased more quickly than soaring prices and were on a par with those of their American counterparts. Indeed, coal mining was perhaps the leading sector within the workers' movement. Certainly, it loomed large in the history of militant actions at the point of production: during the years 1914–20, 12 percent of all strikes, 20.5 percent of all workers involved in strikes, and 23 percent of all time lost to strikes were accounted for by miners. But other industries and trades were also advancing. Workers in logging and sawmilling went on strike, and in 1918, the first public-sector strike occurred when the Letter Carriers' Union struck the Post Office. This context of escalating wartime militancy was supplemented by developments that led to a radical critique of the class nature of Canadian society.

The war years were also the years of the "Red Scare," as the Bolshevik Revolution of 1917 raised the spectre of communism for the first time in North America. When the Western Labor Conference declared its full acceptance of "the principle of proletarian dictatorship as being absolute and efficient for the transformation of capitalistic private property to communal wealth," sending its fraternal greetings to the Russian Soviet Government and the German "Spartacans" recognizing that they had "won first place in the history of the class struggle," it was expressing one part of this process. Prime Minister Robert Borden's fears of western labour's "absurd conceptions of what had been accomplished in Russia" were but another part of the same development. It was in these years, as the Royal Canadian Mounted Police's official historian, S.W. Horrall, has recently reminded us, that the Force was born. The counter-revolutionary panic of the Canadian ruling class cultivated a sense of need, and the regionally limited Royal North-West Mounted Police was merged with the Dominion Police, hurriedly converted to a national police force. The RNWMP entered the national arena, experienced in the art of countersubversion. By April of 1919 it had managed to infiltrate every important revolutionary organization in the west, and two of its agents had been delegates at the Calgary Western Labor Conference in March. The enhanced powers of the state in wartime, secured by the War Measures Act of 1914 and expanded in subsequent Orders in Council and initiatives by the Secretary of State established mechanisms to "register" and restrain supposed "enemy aliens," impose censorship, and disrupt socialist organizations. All these powers were exercised in the wartime climate of statism and anti-Bolshevism. The repression of the war years continued into the postwar reconstruction period. Alien registration, prohibitions on movements and the freedom to possess firearms and to publish newspapers in "foreign" languages, forced labour, deportations, the banning of certain organizations, and private vigilante actions unpunished by the state confirmed the radical beliefs of many ethnic workers, at the same time that it drove less resolute immigrants into passivity. Almost 200 immigrant "anarchists and revolutionaries" were rounded up in summer raids that followed the outbreak of the Winnipeg General Strike. While Canadian workers fought for democracy abroad and, in the aftermath of the war, mutinied, rioted, and struck for better conditions for themselves and other soldiers, those on the home front were engaged in their own war for the rights of citizenship. The war for democracy at home was waged most forcefully in the Alberta coalfields and in the munitions industry, where a 1916 strike in Hamilton challenged state, employer, and the powerful appeal of "patriotism."

Explored recently by Allen Seager, "the great fight for democracy" in the coal communities of Alberta commenced in 1916/17 with a series of limited victories that won war bonuses, wage increases, and the repeal of some harsh clauses imposed on the men under the adverse conditions of 1915. Another strike in 1918 secured further concessions, and the miners returned to work. As their union, the United Mine Workers of America, was recognized by the bulk of the operators, and conditions and wages were better than those previously known by the foreign-born and native English-speaking miners, the mines should have been models of social stability and contentment.

Pinkertons, government spies, and employers interpreted the situation differently, however, and saw the ideological and social components of an alternative culture of resistance. One miner militant was a firm believer that "as soon as this war is over . . . things will be a lot better for the working men and women . . . this will be what the Aristocrats and Plutocrats will call Anarchy . . . then the men that are living off the earnings of us poor devils will either have to work or else not eat." A workers' mock parliament in Blairmore defined the community's war aims as "the establishment forever of government for, by and of the people." In Drumheller, colliers built a new Miners' Institute where they held union meetings. Here were signs of an emerging autonomy, the creation of an institutional foundation for the "new culture," the "working-class culture," that the *One Big Union Bulletin* saw at work in the coalfields in 1919. As nearly 7,000 workers walked off their jobs in District 18 in May of 1919, enforcing the first 100 percent strike in the Alberta mines (pulling out the unionized maintenance men, thereby threatening not only capital's profits and production but its property), something of the strength of that culture was felt.

Even within the confines of more conventional forms of social interaction between capital and labour, the war years were ones of class polarization and unprecedented militancy. The International Association of Machinists, for instance, was a union struggling to establish itself in the early twentieth century, and fought major strikes on the Grand Trunk Railway in 1905–7, against the CPR in 1908, in Kingston (1902–5), and in Toronto (1907–9). But the most dramatic confrontation unfolded in Hamilton in 1916.

On Monday, 12 June 1916, approximately 2,000 workers struck over 30 Hamilton plants engaged in the production of munitions. Among the plants affected were the Steel Company of Canada, Canadian Westing-house, the National Steel Car Company, and Dominion Steel Foundry, a representative sample of monopoly capital's leading firms. Myer Siemiatycki's discussion of the strike stresses the range of workers drawn to the strike and the hostility of the bosses and the state. Nine hundred unionized machinists affiliated with the IAM, 338 associated with a rival craft body, the Amalgamated Society of Engineers, and 800 unskilled unorganized shellmakers came together in a struggle for improved conditions that escalated quickly into a challenge to capital. Employers formed an Association and attempted to fan the flames of public opposition with patriotic hysteria. After a month-long battle, the machinists were forced to return to their jobs. Less radical than actions in the west, waged by supporters of the OBU, such struggles pushed workers toward new awareness. "If the machinists of the world were to strike today," said the oldest member of Hamilton's IAM local, "this war, large as it is, would immediately cease, the world would stand still, because this is a war of machines and an age of the same." Advances in consciousness of this order were a step forward for the working class. A product of the war for democracy within the workplace, they would find their clearest expression in 1919, when the labour movement made its most dramatic stand to date.

General Strike

Nineteen-nineteen was a year of strikes. More than 320 were fought, far exceeding the number of strikes in any previous year. The number of workers involved in conflicts and worker-days lost to strikes also peaked, as did the numbers of workers organized in unions. Between 1917 and 1919, the number of workers striking rose from 50,000 to 79,000 to 149,000. In 1919, the Labour Department began calculating time lost to strikes as a percentage of time worked annually. That percentage was 0.6 in 1919, a figure yet to be surpassed. Most important among these strikes led by metal tradesmen, machinists, and transportation workers was of course the Winnipeg General Strike, which spurned Canadian labour to action across the land, stimulating sympathetic work stoppages from Vancouver Island to Amherst, Nova Scotia.

The General Strike is perhaps the central event in the historiography of Canadian labour history. Originally viewed as a conspiratorial attempt to establish a soviet-style government, contemporary schol-arship has revised the generally held view of this confrontation, casting the struggle as a battle to improve wages and working conditions and to implement the essential structures of collective bargaining. This revisionist stance has drawn upon a reasoned reassessment of evidence, although it has also often been based on the anti-Marxist social democratic premises of the late 1940s and 1950s. This new analysis has clarified the strike's aims, but does not offer any explanation as to how nonrevolutionary demands can, in specific circumstances, form the foundation of a challenge to authority that proves radical, even potentially revolutionary in its implications.

David Bercuson's *Confrontation at Winnipeg* provides the essential chronology and narrative of the conflict. Class relations in the city had undergone a certain polarization as early as 1906, when strikes by street railway workers, machinists, blacksmiths, and moulders had engendered antagonism. Prewar depression, wartime inflation, and workplace militancy further set the stage for the reconstruction period. With labour leaders warning of the necessity to "adopt stringent measures to force a recognition of [worker] rights," and radicals and socialists firmly implanted in the institutions of the workers' movement, the city was a centre of early discussion of the efficacy of a general strike. The return of soldiers, many of whom were still unemployed, the socialist and social democratic commitment of the ethnic community, and the prospect of forming One Big Union in the west and of gaining Bolshevik victories in the east all created an explosive climate.

May Day, 1919, provided the spark. Building trades workers demanded wage increases to offset what they claimed was a 57 percent decline in the purchasing power of their earnings over the years 1913–19. However, the Building Trades Council employers complained of a recession in construction, an impasse was quickly reached, and May opened with the traditional spring strike. Similarly, among metal trades workers, the last week of April was a time of discussion. Asking for

TABLE 4.3   Real incomes among Winnipeg building and metal trades workers (1900–1918)
(Approximate percentage gain or loss over selected years)

Group	1900–1905	1905–1909	1909–1911	1911–13	1913–15	1915–18
Bricklayers	+5%	−1.6%	+8.9%	−27%	+11.4%	−21%
Carpenters	+21%	+12.8%	−3.6%	−15%	+21.5%	−12.5%
Electrical Workers	+16.5%	+13.4%	−3%	−11.9%	+61%	−25%
Painters	+2.9%	−9.9%	+29.2%	−11.5%	+17.9%	−13%
Plumbers	+9.8%	+6.0%	−3%	−16%	+21.6%	−18%
Stonecutters	+12.3%	−18.4%	−11.2%	−9.6%	+26.1%	−23%
Builders labourers	+21.3%	−9.9%	+6.6%	−16.7%	+21.6%	−5.5%
Blacksmiths	+5.8%	−3.3%	−4.3%	−16.6%	+18.1%	+6%
Boilermakers	−1.2%	+9.7%	−10.8%	−16.7%	+21.6%	−3%
Iron Moulders	+5.8%	−2.5%	−4.2%	−10.7%	+21.6%	−3%
Machinists	+8.9%	−7.6%	−2.8%	−20%	+39.6%	−4%
Sheet Metal Workers	—	—	−7%	−8.4%	+21.6%	−8.6%

Adapted and simplified from Joseph Harry Sutcliffe, "The Economic Background of the Winnipeg General Strike: Wages and Working Conditions." M.A. thesis, University of Manitoba, 1972.

higher wages and the 44-hour week, they did not make demands for union recognition. But the employers were resolute in their opposition; of the 28 schedules submitted to various shops in the city, answers were received from only three. The larger employers, particularly, were adamant in their refusal to bargain. As a result, the workers unanimously agreed to strike, closing down the metalworking shops on May 2 for the third time in as many years. The issues were far from revolutionary: union recognition, the eight-hour day, and wage parity with the better-paid railway shop workers.

Other workers were embroiled in similar controversies. Telephone operators had come to a confrontation and nearly gone on strike while street railway workers and even the policemen's union were locked into negotiations with their employers. The weekly Trades Council meeting convened in this atmosphere of discontent. Workers became irate when they heard testimonies of the arrest of a German metalworker, of labour spies and government-hired *agents provocateurs*, and of increasing employer hostility to unionism. Winnipeg seemed to be emerging as a test case; across Canada, labour's eyes were focussed on their struggles, claimed the radical R.B. Russell. He exorted workers to take "No more defeats," as the working-class standard. Amidst "tumultuous applause and scenes of the greatest enthusiasm," the Council voted to take up this rallying cry with a general strike. On 13 May, the Council met again to report the overwhelming support the proposal of a general strike had received from the city's organized workers: they endorsed the action by a vote of 11,000 to 500, and the general strike was called for 15 May 1919. Over 22,000 (eventually as many as 30,000 to 35,000) workers would take to the streets, the bulk of them unorganized workers, in a city populated by 175,000 people.

By the early evening, Winnipeg was paralyzed. The strikers controlled the press, putting out the *Special Strike Edition* of the *Western Labor News*, the police were sympathetic to their cause, and the Central Strike Committee functioned as a labour government. The Labor Temple saw a steady stream of employers marching to its door, begging permission to carry on essential services such as milk delivery, a reversal of roles of subordination that pleased the radicals among the leaders of the strike. By early June, as Donald Avery has stressed, ethnic workers like Oscar Schopperlie (later to be arrested and deported) were growing more and more successful in their efforts to bring immigrant organizations and the strikers close together, while radical leaders had penetrated the ranks of returned war veterans. Thus, the strike became something more than a struggle for mundane workplace and bargaining rights, and its constituency expanded beyond the ranks of the skilled Anglo-Saxon craftsmen among whom it had originated. In this movement of working-class initiative and innovation, nonworkers saw dissidence and challenge that had to be eradicated.

A Citizens' Committee of 1,000 moved quickly to suppress the Winnipeg strikers, sweeping aside the issues of collective bargaining in hysterical condemnation of the "deliberate, criminal and fantastic attempt to make a revolution." Closely in touch with the municipal, provincial, and especially federal levels of government, the Citizens' Committee served as capital's watchdog in its moment of crisis. Expenses incurred were, on several occasions, paid by the government in Ottawa, which kept close watch on the proceedings to determine if any of the strike leaders' actions were "seditious or treasonable." Many of these so-called Bolsheviks were actually labourites, Liberals, or Conservatives; on the 15-member Central Strike Committee only R.B. Russell was a known advocate of the OBU, which had yet to be formally constituted. The Strike Committee kept workers off the streets and confined to mundane tasks of keeping the city going, a stance of moderation that served only to further enrage the political and entrepreneurial "leaders" of Winnipeg. "By Permission of the Strike Committee" was a symbolic but tangible reminder that business was functioning in a manner far from usual. As pressure mounted, nativist attacks on aliens and "foreign Bolsheviks" increased, and the federal government intervened, Gideon Robertson dismissing all the postal workers who refused to report for their duties. Arthur Meighen, Minister of the Interior and future prime minister, condemned the "revolutionists of various types, from crazy idealists down to ordinary thieves" who threatened those Winnipeg economic interests with which he was closely allied.

Pro- and antistriker forces clashed across the city, many war veterans casting their lot with the workers, but other soldiers proclaiming their opposition to extremism and labour radicalism. Parading supporters of both sides merely exacerbated tensions, which reached a new high in the second week of June, when 240 policemen were dismissed for their suspected sympathies with the workers. When 1,800 "special police" were recruited by the Citizens' Committee responsible for public order, the crisis was nearing its violent resolution. Between 16 and 21 June the RNWMP raided labour halls and strike leaders' homes, arresting and imprisoning key spokesmen, as labour mounted a countrywide protest culminating in a silent parade that was attacked by the special police and the Mounted Police, injuring 30 and killing one. Aldermen John Queen and A.A. Heaps, R.B. Russell, Rev. W. Ivens, editor of the *Western Labor News*, and six others, four of whom were "foreign Bolsheviks," were jailed, and when some of their duties were taken over by a new corps of strike leaders such as J.S. Woodsworth and Fred Dixon, another wave of incarcerations followed. On 26 June 1919, after six weeks of constant battle, the strike was declared over, the Central Strike Committee urging labour to "speak in no uncertain terms at the next municipal election." Defeated but not demoralized, the Committee insisted that, "Labor must fight on until she wins the long war for freedom."

Labour radicalism had failed the test of 1919. For all the revolutionary rhetoric, working-class initiatives had emerged out of the course of events, rather than guiding those events in a strategic assertion of programmatic change. The more aggressive and disciplined actions came from employers and the state. Winnipeg's General Strike revealed, as had no other single development in the 1895–1919 period, the power marshalled by state and capital in the age of monopoly. It told, as well, of the price to be paid if that power was not recognized and opposed with workers' organizations of equal power, with class directives, preparations for all eventualities, especially those of repression, and extensions of workers' autonomy and authority. David Simpson, founding member of the policemen's union, recalled in 1979 the impact of the state's assault on the workers: "After the arrests the strike was bust, blown away." Blacklisted, forced to flee the city and then to return to work as a bailiff, Simpson felt something of the long-term consequences of the strike's defeat. A lost moment in the history of the Canadian working class, the General Strike of 1919 led, like the collapse of the Knights of Labor, into a new period of profound dissolution within the working-class experience.

The Fragmentation of Working-Class Culture

At a superficial glance, the General Strike in Winnipeg and the emergence of western labour radicalism seems to represent an unprecedented consolidation of class consciousness. General or sympathetic strikes erupted in Brandon, Regina, Saskatoon, Calgary, Edmonton, Medicine Hat, Prince Albert, Prince Rupert, New Westminster, Vancouver, Victoria, Amherst, Toronto, Lethbridge, Fort William, and Port Arthur. Within French Canada and southern Ontario, workers reacted more cautiously, but Montreal and Toronto were nevertheless centres of sympathetic activity. At a 22 May 1919 strike rally of Canadian Vickers plant employees in Montreal, approximately half of the 4,000 later involved in the strike passed resolutions promising material and moral support to the Winnipeg strikers. Although Montreal failed to mount a general strike in support of the western workers, it was far from acquiescent. By mid-June, nearly 13,000 workers were on strike in the city; rallies in favour of the Winnipeg General Strike and OBU propaganda produced a volatile atmosphere in which workers' militancy and radicalism were apparent.

A similar situation existed in Toronto, where, from the time of the Russian October Revolution well into 1919, revolutionary socialists had been leading a campaign against capital. By May 1919, demonstrations of 5,000 would be headed by banners declaring, "We Fought for Democracy — Not for Capitalists." Future communist leader, patternmaker Jack MacDonald, placed the new demands of labour squarely before the workers' movement. "We want the world for the workers," he yelled, "and we are going to have it." Strikes erupted among many of the skilled craftsmen. On 30 May, a general strike was called; 12,000 responded, although four days later they were back at work. MacDonald insisted that the struggle was far from over. Labour, he claimed, was fighting "for control of the means of production."

These and many other similar developments show 1919 to be a unique moment in the history of Canada's working class. In Winnipeg, the workers' movement left its mark on the local political scene, as J.E. Rae has shown, well into the 1940s, if not to the present day, with a noticeable pattern of confrontation between labour and citizens' league candidates continuing to characterize debate on the city council. The symbolic power of a general strike, moreover, would retain a privileged place within the Canadian labour movement, and would be drawn upon once more, in the difficult years of the 1970s. Among historians, too, Winnipeg 1919 is considered to be significant, and synthetic accounts of Canadian labour generally treat the confrontation not as an event in the history of labour, but as the very starting point of Canadian labour history. "Labour's trauma started at Winnipeg in 1919," writes Irving Abella. "Until then its horizons seemed unclouded and propitious." Kenneth McNaught places his analysis of the General Strike in somewhat different, if complementary, terms: ". . . the Winnipeg strike was a most significant occurrence in Canadian history, if for no other reason than that it was the first and only time in Canadian history that a majority was split clearly into two opposing classes." Such views, however correctly they point to the importance and novelty of 1919, obscure the extent to which the general strike also represented an essential continuity with the nineteenth-century workers' movement, which had shifted from central Canada to the west, in the twentieth-century conditions of monopoly capital, state intervention, labour-market segmentation, and the fragmentation of a relatively homogeneous working-class culture. To see Winnipeg 1919 in these terms is to comprehend both its vitality and its shortcomings, claiming prominence of place for both its tangible successes and ultimate defeat. It is to place a central, if atypical, event at the base of the interpretation of an epoch and to argue that Winnipeg 1919 represented not only the beginnings of labour's new history but, equally, the end of one phase of working-class experience. With the victory of the employers and the state in 1919, the "Indian Summer" of working-class culture came to a close.

For the Winnipeg General Strike was *not* the first event during which Canadian society had been polarized along class lines: that had also occurred in the 1880s, when an eclectic radicalism bred of entrepreneurial capital's undisputed conquests captured the sympathies of the class, structured such attachments into an institutional context — the Knights of Labor — premised on the need to organize all workers, and conditioned a moral universality of opposition, challenge, and alternative unprecedented in Canadian society. Much of this happened in the Canadian west in the years from 1899 to 1919. Capitalist development there had lagged notably behind that of central Canada in the late nineteenth century, but in the Laurier years of the wheat boom and the integration of the west into the very centre of the Canadian social formation, the material foundations of class distinctions emerged starkly and quickly.

This was a classic case of the shifting locale of the industrial frontier: that frontier had gravitated from east to west over the course of the nineteenth and early twentieth centuries. In the years before 1850 the "industrial frontier" was stunted by the hegemony of commercial capital, but it nevertheless thrived in the shipbuilding centres of Quebec City and Saint John. By the 1850s, manufacturing and entrepreneurial capital became established, and the industrial frontier passed into central Canada, encompassing a region bordering the Great Lakes and the St. Lawrence, stretching from London to Montreal. That frontier spawned monopoly and the integration of finance and industrial capital. In the epoch dominated by these forces, wheat, on the one hand, and other new staples like coal, lumber, and nonferrous metals, on the other, emerged as the foundation of resource-based capitalism in the east and, more particularly, in the west. Each of these industrial frontiers produced distinctive working-class structures, both in terms of organization and social and cultural life. Uneven economic development conditioned a specific unevenness in class formation.

Western labour radicalism from 1899 to 1919 was thus in some sense the counterpart of central Canada's labour upsurge of the 1880s. The links here are quite direct, from the Western Federation of Miners, a body tracing its origins to the Knights of Labor, to the attachment to the One Big Union shared by the Knights, the IWW, the socialists, and the OBU. Early socialists like George Wrigley, Phillips Thompson, Richard J. Kerrigan, and others found their way from the Noble and Holy Order to the radical socialist and industrial-union formations of the early twentieth century. It is true that the economic, sociological, and ideological climate of the west at the turn of the century was quite different from that of the east in the 1880s, and this resulted in a western radical movement that differed somewhat from the old eclectic radicalism. By the time industrial development arrived in the west, capital had already entered its powerful monopoly phase and the state had begun to use interventionist measures to support capital. At the same time, the workers' movement had undergone an ideological evolution that was a product of peculiarly North American dealings with corporate capital and of international developments led by European revolutionaries. This new, composite ideology clarified the deficiencies and ambiguities inherent in the eclectic radicalism of the 1880s. Nevertheless, such developments did not give rise to an unambiguous class consciousness and solidarity. Indeed, at the pinnacle of western labour's revolt in 1918/19, working-class radicalism was characterized by an eclecticism not unlike that of the presocialist moment of the 1880s in central Canada. In the new conditions of the twentieth century, diverse strategies that covered the spectrum of "pure and simple" international craft unionism, labourism, Christian socialism, syndicalism, and revolutionary Marxism competed for workers' allegiances. Where the ideological eclecticism of the 1880s had resulted in a movement that was sometimes hesitant and nonpragmatic, the radicalism of the turn of the century (especially in the west) consisted of a fragmented and contentious, if more advanced and sophisticated, body of competing ideologies and organizational directions. If these ideologies and strategic directions appeared to come together in the upheaval of 1919, however, it was through the suppression of difference rather than explicit debate and a formally established united front. Instead, an eclectic radicalism infused with new socialist principles reemerged in the exuberance of wartime militancy, international working-class advance, and a climate in which proletarian victory seemed possible. Labourite and socialist, syndicalist and revolutionary, Christian moralist and pragmatic unionist were drawn into labour's struggles. An uneasy unity then splintered forever as the grim reality of repression imposed itself in 1919/20. Across Canada the lesson of 1919 was brought home to the working class in blunt and unequivocal language: to fail to take into account the combined power of capital and the state was to court decisive defeat. The class stand of 1919 thus proved as unsuccessful as the eclectic radicalism of a previous era. It also faced stronger opposition. As it had earlier, eclecticism gave way to more focussed forms of dissent: communism, social democracy, labourism, a return to partyism, or the contest between industrial unionism and craft forms of organization. These were the paths followed in the 1920s and 1930s.

This ideological and organizational fragmentation was reinforced by demographic change. In the 1880s, the Knights of Labor had succeeded in minimizing ethnocultural divisions within the working class. However, this vitally important achievement extended only to English-speaking and French-speaking workers who were accustomed to life in industrial-capitalist Canada. Irish and non-Irish, Catholic and Protestant, had been brought together. Even in French Canada, where language and culture posed acute problems of unity, the 1880s saw a number of common responses to a range of common problems among members of the working class. In the opening decades of the twentieth century, with immigrants flooding the labour market, ethnic divisions became more distinct. While significant and historically creative efforts to bridge the gaps of ethnic heterogeneity were made, especially in the west and in the radical enclaves of urban industrial-capitalist Canada, no real unity between indigenous and immigrant workers was achieved. Immigrant workers formed the backbone of a reserve army of labour, were isolated in specific job ghettoes and urban slums, and were victims of ethnic prejudice. Whether considered as "dangerous foreigners" given to radicalism, communalists prone to the violent and chaotic resolution of specific grievances, or slovenly and docile workers incapable of sustaining working-class institutions of self-defence, the immigrants were far removed from their English-speaking counterparts in the newly restructured Canadian working class.

Even within the immigrant working class, moreover, there were divisions of significance. At the most basic level, the disciplined socialism of the Finnish community contrasted with the violent strikes undertaken by Italian and Greek workers at the Canadian Lakehead (as described by Jean Morrison). These are broad generalizations, of course, and each immigrant community contained various elements which can be understood only after careful investigation of the immigrants' old-world experience and their regional and occupational situations in Canada. Much detailed historical study of this area has yet to be done, and where it has proceeded, as in Varpu Lindstrom-Best's analysis of Finnish socialists, Allen Seager's portrayal of immigrant-dominated coal towns in Alberta, or Robert Harney's, Bruno Ramirez's, and Michael Del Balso's studies of Montreal's Italians, no constants have emerged.

Such complexity was at the root of diverse experiences, and tied into the ideological fragmentation of the Canadian workers' movement at the turn of the century. Some immigrants, of course, like their unskilled English-speaking counterparts, were forced into positions of subordination. In centres of heavy industry such as Hamilton, where the Steel Company of Canada was growing and consolidating its operations, the years 1905–20 witnessed the introduction of large numbers of such immigrant workers who were effectively segregated within the company and the city. Exploited mercilessly, they offered protests that were generally ineffective. Similarly, Slavs in the northern work camps were described by early sociologist Edmund Bradwin, admittedly in ethnocentric or racist terms, as "just plodders in the day's work — withal, that pliant type that provides the human material for a camp boss to drive."

But not all immigrant workers were so easily cowed. Within the communities of the Ukrainians, Russians, Jews, and Finns, for instance, were some workers who were early recruits to socialism. When state efforts to force Ukrainian miners into wartime camps were facilitated by the racist and self-interested collusion of Anglo-Canada and Italian colliers, *Robotchy Narod* (a radical Ukrainian newspaper, whose name meant *Working People*) called upon its readers not to abandon principle in the face of betrayal by class allies: "Let the inflated English chauvinistic miners run our brothers out of Nanaimo, Fernie and other places; let them put them in camps. We will survive this misfortune and not only will we remain faithful anti-militarists but we will try to teach those workers who have gone crazy over chauvinism." Familiar with the social democratic experiences and movements of their native lands, such immigrants had been attracted to the Socialist Party of Canada in the years 1905-9. But even here, an apparent unity gave way to fragmentation as the immigrant socialists left the SPC in 1910, to form the radical base of the Social Democratic Party. Further splits would occur along ethnic lines: the immigrant sections of the SDP broke from the more moderate labourite Anglo-Saxons led by Jimmy Simpson, and after 1917 a proliferation of revolutionary foreign-language federations were established. Even among ethnic workers whose commitment was obviously to class solidarity and revolutionary socialism, fragmentation rather than ideological agreement came to be the norm.

The availability of large numbers of immigrant workers provided the human material out of which the reserve army of labour was fashioned. It also fed into labour-market segmentation that was accepted complacently, as evidenced by the comment of one contractor at the time: "We distinguish white men. Austrians and Italians we don't call them white men. I don't know that it's hardly fair but it's customary." The already-segmented labour market characterized by a dichotomy between skilled and unskilled workers, was further complicated by ethnic heterogeneity. Gender distinctions also exacerbated such job divisions, creating even more complicated hierarchies in the world of work. Certain types of jobs, including laundry work and the sweated, subcontracted, and subdivided sectors of the garment trades, became female job ghettoes; technological and marketing innovations led to the proletarianization and, in some cases, feminization, of accounting, general office work, clerical tasks, and sales. One Toronto bank increased its female staff from 200 to 8,000 in two years. The predominance of women in teaching, which was a nineteenth-century phenomenon, continued apace in these years and, as in other female work sectors, poor conditions and low wages prevailed. Such female labour was isolated, and while efforts to unionize were made, they were far from effective. Attempts to organize, as Wayne Roberts and Star Rosenthal have shown in studies of Toronto and Vancouver, were frustrated by workplace ecologies that defied collectivity, by employer hostility, and by demographic realities (most female workers were young and single and, after a period within the workforce, often left to engage in unpaid domestic labour). Especially striking is the degree to which the woman's place in working-class society had been devalued since the 1880s, when the class and women's questions had intersected. Craft unions, compared to the Knights of Labor, served women poorly, and remained even more inhibited by the conventional wisdoms of the age. Women's activities were, for the most part, confined to label committees and female auxiliaries. Even in the radical west, where women were central as part of a wide-ranging network of community support for workers' initiatives, the basis of the labour movement — coal miners and urban craftsmen — was such that women were often mistakenly perceived to be on the margins of the class struggle, their interests focussed on the family. Here, too, was an area of fragmentation, undercutting the cultural cohesion of the working class.

Finally, beyond ethnicity and gender, lay the fragmentation of region. Always a potent force in Canadian historical development, it had, among working-class advocates, been diminished by the cross-country upsurge of Knights and Workmen in the 1880s. By the turn of the century, however, as the west began to organize, regional identification intersected with debates over craft versus industrial organization. From Slocan, British Columbia, one miner wrote: "Now there are thousands of old-line K of L's in the WFM and the unsavory acts of the AFL officials have not been altogether forgotten." In 1919 at the Calgary Conference, the radical advocates of one big union in the west separated themselves out from what they considered the craft-exclusionist east. (This was something of a misnomer, given radicalism's strength in certain urban centres and industrial unionism's vitality in the coalfields of Nova Scotia.) Radical west and conservative east split at the Lakehead, with a literal island of regional and radical identification floating to the east in industrial Cape Breton. In Quebec, where francophone and anglophone workers had united in the 1880s, these years saw the beginnings of a unique working-class experience that would progress over the course of the twentieth century. In opposition to the international unions, the first Roman Catholic *syndicat* was formed among paper workers in Chicoutimi in 1907. Over the course of the next 14 years, Catholic unionism grew in Quebec and by 1921 claimed 26,000 members organized in 96 *syndicats*. Endorsed by church and state, these workers, affiliated with the Confederation of Catholic Workers of Canada (Confédération des Travailleurs Catholiques du Canada — CTCC), initially formed a conservative and religiously ordered counterpart to both internationalism and socialism. Regionalism had become a potent source of fragmentation within the working class.

These forces of division weakened labour's capacity to resist monopoly capital. Its growing power and the repressive thrust of the state undermined workers' efforts to establish the unambiguous solidarity that was certainly required at this particular moment of crisis. Much of the cohesion within the working class that had developed in the late nineteenth century survived during the 1895–1919 period, albeit in different forms. But against the new initiatives of capital and the state, working-class unity did not prevail. Summer had passed, and an Indian Summer was about to give way to winter. The Canadian working class entered the 1920s defeated and fragmented. Clinging to legacies of the 1880s and 1919, its diverse cultures fought separate battles, instead of drawing on common experience. In the years to come, new developments would also erode the very substance of traditional working-class culture as a commercialized mass culture took root. And at the point of production, new assaults on the surviving remnants of working-class organization and mechanisms of self-defence were being mounted.

Chapter 5

Dissolution and Reconstitution, 1920–1939

> Whoever understands history even slightly knows that every revolution has provoked a subsequent counter-revolution.
>
> Leon Trotsky (1935)

The Social Formation

The 1920s and 1930s were monopoly capital's years of boom and bust, its moment of consolidation followed by deep crisis. World War I proved to be monopoly capital's "adolescence," separating out its years of maturity from those of its infancy. "Before 1914, business life was increasingly dominated by the close connections between finance and industrial capital, and by economic concentration and mass production." These methods were developed further in the late 1920s as Canada emerged from a postwar recession to take its place within the world capitalist order, a place that would be shown, in the collapse of 1929, to rest on a precariously unstable material foundation. The country and its working class were plunged into a depression both unexpected and unprecedented in its severity. The Liberal and Conservative parties retained their hold on the electorate, although new challenges arose in the form of third parties of dissent. But the forceful initiatives were taken by the Liberals, and Laurier was succeeded by the architect of class conciliation, William Lyon Mackenzie King. His term as prime minister — broken only briefly in the 1920s and early 1930s — provided labour with a promise of participation in decision making that would prove as hollow as it was appealing.

In the 1920s, new patterns of investment and corporate organization were pioneered, facilitating concentration not only of industry but also of chartered banking. Much of this activity centred on resource-based industrial development, the new staples of hydro-electricity and pulp and paper being of particular significance. The bases of many of Canada's contemporary corporate giants were laid in this decade:

especially noteworthy was the creation of a series of investment companies. Among the most powerful were the Brazilian Traction, Heat & Light Company (1912), Power Corporation (1925), and Alcan Aluminum Limited (1928). Such holding companies, as Jorge Niosi argues, provided one way of centralizing and concentrating economic power. Mergers presented another complementary path, and, beginning with the formation of the British Empire Steel Corporation in 1920, which amalgamated the coal and steel interests of Nova Scotia, the decade was dominated by a wave of industrial conglomerations. In the merger movement of 1924-30, 315 such mergers took place, involving firms with assets of nearly one billion dollars. Such concentration of economic power established monopoly as the dominant force within the economy, and in the next merger wave, the dimensions of concentration were substantially reduced. From 1931 to 1935 only 232 mergers involving less than $400 million in assets took place.

Much of the actual joining of corporate interests was orchestrated by financial intermediaries, investment houses such as Wood Gundy and Company or the chartered banks with which they were closely associated in de facto partnerships. Wood Gundy, for instance, "created" Canada Cement in 1927, Canada Power and Paper in 1928, Simpson's Limited, and the reorganized BESCO, or Dominion Steel Corporation, in 1928. Allied with the Royal Bank, Wood Gundy was represented on the boards of 50 of the largest Canadian corporations by J.H. Gundy and was at the centre of some of the most spectacular bankruptcies in the history of Canada when economic collapse took some of its offspring in the early 1930s. The banks, for their part, also concentrated their power, and from a high of 51 banks in 1874, declined in number to 36 by 1900 and a mere 11 in 1925. Three of the largest — the Royal Bank, the Bank of Montreal, and the Commerce — accounted for about 70 percent of banking resources in 1927, and in alliance with a range of investment houses, trust companies, life insurance companies, and industrial corporations, attained a previously unmatched consolidation of economic power and authority.

Concentrated forms of production stimulated real manufacturing output, which grew at a compound rate of four percent between 1919 and 1925 and at the exceptionally high level of 9.8 percent between 1926 and 1929. American capital flowed into Canada to exploit this economic potential until, in 1934, there were 1,350 U.S. firms operating within Canadian territory. Thirty-six percent of these corporations had been established between 1920 and 1929 and a further 26 percent in the years 1930-34. As a percentage of foreign investment in Canada, American capital more than doubled between 1913 and 1926, rising from 21.5 to 53 percent.

American capital was particularly active in resource-based production and in the new mass-production consumer-goods industries, epitomized by the wholesale control of Canadian automobile production by Ford and General Motors. In mining, American-dominated giants like the Sudbury-based International Nickel Company of Canada were products of the 1920s, and forest resources crossed the border at increasing rates to fulfill expanding needs. As the 1924 royal commission on pulpwood revealed, as much as 30 percent of particular regional timber lands were leased or owned by foreign capitalists, the bulk of them from the United States. Within the automobile industry — a symbol of the expanding production of the 1920s — Ford and General Motors were drawn to Canada to exploit domestic sales and to operate within the tariff walls of the British Empire, selling to overseas markets. By 1929, 250,000 cars were produced annually in Canada, of which 100,000 were exported. So pronounced was the American impact on the Canadian economy that by the 1930s U.S. capital controlled almost one-quarter of the manufacturing in Canada, and in automobiles (82 percent), electrical apparatus (68 percent), rubber goods (64 percent), machinery (42 percent), and chemicals (41 percent) the dominance was even more pronounced.

The combined processes of consolidation and Americanization of Canadian capitalism stimulated technological change and automation. In the 1930s, 30 percent of new mining equipment was imported, drawn largely from the United States. Because American investment was concentrated in large industrial firms capitalized at over $200,000, economies of scale were implemented freely, sustained by branch-plant profits between 1926 and 1933 of nearly $550,000,000. To compete with such giants, indigenous Canadian capital was also forced to modernize. Drawing upon new energy sources, especially hydro-electricity, the manufacturing sector expanded greatly. Between 1911 and 1931, the installation of electric motors in Canadian manufacturing establishments increased sixfold in Ontario and forty-fivefold in New Brunswick. Other innovations and developments — refrigeration, steel ships, rail and road penetration of the North, and the discovery of new mineral deposits — contributed to growth, pushing capital formation and Gross National Product to near-record highs in these years.

But for all this expansion, there were serious imbalances within Canada, as well as a critical lack of stability in the world capitalist order, which provided much-needed markets for Canadian exports. Domestically, the prairie wheat sector never recovered from the depressed prices of the postwar years, and was overextended well beyond levels sustainable by peacetime prices for foodstuffs. Cultivated acreage actually declined. In certain key sectors, central Canada produced 90 percent of net production, and within the Atlantic region the dislocations bred of shipbuilding's unambiguous collapse and of the weakness of the coal and steel industries were patently obvious by the late 1920s. Finance capital systematically underdeveloped the region and cultivated dependency on central Canadian needs: after 1928, Cape Breton was called upon to stock the national labour market and provide a reserve capacity for national energy and steel needs, while in the Maritimes as a whole, 42 percent of the region's manufacturing "disappeared" in the years 1920–25.

Built upon consumption and its seemingly endless elasticity, the economy of the 1920s was nearing its breaking point: overproduction seemed endemic, the overextension of credit an unhealthy indicator of the lack of stability in the "boom" of the twenties. The automobile companies of Windsor and Oshawa, for instance, were willing to drive 400,000 cars off the assembly lines in 1930, although Canadians already owned 1,000,000 cars and never, in any year, had more than a quarter million been sold. The beginnings of economic crisis appeared visible to some, even in the midst of a bloated prosperity. A reversal of twentieth-century population-movement trends resulted. Prior to 1920, 1,200,000 Americans had entered Canada from the United States as opposed to 900,000 Canadians who had emigrated south. But the 1920s saw a turnabout, with a drain of 700,000 to the United States.

International markets, too, had reached their limits and could no longer absorb Canadian goods: agricultural exports dropped in value from $780 million in 1928 to just $253 million by 1932. The world capitalist order, perched precariously on the edge of war debts and excessive supplies of primary products, took a turn downward in 1928/29. In Canada, where economic boom was heavily dependent upon such primary products, the effects of worldwide depression were felt immediately. Excess production had been the norm before 1930. In newsprint, for instance, the years 1913–20 and 1920–29 each saw production triple, with Canada producing 65 percent of the world's total, 90 percent of which went to the United States. After the downturn, such excess production was curtailed, regional economies abandoned, and workers thrown out of employment. The bubble of the 1920s had burst.

Within a few years, real GNP declined by almost 30 percent, the value of exports was reduced by 25 percent, new investment dropped to only slightly more than 10 percent of its 1929 level, and unemployment hovered around the 25 percent mark. More than one-tenth of the Canadian population was dependent upon relief. Diverse regional experiences led to a range of responses to crisis, but the Conservative and Liberal political leadership of the country offered little in the way of alleviation. R.B. Bennett presented his "Iron Heel" and then his "New Deal," while King preferred to retire behind constitutional questions or draw inspiration from criticizing Conservative failures. "King or Chaos," not a disciplined response to crisis, carried the Liberals to victory in 1935.

It was left to others — communists, social democrats, community groups, industrial unionists, relief advocates, the unemployed — to articulate new needs in the deteriorating context of the 1930s. That they did so only with modest success was in part a consequence of monopoly capital's unique capacity to undercut the foundations of solidarity. For it was during these years that the promise of the consumer society was first held before workers, a society based on a materialistic pluralism that broke down the class-based cultures of an earlier epoch. This initial influence of mass culture coincided easily with the fragmentation of working-class culture that had emerged between 1895 and 1919. Rooted in the false sense of prosperity of the 1920s, this promise of consumerism played a role in placating working people in these years of collapse. Moreover, it proceeded out of the routing of the workers' movement in the 1920s, a decade of antiunion violence, strikebreaking, wage reductions, and industrial paternalism. When depression struck with all its force in 1930/31, labour was stripped, in large measure, of its institutions and political traditions of radicalism.

Labour Defeated

Capital's relentless quest for hegemony quickened its pace in the early 1920s. Labour, at the centre of social and political life in 1919, seemed to take two steps backward for every forward leap taken by its adversary. Wage cuts, paternalistic schemes, technological/managerial change and increasing concentration of economic power left workers at the mercy of ever more powerful employers. With defeat after defeat, union membership declined precipitously, dropping from almost 380,000 in 1919 to 240,000 half a decade later. Membership in the Trades and Labor Congress of Canada fell from 173,463 in 1920 to a low of 103,037 in 1926. Established craft unions suffered severe setbacks, while in specific sectors — agricultural implements, meat packing, construction, and oil refining — industrial councils brought worker and employer representatives together in a Mackenzie King-inspired attempt to bypass traditional forms of worker organization and collectivity. Estimates from various sources indicate that between 145,000 and 200,000 workers were represented by such councils in the 1920s. The industrial council movement, closely associated with Canadian subsidiaries of American corporate giants such as Imperial Oil, International Harvester, Bell Telephone, Swift's, and Consolidated Rubber, also thrived among indigenous Canadian firms, especially at Massey–Harris in Toronto. Such businesses epitomized the open-shop tendencies of the day, and only encouraged labour's fortunes to decline.

Radicalism was on the wane, with the once influential Socialist Party of Canada defunct, and the advocate of industrial unionism, the One Big Union, slipping into obscurity. Although the OBU may well have drawn over 50,000 to its ranks in 1919, factionalism, repression, employer hostility, and depression eroded this strength until, in 1927, only 1,600 paid dues. Surviving well into the 1950s, the OBU was little more than a nominal presence.

It appeared that the strike was also about to go the way of radicalism, and militancy tapered off noticeably in the post-1919 climate of hard times and antagonism to job actions. In 1921, the Department of Labour reported more than 85 strikes against wage cuts, the bulk of them ending in defeat for labour. This set the stage for the twenties.

As Ian Angus and Stuart Jamieson have shown, if one takes the prewar years (1901–13) as a norm, comparing them to the years from 1922 to 1935, the number of strikes waged dropped, workers participating in strikes declined, and striker-days lost plummeted. Outside the coalfields, where the 1920s witnessed a series of violent confrontations, Canadian labour seemed submissive. It had been forced into quiescence. Between 1920 and 1932, according to the *Labour Gazette's* sometimes unreliable categorizations, 352 strikes were won by the working class, 549 were clear employer victories, and a further 346 were said to have ended in compromise, often a euphemism for a labour defeat. Even if "compromise" outcomes are regarded as a partial victory, workers lost 44 percent of all the strikes engaged in during these years. Noting that the vast majority of these battles were fought to resist wage cuts or to protect union status that had come under attack, it becomes obvious that strikes were often waged as defensive efforts to prevent substantial loss, rather than to strive for new gains. Clearly, this period was one of marked deterioration in labour's power. (See Table 5.1.)

Much of labour's defeat can be attributed to the particular social formation of the early 1920s, when monopoly capital had full control over Canadian workers. In this sense, defeat was a structural consequence of the increasing power of the employers, a power that was, for the most part, unmatched in working-class circles. An explanation of labour's defeat rests, therefore, on an appreciation of the initiatives taken by capital and sustained by the state, which became increasingly repressive with the creation of the Royal Canadian Mounted Police in the aftermath of the Winnipeg General Strike. A part of these initiatives were felt most acutely in the realm of culture, where older, community-based forms came under assault in the faint beginnings of the attempt to fashion attachment to the mass society. The working class was not only coerced into retreat; it was enticed into the classless cul-de-sac of consumption.

Mass Culture: The Fragmentation of Class

The character of mass culture and its impact on class relations remains an unstudied phenomenon, and much of what follows is inferential and speculative. But there can be no doubt that the 1920s saw the decisive

TABLE 5.1 Strike activity index, 1914–35 (1901–1913 = 100)

Year	Total all industries			All industries except Coal mining			Coal mining only		
	No. of strikes	No. of strikers	No. of workdays	No. of strikes	No. of strikers	No. of workdays	No. of strikes	No. of strikers	No. of workdays
1914	50	38	68	50	34	50	45	60	93
1915	50	44	13	45	41	20	134	65	4
1916	95	102	33	94	72	39	119	266	24
1917	127	195	155	117	155	127	313	410	193
1918	183	309	117	154	267	122	183	540	43
1919	267	577	468	265	652	713	299	223	126
1920	256	234	110	241	227	165	522	267	33
1921	134	109	144	133	126	240	149	32	10
1922	83	170	210	67	81	172	313	583	263
1923	68	133	92	53	63	88	343	458	99
1924	56	133	178	46	61	49	224	467	359
1925	69	112	164	59	48	36	253	411	343
1926	60	92	37	51	72	55	239	186	12
1927	57	86	21	45	27	23	299	367	18
1928	76	68	31	70	59	32	208	111	29
1929	70	50	21	69	47	83	119	67	2
1930	53	53	13	44	35	16	224	137	8
1931	68	42	28	66	40	46	134	47	4
1932	88	91	35	70	70	29	493	70	44
1933	97	103	40	87	110	67	313	67	11
1934	150	177	79	138	161	114	388	252	30
1935	95	129	40	76	128	53	253	135	22

SOURCE: Ian Angus, *Canadian Bolsheviks: The Early Years of the Communist Party of Canada* (Montreal: Vanguard, 1981), 135.

shattering of old cultural modes, and their replacement by a range of cultural activities that redefined experience in such a way as to undercut the vitality of working-class experience. By the 1920s the material foundations of the localized and often class-based cultures of an earlier epoch were being undermined by new products, concentrated control, the expansion of urban markets, and monopoly capital's campaign to profit from marketable forms of culture. Culture, once based in social group or community experience, was in the throes of transformation: spectator sports, the rise of the mass media, and the power to overcome distance transformed culture into a purchasable commodity. Throughout these years the collective endeavours that had formed the foundation of nineteenth-century working-class culture were replaced by privatized forms of leisure, which increasingly turned on the purchase of a particular commodity. In spite of its capacity to reach and exploit huge markets, mass culture was an individualized activity that moved workers away from social interaction and into the confines of the unit of consumption, the nuclear family.

In order to integrate a stratum of Canadian workers into the margins of consumer capitalism, it would be necessary to increase the disposable income of the family and to provide sufficient leisure time to allow numbers of workers to divert earnings previously earmarked for basic necessities into new realms of consumption. Specific reforms establishing old age pensions and allowances to the blind, to widowed mothers and to orphans undoubtedly secured, for some working-class families, a portion of income once diverted to needy relatives. Minimum wage legislation for women and children may have buttressed the family wage. Shorter hours — the eight-hour day became the norm in many sectors — allowed at least some industrial workers time to consume. To be sure, the 1920s was hardly a decade of unambiguous advance, as Leonard Marsh pointed out in a pioneering 1931 survey and Terry Copp has recently reiterated in his study of Montreal. Real wages did not rise dramatically. But if a series of studies poses contradictory assessments of the material well-being of the class, a trend does seem clear.

Average wage rates across the industrial spectrum peaked in 1920 and, according to statistics compiled by Urquhart and Buckley, reached a point not surpassed until 1940. Purchasing power, low in the spiralling inflation of 1919/20, began an ascent in the recession of 1921 and continued to climb in the prosperous early-to-mid-1920s, plateauing during the latter half of the decade. By 1928 it was possible, for the first time, for the average male manufacturing worker to raise a family on his wages alone, while it was only in the 1920s that the average woman worker rose above a starvation wage and status of dependency. As figures from the *Labour Gazette* indicate, the cost of the weekly family budget, computed on the basis of average prices in 60 Canadian cities, dropped from over $26.00 in November 1920 to just over $21.00 in

November 1927. Nevertheless, these averages distort as much as they reveal, and while the material well-being of the working class as a whole advanced in the 1920s, considerable numbers of people suffered decline. In 1929, it was estimated that a family of four needed $1,200 to $1,500 to survive in minimum comfort, but 60 percent of Canadian working men and 82 percent of labouring women earned less than $1,000 yearly. The family wage was still likely crucial if working people were to get a grip on even a small piece of the promise of mass culture. Too much stock cannot be placed in these and other available figures, then, but on balance it does appear that workers likely found their disposable incomes increasing over the 1920s, especially in the "flush" years of 1923 to 1925, a development that was paralleled by escalating productivity of labour and capital and rising real Gross National Product.

Moreover, even if the economic collapse and unemployment of the thirties made a mockery of working-class purchasing power for thousands, those fortunate enough to have work continued to be influenced by the consumer society. Drastic cuts in wages were outpaced by price declines that resulted from decreased demand for goods. As a consequence, real wages may well have risen; from 1929 to 1933 money wages declined by 14 percent, but the cost-of-living index fell by almost 22 percent. Goods which had cost $10.00 in 1926 could be purchased for $7.50 six years later. Some employees, such as full-time civil servants, actually saw their standard of living increase by as much as 25 percent during these years.

It was because of these developments that the 1920s witnessed increasing expenditure on a wide range of consumer goods: automobiles and radios, household appliances and furnishings, and less durable commodities in the entertainment field. Per-capita consumption of automobiles in Canada was second only to that in the United States, and Canadian production surpassed that of the United Kingdom and of major western European countries such as Germany and France. Almost one in seven Canadians over the age of 14 owned a car by 1930, and although the bulk of such automobile purchasers were not workers, many of them must have been. The automobile craze, accelerated by easy credit, declining costs of products and fuel, and suburban expansion, helped to transform the nature of working-class experience. It separated work and leisure decisively and structured working-class life in new ways. No longer did workers necessarily have to congregate in neighbourhoods near their jobs, ride to work on the same streetcars, or travel to outings, sporting affairs, or holiday excursions in large groups on rented railway cars or teamster-driven waggons. Instead, some could travel to and from such events in their own car, with their own families. Often they withdrew from participation to savour the more private joys of a family picnic.

The radio served a similar function, and contributed to the breakdown of localized participation sports like baseball that thrived upon specific neighbourhood rivalries, work-related cultures, and class allegiances. Union leagues, common at the turn of the century, survived, and in some centres baseball teams even preserved a class character rooted in the 1880s but transformed by new ideological currents and economic developments. On Hamilton's "Mountain," the all-star team was an independent group called the "Marxian Youth." But this was a rare occurrence, and company leagues, part of capital's paternalistic conquest of working-class initiative, were more common. As radio began to broadcast professional events, sports like baseball and boxing became less class and local oriented and more mass directed. Radio drew large numbers of listeners around the family table or living-room mantel to hear of the conquests of Jack Dempsey, Gene Tunney, Babe Ruth, and numerous other athletic celebrities who were becoming known across the continent.

Mass culture was thus developing from the same concentration and Americanization that dominated the economy as a whole. Radio emerged immediately after World War I, and particularly in border cities, on the prairies, and along the St. Lawrence–Great Lakes System, American broadcasting was heard. Most of the stations were owned by powerful newspaper companies like the *Toronto Star* and *La Presse*, and like the papers, took much of their news reporting from U.S.-based services like Reuters or Associated Press, even as early as 1923. As a result, radio stations resisted attempts in the late 1920s and 1930s to initiate public regulation. A nascent Canadian film industry was quickly eclipsed in the 1920s by American production, and with the rise of Hollywood in the 1930s, the collapse of any Canadian film industry that existed was assured. As early as 1919, similar trends within the sphere of mass-circulation magazines roused the ire of Canadian nationalists. Over 300 such American magazines inundated Canada in the 1920s, led by the immensely popular *Ladies' Home Journal*, *Saturday Evening Post*, and *McCalls*. "The mentality and morale of impressionable young Canadians is being merged in the reeking cloud of lower Americanism," complained the *Vancouver Star*, "Something should be done to dam this trash flowing over the border." Government tariffs, the "high" culture nationalism of painters associated with the Group of Seven, and efforts of the Canadian Authors' Association did little to stem the tide of mass culture sweeping into Canada. American publishers and film producers simply jumped the tariff wall and found a ready audience among Canadians.

This commercialization and diversification of culture necessarily affected the character of working-class life and consciousness. Workers in the 1880s had cultivated an associational network deeply connected with the realities of work, but by the 1920s, radio, automobile, and increased levels of disposable income undercut the experience of collectivity. It was replaced with individualized family-centred activity, emphasizing classless concerns, consumption of consumer goods, and freedom of movement that led workers beyond the earlier confines within which work or neighbourhood allegiances had been conditioned. The more economically and socially privileged Canadian workers — the English-speaking skilled stratum — probably reaped the benefits of these developments along with some semiskilled workers. Immigrants, however, were largely excluded from the luxuries of mass culture, occupying, as they did, the lower rungs of the wage hierarchy. But they could, by ruthless underconsumption and communal pooling of resources and skills, acquire their own homes. Tightly knit ethnically homogeneous communities thus evolved, further separating the English-speaking and the non-English-speaking, widening rifts that had first appeared in the post-1900 years and nativist upsurge of World War I.

By the 1920s, the fragmentation of the working class had proceeded well beyond that of the 1895–1920 period: ethnic workers gathered on their porches, native Canadians huddled around the first automobile purchased on their block, older workers listened to the radio, and younger members of the working class read mass-circulation magazines at their lunchbreaks and danced at night to the sound of American bands. With working-class institutions like the union, the Labour Church, and the radical club no longer at the centre of social and cultural life, and with employers quick to deride the accomplishments of collectivity, mass culture and corporate strategies combined to stress acquisition and individualism. All of this made organization and the development of working-class political opposition much more difficult than in the past. Further problems emerged out of that perennial point of division: gender.

Women of the New Day

The 1920s have often been viewed as bringing in a new day for women in general and for women workers in particular. Suffrage agitation, largely a middle-class activity but drawing working-class advocates such as Flora MacDonald Denison and Helena Gutteridge to the cause of votes for women, developed from the 1880s and peaked in the World War I years, winning women the franchise. Women workers entered new jobs during the war years, helping to fight the battle for production and widening women's access to employment for a brief period. "The great increase in the number of women employed during the first decade of the century dipped over the years 1910–20, but increased again in the 1920s, when the percentage of women over the age of ten in the total labour force rose from 15.5 to 17 percent. Old trends continued, however, and 90 percent of the women engaged in wage labour were single. Nevertheless, married and divorced women gradually entered the labour market, comprising roughly 17 to 20 percent of female workers. As Mary Vipond has shown, mass circulation magazines depicted great transformation in the role of women, and in the legislative sphere, provincial minimum wage laws affecting women were passed in seven provinces between 1917 and 1920. But appearances proved deceiving. Women's working lives were modernized, and the processes of innovation, concentration of capital, and mass culture's expanding workforce led to more opportunities for women in the clerical, service, and sales spheres. Nevertheless, working women still suffered from lower pay, marginal status, and subordination to patriarchal authority. They also remained outside the mainstream of unionism, with one superficial assessment of their organizational potential claiming that they did not "seem to possess that spirit of solidarity characteristic of men in industry."

The emerging mass culture was itself a factor of considerable importance in the development of female employment ghettoes. Domestic labour, almost the sole service employment for women in the late nineteenth-century, was supplemented by waitressing, as the number of restaurants proliferated in the 1920s. Between 1919 and 1929, the number of telephones in Canada doubled, creating new employment opportunities for female operators, who were often judged to be suitably malleable material for efficiency-conscious bureaucrat-run corporations like Bell Telephone and Maritime Telephone and Telegraph. At these companies, employee "team spirit" was cultivated in the interest of profit. Marketing innovations, especially the growth of chain drug and grocery stores such as Loblaws and Tamblyns and the continued expansion of mail-order department stores, also attracted women to wage labour, although it locked them into menial sales positions. Among typists, stenographers, and female clerks in the federal government this structured inequality was also an unwritten rule of the workplace. In many of these occupational settings, as Veronica Strong-Boag's recent depiction suggests, the social relations of production were privatized, subject to an authoritative male supervision, and conventionally defined as temporal due to the single "girl's" tendency to flee wage labour upon marriage, assuming woman's proper station of wife and mother. Such was not the stuff of which unions or persistent resistance were built.

In manufacturing there was a greater trend toward collectivity, as women reacted sporadically to the conditions prevailing in the low-wage competitive sectors of clothing, textiles, and food processing, among others. But a multitude of forces served to undercut solidarity. Caught between innovating employers and craftsmen who were especially protective of their jobs because of threats of dilution and displacement, women were often barred from skilled, well-paid employment.

This did not, of course, mean that resistance on the part of women was impossible, simply that it was less visible than even the modest challenge raised by male workers. Strikes, though far from common, were an indication of growing resentments. Textile workers in Stratford (1921), waitresses in Calgary (1923), match workers in Hull (1924), cotton mill workers near Welland (1924), telephone operators in Halifax (1925), and knitters in Hamilton (1928) were but some of the female strikers of the decade. As women workers faced scabs, hostile foremen, police, and hired thugs, they were not reluctant to use physical force, and in a 1926 Monteal Amalgamated Clothing Workers strike, four teenaged girls were charged with assaulting a constable. At E.B. Eddy's match company in Hull, striking women employees were dismissed as the corporation shifted its operations to a Deseronto plant, a tactic available to mobile and diversified monopolies. Their response was to seize, push, jostle, and hit a manager and, after some time, they resecured their positions, although their demands that forewomen be hired and union activity allowed were eventually denied. Other struggles turned on women's attempts to resist managerial authority, and in 1929, female employees struck Hamilton Canadian Cottons Limited so that "things [would] be like they were before the efficiency experts came along and changed them." Such collective challenges to capital may well have been buttressed by individual acts of sabotage, absenteeism, and worker turnover, but in the end they more often than not came to little.

The working women of the new day thus found themselves facing limited horizons. Conditions at a wide range of work settings were either hygienically deplorable, as in the case of many industrial factories, or routinized, as in the case of clerical/communications work. Regardless of whether women worked in service, manufacturing, or commerce and finance, they found themselves assigned to the lower rungs of particular job hierarchies; advance to positions of authority or skill was a most uncommon development. Wage discrimination was notorious to the point of being institutionalized: between 1921 and 1931, women sold their labour power for 54 to 60 percent of the male "price," revealing a structured continuity in inequality that reached back into the nineteenth century. Even with legislative reforms on the issue of minimum wages, few gains were recorded, so obdurate were the companies and so poorly informed and ill-protected the woman worker. As Strong-Boag concludes, in the 1920s "sexist discrimination remained an integral feature of economic organization, however modern."

Although this did not cause female workers to become passive and acquiescent, it did condition a measure of escapism that was encouraged by aspects of the new mass culture of the time. Dances like the

Blackbottom or the Charleston were a way of relieving the drudgery of alienated labour, while "in a dress factory" conversations might turn, not on the union or radical politics, but on "dress and boys and movies all day long." After work, "the girls all fix[ed] themselves up, the paint and powder [was] put on thick, and they pretend[ed] not to be working girls." This had always been a part of the working woman's experience, from the first Lowell mill girls to the operatives of the 1880s. But in times past, the sheer quantity of consumer goods and activities had been much restricted, and the overwhelming influence of the mass media literally nonexistent. Worker organizations like the Knights of Labor, with their soirees, dances and musical entertainments had supplied a culture that young working women found nowhere else—a culture in which a message of reform and the need for leisure came together. By the 1920s, the Knights of Labor no longer existed, and many of the new cultural pursuits available played no part in raising women's consciousness of their place as workers. For another segment of the working class, the facade of mass culture and the restrictions of dependency were of little concern. Coal miners, working in an industry facing constant crisis, found the 1920s a period during which they were forced to battle for their very lives.

Blood, Guts, and Culture on the Coal

"Blood on the coal" was a gruesome reality for Canadian miners. It shaped attitudes toward the operators and conditioned a particular defiance in union workers, who fought to win "compensation fully compatible with the dangers of our occupation." Between 1871 and 1939, more than 1,600 men were killed in Nova Scotia mines, while in Alberta, over 1,000 died in the years 1905–45. Given the dangers of mining, the impossibility of rigid supervision, and the negligible impact of machines in the mines, coal miners cultivated a pride in their work and a code of ethics that followed class lines. "We built up a certain pride. This is mine. This is my section of the mine," recalled one Cape Breton miner. In Alberta and Cape Breton coalfields in the opening decades of the twentieth century, this pride was centred in the rise of effective unionism. By 1917 in Nova Scotia and by 1920 in Alberta, the United Mine Workers of America represented coal miners in the east and in the west: the history of this ascendancy was not always an honourable one, and in Alberta it had been generated in a conspiratorial drubbing of the One Big Union that involved the federal government, the coal barons, and the international officers of the UMWA. To the east, nothing this sordid had taken place (the international union's moment of disgrace would come later, in 1923/24), although the rise of the UMWA involved a contentious jurisdictional battle between the militant international union and the more collaborationist remnants of the old, and thoroughly discredited, Provincial Workmen's Association.

Recent histories of mine workers in the 1920s by David Frank and Allen Seager provide rare insight into the complex interaction of economic factors, cultural traditions, and ideological currents in the battles of the 1920s. For if the rest of Canadian labour was in retreat, the coal miners refused to capitulate in the face of employer hostility and the weakening of the industry. Coal mining accounted for almost 17 percent of all strikes in the 1920s, 49 percent of strike participants, and 52.5 percent of striker-days lost across the country.

The miners could not have chosen a more inopportune time, in terms of traditional collective bargaining moments, to wage their fight. Just as a rejuvenated miners' movement peaked, the coal market became saturated, and by the end of the 1920s the coal miners' movement was in disarray. Oil and electricity were replacing coal, and marginal mines, thrust into production in World War I, were closing. Prices for coal dropped 50 percent between 1920 and 1929.

Overproduction in American fields resulted in the flooding of central Canadian markets in the immediate aftermath of World War I. Cape Breton's traditional markets were virtually captured by competitors, and inadequate tariff protection and high transportation costs ensured that throughout the 1920s Nova Scotia coal sales would be undercut by an unstable market. Production and miner-days worked in Nova Scotia fields dipped 33 percent between 1917 and 1921. The newly created, financially unstable BESCO and its Montreal-based magnate, Roy ("the Wolf") Wolvin, sought to break out of this impasse by making wage cuts, workers' pay comprising 60 percent of production costs at the time. When BESCO negotiated its first contract with 12,000 employees in 1921/22, it proposed a 33 percent wage reduction, setting the stage for four major strikes that would total almost 2,150,000 miner-days of strike activity. Indeed, as Frank notes, these were years of constant confrontation, and between 1917 and 1926, at least 64 strikes were fought by the miners over wages, political concerns, the status of the union, the length of the workday, and a range of other issues that included the right to celebrate May Day or take one-day holidays to "discuss" questions of vital importance to the mining community. Out of this context of conflict surfaced workplace militancy that embraced the mundane slowdowns in the form of restriction of output, as well as more spectacular actions such as the 100 percent strike. Motivated by radical ideas extending from moderate labourism to Bolshevism, the miners demanded workers' control, fought battles against the international union bureaucracy, and assaulted the "pluck-me" stores. Community solidarity was pitted strongly against corporate arrogance and economic might.

Antagonism grew, not only at the coal face, but on a foundation of traditional cultural attachments enriched by more recently established institutions, ideologies, and practices. While the Cape Breton fields were not ethnically homogeneous, they were dominantly Scots Catholic, and miners drawn from other national/ethnic backgrounds had been assimilated into the local milieu to some extent by the 1920s. The Scottish moral and clan tradition translated into the miners' collective condemnation of the "tyranny" and "slavery" to which they were subjected. Although a devout people, these Scots Catholics were disappointed in the established churches' ties to the corporations and, although they remained members of the church, they distanced themselves from those clergymen who appeared too willing to subordinate miners' needs and aspirations to company profits and policies. Drawing upon religious commitments, the *Maritime Labour Herald* proclaimed its 1922 "Christmas Message": "The social revolution is the economic fulfillment of the gospel message."

Oral traditions reinforced this essential process of cultural adaptation and, like forms of struggle at the point of production, embraced subtle and ironic methods of rebellion as well as more unambiguous and open revolt. In a society comprised of Scots with similar or identical surnames, nicknames, for instance, might reflect grievances with the wage and its injustice, as well as a means of identification. Sandy MacDonald found one payday that, after a series of company deductions, he had collected a mere two pennies. "Did you have a good pay?" he was asked. "Well, yes," came his sardonic reply, "I had a very big pay." When the miners told this story, Sandy was popularly christened "Big Pay" and his sons the "Big Pay" MacDonalds. More direct means of political expression also emerged out of the oral tradition as militant poets and storytellers like Dawn Fraser championed the people's interests in epics that might arouse the class passions of thousands of discontented miners. Bitter in his denunciation of that "monster," BESCO, Fraser wrote lines of condemnation in the near-starvation conditions of the winter of 1924/25:

> When the mines closed down that winter
> He had nothing left to eat,
> And he starved, he starved, I tell you,
> On your dirty, damned street.

Fraser's "The Case of Jim McLachlan" chronicled the "dark and dismal days of old" (it was supposedly recounted to children in 1994), when "the world and all was ruled by Gold," closing with a class exhortation:

> Bend, Labor, bend; pick up your cross;
> Bend, break and bleed to feed the Boss;
> Bend, break and bleed? Ah, damn it, NO!
> Fight on, fight on, let's go, LET'S GO!!

The solidarity reflected in these cultural traditions helped to sustain

Cape Breton miners over the course of mass struggles that ended in defeat in 1923–25 when the international union challenged the district's right to strike, suspended its autonomy, and removed its radical and popular leadership. Violent clashes between strikers and scabbing maintenance workers and police polarized the community in a 1923 strike called in sympathetic support of striking Sydney steel workers. It ended in a show of the armed and legalistic might that monopoly capital could use to suppress worker dissent. The miners' president Dan Livingstone and its secretary-treasurer J.B. McLachlan were arrested, and the latter was tried and convicted for seditious libel. McLachlan's jailing and the crushing of the union reinforced corporate arrogance, epitomized in Wolvin's contemptuous challenge that the miners could not "stand the gaff." But stand it they did, even to defeat, and Wolvin and BESCO, after riding the union into the ground in 1925, succumbed to bankruptcy in 1928. At this point, the coal industry in Cape Breton was able to survive only on government subsidies.

Unlike the Cape Breton mining community, the Crow's Nest Pass was not dominated by any single ethnic group. The coal towns of Alberta and southeastern British Columbia had taken in a great part of the mass immigration of 1895–1919. Coal communities like those at Blairmore, Drumheller, or Hillcrest were populated mostly by European peasants, many of whom, before coming to Canada, had "never [seen] a mine in their life . . . ." This ethnic diversity, in which Anglo-Saxon workers rarely comprised more than 25 percent of the mining workforce, created some of the fragmentation that led to the dissolution of working-class unity. Immigrants were commonly employed as strikebreakers. However, the widespread impact of the OBU in the western coalfields, did play a part in the upheaval of 1919, establishing support for the slogan, "No Alien but the Capitalist." Out of the immigrant cultures, the coal miners fashioned class purpose and forms of resistance that would help to sustain them through years of battle, from 1922 to 1926.

United Mine Workers' District 18, like the Nova Scotia District 26, was the centre of a series of bitter disputes in the years 1922–26, as class war erupted in the coal-mining west. In a district-wide strike in 1922, western coal miners joined forces with their brothers in Nova Scotia and the United States, taking 500,000 North American miners out of the pits. A seven-month battle followed, lasting from April to October 1924. Led by the United Mine Workers of America, these struggles, like those to the east, were mounted to oppose proposed wage cuts (of 50 percent) designed to buttress a declining industry. Involving 8,000 to 10,000 miners, the constant confrontation in the mining west came to a head in the 1924 strike, which saw the usual opposition to the companies complicated by worker resentment of the international union's conciliatory tactics and refusal to endorse the 100 percent strike that would include the withdrawal of maintenance men and thus threaten the property holdings of the owners. With militant miners parading under banners adorned with the hammer and sickle, proclaiming, "NO SURRENDER, NATIONALIZATION OF THE MINES," the UMWA literally abandoned the district; by the end of 1925 the international, where it survived, was little more than a "company union," and the name of its leader, John L. Lewis, a dirty word in "wild rose country."

Defeated or not, the radicalism and solidarity of the coalfields had served as an impressive demonstration of the miners' fighting capacity. Against the drift towards fragmentation and acquiescence, western miners, like their eastern counterparts, forged a movement of alternative that proceeded from work-related experience and grievance, but became consolidated within the community. Exploring the fabric of this experience has led Allen Seager to conclude that "a real flowering of genuine proletarian culture" took place in Alberta's coal towns in the 1920s. The Women's Labour League in Drumheller established childcare facilities "free from bourgeois influence," while meetings, boxing matches, and poetry recitals in the district brought together English, Irish, French, Scots, Italians and Ukrainians.

Thus, miners in east and west differed from other workers at the time in that they comprised a front that battled capital at the point of production. They were also culturally distinct from their contemporaries. As part of a community under seige, the miners could not afford to participate in the emerging mass culture. Their cultural activities — building and filling halls, reading and writing poetry, even coining nicknames — were natural extensions of their class experience and struggle, rather than consumerist means of escape. Leisure was characterized by collective creativity and, as in a similar moment of cultural achievement in the 1880s, the outcome was one of integrating aspects of the dominant culture, such as religious beliefs, the status of women, and the place of education and literacy into the purposes of the class. Culture was thus intimately linked with class experience in the mining community, and, unlike so many other working-class sectors in the 1920s, the coal miners believed and acted as if "the capitalist system as they knew it was coming to an end."

This was a product of exploitation in the mines, of course, but it was also a consequence of oppression in the cultural sphere, and efforts to overcome it. A part of such opposition was generated spontaneously, out of the conditions of existence. But much was also orchestrated by class leaders, and the miners, more than any other working-class group, were led by a new breed of radical, the communist. A Finnish-Canadian miner's wife recalled her "moving" introduction to the Finnish Socialist Organization, when she first sang the *International*. May Day paraders in Glace Bay marched under "the biggest red flag in Canada" (20 feet by 12 feet) and slogans like, "Workers of the World, Unite" and "Long Live Communism." Communism entered the culture of Canadian workers most vibrantly in these years of the 1920s, when, in the context of labour's defeat, the left-wing of the workers' movement consolidated, challenging capital at the very height of its power.

Communism

Communism developed surreptitiously in Canada, forced underground by the repressive and nativist assault on radicalism and the "Red Scare" of 1919. Born of industrial crisis in Canada, the convergence of various radical streams previously allied with other organized constituencies, and the example of the Russian Bolshevik Revolution, Canada's first communists put forward a seven-point program on 30 April 1919. Calling for "the forcible seizure of the governmental power and the establishment of the dictatorship of the proletariat," they advocated the confiscation of private property, the destruction of capitalist institutions, and worker control of society. "Your only hope lies in revolution — the sweeping away of this rotten system of exploitation," their clandestinely distributed leaflet proclaimed. "You must achieve a victory over the capitalist class so that you can celebrate May Day along with your fellow-workers in Russia." This communist message was delivered to working-class neighbourhoods, not in the radical west or the militant coal towns, but in Montreal and in southern Ontario industrial centres.

After overcoming some initial factionalism and organizational divisions, a secret convention of communists met near Guelph, Ontario, in 1921 to formally constitute the Communist Party of Canada (CPC). Among the early figures of Canadian communism were Mathew Popowich and John Navisisky of the Ukrainian Labor Temple Association in Winnipeg; John Ahlqvist and John Latva of the Canadian Finnish Organization; the patternmaker and archetypal proletarian, "Moscow Jack" MacDonald of Toronto; an Irish-born lithographer, Tom Bell, once affiliated with Ontario's Socialist Party of North America; Bill Moriarty, an English emigrant and one of the first SPC members to join the communist movement; former SPNA founder and school teacher, Florence Custance; and the leading intellectual, Maurice Spector. Spector was only 23 at the time of the Guelph meeting, but he was already a theoretician of stature who had been a member of the Young Socialist League (the SDP's youth section), a contributor to socialist newspapers, a student activist and editor of the *Toronto Varsity*, and an early advocate of the United Communist Party of America. Joined by a committed core of other early communists, among them the machinist and future party head Tim Buck, this body of working-class advocates took the message of communism "to the masses" in the early-to-mid-1920s. To better reach a large constituency, they created a legal party, the Workers Party of Canada, and established a newspaper, *The Worker*. The underground apparatus simply fell into disuse. While its membership consisted of 4,800, the bulk being affiliated with foreign-langauge federations, the Workers Party exerted an influence within the Canadian working class far out of proportion to its small numbers.

Communists were active in the Canadian Labor Party, contributing to municipal campaigns in Toronto, Vancouver, and elsewhere, and by early 1923 had won the Workers Party provincial affiliation in Quebec, Ontario, and Alberta. For three years, they offered a vocal and substantial opposition to conservative craft union leadership within the Trades and Labor Congress of Canada, opposing the presidency of Tom Moore. In 1923/24, Workers Party presidential candidates at the annual TLC conventions received approximately 25 percent of the vote. They drew upon the old OBU constituency, the artisan-immigrant quarters of cities, and the coal towns of Districts 18 and 26, which they virtually controlled in the embattled years of 1922/23. In Nova Scotia, Tom Bell edited the *Maritime Labor Herald*, while J.B. McLachlan and "Red Dan" Livingstone led the miners toward affiliation with the Red International of Labor Unions and strong statements of political purpose: "We proclaim openly to all the world that we are out for a complete overthrow of the capitalist system and capitalist state, peaceably if we may, forcibly if we must, and we call on all workers, soldiers, and minor law officers in Canada to join us in liberating labour." As McLachlan was railroaded to prison and District 26's UMWA charter revoked by the international office, a Cape Breton communist and former prize fighter, Lewis MacDonald, led Drumheller's miners in a sympathetic work stoppage. Known as "Kid Burns," MacDonald was both a communist and a nativist; he epitomized the strength and weakness of the class in these years. It was his radicalism and his atheism, however, in conjunction with assault charges stemming from a 1925 strike confrontation, that earned him incarceration in 1926. Further to the west, the Workers Party gained access to the important voice of British Columbia's workers, the *B.C. Federationist*, and although control of this paper produced serious divisions and unhappy political consequences, it did speak of the Communist impact in trade-union circles.

As labour across Canada retreated, as the coal miners suffered defeat, and as cautious practice and conservative ideas gained widespread credence in restricted groups within trade-union circles, the ethnic communists turned inward. In the early period of Communist Party development, as Ian Angus shows, the autonomy allowed the foreign-language sections permitted such development. The Canadian movement itself was also distant from movements in other parts of the world, as it struggled to devise tactics and a strategy that would implant communism within the consciousness and activities of Canadian workers. But in the years 1923–29, the Communist International experienced a profound Stalinization, and communist parties around the world were subordinated to the needs of "socialism in one country."

The potential of the early 1920s, fading in the face of domestic circumstances that were anything but propitious, was further undermined by Moscow-conceived policies and directives that stripped the Canadian Communist Party of its independence, casting a competent leader aside, and submerging the movement in a sectarianism that alienated it from the ranks of labour and much of its membership. The beneficiary of this development was Tim Buck, whose ascent to the leadership of the party was accompanied by the creation of a "cult of the personality," and the expulsion and slandering of leaders like Spector, MacDonald, and Custance. But the most emphatic loss of this period, concentrated in the years 1928–31, was that of many ethnic members and their loyalties to communism. Under attack by the Comintern since 1925, these groups were supposedly enclaves of "opportunism, federalism, and nationalism," and the word came to the Canadian Party that communist work must be based on occupation rather than language. As the central proponent of this new line, Buck earned little respect among the party's Ukrainians, Finns, and Jews, and demands were made that he be removed from the leadership. The tension within party circles mounted in 1928, as Stalin predicted the imminent collapse of the capitalist world order and called for immediate working-class mobilization, thereby implicitly challenging the very right of ethnic language sectors within the Canadian movement to exist. Such "Bolshevization" drew its blood in 1929, as numbers of Finns were suspended and others left the party in disgust. By 1930, the Comintern's position on "Bolshevization" had stiffened, Ukrainian and Jewish comrades were hostile to the leadership, and the foreign-language associations were saved only by ethnic leaders' recantations. These hollow confessions of "guilt" acted only as a cover-up of the internal crisis of the party, and left a residue of suspicion and hostility among the remaining ethnic communists. The fragmentation of class, once superseded by communists, rose to the surface again.

This crisis was a product of the so-called "Third Period" of the international communist movement, although it originated in the mid-1920s. Prior to 1928, the Party had been engaged in "mass propaganda, maintaining and broadening the party contact with the masses, preparing and training the reserves of the working class and educating the party cadres." But between 1928 and 1935, the communist leadership stressed that the radicalization of the masses was now a fact of social and political life, and that the task before workers was to foment revolution. "Little do [people] realize," said Stewart Smith, an early Buck ally and recent graduate of Moscow's Lenin School, "that in a very short time the streets in Toronto will be running with blood." Communist strategy thus centred on the creation of dual unions, the conquest of the streets (where much communist and workers' blood indeed would flow), and a divisive assault on social democracy and reformism within the workers' movement. In this period of revolutionary posturing, much was lost on the cultural front, as well as in the industrial and political realms. These were years that set the stage for the acceptance of the irrational, for blind faith in the "line," however far removed from Canadian reality it may have been. They served as an introduction to the drastic shifts in communist policy resulting from the wartime needs of the Soviet Union. As such they have presented historians with ample ammunition to disparage and discredit the entire communist experience, to denigrate the accomplishments of rank-and-file communists, and to erase the achievements of militancy, struggle, and resistance from the pages of Canadian history. But an examination of the depression years — the struggles of the unemployed and of industrial unionists — will point to a more favourable part of the communist record.

Working against Not Working

The economic collapse that was underway in 1929 reached its lowest point in 1932/33, and among Canadians, the wheat farmers of the drought-stricken prairie west, the marginal small business people, the young with no employment possibilities, and the working class, especially those without skills, suffered the most. Statistics reveal much, but convey only a sense of the dimensions of the problem, and are subject to great variation because of the lack of uniformity in their essential foundations and definitions.

From any point of view, however, the assessment is the same: more Canadians were out of work during the 1930s than at any previous time. Over the course of the entire decade conservative estimates placed the unemployed at ten percent of all wage earners. The winter months of 1933 were the worst, and figures compiled for the prime minister stated that over 32 percent of all wage earners were without work. Almost 20 percent of the *total* civilian labour force was unemployed. By 1937, such compilations revealed a drop in these unprecedented rates of unemployment, with 12.5 percent of wage earners looking for jobs; but in 1938/39 the figures rose once more. Not until the war machinery was in high gear in the early 1940s did unemployment cease to be a problem. The capitalist order overcame one moment of crisis only when another was substituted.

These measures of unemployment were reflected in similar statistics revealing dimensions of workers' economic dependency. The most important data centres on the massive numbers of people who could not survive from one year to the next without public aid. Between 1933 and 1936, about 12 percent of all Canadians received emergency relief, while another five percent relied upon charitable aid, mother's allowances, or old age pensions. More than 1.5 million were reduced to the humiliation of state dependency; this, in a total population of ten million. Charlotte Whitton, of the Canadian Welfare Council, estimated that in 1935, 1.9 million were public dependents, roughly 20 percent of the entire population. As one authority, Leonard Marsh, commented at the end of the decade, the fine distinction between unemployed and unemployable had become increasingly obscure.

Yet little was actually done to confront the vast problem of unemployment and deteriorating standards of life. In the cities, single men were often not entitled to relief (in Kingston, for instance, the unmarried were eligible for only one day of relief, enough, presumably, to let them leave town). Moreover, in many municipalities, such as Montreal, married and unmarried relief applicants were required to establish proof of consecutive residence in the city of six months to three years. Other barriers were also erected, in what appeared to be almost a deliberate attempt to keep the indigent away from relief offices and off of relief rolls. Montreal, for instance, restructured its relief apparatus three times between 1931 and 1937. In Kingston, a public clamour initiated by the *Whig-Standard* secured the dismissal of a relief officer who was a former labourer. In his stead, a "concerned" public placed an army major, whose military background, it was claimed, suited him well to the role of dispenser of relief.

Strict controls were developed within which relief "benefits" could be "consumed." Cash was never simply handed out. Instead, ration cheques were issued, and rents and light and gas bills were paid directly to landlords and utility companies by the relief office or the city. Everyone dealing with a relief recipient would know that he or she was "on the dole." Grocers, dealers, and vendors were often sent special "menus" or food lists, and were told to censor relief purchases. In Ontario, as elsewhere, liquor could not be bought by relief applicants, and those sustained by relief were forced to disconnect their telephones, if they had one, surrender their driver's licence, and deduct all casual earnings from their relief payments. Across the country municipalities responded to the depression unevenly within a set of individually defined rules and regulations. For some, the burdens of providing relief were particularly taxing, and in British Columbia, five municipalities were eventually forced into virtual bankruptcy and placed under the scrutiny of a provincially appointed commissioner. Not until August 1941 did national unemployment insurance legislation come into effect, a measure that one historian of these years, June Macpherson, has described as "too little too late."

This summarizes the official response to the debilitating and catastrophic impact of these years. Within such confines, the experience of the working class and, hence, the development of its culture, turned on the response to joblessness and destitution. Some workers became resigned to their lot, and appealed to authority for some tangible dispensation that would carry them through these difficult years. They wrote, in prose that spoke only of the immediate needs of survival, to the millionaire prime minister, R.B. Bennett. Between 1930 and 1935 thousands appealed to Bennett, and Linda Grayson and Michael Bliss have assembled 168 such letters in a collection called *The Wretched of Canada*. Western farmers, urban dwellers, the elderly, students, and industrial workers begged for Bennett's aid: five dollars, a suit of clothes, a chance in life. But others were demanding, and far more critical. A Toronto carpenter attacked Bennett in 1934: "Us fellows down here are getting fed up with all your paper talk, what we want is action and pretty quick, we have been bluffed along by your big talk. Why don't you cut off about 2 or 3 thousand dollars from these big men and put men to work out of it what your doing is taking all you can get your hands on taxing us poor people so as you can make enough money to go to Florida for a vacation." From British Columbia came this terse close to a letter of condemnation: "this will take my last 3 cents, but we hope it goes to the bottom of *you*, and that you will hand us out *both work* and *living wages*. You have caused lots of people to kill their families . . . . Now you are trying to get war going to make yourself richer. Well R.B. Bennett, I hope you get your share of bullets." Leo Gadali of Toronto simply enclosed a newspaper clipping announcing the suicide death of an unemployed bookkeeper, commenting: "I would say the Dominion Government was the murderer of this young Canadian, in that it is in their power to do something for the unemployed, but have not done so." Letters like these demonstrated to political authority the social forces that could potentially lead to a movement of opposition.

Leaders in the struggle against unemployment and destitution came from many quarters, but the communists were among the most active. While the craft unions followed an understandable, if unheroic, policy of retrenchment, concentrating on maintaining the dues-paying standing of their own members, the CPC and its organized voice within the labour movement, the separatist Workers Unity League (WUL), tackled the problem of unemployment. From city to city tactics varied, and in some instances, the communists functioned, not in bodies affiliated with the WUL-created National Unemployed Workers Association (NUWA), but in other organizations and workers' councils. Communists led a campaign for "work or wages" as early as 1931, helped to gather over 300,000 signatures on a petition demanding a National Non-Contributory Unemployment Insurance Bill, used the Canadian Labor Defence League to protect the rights of demonstrators and workers involved in processions, staged parades and protests around the unemployment issue, and provided speakers at meetings.

Across Canada, they orchestrated events within an emerging movement of the unemployed. In Montreal, communist agitation stimulated Mayor Houde to provide shelter and relief for many of the city's unemployed, and in 1934 the *Montreal Star* reported that the mayor thought "it worth the money to know that these men are living peacefully in the refuges and not plotting any kind of revolutionary movement." After a riot of the unemployed resulted in a series of arrests, the communist-based Canadian Labor Defence League provided bail. Mass demonstrations in Burnaby, British Columbia, called by the NUWA, demanded work at union rates and immediate relief of $250,000. In North Vancouver, the NUWA led a "strike," in which relief workers picketed a public works project. Supported by "comrades" from Vancouver, the strike was meant to protest the voucher system, and the confinement of relief to food purchases. As Bettina Bradbury notes in an unpublished study of the unemployed in the Vancouver area, such actions often resulted in victories for the relief workers. They pressured officials like Burnaby's Reeve W.A. Pritchard, who had been arrested in the aftermath of the Winnipeg General Strike, to demand a more comprehensive federal involvement in the responsibility for relief.

In the separate Dominion of Newfoundland, however, the Canadian federal government obviously could not play a role. Government revenues declined sharply during the early 1930s as fish prices plummeted; costs of relief soared, even when individual monthly allowances were set at the staggeringly low level of $1.80 per adult. With its credit no longer extendable, the government was unable to pay debt charges out of incoming revenue, and after a 1933 royal commission investigated the situation, the Dominion of Newfoundland suspended operations and placed itself under British rule. But this was merely the official response to popular forms of resentment that had already swept political authority aside. A riotous crowd of 10,000 attacked the legislature in St. John's while the House was in session in April 1932, looting government offices and destroying files and records. Parliamentary government was suspended as government liquor stores were pillaged and streets were barracaded and littered with debris and smashed office equipment. Not until a militia of ex-servicemen was sworn in and a British cruiser summoned to the port was some form of order restored in St. John's. Three years later, the city's unemployed formed a more disciplined contingent, headed by a committee of five that demanded specific reforms and acceptance of their list of those suffering from want of work. "We want work, not dole — which is poison to an independent industrious people as ours is," they declared. Ignored by the ruling British commissioners, the unemployed mounted protests and another riot ensued. Although four of the five leaders were arrested and tried, none was convicted by the sympathetic jury.

Similar bodies were more successful in wringing concessions from local and regional authorities. The Ontario Federation of the Unemployed, the Quebec "Front Populaire," the Verdun Workingmen's Association, and the East York Workers' Association are among the better known. Most locales of any industrial significance likely gave rise to a movement of the unemployed. Where communists were not present or were weak, socialists might take the lead; conservative and liberal working people were also commonly involved in a number of initiatives.

In the East York Workers' Association (EYWA), studied by Patricia V. Schulz, militancy, radicalism, and conservatism coalesced, as communists, socialists, and conservatives shared grievances against the relief system. By 1934, the EYWA had enrolled over 1,600 members, and meetings drew more than 800 to nights of entertainment, song, and discussion of Marxism and political economy. A train of visiting speakers drew up to their door: Salem Bland, J.S. Woodsworth, Angus McInnis, Frank Underhill, Jack MacDonald, and J.L. Cohen. Women's groups were formed, mass meetings called, a strike launched, and political affiliation to the recently established Co-operative Commonwealth Federation (CCF) endorsed. This occurred in the face of communist opposition and earlier attempts to set up a rival organization of the unemployed. Radical and conservative were able to coexist because, in the words of one ex-member, "at that time most everybody felt just a little bit revolutionary and I think that it got to the point of desperation that something radical had to be done to better living conditions."

As a thoroughly typical instance of the activism of the unemployed, the EYWA was a product of troubled times and constituted authority's inability to provide for people thrown out of work. It and its counterparts drew upon cultural forces and economic grievances to fashion a social and political challenge. When organizations of unemployed workers from eastern and southern Ontario met in June of 1933, they had common complaints, but were drawn into dispute over whether to sing *God Save the King* or the *International*. No symbol was more potent than the Union Jack, which might be draped over a tenant's door as a protest against eviction. The ideological and cultural fragmentation of a sector of the working class, so apparent in the 1920s, was for a brief moment overcome.

Nowhere is this more evident than in the work camp agitations of the single unemployed. Cut off from relief, stigmatized when they were reluctantly given aid, and directed to isolated work camps where they could be forgotten, these unmarried, unemployed men occupied a particularly tragic place during the depression years. Ignored by most, they were courted by the communists, who formed an organization, the Single Unemployed Workers' Association, to appeal directly to their needs. In the work camps themselves — Saskatchewan alone had 23 — they organized Relief Camp Workers' Unions, and conducted propaganda campaigns designed to heighten the already tense atmosphere of the camps.

Labour efficiency on some relief sites was less than 50 percent of that of ordinary labour and declined further as time passed. Resentments quickly surfaced, and were merely exacerbated by the incompetence of some of the senior supervisory staff, military discipline, poor medical care, and irregularities in the payment of wages or the allocation of rations, some of which were pilfered by supervisors.

As Lorne Brown has noted, unrest spread from camp to camp in the spring of 1933, continuing well into 1934. Camps large enough to report to the Department of National Defence experienced 57 disturbances between June 1933 and March 1934. At an Ontario camp in Long Branch, 700 inmates refused to work, shutting down the relief operation. Thousands of men were expelled from camps for disciplinary reasons, and more than a score received prison sentences resulting from their role in demonstrations and violent disturbances. Wasted lives and seemingly calculated indignities by an arrogant and authoritarian supervisory personnel bred discontents that erupted in 1935.

The major protest occurred in April 1935, when 1,500 relief camp workers in British Columbia "struck" and descended upon Vancouver, demanding "work and wages." After two months, in which they failed to elicit a response from the national government, they began a trek to Ottawa. Buoyed by a straw vote of almost 27,000 endorsing the abolition of the camps and immediate relief for the strikers, generous donations to the reliefers on "Tag Days," and a May Day march of more than 15,000, a core of unemployed "rode the rails," destined for Ottawa. Communist-inspired and -led, headed by Slim Evans, the On-to-Ottawa Trek picked up supporters along the way, drawing men from the relief camps of the west and generating enthusiasm and warm welcomes in the towns of the interior and the prairies. Their travelling display of the grievances of the single unemployed was halted in Regina on Dominion Day, when RCMP forces and the trekkers clashed in a battle designed to stop the protesters before they gained too much momentum and before they had a chance to reach that centre of western Canadian radicalism, Winnipeg. When the Regina Riot was over, one policeman was dead, many trekkers were injured, and a hundred protesters found themselves in jail: Bennett's 1931 declaration not to "put a premium on idleness" had been translated, through the coercive might of the state, into a reality.

Other protests would be launched: a strike prevented work in one Saskatchewan camp in December 1935 to January 1936, and in 1938, a veteran of the On-to-Ottawa Trek, Steve Brodie, led 1,000 jobless men to occupy Vancouver's post office, art gallery, and a major hotel. Like the trek, however, it ended in a violent confrontation on 19 June 1938. By this date — known as Bloody Sunday — the camps had long since been disbanded, and the unemployed were once more a part of the more general process of resistance in the cities. With war literally around the corner, the need to work against not working was coming to an end.

One historian, Desmond Morton, has dismissed much of the WUL-led unemployment agitation with a cynical turn of phrase. "A union of the unemployed," he states, "is composed of members who want to get out." This, of course, is true, but it is no less true that a union of wage workers is about something other than wages, forged by people who know, pragmatically, that they labour for a living, but have aspirations that make them something more than automatons who draw their weekly paycheques. Organization is also about dignity and collectivity, which are cultural as well as economic matters. In creating one of the first truly mass movements of the unemployed — there had been other stirrings among the workless in the 1850s and 1870s — workers of the 1930s raised the demand of "work and wages" at a critical point in history when such a claim to essential human rights necessarily extended beyond the economistic. The resulting agitation certainly produced little in the way of lasting organization, and even less in terms of combatting the causes of depression. But these are not the sole criteria by which one must judge the movement of the unemployed. There were other accomplishments not easily charted along the Whiggish and linear process of organized labour: of standing up to the state, of fighting for human rights rather than succumbing to resignation and defeat, of taking up the cause of those for whom no one battled. In all of this, the unemployed drew upon the spontaneous energies of class experience, as well as the disciplined leadership of communists, socialists, and other nonaligned militants. They charted paths that would be followed by others on the industrial union front, and that would find expression in agitational propaganda and proletarian literature. And in doing so, they intersected with nonworking-class elements that saw in capitalism's crisis of the 1930s the need, not for a communist revolution, but for progressive, if moderate, socialist reform.

Reformism

Although the communists made considerable achievements in the struggles of the unemployed, the Party and its cadre charted a nearly suicidal course in these early depression years. The WUL, certainly pioneered new strategies of class action, and was intimately involved in the early history of industrial unionism in the mass-production sector. But it was also isolated from the masses of workers affiliated with unions, Canadian and international, that had little concern with revolutionary politics. One part of this process of isolation was internal, and stemmed from factionalism, an exodus of members in the 1929–31 years, and the beginnings of the slavish adherence to the now thoroughly Stalinized Communist International. But another part was imposed from outside the party. The Trades and Labor Congress expelled communist unions in the late 1920s, and the state responded to a "Red Scare" by outlawing the CPC in 1931 and jailing eight of its leaders. Employers, too, opposed all radical initiatives. These factors set the party in the direction of a sectarian and irrational adventurism, which made a parody of communist calls for the "United Front." Once an integral part of the workers' movement, communism became part of the periphery, eschewing close relations with mass labour parties and a wide range of reformers.

By 1929, progressive socialists like J.S. Woodsworth were regarded as the "most dangerous elements in the working class," and Jack MacDonald summed up the communist view when he characterized Woodsworth as "the main representative of the bourgeoisie in the ranks of the working class." It was not uncommon for communists in this period to condemn all those outside their ranks as "social fascists," an uncomradely designation that created divisions even within the communist-led movement of the unemployed. Such a sectarian stand did much to marginalize the party. It seemed that the achievements of the communists among the unemployed and the unorganized were made in spite of the sectarianism of "official Marxism." Because so many rank-and-file communists were such dedicated and able organizers, and because they willingly defended the jobless and members of the new industrial workforce, a great deal of historic importance must be attached to their activities in the 1930s. But the policy and practice of the party dictated that it would not lead a generally leftist upsurge. At the very moment that labour needed a political leadership of the left, the Communist Party was embroiled in a theatre of confrontation with which only one segment of the Canadian working class could identify. In abdicating its larger responsibility, and substituting for it ritual exhortations of revolution, the CPC created the conditions in which social democracy would experience its rebirth. Mostly dormant in the 1920s, the proletarian social democracy of the early twentieth century had drawn largely upon the urban immigrant masses. As progressive farmers and moderate, religious anglophones kept social democracy alive in the 1920s, its character was altered to some extent. In the 1930s, it would be a movement of intellectuals, farmers, and a few assimilated, but more often Anglo-Canadian, workers.

The social democracy of the 1930s had its roots in the social gospel, an early twentieth century crusade to transform religious concerns into demands for the reform of society, in the farmers' agitations of the war and immediate postwar period, and in the class conflict associated with 1919. Its early leaders were J.S. Woodsworth and William Irvine, both alienated clergymen who abandoned their churches to lead a small but influential parliamentary group of dissidents that would be known as the "Ginger Group" in the 1920s. By 1930 Woodsworth and his allies in parliament were searching for new means to combat the increasing unemployment and acute poverty of the depression. In William Irvine's office in the Parliament Buildings, on 26 May 1932, "co-operating independent" MPs agreed to form a "Commonwealth Party." Two months later, as representatives of western labour groups, farmers' organizations, and socialists affiliated with declining parties met in Calgary, the new movement christened itself the "Co-operative Commonwealth Federation (Farmer Labour Socialist)," and proclaimed its intention to establish a political program that would regulate production and exchange according to principles of human need, rather than profit.

Over the course of the next year, the early CCF aligned itself with the League for Social Reconstruction. Formed in 1931, and headed by historian Frank H. Underhill, McGill law professor Frank Scott, University of Toronto social scientist Harry M. Cassidy, and economist Eugene Forsey, the LSR was the Canadian counterpart of the Fabian Society: concerned to distinguish itself from the communists and the fascistic "national socialists," it prefaced every statement with a note regarding its "democratic" allegiances. Among the LSR's demands were public ownership and operation of transportation, communication, electric power, and other monopolistic industries; nationalization of the banks; the establishment of cooperative institutions to produce and merchandise agricultural goods; social legislation to secure worker rights, including freedom of association and insurance against accident and unemployment; publicly organized medical services; graduated income and inheritance taxes; and a foreign policy securing international cooperation, disarmament, and world peace. Explored fully in a recent study by Michiel Horn, the League for Social Reconstruction represented the social democratic intellectual response to the Great Depression and world crisis. The democratic reformers affiliated with the League, however, had little connection with labour or farmer groups, and conceived of their roles as educational. They directed their efforts at the intelligensia and used their positions to gain platforms from which they posed a running critique of the lack of public policy aimed at overcoming the distress of the early years of the depression. They also fought for essential civil liberties, defending communists like Tim Buck, for whom they had no great love, from the repressive assault of the state. By 1933, there were more than 17 branches of the LSR in Canada, with a membership of 500.

Originally founded as a nonpartisan body, the League, led by Underhill, was drawn to the CCF. It played no role in the Calgary conference that created the CCF, but late in 1932 Woodsworth was urging Underhill and Scott to help draft the new party's manifesto. To accommodate nonworking-class/farmer supporters of the new movement, CCF clubs, in which LSR members could function easily and comfortably, were established. These progressive intellectuals were not above an élitism that made them uncomfortable in the "coarse" ranks of the people for whom they advocated change, and many were unsure of whether they could embrace an organization considered "socialist." When the CCF's Regina Manifesto was drafted on 19 July 1933, Underhill, Scott, and other League members could congratulate themselves on their efforts: whole segments had been written by them, and the academics had an important hand in redrafting those sections they had proposed but that were rejected by the CCF's 1933 convention.

As Norman Penner has argued, the Regina Manifesto was a parting of the ways in the history of Canadian socialism. Unlike all previous socialist bodies, the CCF was "a federation of farmers, labor and socialist organizations," rather than a working-class body. Not only did the Manifesto reject violence as a means of change, but it spelled out clearly that it would seek "its ends solely by constitutional methods." Oriented toward immediate reforms, 14 of which were spelled out in the Regina statement, the CCF was dedicated to "the eradication of capitalism" through ameliorative reform and parliamentary debate rather than revolutionary action. After years of left-leaning ideological debate, the Regina Manifesto represented a return to the eclectic radicalism of the 1880s. But within the context of extreme crisis, with the uncompromising CPC pursuing revolution and a denigration of reform, the CCF's program offered much to alienated intellectuals and socially aware small property owners, as well as to devastated farmers and some embattled workers. It became the embodiment of Canadian socialism, identified with public ownership and nationalization.

In spite of its appeal, however, the CCF in the 1930s was not a working-class organization. When workers gravitated to the CCF, it was through already established labour-political channels: remnants of the ILP, the Canadian Labor Party, and the Socialist Party of Canada found their way into the new movement. Local unions could affiliate, but few did, and there was no constitutional means by which national unions could cast their lot with the CCF. While CCF leaders like Woodsworth spoke for labour in the House of Commons, they did so unofficially. Contacts between the CCF and the labour movement, then, while present, were only barely formalized and structured into political alliance. The CCF would not officially associate with the labour movement until the 1940s, well after the emergence of industrial unionism that rocked class relations in Canada in the post-1936 years.

Industrial Unionism

Industrial unionism predated the 1930s. In certain sectors, most notably mining, it had existed before the turn of the century, and both the Western Federation of Miners and the AFL-affiliated United Mine Workers of America were de facto industrial unions. Other craft associations, including early union efforts in some realms of the garment trades or the steel industry, flirted with industrial organization. The Knights of Labor upheavals of the 1880s and those of the One Big Union in 1919/20 constituted attempts to introduce industrial, rather than craft, organization. But it was not until the establishment of mass production during the age of monopoly capital and the technical and managerial changes of the twenties and thirties that industrial unionism became a presence in the Canadian workers' movement.

Communists set some important precedents in the early-to-mid-1920s. As members of the Trade Union Educational League, activists like Buck supported the amalgamation of the craft unions in 1923, but as this was before the Third Period of revolutionary upsurge and dual unionism, they worked within existing trade union structures. Only when established craft unions collapsed, as with the UMWA western debacle of 1923–25, did communists endorse the creation of new organizations. Along with social democrats and unaffiliated militants, they led a minority of western miners in the creation of the Mine Workers Union of Canada in opposition to the employers and their tool, the UMWA, clearly identified by 1926/27 as a company union. While it claimed a national membership, the MWUC attracted few eastern coal miners. Although communists played a pivotal role in District 26, cultivating antagonism to John L. Lewis, eastern miners remained associated with the international union for a time. Only in Westville, Pictou County, did the MWUC attract a following. But the miners withdrew from the Canadian union in 1928 when the Canadian Legion red-baited its radical international ties. When the Legion, a community social centre, took the harsh step of barring the MWUC miners from its premises, cutting them off from entertainment and leisure activity, the workers surrendered their charter.

Western miners were therefore the strength of communist trade union work, just as the immigrant quarter was the CPC's most productive recruiting ground. One opponent in the 1940s argued that the communist presence in the mass organizations of the ethnic community allowed them to conceal their seditious actions "under the guise of cultural, educational, and athletic activities, in order to lure more flies into the web." Whether this was true or not, their community involvement did give them a base from which to champion the cause of industrial unionism. By 1929, communists had led the way in a number of industrial union drives. They controlled the Mine Workers Union of Canada and the Lumber Workers Industrial Union, which drew its main sustenance from 1,000 to 2,000 Finnish workers in Northern Ontario. In the doldrums of the 1920s, these unions launched a number of strikes, and Alberta miners participated in at least seven confrontations with the operators between 1926 and 1929. The lumberworkers of the Algoma District gained a reputation for radicalism through their participation in May Day demonstrations, support for cultural agitation-propaganda, commitment to publishing their own ethnic newspaper, and militant job actions in the strikes of 1928/29 in the Port Arthur, Cochrane and Thunder Bay region. Communists were also prominent in the Auto Workers Industrial Union, claiming a 1928 membership of almost 700 in three locals, and in the Industrial Union of Needle Trades Workers. This last body was supported by militant garment trades workers expelled from the International Ladies Garment Workers Union and the Amalgamated Clothing Workers. The LGWU briefly organized in Windsor, a difficult city in which to gain support, while the ACW consolidated its membership in Winnipeg, Toronto, and Montreal.

These unions, and a number of communists active in them, made common cause with the All-Canadian Congress of Labour, formed in 1927 by A.R. Mosher of the Canadian Brotherhood of Railway Employees, a body expelled from the TLC in 1921. An unlikely alliance of nationalists, radicals, and conservatives, joined by a superficial commitment to industrial unionism, the ACCL was by no means a centre of Canadian trade union unity. Built upon implicit and explicit hostilities to the centralization of international unions and to the craft-dominated Trades and Labor Congress of Canada, the ACCL was a temporary meeting ground for communists and reactionaries. The former were in the initial stages of subservience to the shifting "lines" of a Stalinized Communist International; the latter were an opportunistic trade union grouping, which eventually opted for "co-operation between capital and labour" in order to oppose American unions in Canada. By 1929, the ACCL's policy of "Canadianization of labour organizations" looked more to the state and the employer than it did to worker initiatives and militancy. It never succeeded in capturing the sympathies of Canadian workers, and likely won no more than 50,000 adherents, approximately one-third of the membership of the TLC.

Communists were drawn to the ACCL through a combination of indigenous developments and changes originating with the Communist International. The conservatism of the AFL–TLC pushed some toward alliance with secessionists like Mosher, and within the party there were some who saw the need to address the influence of American imperialism. But the deciding factor was far removed from the peculiarities of Canadian conditions, and related more to the broad searching out of new orientations to trade union work that proceeded, often, from Stalin's rigidly formed and poorly conceived theoretical "laws of motion," some of which made abrupt turns in this period. From 1928 on, there was a movement away from the Leninist practice of the early-to-mid-1920s, when communists were instructed to "bore from within" established trade union centres to win the masses to communism. Instead, greater emphasis was placed upon the treacherous role of the reformist leadership of the trade unions, and the need to build autonomous revolutionary organizations. This was the trade-union component of the Third Period, and had been prefaced by Stalinist directives to Canadian communists to concentrate less on TLC unions than on the "progressive" ranks of the nationalistic ACCL. However, the most substantial new development came in October–November 1929, when both the TLC and the ACCL were attacked as "the bulwark of the Canadian and Anglo-American bourgeoisie." Early in 1930, the Communist Party followed the logic of this denunciation and formed the Workers Unity League (WUL), dedicated to creating new unions under communist leadership and displacing the established trade-union centres. The WUL served, in effect, as a complement to other bodies, including the TLC. By no means a majoritarian tendency within the labour movement, it nevertheless attracted more than 40,000 to its ranks by 1932.

Dramatic confrontations involving the WUL included the bloody Estevan-Bienfait, Saskatchewan, strike-riot in 1931, which left three miners dead at the hands of the police, firemen, and the RCMP, and the Stratford furniture workers' battle of 1933, where the intervention of the state again secured victory for the employers. But the lessons of such defeats were not lost on workers across the country, whose resentments of the military arm of political authority increased considerably in these years. Across the country, other strikes unfolded and similar results ensued: John Bracken used the RCMP to crush communist-led workers in Flin Flon, while British Columbia miners' picket lines were dispersed by bulldozer-driving police. On Vancouver Island, Cumberland workers lost their struggle to attain collective bargaining rights, a conciliation board condemning the "communist agitation" that opposed a company that had managed to stifle organization in its mines for 66 years. Eastern miners, unaffiliated with the WUL, were more successful, and McLachlan launched a series of job actions in 1931/32, many of them ending in victory, securing the workers a rotation system that divided available work among union members in the face of mine closures and mass layoffs. In 1932, they formed the independent but communist-led Amalgamated Mine Workers of Nova Scotia that existed until 1938.

Aside from defensive struggles led by the two internationally affiliated garment trades unions, the WUL provided much of the strike leadership of the early 1930s, substantiating communist claims that they led 75 to 90 percent of the strikes in the years 1932–34. Among the Canadian workers encouraged to strike action under the banners of WUL-unions in the years 1931–35 were Montreal garment workers, sawmill workers in New Westminster, British Columbia, lumberworkers in Northern Ontario, loggers on Vancouver Island, fishermen on the Skeena and Nass Rivers of British Columbia, longshoremen in Vancouver, textile and furniture workers in Toronto, Kitchener, and Waterloo, chicken pluckers in Stratford, and miners at Noranda–Rouyn. Quebec furniture workers, teamsters and shoeworkers across western Ontario, and, most importantly, automobile, steel, and rubber workers in central Canada, were also organized by the WUL, which was active in Windsor, London, Hamilton, Toronto, Montreal, and Sydney. At the very moment that the WUL appeared to be on the threshold of an organizational breakthrough in the mass-production sector, however, new imperatives came from Moscow. In conjunction with indigenous North American developments discussed below, these altered Canadian communists' practice in the labour movement. The rise of fascism, according to Stalin's spokesman, Dimitroff, necessitated a "United Front," and demanded the disbanding of all dual unions and an end to labour's divisions. The WUL was to liquidate itself, transferring its members back to the appropriate unions associated with the TLC. J.B. McLachlan, among others, refused to chart such a course, and resigned from the Communist Party; he died later in the decade.

The call to return to the fold coincided with developments of immense significance in the United States, where John L. Lewis was putting aside his collaborationist, red-baiting clothes of the 1920s to don the late 1930s cloak of working-class spokesman, championing the cause of industrial unionism and organizing the unorganized. Always aware of the impact of symbolic gestures, Lewis crossed the floor of the 1935 AFL convention to land a punch on William L. ("Big Bill") Hutcheson, president of the craft-conscious and exclusivist Brotherhood of Carpenters and Joiners. That act announced publicly the birth of the Committee of Industrial Organization, later renamed the Congress of Industrial Organizations (CIO). The ties between Lewis and the American Federation of Labor were severed. In conjunction with what was perceived to be Roosevelt's encouragement of unionization under various disputed sectors of his New Deal, this led to an unprecedented organizational boom in the United States.

The CIO had no official presence in Canada, but as its historian, Irving Abella, notes, communist activists and rank-and-file workers were captivated by the great breakthroughs being made by a revived labour movement to the south. By 1936, with some signs of industrial recovery present, Canadian labour also appeared to be on the move once again: union membership had climbed approximately 15 percent over the course of the previous year, and stood at almost 325,000, which represented a greater expansion of union ranks than had occurred at any time since 1919/20. In steel, textiles, and mining, the CIO attracted Canadian workers, although the lack of funds and support from Lewis retarded growth. Sit-down strikes broke out in Chatham, Windsor, Oshawa, and Point Edward in 1936/37, demands ranging from the establishment of union shops to increases in wage scales. Once more, the state intervened, this time with Ontario premier Mitchell Hepburn struggling to keep the CIO from organizing in the province, proclaiming that law and order would be preserved and invading unions turned back at the border. At Oshawa auto workers won the key strike in a series of labour–capital clashes through subterfuge. Denying affiliation with the CIO, union negotiators Charles Millard and J.L. Cohen (the former, a war veteran associated with the CCF and president of the local union, the latter, a radical Toronto labour lawyer) achieved almost all of the workers' substantive demands. The process of denying acknowledgement of the role of the CIO, pointed out a defiant Millard, was "just child's play." The Oshawa strikes of February–April 1937 were, like an earlier confrontation in 1928, "a demonstration that the spell of industrial slavery [could] be broken down even in the automobile industry." Despite his posturing and reliance upon tactics of repression, Hepburn had proven, in Abella's words, "the most successful organizer north of the border." Thus, Oshawa created a CIO presence in Canada in the absence of actual CIO organizers. (Lewis appointed only one recognized CIO leader, Silby Barrett, directing the leader of the UMWA to organize Nova Scotia steel workers at the Sydney DOSCO plant into the Steel Workers Organizing Committee, or SWOC.) The drive toward industrial unionism was continued by able young communists under the guidance of J.B. Salsberg. Some early successes resulted, but lacking organizational backing of any magnitude, they quickly dissolved. In Quebec, Hepburn's antilabour policies were surpassed by those of Maurice Duplessis, whose repressive Padlock Law was used to confiscate SWOC records and to disband the 1,000-member lodge in Montreal. Employers followed such state actions, and refused to bargain with the struggling CIO lodges. In March 1938, only 16 percent of the SWOC recruits who had signed in 1937 were still paying dues.

State and employer opposition to the CIO was exacerbated by political wrangling and factionalism, as communists and social democrats literally came to blows in union circles. Even "Mr. CIO," Charlie Millard, was driven out of the United Automobile Workers, where his anticommunism won him little support from the essentially communist leadership. He was immediately hired as the CIO regional representative in Ontario. However, he encountered serious difficulties, for by the time of his appointment, May 1939, the CIO and the cause of industrial unionism were in decline: membership, which had stood at 65,000 in 1937, dropped precipitously. Unions in auto and steel lost thousands, while the wood and rubber workers experienced losses of one-half to one-third of their membership. And in January 1939, in a move that spoke more to the concerns of American craft union leaders than to the needs of the Canadian workers' movement, the Trades and Labor Congress of Canada suspended all the CIO unions affiliated with it. Repudiated by his own union, yet expected to orchestrate activities among other trade bodies also led by communists, Millard faced months of turmoil. The situation continued to deteriorate when, later in the year, the CIO unions were officially barred from the TLC. By mid-1939, the CIO reported that of the nearly 1,300,000 Canadian workers in its jurisdiction fewer than 5 percent were organized and affiliated with the Congress. Most workers were living below the minimum subsistence level, and Canadian workers, unlike their counterparts to the south, lacked legislation protecting their rights to organize. The workers' movement, after such impressive progress in its attempts to reconstitute a unity and solidarity all but destroyed in the 1920s, had been dealt a series of blows by state forces, obstinate employers, internal ideological disagreement, and a return to depressed business conditions that would not lift until war resuscitated the world economy. Not until the 1940s would the euphoria and promise of the early CIO years, comparable in their intensity to the upsurge of the 1880s, again spread among Canadian workers, leading to militant action and dramatic advances for the working class.

Agitprop/Prolit

The crisis of capitalism, the rebirth of social democracy, the rise of industrial unionism, and communist agitation among the jobless combined to bring the working class to the forefront of the public consciousness. This awareness was deepened through unprecedented activity on the literary front as the written word became a potent weapon in the class struggle. As Frank Watt has stressed, a literature of protest paralleled the rise of capitalism in Canada, and was especially pronounced in the labour upsurge of the 1880s, producing a range of critical writing that was reflected in the social gospel-type novels of the 1890s. With the escalating class conflict of 1919, new journals of social criticism were founded, led by *Canadian Forum*, which aimed to "secure a freer and more informed discussion of public questions." In the 1930s, this organ would be used regularly by CCF and LSR writers; *Forum* exemplified the restrained radicalism of an intellectualized social democratic milieu, although it did have room for communist commentary, especially with J.F. White as its editor. During the depression years, it was joined and challenged by a major anticapitalist literary movement. For the first time, plays and short stories, literary magazines and cultural journals, intersected with the class struggle producing a substantial agitational propaganda and a proletarian literature.

Communist journals such as *Masses* (1932–34) and *New Frontier* (which began publication in 1936) provided a public outlet for left-wing writers and intellectuals affiliated with the Progressive Arts Club. Evolving out of a Saturday afternoon discussion group set up by poet Abraham Nisnevitz, the Toronto-based Progressive Arts Club was active in the late 1920s, and by 1932 included sections for writers, artists, and theatre workers. Among the more active were Dorothy Livesay and future historian Stanley Ryerson. Theatre troupes developed around the

Workers' Experimental Theatre in Vancouver, Winnipeg, Montreal, and Toronto. Plays like Ryerson's "War in the East," an antiimperialist piece depicting Japanese soldiers who refused to fight the Chinese, and Dorothy Livesay's "Joe Derry," a children's pantomime about the arrest of a communist cadre, were performed throughout Ontario in the summer of 1933. The direct appeal of agitprop theatre, on the picket line or in the street, was an innovation of considerable importance, and a strength of the workers' movement. There was tangible appeal in the unemployed themselves staging a play about their situation, as in Trevor Maguire's "Unemployment."

There was appeal as well in a series of short stories and poems published in literary journals. B. Gluckman's "Juggernaut" appeared in the *Canadian Forum* in 1932, a timely and blunt condemnation of life in an automobile plant. *Masses* and *New Frontier* carried similar stories. One, J.K. Thomas' "Production," captured the tension and drudgery experienced by women on piece work in a Burlington, Ontario, canning factory:

> The factory settled down to its monotonous routine of the day. The machine that sealed the cans persisted in its maddeningly exact rhythm, and its hellish noise. The belt rotated endlessly. The air smelt of boiled tomatoes. The women shifted from foot to foot seeking some relief from their tired feet. Their fingers moved deftly and rapidly. Their faces had a dogged look, except where one knocked on the table with her knife to call the inspector to check her basin, then they would look impatient.

Poets appearing in the *Canadian Poetry Magazine* addressed similar subjects, with works on "Hunger" and lines of verse addressed "To a Generation of Unemployed." Nathaniel Benson's "Depression Chants" was one of these:

> The railmen, teachers, clerks, and boys
> Who never earned a wage
> Are stricken swift with thundrous jears,
> With helplessness of age.

"Social Notes," by Frank Scott, struck a more political chord:

> After the strike began
> Troops were rushed
> To defend property.
> But before the trouble started
> Nobody seems to have bothered
> To defend living standards.

As Watt notes, it was not so much the artistic merit of such work that was at issue, as it was the attempt to create an entirely new aesthetic in the literary realm. Agitprop, proletarian literature, and a people's poetry forged a movement towards contemporaneity, political purpose, and realism in the arts that had been woefully lacking in the Canadian tradition.

In art, too, the depression exerted an influence. *All That Our Hands Have Done*, an illustrated history of Hamilton workers, tells how Leonard Hutchinson switched from painting to printmaking in the 1920s, so that ordinary people could afford his artistic creations. By the time of the Great Depression, however, his work was considered political commentary, and he strove to "make a record of the terrible injustice that was thrust upon these people." His slogan was, "Wherever people worked, I'd be there," and he claimed to have glimpsed "the bravery of them — they had the spirit in them that you couldn't kill." A small November 1981 exhibit of Hutchinson's work depicted farm labourers, logging camps, main streets in small-town Ontario, and Port Dover's fishing boats. As John Bentley Mays, art critic for the *Globe*, suggested, these artistic endeavours were and are "documents of real working life, . . . a resolute, important, and little-researched experiment in Canadian socialist realism." Convinced that there was a need to fight back and to oppose the authorities, Hutchinson was "called an agitator, bolshevik, Communist, Marxist — everything under the sun." As curator of the local art gallery, he taught classes on art to young children and bought classical works, but he also opened up the basement to vagrants and used his woodcuts and prints to address obvious social issues that were easily identifiable in their titles: "Breadline" and "Protest." Accomplished artist, elected associate of the Royal Canadian Academy, Hutchinson was part of a struggle to bring "high" and "low" culture together in an understanding of the depression that would lend itself to solutions and activist intervention.

A literature of protest was thus united, on the left, with a popular art of protest that defied the forces of mass culture. With consumption undercut by depression, with the organs of mass culture championing political solutions that many knew to be bankrupt, a culture of protest emerged in the 1930s. It appeared in street theatre, among the unemployed, at the factory gate, within literary and artistic production, and in the evolution of socialism and communism. That it was unable to consolidate itself in the political realm, to effect the transformation of the social order that it attacked, remains an issue of considerable magnitude.

The Legacies of Fragmentation

The 1920s and 1930s had seen labour's dissolution in the period of capitalist hegemony and its attempted reconstitution in the crisis-ridden decade of the Great Depression. Gains were registered and advances made, but on the eve of World War II, the Canadian labour movement was fragmented, its militant sectors in retreat and its conservative sectors drawing inward. Regionally, the radical miners' movement of the east was in disarray, while the western-based Mine Workers Union of Canada, which had waged over 40 strikes in the early 1930s, involving most of its 3,000 members, had been liquidated within the UMWA's District 18.

In Quebec, the advances of the workers' movement were also nearly nullified. The CIO's major triumph, after a WUL defeat in 1934, was the 1937 recognition strike of the International Ladies Garment Workers Union. Five thousand workers struck and succeeded in cutting women's hours of work from 80 to 44 weekly, securing a wage increase of more than 30 percent, and winning approval of a closed shop. Yet, even in the midst of victory, solidarity was undercut, the Catholic *syndicat* opposing the ILGWU, which in turn accused the rival confessional union of "selling out" the workers through personal deals between the priests and the employers.

The Confédération des Travailleurs Catholiques du Canada (CTCC) was formally constituted in 1921, organized in 120 locales with a declared membership of 45,000. (Effective membership may have been much lower, possibly 17,600.) Based on the Church's role in developing study groups among autonomous Canadian trade unions during the World War I years, the CTCC emerged out of a close and working relationship established between the priests and francophone trade unionists. In the ensuing dialogue, workers' leaders explained tactics and the realities of class distinctions separating labour and capital, while the Catholic priests interpreted the papal encyclicals. The confessional unions that were amalgamated in the CTCC, all led by priests or aumôniers (chaplains), were thus rooted in a two-sided interaction, explored in a recent study by Jacques Rouillard. On the one hand, Catholic confessional unionism grew out of the Church's bitter antagonism to socialism and the godless materialism associated with international unionism. On the other hand, *les syndicats nationaux au Québec* were a product of the resistance to Gompers' insistence that Canada be treated as "a state federation of labor." At first, Quebec workers in the *syndicats* appeared overly quiescent, as the priests' prohibitions of sympathy strikes, justifications of private property, and rationales for hierarchical social relations all created barriers blocking class struggle. Resisting the internationalism of the American Federation of Labor craft unions in the interests of Quebec's national survival, Catholic unionism was more concerned with preserving the status quo than with militant defence of workers' material interests. But in the harsh climate of anti unionism in the 1920s, employer hostility forced the hand of Catholic unionism: workers ceased to adhere strictly to church doctrine, priests adopted more militant postures, and opposition to the international unions faded.

Both the internationals and the *syndicats* suffered losses during the

1920s and their common plight encouraged them to combine forces. Rouillard shows that by the end of the decade the two rivals were linked in joint legislative and strike activity. As AFL leaders softened their attacks on the CTCC and avoided comment on the church, the confessional unions endorsed the closed shop, the eight-hour day, and collective bargaining procedures. As early as 1925, the CTCC had repudiated its own origins, taking its stand with the workers' movement. Father Maxime Fortin declared that the days of exhorting workers to "practice renunciation" were over, that no longer would Catholic labor devote itself to "fighting the International." Instead, like all unions, the *syndicats* would "take care of the interests of the working class."

Still, there were differences between the confessional bodies and other labour unions. Separate union centres still existed, and sometimes they opposed each other. The trade unions also continued to be more militant than the confessional unions. One estimate claims that between 1915 and 1936 more than 500 strikes were waged in Quebec, involving over 150,000 workers. The confessional unions apparently led a mere nine of these struggles (4,300 workers), and they were still regarded by many outside their ranks as thoroughly compromised in the arena of class struggle. Forced into joint action at times, the internationals and the confessionals harboured deep distrust of one another. A Canadian trade-union leader, writing to an AFL spokesman in 1927, claimed that the best policy to pursue was to "pay little or no attention to these rival dual national Catholic . . . movements, thereby allowing them to peter out over time."

But as the CIO swept into Canada in the 1930s, it stimulated expansion among all unionized workers, and the CTCC grew to its pre-1940 peak of 52,000 workers associated with 285 locals in 1937. In this climate of union growth, CTCC and AFL–TLC unions again found themselves fighting similar battles. CTCC condemnation of trade-union violence and calls for the arrest of foreign communists and rival unionists (all of which had divided confessional and international unions in the early years of the depression) no longer appeared relevant as hitherto unorganized industries such as asbestos mining and shipbuilding became the sites of bitterly contested strikes.

The most dramatic struggle turned on efforts to secure recognition of the National Textile Federation of the Canadian and Catholic Federation at the Dominion Textile works in 1937. Strikes erupted across the industry, and much of the malingering conservatism of the confessional unions was broken down as an American manager was kidnapped, driven to the United States, and told to stay there, or as an inkpot was thrown in the face of the president of the Dominion Textile Company. But the union was nevertheless defeated, ushering in a new period of traumatic decline for the confessional unions. As the CIO achieved some significant breakthroughs in Quebec in the late 1930s, the Catholic unions lost prestige. After almost two decades of attempts to bring together the rival sections of the trade-union movement in Quebec, they remained apart. Labour's divided ranks were no doubt weaker for this disunity, and whatever temporary gains were registered by the CIO before 1940 were more than offset by Catholic union losses.

Regional and religious peculiarities also coloured the Maritime response to the fluctuating fortunes of these years. In the late 1920s and 1930s, the Antigonish Movement flourished in eastern Nova Scotia, and gained a foothold in New Brunswick and Prince Edward Island as well. As an attempt to organize adult education to stimulate self-help, cooperation, and associations of social action, the Antigonish Movement was led by clergymen, professionals, and government employees centred in the Extension Department of St. Francis Xavier University, bringing together farmers, fishermen, and coal miners. By 1938, it had organized 1,100 study-for-action clubs, 39 cooperative stores, and almost 40 other cooperative plants, factories, or purchasing associations. Courses in "the Antigonish Way" were offered, enrolling people in discussion groups where socialism, unionism, and cooperation were extolled. Part of a long history of regional grievance, the Antigonish Movement emerged out of the dissolution of the 1920s, which saw the farmers' political challenge discredited, the Maritime Rights Movement collapsed, and the coal unions assaulted by capital and divided by rifts between moderates and militants.

Conflicts also existed between the craft and industrial unionists. In spite of efforts to preserve some form of unity, the emergence of the CIO unions and the hostile reception afforded them by the TLC separated the labour movement into opposing camps. After being expelled from the TLC in 1939, the CIO unions formed an alliance with Aaron Mosher's All-Canadian Congress of Labour, a body ostensibly antagonistic to international unionism. After the Oshawa auto workers' strike of 1937, Mosher had congratulated Ontario premier Hepburn's attempt to "curb domination by foreign agitators and Communists." But the ACCL, as it had been when it was connected with the communist-led Canadian unions of the late 1920s, was as opportunistic as it was nationalistic and reactionary. It needed the buoyant CIO to keep its sagging fortunes from receding from view. And within the CIO there was an emerging social democratic leadership sector that saw in the ACCL a force that could be directed against the communists, who could control policy in the SWOC, UE, Fur Workers, and Mine Mill, as well as holding considerable power in the UAW and the United Shoe Workers.

The 1930s ended, then, with Canadian organized workers aligned with the newly established Canadian Congress of Labour (CIO–ACCL), the TLC, or the Quebec Canadian and Catholic Confederation of Labour. Many more workers, however, remained unorganized; fully 83 percent of the nonagricultural workforce did not belong to unions. Divisions of ethnicity and gender remained of considerable importance, and sectional and regional barriers remained. As late as 1939, for instance, the 638,000 women employed in waged pursuits formed a mere six percent of the total labour force and but a minuscule portion of unionized workers. In certain provinces, such as Quebec, where women still did not have the vote, there was direct opposition to their working in industrial situations, and across the country they were concentrated in poorly paid industrial and unskilled economic sectors. They presented a visible reminder of the divisions that fragmented the class experience.

So, too, did the extreme case of the racially divided workforce in British Columbia, where militancy and class consciousness were diminished by white antagonism to Indian and Asian (Chinese, Japanese, and East Indian) members of the population. These disparate groups comprised 8 to 12 percent of the population in the years 1920–40 and, like women, were structured into the lowest-paid categories of a highly segmented labour market. While historians like W. Peter Ward have perhaps overestimated the extent to which such divisions undermined class, these social cleavages did present a significant barrier to unity. The Chinese, of course, had been working in Canada since the nineteenth century, and the working-class opposition that they faced was quite pronounced during the 1880s. But in that earlier context, the Chinese had been the only exception to the rule of class solidarity. By the 1920s, however, a multitude of eastern and southern European immigrants had entered the labour market. To be sure, these ethnic minorities sometimes encouraged radicalism and often joined with their English-speaking counterparts to resist the encroachments of capital. But they were also potential strikebreakers, and employers and the state did much to see that they were used to segment the labour market. In conjunction with the antagonisms of the native-born Canadian workers and the immigrants' cultural distinctiveness and ethnic loyalties, these factors ensured that ethnicity was as much a force that destroyed class unity as it was an agent that contributed to collectivity.

Anticommunism had also begun to influence numbers of trade-union leaders, social democrats as well as conventional liberals and conservatives. Among rank-and-file workers, the Communist Party's many "turns" had introduced them to the instability of the more militant fighters within the workers' movement. Nothing would serve to discredit the communists more than the shifts in policy that emanated from the Hitler–Stalin Pact of 1939 and the German invasion of the Soviet Union in 1941. Subservient to the needs of "socialism in one country," international communist movements were expected to reorient themselves immediately to Stalin's directives. Canadian communists were among the most pliant. From being staunch advocates of class unity against fascism in the 1935–39 period, they turned to attack Canadian capital and the state in 1939–41, arguing that these warmongers must not be supported. With German tanks rolling toward Moscow in June of 1941, however, the Communist Party changed course and became the agent of employers and the government, going so far, in some unions, as to secure no-strike pledges and whip the membership into patriotic fervour for the progressive cause of Mackenzie King's liberalism. Honoured more in words than deeds, such "pledges" were broken regularly in a 1942/43 strike wave, but they did provide anticommunist forces with a forceful critique of the CPC's claim to be a voice of the working class. Many workers considered that the war and the defeat of Hitler had become the sole concern of communists in the labour movement, and it was difficult, once the war ended in 1945, for the party to reestablish credibility as militant spokesman for the workers.

With labour thus divided and subjected to conflicting and shifting ideologies, Canadian workers entered the 1940s unsure of their status and politically ambivalent. Social democracy had consolidated some support among labour in British Columbia, Winnipeg, Cape Breton, and Ontario, but it was preeminently a farmer's movement, with its most tangible electoral strength in Saskatchewan. Unable to win more than eight or nine percent of the federal vote in the years 1935–40, and running poorly in the industrial heartland of Ontario, where it secured only six percent of the provincial vote in 1937, the CCF was a party in search of a labour constituency. Liberalism remained the political choice of the majority of the Canadian population, worker and nonworker alike. As King had absorbed the protests and challenges from the farmers' movement in the 1920s he may have felt confident in his abilities to accommodate labour's emerging political voice. But in the late 1930s, the Liberal regime of Mackenzie King actually did little to encourage labour's support. In the 1940s and 1950s, war and the resurgence of mass culture and consumer capitalism set the stage for a new chapter in the unfolding drama of the social relations of labour and capital. Workers began to search out a new legitimacy and raise the challenge of a unified political voice that would speak for the working class.

Chapter 6

Class and Movement, 1940–1980

No, I ain't gonna work on Maggie's farm no
more
Well I wake up in the morning
Hold my hands and pray for rain
I got a head full of ideas
That are driving me insane
It's a shame the way she makes me scrub the
floor
I ain't gonna work on Maggie's farm no more.

No, I ain't gonna work for Maggie's brother no
more
Well he hands you a nickel
He hands you a dime
He asks you with a grin
If you're having a good time
And he fines you every time you slam the door
I ain't gonna work for Maggie's bro.: er no
more.

No, I ain't goona work for Maggie's pa no more
Well he puts his cigar
Out in your face
Just for kicks
His bedroom window
Is made out of bricks
The National Guard stands around his door
I ain't gonna work for Maggie's pa no more.

Bob Dylan, "Maggie's Farm,"
Bringing It All Back Home (1965)

The Social Formation

Dylan's lyrics introduce some central features of the post-1940 years. They are themselves a part of a larger cultural phenomenon, the Americanization of mass culture that accelerated in these years, going well beyond the beginnings of this process that were established in the 1920s. Especially in the late 1950s, when Diefenbaker was in power, the invasion of things American created a resistance that culminated in the O'Leary Commission's 1961 report recommending that restrictions be placed on U.S.-controlled magazines like *Time* and *Reader's Digest* that, because of their mass circulation, played such an influential role in the Canadian marketplace. But as Frank Underhill stressed early in this period, the mass culture of these years was not characterized only by increasing American content. It was also, at root, a democratizing force, and it was in the 1940s and 1950s that the promise of the 1920s, the extension of consumer potential, was widened considerably. And as material acquisition became a common feature of working-class life, mass culture in the 1960s and 1970s became more complex and diverse. By this time, all spheres of mass culture proceeded from market considerations and profitability, and Dylan, no less than televisions, cars, refrigerators, and homes, was a commodity. But he was a peculiar commodity, one that in its essential dependence upon acquisition conditioned accommodation to capitalist structures at the same time that it could convey a message of resistance and questioning of the social order. Mass culture fulfilled certain consumer demands in the 1940s and 1950s, and in the postwar years consumption declined only in 1948. In the 1960s and 1970s, new products and cultural developments pushed an increasingly commercialized mass culture toward limited forms of dissent that extended beyond conspicuous consumption.

The new mass culture itself flowed out of demographic and economic developments. Until at least the late 1960s, the Canadian economy expanded impressively, and output increased yearly with the exception of 1945/46 and 1954. Immigration, inconsequential during depression and war, was revived, and 1.5 million new Canadians arrived between 1948 and 1957. Population rose substantially in the years from 1945 to 1980, almost doubling to approximately 24 million, while the average family head's real income between 1944 and 1978 also increased from about $2,500 to $5,400. Such figures, of course, make no allowance for those intangible losses — in the environment, in personal satisfaction, in the quality of life — but they do speak to particular gains. As an absolute magnitude as well as a percentage of the labour force, unemployment fell in 1947, 1948, 1951, 1955/56, 1959, and 1962–66. In the early 1950s, unemployment generally stayed at between 2.5 and 5 percent, but in the downturn that followed the Korean War, it climbed to almost 6 percent, while in the 1956–59 recession it soared from 4 to roughly 10 percent, which was dangerously close to 1939 levels. Between 500,000 and 750,000 people were jobless. "It's a crying shame that in a country with all the natural resources we have, we have to see people on the street," declared an autoworker in 1958. By 1960, however, the situation was improving, although between 1951 and 1971 for every 100 jobs created, 117 men and women entered the labour force. The Maritimes and Quebec fared particularly poorly with the comparable regional ratios standing at 128 and 120 to 100, respectively. Still, unemployment dropped yearly until 1966, when it was approximately 3.75 percent, although it rose to almost 8 percent in 1976, and soared to over 12 percent in the 1980s.

As a result, many workers in the 1950s and 1960s had greater capacity as consumers, and this prosperity was enhanced by demographic trends. Because fertility rates decreased in the depression-ridden 1930s and during the World War II years, Canadian society was particularly devoid of youth throughout the 1950s and early 1960s. This was one of the factors leading to the postwar "baby boom," which peaked in 1959. "Today," wrote A.R.M. Lower in 1958, ". . . the five-room bungalow [is] the object of life and every woman in sight [is] pregnant." The children of this epoch would become the young workers of the years after 1965, men and women who had known little of the immediate postwar economic expansion, but whose expectations arose from their parents' lifestyle and the economic buoyancy of the early 1960s. However, this prosperity did not continue, and the 1965–80 period would be one of inflation, unemployment, industrial crisis, and political turmoil. All the consumer "attractions" of the 1950s, when durable goods, cars, gasoline, housing and land were relatively inexpensive and earnings seemed high, were about to disappear. The norm of two cars, a home in the suburbs, and four children became increasingly difficult to attain. However, the urbanization that helped to establish this norm still continued. The percentage of the labour force employed in the agricultural sector declined from 24 percent to less than 6 percent between 1940 and 1970. By 1956, two out of three Canadians depended on urban sources of employment.

It was in this context that workers began to conceive of alternatives and to develop new strategies of resistance. No longer circumscribed by the need to fight for survival wages, workers came forward with a new set of demands. With essential rights of association and collective bargaining established during the 1940s, when organized labour finally attained legitimacy, the workers' movement of the 1950s consolidated wage and condition agreements in many industries and often attained compulsory checkoff of union dues through a formula devised by Mr. Justice Ivan Rand. Fragmentation among labour's institutions was even overcome to some extent in the 1955/56 merger of the Trades and Labor Congress of Canada and the Canadian Congress of Labour.

Such accomplishments provided the foundation upon which a youthful and demanding working class launched a new series of initiatives after 1964. The sixties began with the smallest amount of time loss from strikes and lockouts since World War II, and fewer numbers of strike participants than in any year in the 1950s. But from this modest beginning, strikes increased throughout the early 1960s and attained an unprecedented peak in 1966, when over 617 strikes involving more than

410,000 workers cost corporations over 5,000,000 worker-days and 0.33 percent of working time. Especially noteworthy were the "wildcat" strikes, "illegal" walkouts not sanctioned by unions and often undertaken to resist the ratification of contracts negotiated by union officers but rejected by the membership. Such strikes were often violent, and defied convention and attempts to impose legal restraints. They numbered in the hundreds in 1965/66, when they comprised 20 to 30 percent of all conflicts. As industrial relations "experts" were quick to observe, these struggles represented a departure from the traditional confines of class relations: "Much of this unrest is characterized by militancy that is less the product of labour leadership than the spontaneous outbreak of rank-and-file restlessness. . . . In some cases the rank-and-file have been rebelling as much against the 'union establishment' as against the 'business establishment.' In this oppositional stance "breakaway' " unions emerged, the nationalistic antagonism to the American-based internationals that had been dormant since the founding of the ACCL in the late 1920s resurfaced, and raiding (one union's attempts to draw another union's members into its ranks) became a critical problem for the labour movement, causing strains and tensions within the newly forged merger of 1956. Quebec's rejuvenated Catholic *syndicats* challenged international unions, and drew new strength from a socially conscious unionism that blended Québécois nationalism, militant syndicalism, and political action in a common front that united labour, cooperatives, and community groups in opposition to capital. Across the country, new groups were on the march, with civil servants, provincial employees, and postal workers leading a contingent of public-sector unionists, many of whom were women.

This resistance on the part of labour did not develop spontaneously, of course, but as a result of new types of worker exploitation. Technological change was altering the working environment at unprecedented rates. While many crafts had already been undermined before the war, others did not become obsolete until after 1945. Between 1950 and 1957 the proportion of diesel locomotives used on the railways rose from 25 to 80 percent, and other improved equipment, as Rosemary Spiers has shown, allowed the CNR to develop the "run through," in which trains no longer stopped at particular terminals for servicing and crew changes. The layoffs resulting from such developments were a prelude to those of the 1980s, when the Liberal government would terminate much of CN's VIA Rail service. Whole communities were decimated in the process, and the number of employees on the Canadian National declined from nearly 128,000 in 1952 to fewer than 80,000 in 1971. Other work sectors were devastated by technical change as well, the skilled crafts being among those most affected, often losing 70 percent of their numbers. From the end of the Korean War to the 1970s, the railway workforce as a whole declined by 40 percent.

Throughout the 1950s, the railway brotherhoods did little to oppose this development, but by 1964 the "run through" caused a number of wildcat strikes, prompting a royal commission under Mr. Justice Samuel Freedman of the Supreme Court of Manitoba. In a controversial ruling, Freedman recommended that employers should be required to negotiate on technological changes implemented during the life of a union contract.

Not until 1973 was federal labour legislation passed to lend some authority to Freedman's decision, but the legislation has proven, over the course of the last eight years, a dead letter. As Wilfred List has suggested recently, "Parliament either deliberately or through lack of appreciation of the matters involved clouded the whole area of dealing with technological change under the law so as to make the legislation almost meaningless." Government actions such as this prompted the United Steelworkers of America to demand a technological bill of rights: at Hamilton's International Harvester plant a robot now does the work once done by six steelworkers. As Wallace Clement has pointed out, the 1970s saw vast technological changes in INCO's mining methods until workers in the pits became little more than machine tenders. In Grande Cache, Alberta, open-pit miners work under the supervision of a computer system that monitors them and their automated tools minute by minute. Indeed, the microelectronics revolution of the late 1970s threatens the very existence of the human component of work in the office and in the industrial workplace. The labour movement now feels, with some justification, that microprocessor-equipped machines will soon be able to "learn" complex tasks from skilled workers and then repeat them endlessly, driving workers from their jobs.

Employers, as Dylan's song implies, rely on more than their power at the point of production, as substantial as that is. They are also able to draw upon the support of the state, and if militaristic intervention in the social relations of production was not as dramatic in these years as it had been under Laurier, King, Bennett and their provincial counterparts of the earlier years of the century, state intervention after 1940 was far from nonexistent. Nowhere was this more apparent than in Quebec, where the Dominion Textile interests in Montreal, Valleyfield, Montmorency, and the Eastern Townships were consistently defended by the provincial police forces in the 1940s and 1950s. Trudeau himself helped to crush the striking Lapalme mail drivers in the late 1960s, and in 1969, in a preface to the October Crisis of 1970, soldiers were sent to Montreal to buttress provincial police as over 5,000 Montreal firemen and police struck work and the *mouvement de libération du taxi* attacked its competitor, the Murray-Hill Bus Lines, exchanging rifle fire that left a policeman dead. Injunctions, increasingly opposed in the 1960s, lent the armed might of the state legalistic cover, while a Task Force on Labour Relations, headed by Dean H.D. Woods of McGill University, was commissioned in 1966 to search out the cause of industrial rebellion. The task force offered some suggestions of how conflict might be "managed," suggesting that employer associations should provide material concessions that would placate unions and that government should protect individual union members' rights from violation. In the end, the task force could simply reassert what both capital and labour had known for more than a century: workers and employers occupied distinct ground, and within overlapping territory, relations were governed by adversity.

In some ways the state made more effective use of the carrot than it did of the stick, and these years saw the birth of the welfare state. Concessions to labour were wrung from the state in the late 1930s and early 1940s, and from 1943 on, when Leonard Marsh issued a rejected but influential report on social security and a "comprehensive" scheme to embrace health insurance, family allowances, unemployment insurance, children's allowances, and workmen's compensation, the potential of a benevolent Ottawa was ever present. Unemployment insurance had been but one of many of the consequences of the depression, with the Unemployment Insurance Bill passing the House and Senate in 1940. Later to arrive on the scene, but equally significant, were hospital insurance acts, pioneered by Tommy Douglas' CCF government in Saskatchewan in 1946 and followed by British Columbia, Ontario, and, eventually, the federal government (in 1957). Universal old age pensions were adopted in 1951, through agreement between provinces, which essentially controlled the domain of welfare, and the federal government, then headed by Mackenzie King's successor, Louis St. Laurent. In the 1960s, these developments were amplified and extended as the federal Liberals launched a nationwide war on poverty, advocated medicare, and strove to overcome long-standing economic imbalances among the regions. This had been a persistent and vocal complaint for many years, but had grown more urgent after the provincial opposition to the Rowell-Sirois Report had culminated, in 1941, in Hepburn's attack on federal authority and his withdrawal from the Dominion-Provincial Conference with the words that he would "leave these wreckers of Confederation . . . to carry on their nefarious work". Canada's governments spent increasing sums on health and social welfare, approaching 24 percent of their total outlays: in 1950 the cost was one billion dollars; 20 years later it approached nine billion. Despite this expenditure, however, a 1976 federal study conceded that between 1951 and 1973 the gap between upper and lower income groups actually widened.

These government expenditures have been interpreted by some as proof of the selfless concern of the state and its agents. It was, in fact, "the price Liberalism [was] willing to pay to prevent socialism," as the *Canadian Forum* commented in the 1940s. As Mackenzie King knew well, such social legislation was fundamentally conservative in intent, and was passed to dampen discontents that emerged from the rising expectations of wartime prosperity. After war, when the possibility of recession was great and when entrepreneurial magnates like C.D. Howe virtually controlled the political economy, welfare measures were even more important and necessary, although Howe seemed at times unable to grasp this elementary political reality. He had, according to King, "the employer's mentality."

Americans with whom Howe dealt during World War II, when he was Minister of Munitions and Supply, noted that he was one of only two Liberal officials "at home with, and consequently able to deal, without a sense of inferiority, with the representatives of money." By the early 1950s, when Howe had passed through the ministries of Reconstruction and Trade and Commerce and orchestrated the Department of Defence Production, the creation of which had been inspired by the Korean War, *Fortune* correctly noted that Howe had created "a businessman's country." This new "Dominion of Howe" was committed to American defence policy, was unequivocally anticommunist, and had, over the previous two decades, issued a wholesale invitation to U.S. capital to take over Canadian resources and manufacturing. Foreign-owned industry in Canada rose sharply from $7.5 billion in 1948 to $17.5 billion in 1957. The percentage of American-controlled capital in manufacturing between 1926 and 1976 rose to 40 in the 1950s and climbed throughout the 1960s to a high of 47 in 1970; thereafter, it has declined modestly. A similar development took place in mining and smelting, where the percentages were 55 and 59, respectively, while in oil and natural gas, 1955 represented the pinnacle of U.S. penetration of the Canadian economy, with an overwhelming 73 percent of the industry controlled by American interests.

But this integration of American and Canadian capital did little to decimate the national bourgeoisie. Corporate magnates like Howe, E.P. Taylor, and others reaped the profits of resource-development deals and concentrating economic power. Robert Sweeny's study of financial groups in postwar Canada examines the various connections among industrial, financial, and commercial interests. Other studies, by Porter, Clement, and Niosi, attest to high degrees of concentration within the capitalist sector. Monopoly, established in the early years of the twentieth century, attained new levels of authority and sophistication in the post-World War II epoch of finance capitalism. On the eve of the 1980s, the top 500 Canadian companies accounted for more than half the sales in the country and two-thirds of the profits and assets. More significantly, the leading 25 companies alone produced nearly one-quarter of the sales, profits, and assets. Of this dominant group, 16 were Canadian-owned. According to the Bryce Commission (1977), Canadian capitalism exhibits higher degrees of concentration than other industrial economies, among them the United States, West Germany, Japan, and Sweden. The 1970s saw increases in this trend, with almost 300 mergers in 1974, 449 in 1978, and a record-breaking 511 in 1979. Profits for some of the resulting supercorporations, like Bell Canada, have soared into the hundreds of millions of dollars yearly.

Against such a background, the state's social-welfare offerings appear to have been no more than a palliative. In spite of its overt concern for the economic needs of its population, the state still essentially supported capital. Further evidence of this is found in the countersubversive activities that the government began to undertake in the 1940s. Acting on Igor Gouzenko's 1945 revelations of Russian spies operating in Canada, the government created a special branch within the RCMP to be responsible for counterespionage work. Within a decade, the Special Branch became an independent directorate, called Security and Intelligence, and in 1970 established its autonomy as the Security Service. Recent findings have shown that this wing of the RCMP has been engaged in illegal surveillance and harassment of domestic dissidents, including "left-wing subversives," Québécois nationalists, social democrats, and unionists.

From 1940 to 1980, these and other developments within Canadian society created new challenges for labour. Waves of militancy were pitted against newly developed corporate power, enhanced by technological innovations, and the interventionist state, which was capable of sustaining paternalistic as well as coercive forms of incorporation and repression.

Militancy and Legitimation

The voice of class conflict, virtually silent outside the coalfields in the 1920s, became louder in 1933/34, quieted during the lull of 1935/36 and intensified once again in 1937, only to be stifled by the slump of 1938. But with the escalating wartime needs of the early 1940s and the impact of military enlistments and government expenditures (which meant that productivity climbed during a period of relative labour shortage), conflict increased, reaching a peak in 1943. More strikes were fought in that year than ever before — 402 strikes involving an unprecedented 218,000 workers. In spite of Privy Council (P.C.) Order 7440, limiting settlements to rates established during a period of "reasonable" (in practice, depressed) wage increases, workers were more likely to confront authority than ever before. The wage question became of secondary importance. Most of the struggles were for union recognition, a demand ironically stimulated by P.C. 2685, an empty piece of wartime legislation arguing that fair wages and conditions for workers should be encouraged, along with the right to freedom of association. As employers refused to fulfill the moral obligations set out in this order, labour met with strong employer opposition. The government assured both parties that P.C. 2685 was meant to provide guidelines, but that it was not designed to be coercive. Labour correctly concluded that the government was failing to meet its commitments to unions, and struck for union rights. The number of organized workers doubled between 1939 and 1945, rising to 725,000. The most unionized sectors were those directly involved in the war effort. Almost one-half of the 760 strikes in 1942/43 were fought in the metal-producing and mining sectors, while workers in the clothing, textiles, and wood products areas were also forced into defiance.

The increasing willingness of workers to resort to the strike was paralleled by substantial gains in production, and between 1939 and 1944 economic output increased by approximately two-thirds. Much of this went into war goods and services, but personal consumption also rose dramatically, perhaps as much as 30 percent. Real capital formation, according to Pentland's 1968 report to the Woods Task Force on Industrial Relations, was from 50 to 70 percent higher than the immediate prewar level.

It was in this context of rising output, consumption, and militancy on the economic front that a vital transformation in Canadian labour relations occurred over the years 1939–48. In the present day, Canada is governed by provincial labour codes that cover fully 95 percent of the workforce, the national government retaining power to legislate only with respect to a restricted number of workers who come under federal jurisdiction. However, during the World War II period, full national regulation of workers was in force, and this had the effect of increasing union activity. The ranks of the unionized expanded from over 700,000 in 1945 to just under 1.5 million in 1960.

To curb the mounting number of worker-days lost to recognition strikes, the government enacted P.C. 1003 in February 1944. Like all orders-in-council, P.C. 1003 was meant to remain in effect only for the duration of the war. It guaranteed the right to organize and bargain collectively, established procedures for the certification and compulsory recognition of trade unions with majority support, defined numerous unfair labour practices, and established an administrative tribunal to enforce the order, which continued the King-inspired policy of compulsory conciliation prior to a legal strike. For labour, in spite of many problems, P.C. 1003 was a welcome development, and as Laurel Sefton MacDowell has commented, it was a significant contribution to the wartime curbs "on the previously unfettered authority of management" and introduced "a degree of democracy in industry." P.C. 1003 was, in fact, the first major advance in industrial relations policy since the Industrial Disputes Investigation Act of 1907, another intervention that grew out of a great increase in class conflict.

Immediately before P.C. 1003 was instituted, more than one million worker-days had been lost to strikes in 1943. This stimulated state concern, resulting in majority and minority reports from the National War Labour Board, collective bargaining acts among the provinces, and unique experiments in alleviating class conflict, including the creation of a Labour Court in Ontario in 1943/44. In 1944, the number of worker-days lost decreased by more than half to 490,000, an indication that P.C. 1003 had met some of the demands of Canadian workers. But in 1945, with war at an end, militancy resurfaced and almost 1,500,000 worker-days were accumulated in strikes. One reason for this was of course the return to peace, and the consequent potential nullification of P.C. 1003 and the protections it offered labour. Another explanation lay in capital's hostility to the innovations of the war period, and the refusal of the state to confront "the unilateral authority of employers." P.C. 1003, while extending organizational rights to Canadian workers during 1944, had been enacted like a host of other contradictory orders-in-council under the pressures of the moment, in order to ensure that industrial unrest did not disrupt wartime production.

However, disruptions occurred in 1946/47 when the Wartime Emergency Powers of the government were officially coming to an end. Over 460 strikes were waged across the country in these years, and massive confrontations shook logging and lumbering, metal, asbestos and coal mining, steel, textiles, transportation, meat packing, and automobile and rubber production. Struggles in these industrial sectors involved approximately 175,000 workers and millions of worker-days lost. New breakthroughs in union rights were won, and pioneering wage and hour agreements ratified. Fighting its own war for democracy, Canadian labour won a major battle in 1948 when the Industrial Relations and Disputes Investigation Act replaced P.C. 1003 and the Industrial Disputes Investigation Act, ensuring the survival of labour's wartime gains and legitimacy. The provinces generally followed this federal initiative. To understand more fully the issues in the battles of the 1940s, it will be helpful to explore the nature of mass-production unionism's consolidation in this period and to probe the militancy that won working men and women so much.

Unionism

Unionism made great gains during the war and immediate postwar years, with membership expanding rapidly in both the long-established craft unions of the Trades and Labor Congress and the newly established industrial unions of the CIO, affiliated with the Canadian Congress of Labour. In the TLC, membership soared from 160,378 in 1938 to almost 360,000 in 1946. During the 1940s, the CCL unions almost tripled in number and membership. The original 448 branches expanded to over 1,000 between 1940 and 1946, and membership grew from

100,000 to 315,000 in the same period. It was among workers in the CIO-dominated sectors of resource extraction and mass production that militant action was concentrated.

The new unions of the CIO were a mixed group. Some, like the International Woodworkers of America were the direct descendants of a long line of labour militants that traced their lineage back to the IWW and the WUL. A major struggle was waged at the Fraser Mills strike of 1931, but the more substantial organizational breakthrough came in the early 1940s. Led by left-leaning Scandinavian loggers, the IWA organized 90 percent of the workforce on the Queen Charlotte Islands, won significant support among Vancouver Island workers, and launched a drive to unionize the company towns of the lower mainland, where huge employers dominated life in the community as well as the sawmill. Lumber workers gained their first taste of victory in 1943, an October strike winning them union recognition on the Queen Charlotte Islands and a master contract. In 1946, the loggers led a province-wide strike involving almost 35,000 workers and challenged the government intention of maintaining wartime wage controls. Under the slogan "25–40 Union Security," the woodworkers defied state and employer, demanding a 25-cent-an-hour increase, a 40-hour week, and a range of union provisions, including the dues checkoff. Three thousand strikers marched on the capital at Victoria, while in Vancouver, "tag days" reminiscent of the relief strikers' tactics of the mid-1930s raised thousands of dollars for the workers in spite of the opposition of the Vancouver City Council. Forced back to work by a government order issued by Labour Minister Humphrey Mitchell, the IWA eventually settled for far less than its original demands. But a contract was secured, as well as partial union security, and organization boomed. Ten thousand workers joined the union during this tumultuous confrontation, raising the membership of the B.C. District to 27,000. By 1946, the IWA was the largest union in the coastal province and one of the four largest in Canada.

Also of critical importance in the upsurge of CIO unionism, and of the CCL's opposition to the government's wartime policies was the struggle of the International Union of Mine, Mill and Smelter Workers for union recognition. As in logging, workers concentrated in company towns of northern Ontario's mining frontier had a tradition of radicalism, the constitution of Mine-Mill borrowing freely from the advocacy of class struggle associated with the lapsed Western Federation of Miners, active at the turn of the century. But there was also a more immediate structure of subordination to overcome. Union organizer Bob Miner recalled the conditions of the 1920s and early 1930s, when the mine owners kept religious institutions, leisure activities, schools, and housing firmly under their thumbs. "You worked, ate and slept company," Miner noted, and in Dome, near Timmins, children went to bed with prayers of thanks for the livelihood the company town provided: "God bless mommy, God bless daddy, and God bless the Dome." When Miner's father, a communist who once harboured Tim Buck during one of a series of "Red Scares," was asked by a minister and a mine manager to intervene in a carpenters' strike to secure harmony as well as some material benefit for himself, the miner "hit the preacher and knocked him into the ditch." Forced to move from the town because of this rash act, the Miner family felt the ultimate power of the company. It was made clear that anyone who bought their house would be fired.

It was to overcome this kind of autocracy that miners in northern Ontario led a battle for union rights in 1941/42. Local 240 of Mine-Mill demanded recognition in Kirkland Lake, and after two years of listening to CIO officials caution against strike action, petitioned the government for a conciliation board. Previous landmark decisions by government-appointed controllers, such as those at the Peck Rolling Mills in Montreal and Hamilton's National Steel Car Company, had convinced Canadian unionists that they had little to look forward to from state intervention in labour relations. In both cases, union efforts to secure wage increases or recognition were crushed. In Kirkland Lake the situation would be no different. After stalling for a long time, a Conciliation Board was finally appointed, and it recommended recognition of the union; management refused to comply, forcing a confrontation. After more delays, in the form of a government-supervised strike vote, the workers struck. They were immediately attacked by the press, led by the *Globe and Mail* (owned by gold-mining interests concerned with the battle at Kirkland Lake), and chastized for their antipatriotic wartime strike. With winter upon them, the miners were "frozen out." Government intervention, in support of the recommendations of the Conciliation Board, was not forthcoming, although Ontario premier Mitchell Hepburn did provide the mine owners with constables ordered to protect strikebreakers. A costly defeat, the Kirkland Lake strike bankrupted the CCL, and decimated Mine-Mill. Company power returned to the mines.

Bob Miner remembered that for the workers who participated in the strike, "it was pretty well disastrous. They lost their jobs, their homes, everything. "Although his comment supports some academic interpretations that lay stress on the "suicidal" and "disastrous" character of this struggle, Miner, in fact, would not have agreed with such a pessimistic assessment. Like Harold Logan and Laurel Sefton MacDowell he knew that out of the defeated miners' efforts would come "the march toward P.C. 1003." Kirkland Lake produced a committed cadre of labour leaders, brought ethnic groups together, united segments of the TLC and the CCL, earned labour widespread support and, in the end, forced the state and employer to accept change and collective bargaining. Whether or not it had been orchestrated by the employers, and in spite of the vast material cost, Bob Miner remembered the events of 1941/42 as ones of accomplishment: "The Kirkland Lake strike was one of the most advantageous, for the working class as a whole, that ever took place. As a result of what took place there, we obtained labour legislation in Ontario in 1943, which made recognition of unions compulsory once a majority backed the union."

Within the mass-production sector, the gains of this action could be counted in rising CIO union memberships, especially in the electrical and steel industries. The United Electrical, Radio and Machine Workers (UE), for instance, grew out of the development of the electrical industry in the 1920s and the resulting new wave of consumer goods. Predominantly semiskilled, and often female, the workforce in this field had few ideological or organizational benchmarks to guide it in its post-1937 history. Led by communist C.S. Jackson, the UE grew slowly, and won support in plants in Brockville and Hamilton. Prior to the 1943/44 legitimation of labour, it had enrolled a mere 3,000 members, but its real strength began to emerge by 1946, after battles in Brockville, Montreal, and Hamilton. In the last city, the strike at the Westinghouse works was part of a concerted effort to win union rights at a number of plants, Stelco being the most important. One in five Hamilton workers was on strike, and as one participant in the 1946 upheaval recalled: "In those days the union was evangelical, it was missionary. We had the feeling we were building something for posterity, that we were charged with a mission." That sense of mission spread across Ontario, where rubberworkers and steelworkers joined electrical workers in massive 1946 strikes involving almost 30,000 workers and two million working days lost. The president of Stelco's local union, which succeeded in turning back the company's successful early resistance to the Steel Workers Organizing Committee in the 1946 attainment of union recognition, spoke for many workers when he argued, 30 years later, that labour had won benefits "which could not be measured in dollars and cents." In the 1946 challenge to managerial prerogatives, workers had, in union leader Reg Gardiner's words, experienced "the feeling of freedom [that came from] breaking the hold that Stelco had on us." By 1951, the United Steelworkers of America claimed a Canadian membership of 55,000, boasting that average earnings in the industry had more than doubled over the course of the union's brief life. Electrical workers accomplished similar achievements, and by 1947 were supported by 20,000 dues-paying supporters. As an unpublished study by Douglas Caldwell suggests, the UE had managed to grow from a small and struggling body dependent upon American support into a healthy, democratic, autonomous union.

Among auto workers, a similar history unfolded. In spite of the 1937 Oshawa victory at the General Motors plant, Ford of Canada remained an open shop. The Windsor auto plant was the foreman's domain, and while treatment of labour during the war years was mediated by Ottawa's demands and the realization that workers and the production they fostered were needed, it was clear to the men on the line that a return to prewar conditions would leave them at capital's mercy. Tools were often laid down during the war to secure some gains for the union, and walkouts were staged yearly from 1942. Two weeks after the war ended, 10,000 automobile workers struck, and a determined union sought recognition from one of "the most virulent antiunion companies in Canada." To keep maintenance men and police out of the company powerhouse, workers and their supporters surrounded the Ford plant with automobiles and, in a dramatic and ironic blow against the company, locked their cars and went home. One of the most successful pickets in the history of unionism had blockaded a factory with its own products. A nationwide sympathetic strike was discussed, and workers in Kitchener and Sarnia protested with walkouts. The attorney-general claimed that "the actions of the Ford Company strikers . . . constituted open insurrection," but other unionists across Canada voiced their support and offered financial assistance. The strike was eventually settled with the aid of a government arbitrator, Mr. Justice Ivan Rand, whose historic decision that union dues were to be checked off whether or not the individual chose to be affiliated with the union stands as a landmark in the history of labour relations in Canada. In the words of former Ontario labour minister David Croll, it was "a resounding blow for the advancement of labour's rights in our economy . . . a great milestone in the development of labour-management relations as was the initial recognition of collective bargaining." While the trade-union movement would applaud this decision and embrace Croll's interpretation, less than two decades later it would have cause to consider Croll's recognition that Rand had also given security to companies in the form of "protection from wildcat strikes."

The CCL unions were not alone in making progress during these years. Within the TLC, textile workers at the Dominion and Valleyfield works in Quebec waged a strong battle for the same demands as those of the loggers of the west coast in the form of "25–40 Union Security." Marshalling the full power of the state, Duplessis jailed Valleyfield leaders Kent Rowley and Madeleine Parent, while the companies relied upon hired thugs and provincial police to escort strikebreakers to their jobs. Seamen on the Great Lakes faced similar tactics, as their strike for the eight-hour day was undermined by "scabherding" contingents of Ontario provincial police and the RCMP. The federal government intervened to declare the docks public property and denied picketing seamen access to them. A four-year battle was fought by the printers against the Southam newspaper chain in the 1946-49 years, while an industrywide strike of 125,000 nonoperating railway employees in 1950 necessitated the calling of a special session of parliament to deal with a

TABLE 6.1   Large strikes, 1946/47

Industry	Province	Date	Workers involved	Worker days lost
Logging and lumber	B.C.	1946 May 15–June 26	38,000	600,000
	Ontario	1946 Oct. 11–Nov. 4	6,000	50,000
Metal mining	B.C.	1946 July 3–Nov. 11	2,070	149,000
Asbestos mining	Quebec	1949 Feb. 14–July 4	4,650	494,000
Coal mining	Alberta	1946 June 26–June 27	6,500	6,500
	N.S. and	1947 Jan. 31–Feb. 4	14,500	30,750
	N.B.	Feb. 15–May 26	14,919	1,121,000
		May 28–June 11	14,167	160,000
	Alberta and B.C.	1948 Jan. 13–July 31	9,000	289,000
Motor vehicles	Ontario	1945 Sept. 12–Dec. 29	17,000	1,070,000
and parts	Ontario	1946 Jue 8–Oct. 21	3,440	267,000
	Ontario	1948 July 4–Nov. 1	2,58	163,000
	Ontario	1949 Oct. 21–Nov. 22	5,400	102,000
Rubber	Ontario	1946 June 23–Oct. 28	10,146	800,000
Electrical products	Ontario	1946 July 5–Nov. 1	6,271	432,000
Steel	Ontario and N.S.	1946 July 14–Oct. 3	12,496	700,000
Textiles	Quebec	194 June 1–Sept. 9	5,253	321,500
	Quebec	1947 Nov. 3–Nov. 11	6,020	40,000
Meat packing	All provinces	1947 Aug. 27–Oct. 24	13,769	461,500
Shipping (Seamen)	Ontario & Quebec	1946 May 24–June 22	2,500	50,000
Street railways	B.C.	1947 Oct. 20–Nov. 18	2,873	64,000

SOURCE: Stuart Marshall Jamieson, *Times of Trouble: Labour Unrest and Industrial Conflict in Canada, 1900–1966* (Ottawa: Queen's Printer, 1968), 298.

so-called "national emergency." In towns like Paris, Ontario, strikes such as the 1949 textile workers' struggle at Penman's Limited divided communities.

A catalogue listing of these and many other conflicts would enhance our appreciation of the struggles of these years, of the victories and the defeats. But it would tell us very little about the human sacrifice and effort that went into such battles, or of the cultural context within which they unfolded. That remains, for the most part, a hidden history. However, studies are beginning to be undertaken with projects such as the McMaster Labour Studies publication series, which presents descriptions of working-class life and of various campaigns in separate historical periods beginning in the 1930s. One of the more revealing documents of this series is entitled *Organizing Westinghouse: Alf Ready's Story*. It details, through focussing on a single but strategically important figure, the virtually unstudied daily routine of union organizing. It was pitted against a gruff political economy of management, that saw only profit and loss. "You see, in this electrical industry," claimed one Westinghouse boss, "we have to buy many commodities. . . . To us, labour is just like copper, rubber, steel, paint, and so on. It's a commodity that we need. And we're going to buy it for the lowest price we can." Alf Ready did not agree with that view of human beings: "We were slaves," he recalled, "only they didn't have to keep us." He worked to ensure this attitude would not survive. His persistent attempts to establish the UE at Westinghouse included economic demand and political challenge, as well as creative cultural acts, that lent abstract goals a concrete meaning.

Ready began his "art of organizing," for instance, in 1941, with a symbolic destruction of the company union. When the glossy newspaper of this association ran pictures of the company union's leaders, Ready cut them out, mounted their heads on pictures of rats, and pasted them onto a drawing of a cheese, upon which the "rat" union leaders nibbled. He then labelled the creation, "The remains of the Company Union" and hung it in the department from which many of the company union's leaders were recruited, as a protest against those who attempted to curry favour with the employer. "Fellows filed by there by the hour, filed past the bier of the company union," recalled Ready with glee. But the real union remained to be built. Ready circulated through the plant, armed with a pink requisition slip to make it appear that he was on a company errand, and spoke with workers in all areas about setting up a union. His father, a milkcart pusher in the aircraft shop, collected dues. Union slogans and messages were chalked on stairway risers, written on toilet paper, stuck on the wall. One day, as the janitors went to the washroom, workers flooded the shops with shredded paper (the remains of union leaflets) scrawled with the slogan "United we Stand." As Peter Friedlander has shown in a study of the emergence of a UAW local in Hamtramck, Michigan, such symbolic repudiations of the deferential climate of the workplace are far from minor interludes in the class struggle. They are the very stuff of which resistance is built, the foundation upon which more episodic and consequential struggles arise.

From these mundane beginnings, Ready began organizing lunch-hour meetings: "People came from everywhere — it was nothing to see two or three thousand out there on a noon hour." These gatherings in the park brought out an unprecedented boldness. Workers who at first had hidden behind trees to stay out of sight of their supervisors came out into the open. In 1944, UE won a recognition vote by an overwhelming majority, and by 1946 UE's efforts had branched out beyond Westinghouse to other Hamilton plants, including Stelco and Firestone. Community support sustained the unionists during the confrontations of 1946, and with the recognition of essential human rights, workers at Westinghouse won the respect long denied them.

Alf Ready, like many union pioneers in the mines and on the shop floors of mass-production industries was not a radical. But like so many workers who began to organize in the 1930s and early 1940s, he had been motivated by a communist worker. A steelworker named Bert McLure helped Ready with the UE drive and "introduced [him] to unionism." However, for all the successes of industrial unionism in the 1940s, there would prove to be no place for the communists who had led or aided so many organization drives.

Labour's Cold War

Bob Miner recalled that in the struggle to organize the mines of northern Ontario, "it didn't take . . . very long to realize that the people who were doing the work and scrupulously carried out every decision of the union — whether or not they agreed with it — were Communists. That's what influenced me to become a Communist too." Pioneers of industrial unionism, and early organizers for the CIO, communists were a substantial force in the labour upheaval of the 1940s, especially in Mine-Mill, the IWA, and the UE. Within the CCL, one-third of the membership was affiliated with unions associated closely with the Communist Party; one-half of the CIO organizers, at least, were reputed to be communists. At the local level, it was often the communists who led organizational efforts and undertook the routine but vital tasks of keeping fledgling unions from disbanding. This won them the admiration of militants like Bob Miner and the respect of many rank-and-file workers.

Nevertheless, if communist energy and commitment secured the allegiance of many workers, the changeability of official Stalinist Communist Party policy led to a measure of cynicism. As the Hitler–Stalin Pact of 1939 crumbled with the fascist invasion of the USSR in 1941, the communists reversed their policy of attacking the state and Canadian employers to embrace a patriotic defence of Canada and its ally, the Soviet Union. Some unions, like the UE, implemented no-strike pledges, and the Communist Party, driven underground in 1940/41, was renamed the Labor Progressive Party. By 1944, it was publicly supporting the King Liberals in electoral contests and working against its former "social fascist" associate, the CCF. This party had recently scored unprecedented political success and was attempting to win the support of the trade-union movement, in order to gain the strength to form a third-party opposition. The communist and social democratic rivalries of the 1940s exhibited a violence seldom witnessed in the history of Canadian labour. When, after the war, the Communist Party abandoned its conciliatory stand toward constituted authority, the confrontation escalated, exacerbated by the predictable involvement of employers and the state. One part of the emerging anti-Soviet Cold War would be fought out in the trade union movement.

This period, then, has been cast in the academic literature as one of "communist domination" in the labour movement. Appropriating the language of social democracy, academics from Harold Logan to Desmond Morton have argued the case for the CCF and its anticommunist crusaders: Charles Millard, David Lewis, and many lesser lights, such as Shaky Robertson and Eileen Tallman, who were associated with Millard's Steelworkers. Rarely, if ever, is social democratic domination spoken of, and never with the same degree of vitriol reserved for the communists of the 1940s, although CCL secretary-treasurer Pat Conroy regarded young CCF members in the unions as "trade-union illiterates" . . ."whose primary motivation was not to build a labour movement but to capture it for the CCF." This political reading of the history of the 1940s is lent authority by the Stalinist policy of the CPC itself, and a scholarship pitting a "heroic democratic socialism" against the "dark forces" of communism points to the CPC's willingness to alternatively encourage and discourage class struggle as evidence of its disregard for the workers' true needs. Especially in the formative years of the CIO, from 1939 to 1941, when communists were often engaged in leading labour into confrontations that were more harmful than helpful, criticisms of CPC activity are warranted. However, even this does not justify interpretations depicting tragic rifts within the labour movement as a battle between good and evil, an either/or dichotomy that was resolved in the inevitable victory of those practitioners of "the good fight." Irving Abella's *Nationalism, Communism, and Canadian Labour* remains one of the few substantial studies to document all that was lost with the rash of "commie bashing" that broke out in the 1940s. However, even he argues that in particular cases, the demise of communism was necessarily a positive development in the history of Canadian labour. "In the long run," he contends, "the expulsion of the Communists proved a benefit for SWOC." But the Steel Workers Organizing Committee did not exist in isolation. Its anticommunism spread to other unions, and the results were far from beneficial for the labour movement.

A case in point was the British Columbia-based International Woodworkers of America. Under orders from national CCF secretary David Lewis, the CCF dedicated itself to ridding "British Columbia of Communist domination." As Jerry Lembcke has recently shown, this crusade had been preceded by CCF factionalism and opposition to communists in leadership positions in the IWA; one consequence of the divisiveness that emerged from this assault on the B.C. District was a weakening of the organizational drive on the mainland. By 1944, the criticisms directed against communist president Harold Pritchett and his supporters in the IWA had escalated into a disruptive campaign. CCF supporters and outright reactionaries aligned with a White Block that was tied to the conservative American woodworkers of the Pacific northwest, and attempted to break up large IWA locals, rechartering the smaller units under noncommunist leadership: meetings were attended solely to cause antagonism; the union's "no-strike policy" was constantly held up to derision; and communist organizers of proven worth were fired by the international's head officers.

In the postwar climate of anticommunism and the Cold War, the situation deteriorated. Adding to anticommunist feeling was the passage of the American Taft-Hartley Act, which outlawed the closed shop, requiring union officials to file noncommunist affidavits and curtailing labour rights established in the 1930s. Communist leaders from the B.C. District were denied admission to the United States and thus blocked from attending conventions and meetings of the international union. Their resignations were demanded. Union books were audited and poor bookkeeping lent credence to the charges of financial mismanagement. The International conducted a vicious program of red-baiting, enhanced by radio broadcasts in which the "reign of terror" in effect in the Soviet Union was imaginatively portrayed. The CCL and the CCF lent such efforts increased potency, sending Steelworker organizer Bill Mahoney to break the back of the communist labour movement on the west coast. He tackled the Vancouver Labour Council, the British Columbia Federation of Labour, and the IWA. During this time, the communist leadership of the IWA retained the support of its rank-and-file membership, but they had been so harassed by the autumn of 1948 that they seceded from the international union to form the Woodworkers Industrial Union of Canada. The repressive assault of the CCF, the Canadian Congress of Labour, and the Cold War warriors in the international union and the American state had succeeded in reducing the woodworkers to the status they had held in the early 1930s. Between 1948 and 1950, the WIUC attempted to represent its membership in the British Columbia logging industry. But employers were hostile, the Canadian labour movement was unsympathetic, the IWA broke its strikes, and provincial police intervened. At the same time, the Labour Relations Board denied the WIUC legitimacy, often refusing to certify secessionist locals or to sanction the union's strikes. In August 1950, the dissident woodworkers returned to the ranks of the IWA. The communists had finally been defeated.

As the official organ of the WIUC, *The Union Woodworker* correctly asserted that the assault on communism in the IWA had struck a fatal blow to labour unity. "A year ago," it declared in 1949, "the main bulk of the labour movement was more or less united in a common front. Today, it has been driven asunder, transformed into warring factions, with the remnants of the CIO raiding and wrecking in obedience to [a] policy of 'divide and conquer.' A united CIO movement no longer exists." As Abella shows, the anticommunist drive "cleansed" the Steelworkers, the United Automobile Workers, the Leather and Fur Workers, and many other unions. The International Union of Mine, Mill and Smelter Workers, a centre of communist strength and support for the "no-strike pledge" during World War II, was decimated by an attack from "the steal union." Only in Sudbury did Mine-Mill remain, but even there the CIO was the more influential union. "What a friend we have in Jesus, since we joined the CIO," International Nickel employees used to sing, adding in more sober tones that they were "not joining anything but the CIO." Within the AFL–TLC, as Rick Salutin's portrait of Kent Rowley reveals, the United Textile Workers were red-baited into retreat in these years.

Only one organization resisted the tide in this Cold War period: within the United Electrical, Radio and Machine Workers' Canadian unions, communists survived to challenge big business and the state, to attack Millard and his allies Aaron Mosher (president of the CCL) and Pat Conroy (secretary-treasurer), and to pillory the anti-Soviet character of Canada's foreign policy, the Marshall Plan, and the Korean War. Unable to destroy the UE from within, the CCL was forced to expel it upon a technicality late in 1949, and to charter a rival body staffed by those experienced in searching out communist sympathizers. In rejecting a UE appeal to be allowed back into the Congress, Conroy charged that the union's leadership and staff were "prisoner[s] and political slave[s] of the Communist party . . . vassal[s] of Uncle Joe Stalin . . . crawling on their bellies to Uncle Joe Stalin to obtain leadership at the expense of the Canadian workers." With the CCL whipped into an anticommunist frenzy by the onset of McCarthyism in the United States and war in Korea, these words found a warm reception in 1950, and the UE was categorically rejected.

And yet the UE survived, retaining most of its membership in the face of CCL raids and attacks from the state (in Quebec Duplessis virtually outlawed the UE). Rank-and-file members, by no means committed to communism, stayed loyal to their leaders, although the Brockville local succumbed to the second raid of the CCL-backed International Union of Electrical, Radio and Machine Workers in 1953. Recent interviews with UE members conducted by Jim Turk suggest that the communist leadership survived because it cultivated an egalitarian atmosphere of participation, in which established structures linked workers to their union spokesmen. A steward's system bridged the gap between leaders and the led, and executive and membership meetings convened regularly and were attended by the union's leading figures. Among the union's leadership, any attempt to divide the membership was rebuffed by a commitment to operate on the basis of consensus. At the workplace itself, the UE won workers' respect through solid contract settlements, its aggressive handling of complaints, and the avoidance of unnecessary and unpopular strikes. Finally, unlike the steel and rubber industries, electrical manufacturing lacked a range of occupations and a hierarchy of job classifications. Informal work groups in steel and rubber often developed within the industrial union, functioning autonomously rather than processing grievances through the union. In electrical production plants, however, this was a rare occurrence because of the homogenization of semiskilled labour involved in the work process and this, too, facilitated the development of a union closely associated with the rank and file. This meant that the issue of "communist domination" was irrelevant to many workers. The CCF and the distant CCL, rather than locally-rooted communists, appeared to be the interlopers, partisan and irresponsible agents of disruption.

The United Electrical Workers were thus able to withstand the climate of anticommunism that prevailed during the Cold War. Other unions were less successful, even when communists functioned as they did within the UE. During the Penman's 1949 strike in Paris, Ontario, textile workers affiliated with the Trades and Labor Congress felt the sting of anticommunism as editorials in the *Financial Post* and Toronto newspapers criticized "a Communist-inspired and conducted strike" that was said to have torn "the heart out of this once peaceful, friendly community of 5,000." A citizens' league dedicated to the defeat of "Communism and other subversive activities, thereby assuring all God-fearing and right-thinking citizens the right to go about their normal affairs," supplemented the efforts of these distant but authoritative sources. As workers and police clashed on the picket lines, Paris was said to be "shaping up like another Lachute and Valleyfield or any one of a dozen other violence-ridden strikes called by Communist-run unions since the Soviet Union resumed its prewar line of class struggle." Union organizers like Madeleine Parent, Kent Rowley, Val Bjarnason, William Stewart, and Helen Muller were stigmatized as communists. But as research by D.A. Smith suggests, few of the strikers saw these figures in this light. One striker commented that, "I couldn't see anything wrong with Bjarnason, Parent and Stewart. To me they were OK. . . . I think they were just working for working-class people." In conjunction with the repressive capacity of the state and the municipality, the pervasive power of the company, and the fragmented workforce, anticommunism exacted its price from the working class of Paris, and helped to seal the union's fate in defeat. Across Canada, the Penman story was repeated again and again.

Among Canadian seamen, it would take a particularly tragic turn as a union was crushed by the combined forces of capital and state, armed with anticommunist zeal and gangster tactics of intimidation. Precedents had been established for state intervention in the anticommunist battles within the labour movement, and as early as 1944 the Canadian government may well have facilitated the granting of landed-immigrant status to a Textile Workers' Union of America organizer, Sam Baron. In conjunction with other red-baiters in the textile industry, Baron drove Kent Rowley and Madeleine Parent from positions of leadership in the AFL-affiliated United Textile Workers of America. But Baron's influence in Canadian trade-union circles would be negligible when compared to that of another "import" to the Canadian anticommunist labour team: Hal Banks would long be remembered, in the words of one judicial authority, as "the stuff of the Capones and Hoffas -- a bully, cruel, greedy, dishonest, power hungry, contemptuous of the law." His rise signalled the fall of the Canadian Seamen's Union.

The CSU had its origins in the late 1930s, when a communist-led contingent broke from the Toronto-based National Seamen's Union, a unique company union led by Captain H.N. McMaster and his daughter. Famous for its strikebreaking, blacklisting, and racketeering practices, the NSU was quickly displaced and the new organization claimed a membership of almost 6,000 by 1939, enrolling over 90 percent of the seamen working the Great Lakes. Agreements were reached with the bulk of the employers, and connections formally established with the AFL and the TLC. Wartime expansion of Canada's ocean-going fleet provided further growth, doubling the CSU's membership and establishing it as the dominant union on fresh- and salt-water ships by 1947. Soon after the Hitler–Stalin Pact was signed, recently recruited communist Pat Sullivan led a 1940 strike on the Great Lakes that earned the union notoriety for its militant defence of its members and resulted in Sullivan and three of the Seamen's officials being sent to an internment camp. Such confrontations would be rare in the years of Liberal–Labor Progressive Party alliance in 1944/45, but resurfaced in 1946 with a particularly violent clash that won the CSU sole bargaining rights and turned back an aggressive employer offensive.

By this time, however, the union was increasingly forced to take defensive measures. Shippers and the Liberal state colluded to dismantle the Canadian merchant fleet as owners sold their vessels to international buyers, sailed under non-Canadian "flags of convenience," and hired foreign crews at wage rates far below union scale. The Cold War began to back the communist-led Seamen into a corner, and the situation worsened as Sullivan (lent to the TLC as secretary-treasurer in 1943) resigned his Presidency, denounced the CSU as "communist dominated," and established a rival union. This action combined with the American-based Seafarers' International Union campaign to discredit the Canadian union. After a series of bloody 1948/49 battles that extended from the Great Lakes to Europe and saw employers, the state, and red-baiters in both the Canadian and American labour movement pitted against the CSU, the organization was expelled from the TLC in 1949 and its certification revoked by the

Canada Labour Relations Board in 1950. Being "Communist controlled and directed," the CSU was "no longer within the meaning of the Industrial Relations and Disputes Investigation Act." Throughout this time, however, the CSU members stood by their union, and rank-and-file unionists rebelled at their international officers' attempts to drive the Seamen from the ranks of organized labour. One Toronto delegate at the 1948 TLC Convention condemned these actions as "stabbing the seamen in the back . . . stabbing the entire labour movement in the back." The fiercest opposition to the CSU was yet to come, however, in the person of Hal Banks.

The March 1949 strike of the Seamen revealed the unequal character of the opposing forces involved in the struggle against the CSU. As the union protested wage cuts and the abolition of the union hiring hall, major employers signed "sweetheart contracts" with the Seafarers' International Union. To enforce these contracts and to oversee opposition to the CSU, Banks was brought to Canada, his criminal record and unsavoury past virtually ignored by the Montreal courts that granted him citizenship on the recommendations of leading labour lieutenants. Shortly thereafter, armed thugs were dispatched to Halifax aboard CNR trains and, escorted by RCMP forces, opened fire upon seamen picketing a CN-owned steamship. These were but some of "the broad-shouldered boys" that Banks would use to "recruit" for the SIU. As protests mounted, it was clear that the state itself was in bed with the anticommunist drive in the seafaring trade. Transport Minister Lionel Chevrier was "not able to say" whether the Halifax strikebreakers were Canadians, Minister of Labour Humphrey Mitchell downplayed the violence and the strike as a "jurisdictional dispute," and C.D. Howe, ever the voice of capital, judged the whole affair just one more indication of how difficult it was for ship's officers to get "a fair day's work out of the crew." Banks, supported by state, employers, and a powerful segment of the labour bureaucracy, soon vanquished the CSU. A decade later the price of this "victory" over "communist domination" was revealed: 2,000 seamen were blacklisted, not by employers, but by the union; wage costs in the industry declined; employers and union officials defied the law to the detriment of workers in the trade. When criminal charges were laid against Banks he simply returned to the United States, leaving a legacy of collaboration and corruption.

The Canadian labour movement thus entered the 1950s purged of communist influence. Labour's Cold War, effective in most unions, had led to tactics of intimidation and new forms of domination that far exceeded those of many of the communist-led unions. While certain communist organizations had no doubt deserved stiff rebuke on a number of occasions, and while their subserviency to Stalinist directives worked to the detriment of the labour movement, they had, when all is taken into account, achieved much of significance. In spite of the much-publicized wartime "no-strike pledges" for instance, it is clear that communist-led unions rarely imposed such a ruling upon their membership. As the 1943 IWA recognition strike on the Queen Charlotte Islands and the 1941/42 Kirkland Lake Mine-Mill battle revealed, communists participated in militant job actions even during the period of the popular front. Despite the shifting policy of the Communist International, the communists won the support of many workers for one simple reason: at the local level they were capable of sensing the mood and needs of their membership. Nor were communists given to lining their pockets or to packing the union staff with loyal incompetents. As a disciplined cadre, they were often the first to make material sacrifices and to call to task union staff who failed to do their jobs properly. This is not to deny that some shady dealings were made; it is to suggest that they were not the monopoly of the communists. Yet for all of this, the communists had to go. Millard won the day, and as a consequence the labour movement in the post-1950 years would operate on the policy that "Loyalty was more important than ability." During the upheavals of the 1960s and 1970s, that orientation, a product of the internecine struggles of the 1940s, would come under attack as the trade unions were besieged by a younger, more militant rank and file that knew little of the ideological turmoil in which the "old guard" had been forged.

Coming Together

The 1950s marked a point of departure for Canadian labour, as the strains and tensions of the postwar upheaval dissipated in years of relative prosperity. This decade marked the supposed "end of ideology," an appearance conditioned, in part, by the crushing of the communist presence within the trade union movement, and managerial adoption of "human relations" orientations to the perennial "labour problem." Strikes were less common than they were throughout the 1940s and were more often successful in winning wage, condition, and benefit agreements. Survival and defence of basic rights were no longer as central as they were in the 1930s and 1940s. The organized working class appeared to have reached a new plateau of authority and power, and union membership stabilized. The more than 65 percent of workers who remained outside the unions were concentrated in smaller industries and businesses or were part of sectors like the emerging white-collar stratum that, historically, had proved difficult to organize.

Labour's relative effectiveness throughout the 1950s, and the widening parameters of union demands, which increasingly reflected concern over automation, job security, and company-financed benefits, drew some hostile fire from capital and the state, especially during the closing years of the decade, as the economy dipped into recession. Militancy was perhaps most pronounced on the west coast at this time. British Columbia accounted for 28 percent of the large strikes in the decade and about 21 percent of all worker-days lost to labour conflict. In 1952 and 1959, when notable strikes occurred, British Columbia provided 50 to 60 percent of national worker-days lost and workers involved in strikes. Led by lumber and construction workers, many of these struggles were "wildcats," and the regional conflicts of the 1950s prefaced the nationwide rank-and-file revolt of the 1960s. They drew antagonistic response, most noticeable in the passage of the Labour Relations Act (1954) and the Trade-Unions Act (1959). Such legislation placed new restrictions and penalties upon union workers participating in "illegal" strikes and picketing, and defined worker organizations as legal entities that could be sued for a range of damages in the event of their involvement in activities that violated the law.

For the most part, however, the 1950s were years of consolidation for labour. More large strikes were fought in the manufacturing sector of central Canada and the new extractive industries (fishing, lumbering, nonferrous mining and smelting) that had been at the very centre of the organizing drives of the 1930s and 1940s. Conflicts in the auto industry accounted for more than 16 percent of the significant battles of the 1950s. Regionally, too, the trade-union movement strengthened its foundations, although perhaps at the expense of regional autonomy. Newfoundland's union with Canada in 1949 increased the number of organized workers in the country to over the one million mark. The region had seen a range of organizational activities over the course of the nineteenth and twentieth centuries, and seal skinners, craftsmen in various trades, and miners at the Wabana deposits on Bell Island were all active unionists. As Peter Neary has argued in one study of Bell Island and Conception Bay, they had been a unique blend of the traditional and the modern, their culture a hybrid of imposed industrially oriented structures, and the ancient ways of the outports and "Old Newfoundland." But according to William Gillespie, this combination produced a vibrant regional labour movement. At the time of Confederation, Gillespie claims, over 41,000 workers were organized, and when Newfoundland joined Canada these workers became part of the larger national labour movement. Nine years later, under the impact of political integration, international unionism, and the rule of Joey Smallwood, Newfoundland's union membership had dropped to 33,000.

The question of who would control these and other dues-paying workers constituted one aspect of the fragmentation of labour that remained to be resolved in the aftermath of postwar workplace victories and the silencing of communist organizers. The Trades and Labor Congress of Canada, affiliated with the American Federation of Labor, still contended for jurisdictional rights with the Congress of Industrial

Organizations' Canadian Congress of Labour. The purging of communists in the late 1940s and early 1950s, and the resulting suspensions,
merely exacerbated a difficult situation. Unions were "raided" by other
unions, their members enticed away from TLC and CCL bodies on the
grounds that the rival union could provide higher wages and more
lucrative benefits. By 1952, it was clear that labour unity was suffering
seriously from these activities referred to by one CCL delegate as "the
worst attempt at mass raiding in the annals of Canadian labour." Within
the trade-union movement, two positions were forming, one that
supported TLC-CCL unity, and one that dismissed the possibility.
Those who hoped for unity were led by people like R.C. McCutchan of
the TLC's Retail Clerks International Protective Association, who
declared in 1953: "Have you got to wait for the boss to drive you
together? . . . Let's control our Canadian policies to the extent of saying:
'Well, if you Yankees can't get together, we in Canada have brains
enough to do it'." But this advice was rejected, the majority of TLC
delegates aligning themselves with plumbers' leader John Bruce, who
rejected any compromise with the CIO unions. "You can't live with
snakes," he claimed, "and I say they are traitors."

Ironically enough, given McCutchan's mildly nationalistic advocacy of
unity, the first step was taken in the United States, where new leaders
emerged in both the AFL and CIO in 1952. George Meany of the
plumbers (AFL) and Walter Reuther of the UAW (CIO) struck a
no-raiding pact in April 1953, and by 1955 the unity movement in both
Canada and the United States had accomplished its aims. The first
Canadian convention of the united labour bodies convened on 23 April
1956 and even the remnants of the OBU joined the newly forged
national labour organization, the Canadian Labour Congress. A product
of compromise and conciliation, the CLC struck a crucial financial
agreement on dues that stood midway between the monthly member
rate of 4 cents charged by the TLC and the ten cents levied by the CIO.
In the divisive realm of politics, the long-standing divergence between
CIO support for the reform-oriented CCF and the TLC advocacy of
nonpartisanship was overcome to some extent in the agreement to
support a political education department that would play a role in the
creation of a new party linked to trade unions, cooperatives, farmer
organizations, and other progressive blocks. This was possible, of
course, because in the 1950s the CCF was essentially moribund and even
the "old guard" within the TLC recognized that the Liberal and
Conservative parties offered labour no real voice and even worked
against labour in moments of crisis.

But in 1956 it seemed that such moments of crisis could be overcome.
Labour unity was apparently achieved, and with the young Montrealer
Claude Jodoin leading the recently created CLC, it appeared that even
Quebec might be enticed to join. This declaration of unity, however, did

not eliminate fragmentation within the workers' movement.

Before the decade was over, a jurisdictional dispute between the Brotherhood of Carpenters and Joiners and the International Woodworkers of America reminded labour of the fragility of its newly discovered unity. Two powerful corporate interests — Bowater and Anglo-Newfoundland — refused to deal with the IWA, which the workers in the industry embraced, and the government denied the union certification. Joey Smallwood, once a trade unionist, but now a "Father of Confederation," proclaimed his intention of freeing "the loggers of Newfoundland from the tyranny of a foreign union." IWA left-winger Harvey Ladd added to the conflict by threatening that the establishment of the woodworkers' union would preface a revolution in Newfoundland. Smallwood took a swift, arbitrary, and dictatorial course: outlawing the IWA, he set up his own union, the Newfoundland Brotherhood of Wood Workers. Clashes between loggers and police increased, and in one confrontation a policeman was killed; vigilante actions followed. The IWA was routed and the wider labour movement crushed. Under the Labour Relations Amendment Act (1959), secondary boycotts and sympathetic strikes were outlawed and the province was given the right to dissolve any union whose officers were convicted of criminal activities. Between 1958 and 1962, the number of organized workers in Newfoundland declined precipitously to 16,000, while union locals were reduced from 286 to 109. The debacle of organized labour culminated in 1961 when Smallwood handed his union's contracts over to the Carpenters, who refused any CLC interference in their right to represent the Newfoundland loggers. The IWA considered this a high price to pay for the appearances of consolidation. Among Quebec workers, unity was to prove far less significant than a shift away from Catholic unionism to militant syndicalism, a process commencing in the 1920s, 1930s, and 1940s, visible by the 1950s, but not coming to fruition until the 1960s and 1970s. And among many immigrants, structured into low-paid employments, the issue of unity among Canadian workers was secondary to fulfilling basic needs.

Immigrants and Incomes

The rapid economic development of the postwar years, labour shortages in certain sectors resulting from wartime mobilization, and the low fertility rates of the depression era all led to increasing liberalization of immigration regulations. A wave of new immigrants flooded the Canadian labour market after World War II. Between 1946 and 1961, well over 2,000,000 immigrants arrived in Canada, and during the 1950s, immigration played a central role in the growth of the labour force. Two-thirds of the labour force growth of the early 1950s was provided by such new Canadians, while in a less dramatic increase during the less prosperous later 1950s, immigrants contributed to one-third of the expansion. By 1957, the number of immigrant arrivals (282,164) approached the annual figures for the peak immigration years of 1910–13. In metropolitan centres like Montreal, Toronto, and Vancouver the foreign-born population soared in these years, expanding by 172,000 between 1951 and 1961. Across Canada as a whole there were almost 800,000 more foreign-born residents in 1961 than there had been a decade earlier. As of 1961, foreign-born Canadians comprised 15.6 percent of the general population, while their numbers had increased 38.1 percent over the 1950s, outpacing the natural increase of the native-born. Taking pre- and postwar immigrants together, one in five Canadian workers was born outside the country.

Two features of this new immigration are notable. First, the relative significance of British immigration declined markedly. It is true that English-speaking immigrants from the British Isles remained the single most important group in the postwar period, with approximately 475,000 coming to Canada in the 1950s. But the massive influx of Italian immigrants, commencing in 1951 and cresting in 1956–61, brought 250,000 new immigrants to Canada. In the late 1950s, Italians actually outnumbered those from the British Isles, and when taken in conjunction with other groups like the Greeks and the Portuguese, attest to the important place of southern Europeans in the labour market of the 1950s and 1960s. The second notable characteristic of this new immigration was the extent to which it was destined for the workplaces of the land: almost 90 percent of the immigrants were wage earners, with high concentrations (70.6 percent) in the craft, mass-production, service, and recreational sectors. This extended far beyond the labour force involvement of native-born Canadians in similar occupations (57.8 percent). Among labourers, the foreign-born were also overrepresented.

The lot of the immigrant was not an attractive one when compared with that of the Canadian-born worker. But for the immigrants themselves the positions secured in Canada usually represented an advancement, so limited had been the employment possibilities in Europe. Yet in Canada, 48 percent of the postwar immigrants earned less than $3,000 annually, which was near the poverty line for a family, compared to 46 percent of the native-born. Among those who earned over $6,000, the foreign-born contributed 9 percent compared to a figure of almost 12 percent for the indigenous Canadians. Within this generalized pattern, moreover, a wage hierarchy divided British immigrants from their less affluent Polish and Italian counterparts. In the former group, incomes of the family heads in 1961 averaged $5,341, compared to the much lower $3,992 and $2,918 for the latter two immigrant communities. Only through the pooling of family earnings did non-British immigrants of the postwar period narrow the gap between themselves and the native-born in this realm. Nevertheless, to be foreign-born in Canada on the eve of the 1960s was likely to live the reality of life in the lowest wage sector: in the metropolitan centres such postwar immigrants earned, on the statistical average, at least $500 less per year than their Canadian-born counterparts. In this, they were not all that unlike the oldest Canadian immigrants, the French Canadians, whose average personal income in 1961 was $1,383, significantly below the national norm of $1,564 (and this far outdistanced the figures from the Maritimes, which ranged from Newfoundland's $934 to Nova Scotia's $1,197). For workers caught in such structural inequalities, daily life and identification with class demands or the labour movement's particular perspective would no doubt have been different than they were for the more prosperous native-born.

Class and Nation: Quebec

In Quebec, the long-standing struggle between national and interna-tional unions has been mediated by the French fact, by the particular and unique culture and perspective of Quebec workers. The Knights of Labor, for instance, existed far longer in Quebec than in any other Canadian province, and when the Berlin decision of 1902 forced the Knights from the Trades and Labor Congress of Canada, many French Canadian workers in the Knights of Labor were forced to form their own "national" unions. Those attracted to the local assembly of a particular locality and, hence, attached to a set of common experiences, found it far easier to transfer their loyalties to the local Catholic confessional *syndicats* than to join the larger English-dominated organizations of international unionism. The result was the formation of the misnamed National Trades and Labor Congress on 18 September 1903. This maverick TLC, composed of so-called national unions (Quebec's Knights of Labor, despite their affiliation to the Philadelphia-based Noble and Holy Order, considered themselves national unions), represented a conservative, largely French Canadian alternative to the internationalism of Sam Gompers, but it soon lost support, and by 1907 had been severely weakened by internal splits and factionalization.

Out of the ashes of the National Trades and Labor Congress rose the Catholic *syndicats*. These confessional bodies had their origins, as Fraser Isbester has argued, in the confluence of three streams of intellectual and social endeavour. First, they were themselves carried along in the general labour upheaval that swept North America immediately after the turn of the century. Second, the separate structures of French Canadian unionism were manifestations of the popularity of nationalism in Quebec, strong since the execution of Riel, and given new impetus under advocates like Bourassa and Lionel Groulx. Third, the Catholic unions could also trace a part of their origins to the shift toward social action noticeable in the pontifical reign of Leo XIII, dating from 1891.

Conscious of its waning influence among the working masses, the church sought to reestablish its influence among the labouring poor. "The scandal of the nineteenth century," noted one concerned Catholic authority, "was the loss of the working man to the Church."

Catholic unionism, dating from 1907, was thus firmly established in Quebec, and after years of preparatory work, as was noted earlier, the Confédération des Travailleurs Catholiques du Canada (CTCC) was founded in 1921. Most successful in the 1920s and 1930s, the CTCC was led by Pierre Beaule and attracted activists like Alfred Charpentier. A future leader of the CTCC, Charpentier carried the new "gospel" across the province in the early years of organizing. By 1939, the Catholic union centre claimed a membership of almost 50,000, 238 union locals, 18 study circles, a like number of trade federations, 7 regional groups, and 12 city centrals.

In the opening years of the 1940s, as Canadian labour struggled to gain legitimacy, French Canadian workers became increasingly active in the struggles of the time. By 1943/44, the CTCC was involved in more conciliations and arbitrations with various state agencies (57) than it had been in any five years throughout the 1930s: a record-breaking 154 strikes were fought in Quebec in 1942/43, involving 48,000 workers. Much of this activity was conditioned by escalating worker militancy, but corporate autocracy also played a part in the emergence of conflict. Large American-owned firms were not above a practised ethnocentricity, in which they expressed aversion to dealing with French-speaking Catholic clergy. On specific occasions they attempted to destroy all unionism and, failing on that count, encouraged workers to join international unions headed by English-speaking labour leaders.

As labour and capital in Quebec drifted toward an impasse in the 1930s and 1940s, Catholicism itself underwent a mild radicalization. The encyclical "Quadragesimo Anno" issued by Pope Pius XI in 1931 led to this development, establishing workers' rights to shares in the profits of industry. With the rise of Gérard Picard to the presidency of the CTCC in 1945 an older, more conservative generation of leaders was replaced: lay leaders emerged to take the place of priests. A group of aggressive young organizers, among them Jean Marchand, was recruited from Laval University and the traditional tie between church and state was weakened as the newly reordered CTCC broke decisively from the Duplessis regime. In consequence, membership almost doubled between 1943 and 1948, when over 93,000 Quebec workers were enrolled in 428 syndicats, and some of the losses of the 1938–43 years were offset by new advances. By 1955, 100,000 Quebec workers had joined the CTCC unions, and 43 percent of organized workers in Quebec were controlled by the Catholic unions. For the first time in almost 40 years, moreover, these syndicats, although Catholic in form, were less closely linked to the church. Non-Québécois workers diluted the traditional cultural homogeneity of the Catholic unions, weakening the hold of religion, and strengthening more secular working-class concerns, while the inclusion of women altered the traditional character of the *syndicats*.

All these factors led to the militancy and confrontation that was itself a part of the industrial-capitalist transformation of Quebec. Over the course of the 1940s, employment in manufacturing in the province rose by 87 percent, the value of output jumped 312 percent, the volume of production climbed 92 percent, and investment increased 474 percent. Between 1939 and 1950 employment in manufacturing soared by 200,000, an increase in a mere 11 years as great as the gain in the entire preceding century from 1839 to 1939. Approximately 700 strikes were waged during this same period, or approximately 40 percent more than were conducted in the two decades leading up to 1936. One of these strikes, the 1949 confrontation in the asbestos mines of the Eastern Townships, was an example of a type of a conflict between capital, labour, and the state that revealed the level of class polarization emerging throughout Quebec.

As a fibrous and noncombustible product that could be employed in the making of fireproof fabrics and materials, asbestos gained commercial value throughout the 1930s and 1940s. By 1949, production in the noncommunist world was dominated by six producers in the Eastern Townships and their rivals in the Belgian Congo. The largest Quebec concern was the Canadian Johns–Manville company, which created the town of Asbestos. Negotiations between the CTCC unions in the mining towns and the employers commenced late in 1948, the first contract in the industry expiring on 1 January 1949. According to the company representatives, the union demanded wage and working condition changes, the elimination of asbestos dust inside and outside the mills, welfare provisions, recognition of the Rand formula, and the "takeover" of management rights. Capital and labour stood deadlocked well into 1949 and Quebec Department of Labour officials failed to effect a conciliation. With only two possible options — arbitration through legal channels or an illegal strike — the miners walked off the job in mid-February 1949, blocking production in most mines in the region.

A militant solidarity combined with a festive sense of community to oppose state and employer. Over the course of the next four-and-a half months the workers battled provincial police and government condemnation as well as employer determination. Strikebreakers were imported into the townships, workers were evicted from company houses, and mass demonstrations and silent processions brought Quebec nationalists, intellectuals and workers together in the opening scenes of the Quiet Revolution. Religious leaders spoke of the "dishonour to the province of Quebec" and proclaimed their opposition to "the conspiracy" crushing labour. By early May, community polarization and rising tension culminated in striker pickets and barricades by which the workers secured control of the town of Asbestos. Not until the Riot Act was read was "order" restored, but the resumption of legal authority was secured only through hundreds of arrests, police beatings of strikers, and a violent routing of the unionists that engendered much bitterness and resentment. More than a month-and-a-half later, a settlement was reached, but it was to prove an empty one for many of the strikers, significant numbers of whom were not rehired. "Blacklegs" who remained at work were liable to find their cattle slaughtered, barns burned, or windows broken. Perhaps psychologically gratifying, such acts of vengeance did little to win the disgruntled workers material concessions from the companies.

After five months of pitched battle, the workers were left with the bitter aftertaste of defeat. But they had also gained significant successes, which would bolster the workers' position in the 1950s. There had been signs, however faint, of English Canadian labour's support for the strike, and the caricature of Catholic workers' conservatism and caution had been erased. Church leadership in the labour movement, and the links that this had forged among the clergy, the state, and the employers, was weakened; in the 1950s, the CTCC would remain a Catholic body, but the chaplain was more a religious figurehead than a union leader. The longstanding bond between the confessional unions and the Duplessis machine was also broken down as workers came to recognize that the product of such an alliance was repression. By 1952, the CTCC launched an anti-Duplessis Political Action Committee. Asbestos 1949, for all that it cost the workers of the Eastern Townships, stimulated structural reform within Catholic unionism.

Led by Picard and Marchand, Catholic unionists in Quebec continued to encourage the secularization and militancy first introduced in the 1920s and so evident by the time of the Asbestos confrontation. In conjunction with the Quebec-based CIO unions of the Canadian Congress of Labour, the CTCC presented the more radical face of Quebec labour. Together, these bodies claimed the allegiance of approximately 135,000 workers, but the craft unions associated with the Trades and Labor Congress, organized throughout the 1940s and 1950s in the Fédération Provinciale du Travail (FTP), still remained numerically dominant with 130,000 members. All three labour organizations had been united in the Asbestos battle of 1949, but in the years after 1952, the FTP tied its fortunes to the Duplessis government and distanced itself from the increasingly radical and politicized wing of Quebec labour. A strike wave swept through the textile industry in 1952, drawing thousands of workers into the streets. The new vitality of the Catholic workers' movement was apparent in the 1952 strike against the Montreal department store, Dupuis Frères, during which elderly, disabled, and female sales personnel waged a successful struggle for increased wages, the 40-hour week, paid holidays, and union security.

As the company attempted to convert to a self-service operation and as Mayor Camillien Houde denounced the strikers as communists, nationalists in the Quebec labour movement saw that Quebec capital was as oppressive and as exploitative as American or English-Canadian interests. Michel Chartrand, rising union spokesman, pointed out that the CTCC would have no relations with those who "defended the French language while starving those who used it."

With the merger of the AFL–CIO in 1956, Quebec labour overcame some of the organizational and ideological fragmentation that had divided leading sectors of the trade-union movement in the 1952–55 years. The creation of the Quebec Federation of Labour (QFL) in 1956 was followed by the Murdochville Steelworkers' strike of 1957, in which combined CLC–CTCC forces were defeated by provincial police, hired thugs, and strikebreakers, and nearly bankrupted by legal costs. One worker died in the battle, and to this day Steelworkers in Quebec remember the strike as one of the first lessons learned in opposing repression. "Murderville," they recall, told them much of what to expect in their dealings with employers. As the regional economy succumbed to recession in the later 1950s, unemployment rose to over eight percent, but the decade as a whole had seen the wage differential between Quebec and the rest of Canada narrow and the ranks of unionized workers expand modestly: between 1950 and 1960, the Catholic *syndicats* grew in membership, from just over 80,000 to approximately 102,000. During this time of stable and moderate expansion, the CTCC had opposed the Duplessis regime, reformed and secularized its organization, and worked for a more effective unionism that would enhance the bargaining power of its members. During the 1960s and 1970s, the Quebec working-class experience would reveal different features. Just as the Asbestos strike of 1949 signalled the end of an epoch in the history of Quebec workers' movements, the conjuncture of the 1960s — where national and class grievances fused to reorient workers' demands — transformed the character of class conflict in Quebec.

The early years of the 1960s witnessed the beginnings of change. The era of Duplessis and the Union Nationale came to an end as the Liberal party consolidated its electoral strength. The revival of the economy after the recession of the late 1950s simply accelerated the trend toward industrial-capitalist development and urbanization. Finally, within the labour movement itself, Marchand led the CTCC decisively away from its religious origins and, in 1961, the organization was officially renamed the Confederation of National Trade Unions (CNTU). Although this change was motivated largely by secularization, it may also have resulted from Marchand's desire to reassure Pearson's Liberals. By affirming the autonomy of the Quebec unions, he succeeded in checking the drift toward amalgamation with the AFL–CIO unions that had been evident since the 1956 merger and that would have linked the CNTU to the recently established New Democratic Party.

By 1965, then, the longstanding rivalry between national and international unionism within the province resurfaced with a vengeance, and consolidated around a growing hostility between the CNTU, now led by Marcel Pépin, and the internationally based QFL, headed by Louis Laberge. The latter secured a rare independence and autonomy within the CLC on the grounds that his own unions in Quebec were constantly threatened by possible raids and that international unionism in the province was engaged in a constant battle with the CNTU. In 1964 alone, the QFL lost 10,000 members to the CNTU, and over the course of the 1960s the Confederation grew rapidly, from 80,000 to 250,000 members.

This tremendous expansion was the product of more than simple raiding tactics. Indeed, it was linked to the weakening of the CNTU's Liberal ties and its advocacy of militancy on the economic front, reform in the social arena, and radical nationalism in political action. Many factors contributed to the abandonment of Liberalism, including political corruption, antilabour action, and the inability of federalists to placate the grievances of Quebec nationalists. As Trudeaumania swept the country in the late 1960s many of the CNTU union members recalled the new Liberal leader's words to Montreal's mail-truck Lapalme drives ("mangez la merde"). Once enrolled in the CNTU, les gars de Lapalme had resisted poor pay and long hours, forming a cooperative company and winning a mail-delivery contract. But their efforts in the late 1960s collapsed as the Post Office split their contract among a group of new companies. Trudeau's brusque words of dismissal let these and other protesting workers know that they had little to look forward to from a politician whose career had been, ironically, so closely linked to labour's much-heralded awakening in the Asbestos strike. As radical nationalism flourished in the mid-1960s, concentrated in the post-1963 rise of the Front de Libération du Québec (FLQ), alternatives to bargaining within existing political structures grew more and more attractive to militant workers. Grouped around Michel Chartrand's radical core in the Montreal Central Council of the CNTU, militants supported extra-parliamentary forms of social, cultural, and political action.

Far more democratic than international unions, CNTU locals retained more of their dues at the local level, possessed greater independence of action, and were less bureaucratic and centralized than their international counterparts. They supported a range of demands that extended beyond the workplace, backing the McGill–Français movement, opposing the nuclear arms race, condemning American involvement in Vietnam and imperialist aggression around the world, and demanding the release of the imprisoned FLQ leaders, Charles Gagnon and Pierre Vallières. With thousands drawn to this eclectic attempt to address class and national questions, Quebec became the syndicalist centre of direct action in North America, and the CNTU the voice of a broad amalgam of unionists, the unorganized, the unemployed, tenants, and consumers. Rejecting the outright endorsement of the social democratic NDP, the CNTU of the late 1960s sought mass mobilization on three fronts: job action and collective-bargaining efforts; pressure group activities to address particular "consumer" grievances; and, finally, political opposition to specific power structures, especially those operating at the municipal level. Like the Knights of Labor 80 years earlier, the CNTU lent its support to cultural attempts to reconceive the social order, stimulating cooperative buying and selling of goods, establishing publishing co-ops that provided books and mass-circulation newspapers to the developing movement, and financing films and literary works of social and political worth.

Nevertheless, the perennial problem of institutional fragmentation remained, and the CNTU and QFL continued as distinctive bodies. The massive repression of the October Crisis (1970) galvanized working-class unity as much as it stimulated radical resentment. When workers at *La Presse* struck in October 1971, they were supported by a violent demonstration of 14,000. Chanting, "This is only the beginning," the crowd overturned police barricades to vent their rage at an economic and political system seen to be controlled by Drapeau, Bourassa, and the Power Corporation. Less than one year later, the prophetic note of that 1971 chant was thrown in the face of authority. A Common Front composed of the CNTU, QFL, and the Quebec Teachers Corporation embraced nationalist and socialist demands and, on 9 March 1972, rejected government offers of a 4.8 percent wage increase for all public-sector workers. Two-hundred thousand workers responded with a one-day general strike on 28 March 1972, openly defying state directives to remain on the job. On 10 April, after days of fruitless negotiation, the Common Front pulled its members from the province's schools, hospitals, government offices, and other public-sector worksites. "Never again will we be divided," declared Laberge. But this unity was destroyed as the state moved to crush this incipient rebellion. The Common Front was legislated back to work and the three leading figures within the Common Front alliance (Pepin, Laberge, and teachers' leader Yvon Charbonneau) were jailed.

Disputes erupted within the workers' movement as some claimed that the actions of March–April 1972 had been the utmost in extremist folly, destined to lead to frustration, demoralization, and defeat. As in 1919, lack of programmatic direction and the immense weight of authority of the state defeated the general strike.

The Common Front had revealed the workers' potential ability to control the social and economic structures of the entire province of Quebec. At Sept-Isles, St. Jerome, and Montreal, workers seized the reigns of authority in the workplace, liberating themselves from traditional restraints. Equally significant was the Common Front's demonstration of the force of public-sector workers and the volatility of this previously overlooked stratum in the event of confrontation. Indeed, across Canada, to varying degrees, the question of public-sector unionism raised new debates about essential services and curbs that would be placed upon workers' rights in these economically and politically crucial areas. For, like Quebec labour, this new contingent of Canadian workers was beginning to make its presence felt. Two distinct but overlapping strata found their way into the trade-union movement and into public prominence after almost a century of remaining on the margins of organized labour. White-collar and public-sector workers would add new strength to trade unionism's potency, at the same time that they revealed the limited impact that organization could have in specific job classifications and the power of the state to curb working-class initiatives in particular service realms.

New Strengths for an Old Movement

Organization in the public sector dates at least from 1889 when railway mail clerks first formed an association. This early effort was followed by various federal government employee attempts to forge à moderate sense of collectivity in 1909, and organization among the letter carriers and postal workers in 1891 and 1911, respectively. The latter groups would initiate a more militant public-sector unionism, breaking from other government employees in the late 1950s to set up the Letter Carriers' Union of Canada and the Canadian Union of Postal Workers. Together they claimed a membership of 36,000 by the end of the 1960s. That decade, moreover, would see the first wave of conflicts in the public sector, serving as a preface to the even more wide-ranging upheavals of the 1970s.

Civil servants, including British Columbia and Saskatchewan government employees, customs officers, and a wide range of Quebec workers, were adamant in demanding the rights of collective bargaining by the early 1960s. Postal workers, however, took the first steps in this direction. They nurtured a weak recollection of a history of combativity that originated with their support for the Winnipeg General Strike and a 1925 strike broken by some of their own members. In 1965, the postal workers defied the government, the moderate leadership of their unions, and public outrage to extract a wage settlement. As the Post Office introduced automation and the government sought to turn the Post Office into a Crown corporation (a plan not to be realized until the 1980s), workers endorsed militant leaders and continued to demand humane treatment and economic justice.

In 1969, a work-to-rule campaign was initiated, and by 1975, postal workers had waged 30 job actions and strikes directed at issues of technological change, job security, hours, and pay. The introduction of automatic mail processing, based on the postal code, thrust CUPW into the role of arch-opponent of an economistic dehumanization: sorters working on the automated system were being paid 50 cents an hour less than manual sorters. Losing the battle against the code, CUPW remained sufficiently strong to stop the mails in 1975, winning a 30-hour week and a 70 percent wage increase. Amidst charges of "irresponsible elements" within its leadership and condemnation of its illegal actions, the union succeeded in increasing its membership as it broke through the "wage guidelines" established by the Liberal government in the early 1970s. By 1978, with Jean-Claude Parrot leading ·the postal workers, CUPW was continuing to oppose attempts to undercut its authority. The hiring of nonunion casual labour and the union's demand to be consulted on the implementation of technological changes sparked a confrontation in 1978 that ended with the workers legislated back to work and Parrot jailed. In spite of their victories, postal workers still faced supervisors and inspectors whose tactless "handling" of the workers conformed to the military discipline of the barracks from which many of them had come. As late as 1977, after countless studies of the poisoned atmosphere within the Post Office, the case of A.G. Steele, an Ottawa mail sorter, revealed the workers' plight. Accused of misplacing a package, Steele was questioned by his supervisors, taken to a police station, jailed for eight hours while his apartment was ransacked, and approached by a management informer who attempted to make him admit guilt before a hidden recording device. In the end, the Post Office admitted that it had been in error and that Steele had simply rerouted an improperly sorted package.

In addition to the militant confrontations at the Post Office, new developments were reshaping the texture of class relations in other parts of the public sector. The passage of the Public Service Staff Relations Act and two accompanying bills early in 1967 gave 260,000 government employees the right to choose between the strike or arbitration. Months earlier, civil servants affiliated with two workers' bodies that resembled company unions renounced these "staff associations" to create a more aggressive and united organization, the 120,000-member Public Service Alliance of Canada. By the 1970s, PSAC, teachers, and hospital workers associated with the 1963-created Canadian Union of Public Employees, provided the labour movement with a new voice of militancy.

No union so clearly articulates the massive upsurge of public-sector unionism as CUPE. Between 1963 and 1973, it doubled its membership, as it attracted thousands to its ranks every year. In mid-1975, with 210,000 supporters, it became the largest union in Canada. A significant part of this growth can be attributed to its efforts to organize hospital workers in the 1960s, many of whom were denied the right to strike by provincial legislation. These health workers threatened to take to the streets in a 1974 illegal defiance of the Ontario Hospital Labour Disputes Arbitration Act, presenting, like their Quebec counterparts, a "Common Front" to various hospital boards. Wage increases were eventually won, often without recourse to an illegal strike, and the 1974 campaign to secure "catch-up" pay increases for hospital workers encouraged nurses to join the rebellion. In New Brunswick, Nova Scotia, British Columbia, and Manitoba, nurses demanded settlements similar to those won in Ontario. Nurses resigned, threatened illegal job actions, and promised more militancy. Like Ontario's secondary and elementary school teachers, whose 105,000-member unions struck schools in December 1973, these workers discovered their place in a class society and expressed their discontent openly. Challenging the legalistic restrictions that had circumscribed their protests in the past, hospital workers and teachers defied the barriers of "professionalism" to demand legitimate status within the Canadian labour movement. They would suffer through denunciations, state opposition, and attempts to sabotage contract negotiations as they joined thousands of federal, provincial, and municipal civil servants struggling to improve their lot in the mid-to-late 1970s. By 1978, the Liberal government had moved to curb free collective bargaining in the public sector. A movement to "free the servants" (the slogan of an advertising campaign launched by the Civil Service Association of Ontario in an effort to revise the Crown Employees Collective Bargaining Act of 1972) began to confront the authority and opposition of the state.

The organizational explosion in the public sector was, of course, paralleled by similar developments in more traditional union strongholds and militancy was also evident among blue-collar workers, where it often assumed different forms. Moreover, the motivations for the union drives and workplace actions of teachers, health-care workers, and civil servants were not unlike those causing building trades workers, railwaymen, and factory operatives to strike. Double-digit inflation, which was officially 12 to 13.5 percent by 1974/75, reduced purchasing power and led to rising worker demands. Strikes and walkouts increased greatly, and by the mid-1970s, were consuming 0.53 percent of all working time. Railway workers struck for a 38 percent wage increase in 1973, only to be followed by strikes of Ontario hospital workers and public employees who sought settlements that included provisions for 45 to 60 percent pay increases. In this climate, white-collar workers in the private sector, long impervious to organization, were forced to consider the possible advantages of casting their lot with unionized labour.

Many of the workers in the public sector embracing a militant stand for labour in the 1960s and 1970s worked in job settings dominated more by white-collar than by blue-collar employees. Few fit the image of the archetypal proletarian. Yet, as studies by David Coombs and Graham

Lowe reveal, the early years of the twentieth century saw the erosion of status and privilege associated with the prim and proper "black-coated worker," traditionally a male ally and confidant of the employer. As an administrative revolution altered the corporate structure of Canadian capitalism in the early twentieth century, the modern office, staffed by a newly created stratum of clerical workers subordinate to managerial authority, emerged as a central component of the economic order. Between 1901 and 1961, white-collar work rose from a relatively insignificant place among the occupational groups making up the total labour force to a position of dominance, encompassing almost 40 percent of all Canadian workers. By 1971, the clerical subsection of white-collar workers was the largest occupational grouping in the country, with over 1,300,000 working members.

In the workplace experience of these clerks, two developments were of paramount importance. First, the feminization of clerical workers meant that whereas 22 percent of those employed in this sector were women in 1901, 60 to 70 percent of all clerical workers in the 1960s and 1970s were female. As a female job ghetto, then, clerical work was particularly subject to the low wage structure that a patriarchal capital found easy to rationalize. Second, office work was itself increasingly fragmented, routinized, and restructured through automation. In recent years, word processors and microchip technology have revolutionized the office, threatening displacement of entire platoons of clerks and now-expendable technicians. Before the advent of microtechnology, white-collar workers were in greater demand, and employers often used the possibility of career advancement as a means of encouraging employees to work for lower rates. As technological innovation continues to eliminate jobs and to reduce the demand for workers, employers have maintained low wage levels but also reduced advancement possibilities. As one business school professor has remarked: "White collars are where administrators look to save money, for places to hire. It's the law of supply and demand. Once you're in big supply, you're a bum."

Such developments have led to generally deteriorating wage and working conditions. In 1971, clerical workers in Canada saw their wages relative to those of other workers decline ten percent, and their take-home pay was only 70 percent of that of their counterparts in other work sectors. By the early 1970s, the "white collar blues" became a much-discussed issue, and one CLC officer noted that "most large offices are nothing but quiet factories." Subjected to the same insecurities and tedium as factory operatives, white-collar workers had become part of the working class. Many, as a study by Janet Mayer reveals, refused to confront this reality and clung to outmoded conceptions of their unique status and intimate connection with capital: they continued to view themselves as members of the middle class.

Others, however, began the battle for workplace rights, entering the trade-union movement.

The history of office-worker unionization began in the 1940s when the Steel Workers Organizing Committee lent support to bank clerks' efforts to organize under the auspices of the Office and Professional Workers Organizing Committee. Clerks worked in what CIO-organizer Eileen Tallman described as "Neanderthal" conditions. The patriarchal hold of the banks was so firm that even male bank clerks earned meagre weekly earnings and their personal lives were monitored to the extent that they were not allowed to marry until their annual salaries rose to approximately $1,500.00. Bankers apparently felt that this amount would enable the workers to assume family responsibilities and provide for their dependents without "dipping into the till." Rebelling against these conditions, tellers organized locals in Toronto, Vancouver, and Montreal and struck against two banks in the latter city, where young clerks took home only $8.00 to $12.00 per week. Opposed by managers and priests, this first bank strike was crushed, and the office and professional workers' union disappeared, its essentially male leadership drawn off by wartime armed services recruitment.

By the late 1940s, the leading role in organizing white-collar workers passed to the Retail, Wholesale and Department Store Union. After establishing a base in a few dairies, bakeries, and a food chain in 1946, the RWDSU began to organize employees at Eaton's, Canada's third-largest employer and a force that was keeping wages low in the retail field. Bringing together dedicated CIO organizers Lynn Williams and Eileen Tallman, the Toronto-based Eaton's campaign turned on the demand of equal pay for equal work. Struggling to overcome a segmented workforce, in which employees were distinguished by gender, age, wage, and a multitude of job classifications, the organizers learned that the response to unionism varied from one group to the next. Across the spectrum of departments, Williams and Tallman found that a segmented labour force conditioned a fragmentary cultural context that created barriers to unity. Women in part-time sales, working for "extra" family income, were difficult to organize, as were prestige salesmen in heavy appliances or long-time employees selling fine china goods to an established clientèle. Drivers, pressured and structured into persistent overtime, however, were strong union advocates.

Between 1948 and 1952, Eaton's Toronto stores were leafletted and, as in the industrial union struggles of the 1930s, cultural activities were set up to draw workers to the cause. The "Mugwump," a cartoon or *papier mâché* caricature of the worker who could not decide whether or not to join the union, was created to demonstrate the urgency of decisive action and commitment. Banquets, dances, and social affairs were held, all of which proclaimed openly the existence of prounion forces and broke down long-entrenched relations of subordination. Williams created a 44-team league captained by organizers, each of whom had a weekly membership objective. Gains were being registered by the young CCF organizers, but they encountered difficulties as union supporters moved on to other jobs. (Labour turnover at Eaton's approached 35 percent of the staff yearly.) In addition, the company was gaining support through wage increases, the creation of a pension plan, and opposition to the collectivist orientation of the union. Eaton's stalled union certification proceedings until the Christmas season of 1951, when workers were busiest and thousands of casual labourers were hired for a few weeks. Such developments provided the company with a substantial number of workers who would be apathetic enough to fail to vote for unionization. When the votes were tallied the union had lost by a mere 800 ballots, almost 9,000 having being cast. Later efforts came to little and an historic opportunity to win union rights for the workers of a major white-collar employer came to nought.

The defeat of the Eaton's campaign symbolized the constricting potential for white-collar workers that would prevail throughout the 1950s and much of the 1960s. Not until public-sector unionists moved to the forefront of organized labour in the mid-1970s was interest in white-collar organization revived. The CLC led a well-financed attempt to recruit office workers to the Association of Clerical and Technical Employees. But barriers remained, including what Michael Katzemba has described as the fear of "trouble" that is a significant part of the psychology of the office. ACTE was able to enlist only 7,000 new members. The percentage of unionized offices actually declined from 7 percent in 1975 to less than 3 percent in 1976. But fear of the "trouble" unionism entails is gradually being eroded. The increasingly alienating conditions of modern white-collar work, inflationary assaults on the white-collar wage, the disparity between blue-collar union and white-collar nonunion wage rates, and successful union efforts, such as the recent Steelworkers' Radio Shack warehouse victory, have led to changing attitudes. Finally, although there is a preponderance of females among white-collar workers and this sector has traditionally proven difficult to organize, the structural context of women's wage labour and female attitudes to unionization are changing, translating into escalating demands.

Women: At Home and Away

The twentieth century has witnessed a shift in attitudes and practices regarding women and wage labour. Once defined as a stage in the life cycle between two phases of dependency (childhood and marriage), and an undesirable interlude at that, female involvement in paid labour has now become commonplace in contemporary Canada, where large numbers of women work in manufacturing, service, and sales occupations. The female participation rate in the labour force climbed from 16.2 percent in 1911 to 39.9 percent in 1971, almost doubling between 1941 and 1971. Whereas 832,000 Canadian women worked for wages in 1941, over 3,000,000 occupied a like status at the beginning of the 1970s. Such figures point to the partial elimination of traditional prejudices and barriers blocking entry to wage labour, but they mask certain critically important social and cultural realities. For women have always worked, if not for wages, providing a force sustaining working-class households and experience for decades, even centuries. Often casually employed, or marginalized in outwork, it has proven particularly difficult to place women in the usual occupational classifications. Given to voicing their discontents at the workplace by leaving one job to secure another (often the only option for workers who lacked union protection and legal recourse), women workers' visibility has been clouded historically by the high turnover rates in specific work sectors. To discuss women and the working class, however, is to recognize more than the expanding place of women in the labour force and the problems that intrude upon analytical and empirical work in this area. It is also to understand the pivotal role women have played in reproduction — through child bearing and child rearing, as well as in unpaid domestic labour — and in the political economy of the family.

Until the 1940s, the bulk of women employed in wage labour toiled as laundresses, sweatshop workers in the garment industry, or factory operatives in light manufacturing, producing goods like boots and shoes or textiles. As the clerical workforce expanded, women came to dominate the office, and female employment possibilities widened with the expansion of health care that paralleled the rise of the welfare state. Domestic service, the nineteenth century's major female occupation, declined as women were drawn to these more "liberating" jobs. World War I drew many married women into the labour force and, for a brief moment, invalidated long-cherished notions of the distinctions between men's and women's work. A similar process occurred during World War II, when state and employer welcomed some women into the ranks of a labour force depleted by male recruitment to the armed forces. But even in the war-induced "emergency" situation of the early 1940s, as Ruth Pierson has argued, the confinements of domesticity hung over women's entry into war industries. Young single women were recruited first, childless married women next, and finally and reluctantly, mothers. Daycare facilities were established to ease the burdens of this last group. By 1943, more than 250,000 women worked in industrial pursuits of strategic importance to the war effort. Countless others manned the service sector and worked in agriculture: teachers and female students over the age of 15 formed the majority of the almost 13,000-member Farmerette Brigade, whose hard labour at 25 cents an hour did much to keep the country and its soldiers fed.

But, as in the aftermath of the Great War, many of the gains made during the war period were eclipsed with the return to a post-1945 "normalcy." In industrial cities like Hamilton, where women had worked at Stelco, National Steel Car Company, Westinghouse, and Sawyer Massey, work in the primary sector was never completely redefined as a male preserve, but a series of pressures — from the state, the employers, and the returning veterans — constricted opportunities and undermined the sense of women's independence cultivated in the war years.

The family, not the factory, reemerged as the centre of women's lives and, as Hugh and Pat Armstrong have shown, the 1950s and 1960s saw women segregated in occupations designated unofficially as female. More than half of employed women in these decades worked as typists, maids, teachers, waitresses, nurses, telephone operators, tailoresses, clerks, and janitors. As women workers peculiarly adapted to such maternal service-oriented tasks, they earned approximately half the income of their male counterparts and only in rare circumstances did women's wages approach 75 percent of those of men. Poorly paid, such women workers were conventionally seen as duplicating at work what they were supposedly physically and temperamentally suited to in the home. More women entered the labour force than men during these years and married women became more likely to seek employment, so that the proportion of single women in the workforce declined from 80 percent of all female workers in 1941 to 34 percent in 1971. However, throughout most of the postwar period, women's working lives were characterized by subordination and poor pay at the same time that their domestic situations were similarly circumscribed. If unmarried, the woman could support herself and such dependents as she had only through rigorous budgeting and underconsumption. Married women, on the other hand, while contributing to the family wage, seldom did so as the equal of men, whose earnings, on average, made their wives' paycheques appear paltry indeed. In spite of increasing numbers of women who have gained entrance to the professions, the sociological literature reveals that a gender-based structured inequality still predominated from 1950 to 1970, the years when vast numbers of women entered the labour force. Table 6.2 shows occupations that women tended to enter between 1941 and 1961.

Employers, of which the government is among the largest, had successfully secured a pool of inexpensive labour that they envisioned would remain compliant, while the sanctity of the family remained intact. By perpetuating a conception of maternalism that was little more than a rationale for low wages and patriarchal authority, capital once more contributed to inequality within productive relations. Although the situation remained unchanged during the 1950s, exploitative

TABLE 6.2 Leading female occupations, 1941–61

Occupation	1941		1951		1961	
	Female percentage of occupation	Percentage of all women workers	Female percentage of occupation	Percentage of all women workers	Female percentage of occupation	Percentage of all women workers
Stenographers & typists	95.9	9.4	96.4	11.6	96.8	12.2
Sales clerks	41.4	6.8	52.9	8.3	53.6	7.8
Babysitters, maid, & related service workers	96.1	22.8	90.8	9.3	88.9	7.7
School teachers	74.6	7.8	72.5	6.5	70.7	6.9
Tailoresses, furriers, & related workers	67.8	6.2	73.7	6.4	76.2	4.5
Waitresses & bartenders	62.5	2.8	66.7	3.5	70.5	3.6
Graduate nurses	99.4	3.2	97.5	3.0	96.2	3.4
Nursing assistants & aides	71.0	1.0	72.4	1.6	78.9	2.9
Telephone operators	92.6	1.5	96.5	2.6	95.2	2.0
Janitors & cleaners	19.7	0.6	27.5	1.2	31.5	1.8
Totals	74.3	62.1	73.7	54.0	73.6	52.8

SOURCE: Hugh and Pat Armstrong, "The Segregated Participation of Women in the Canadian Labour Force," *Canadian Review of Sociology and Anthropology* 12 (1975), 372.

employers were challenged in the 1960s and 1970s. Within families, for instance, women had already begun to question patriarchical authority. This experience, in part, led to the increasing consciousness of women's oppression in both home and workplace, which was stimulated by the growth of the women's movement in the mid-1960s. On these foundations were built new demands that, by the 1970s, had become common currency within a labour movement forced to confront the "woman question."

The 1940s and 1950s were years of transition in this process. In a study of female cotton workers in Quebec between 1910 and 1950, Gail Cuthbert Brandt delineates a movement away from the traditional two-phase life cycle of the 1940s, in which single women worked in the mills until their early twenties and left the workforce upon marriage. Women moved between two cycles of dependency: as young workers they handed their wages over to their parents; when married, they were engaged in unpaid domestic labour and child rearing, and relied on their husbands' earnings. After 1940, however, more workers were practising family limitation, higher wages allowed earlier ages of marriage, and women workers' life cycles took on a more complex structure. Young women worked for a shorter period before marriage and, after a finite period of child rearing, returned to the workforce as married women, supplementing the family income and expanding the consuming potential of the conjugal unit. Between 1941 and 1951, there was thus a decline in the labour-force participation of female cotton workers in the 25 to 34 age bracket, and a 40 percent increase in the proportion of workers aged 45 years and older. A study of the entire Quebec female labour force by Nicolas Zay contains similar findings. Meg Luxton's oral histories of three generations of home workers in the one-industry town of Flin Flon, Manitoba, demonstrates how housewives in the years 1940-59 experienced the modernization of domestic labour, "financing" the purchase of household commodities through babysitting, taking in boarders or laundry, sewing, providing services such as haircuts or Tupperware parties, and carefully budgeting the husband's wage.

These tendencies, in conjunction with the rapid dismantling of employment opportunity and childcare facilities in the aftermath of World War II, suggest that in the 1940s and 1950s women retreated into the nuclear family. Female cotton workers, Brandt argues, faced technological changes and workplace disciplines that eroded what little autonomy and few skills they had possessed in the 1920s and 1930s. As their youthful working lives were shortened through marriage and they could only return to work in middle age when the working-class family had finally reached an economic plateau, women conceived of themselves as a transient, family-oriented stratum of the labour force. Their concern with the social aspects of collectivity and working-class solidarity in general, and unionism in particular, was correspondingly diminished. In Luxton's study of Flin Flon, it is not so much a sense of class that emerges from her "second generation" of housewives, establishing their families during the 1940s and 1950s. Rather, it is the development of a community of women that is most visible. Their ties to each other, consolidated through moments saved by washing machines, improved kitchen technology, and the mechanization of cleaning, were ultimately forged within a family mediated by the realities of working-class life, but affected deeply by changing patterns of consumption that blurred class distinctions.

Of course, these processes affected men as well as women, and their impact would be felt in realms connected with, but seemingly far removed from, the home. In failing to fight adequately the segregation of women in the most menial and ill-paid work sectors, the labour movement itself bore some of the responsibility for the general drift toward an insular, family-centred culture of consumption, in which the man's wages provided women with money for housekeeping, while the woman's wages, when earned, were easily characterized as "pin money." Mass culture, the appearance of working-class affluence, and the economic climate of buoyancy in the early 1950s lent such developments force, but it was capital, not the working class, that would reap the final rewards, as one strike in northern Ontario demonstrated.

The largest industrial dispute in the 1950s was the Sudbury, Ontario, Inco strike of 1958, a three-month long confrontation that pitted 14,500 workers and their families against the mining company, which lost almost 700,000 worker-days to the strikers. Affiliated with the International Union of Mine, Mill and Smelter Workers (a survivor of the anticommunist purges of the 1940s), the Sudbury workers and their union were crushed in what one workingman later described as "a premeditated smashing of the union." An indecisive union leadership failed to develop a coordinated strike strategy, and appeared to be alienating the rank and file with its undemocratic and arbitrary stifling of discussion in union meetings. A Women's Strike Committee was formed to pressure the company and the union, formalizing the supportive role that many wives and mothers had been playing since the beginning of the strike. But after two months of suffering and deprivation, the majority of Sudbury's women favoured a different approach. Two thousand convened in the Sudbury arena to confer with the mayor, who appealed to their "protective instincts . . . a basic quality of all women here today." This was to prove, in specific circumstances, a variant of Betty Friedan's "Feminine Mystique" of particular use to capital.

Calling for a settlement at prestrike wages, demanding that civic officials intervene to end the strike, and asking the company to assume its appropriate paternalistic responsibilities by providing relief that would alleviate distress in the Sudbury district, these wives defied the union in the interests of the family. "This is a meeting of wives, not of union members," they proclaimed. "Our men are booed down or forced, physically, out of [the union] hall if they ask questions. How do they propose to shut the women up?" In the days to follow, the media made much of the rebellion of the wives, the state was drawn into the conflict, and tensions mounted within the striker community. One unionist assaulted another for causing his name to be removed from Mine-Mill's welfare list. "He took the bread out of my kids' mouths," he stated in explanation. The miners eventually returned to work for a paltry six percent wage increase over three years; Inco had won an unambiguous victory.

As an unpublished study by Bill Pentney notes, miners were defeated partly by the intervention of the wives on the side of settlement; economic recession, corporate power, unwillingness to negotiate, and a faction-ridden union also ensured a less than impressive showing against capital. In the family-bound context of the 1950s, workers and their wives may well have placed primary emphasis upon their particular family unit to the detriment of larger collective interests. But it would be wrong to simply dismiss the Sudbury wives of 1958 as a conservative force buttressing capital's rule. Their assertiveness represented a revolt against the confines of domesticity and femininity, a restatement of social values that had particular relevance within workers' experience: the right to work; the calling to order of a company that wielded its power in an irresponsible manner. Twenty years later, during another strike at Inco, wives would prove a force sustaining militancy and class resolve, reversing the stand that their counterparts had taken in 1958.

Strikes were fought at Inco in 1966, 1969, 1974 (a wildcat), 1975, and, in 1978/79, the longest conflict in the history of Sudbury's miners erupted. Led by local militant Dave Patterson, this last battle turned on issues involving wages, conditions, and grievance procedures, and won the workers union securities and a substantial hourly rate increase. But their costs were also high, including 261 days during which they had drawn no wages. Millions of dollars of support from the United Steel Workers of America sustained them, on one level, but more important, perhaps, was the militant solidarity of the entire working-class community.

A miner expressed this sense of unity in a letter to the *Globe and Mail* that condemned Inco's antilabour stand: "They had misread the workers' will to fight for a decent living wage. . . . The whole exercise was designed to lower the pride of the ordinary workers, to teach the pensioners a lesson for daring to picket Inco's Toronto office and to restrict the effectiveness of the stewards to obtain redress for aggrieved workers". An exemplary role was also played by the strikers' wives, who formed a support group called Wives Supporting the Strike. But unlike the 1958 Women's Strike Committee, this group won the allegiance of many women who feared the conflict would disrupt family life and wipe out the little security that employment had provided. The Wives Supporting the Strike overcame the insularity of the family to develop collective aid, organizing babysitting cooperatives, car pools, mass suppers, and educational groups that provided new knowledge of the issues at stake in the conflict. Women picketed and joined women's demonstrations in Toronto. The actions of these women led to a new awareness of ways in which cultural and political issues could combine with struggles in the workplace in an attempt to establish a more humane society. One woman expressed the new sense of community that she had discovered:

> I'll never be quite the same again. Now I have a vision of another day. I guess I learned that ordinary women like me can fight a big multinational company like Inco and win — can challenge the government . . . . I learned that there are other ways of organizing our daily lives, ways of living as a community together, ways of being husbands and wives that I never imagined before . . . . Maybe all together, we could make a better world.

The evolution that had occurred in Sudbury between 1958 and 1978 can be understood only by examining the development of the women's movement as a whole. During these years, the movement was revitalized after half a century in which it had lain dormant in the aftermath of World War I. In kitchens, offices, universities, and industrial plants, the question of the woman's role became, once again, a topic of discussion. A diffuse and eclectic amalgamation of individuals and groups, the women's movement extended beyond class at the same time that it exercised a powerful influence within trade-union circles.

Women remain less unionized than men. In the mid-1970s, 43 percent of male workers belonged to unions, compared to just 27 percent of female workers. Great provincial variations further complicate this differentiation, with Quebec and British Columbia having the highest degree of unionization among women, Ontario and Nova Scotia the lowest. Yet in spite of the generally poor record in this realm, the rate of unionization among female workers increased markedly between 1966 and 1976. The number of female unionists more than doubled to over 750,000, while women as a percentage of organized labour rose from 17 percent to 27 percent. In the growing public-sector organizations women have become a considerable presence. CUPE's 1976 membership of almost 220,000 was 41 percent female, while in PSAC, various provincial employees' unions, nurses' associations, retail clerks' unions, and internationally affiliated organizations like the International Ladies Garment Workers Union, women comprise from 40 to 100 percent of the membership. Representation on union executives has been increasing since 1975, and approximately 17 percent of such officers are now female. Whereas the number of male unionists increased by 40 percent between 1966 and 1976, the ranks of female unionists expanded by 160 percent. Certainly, unionization of women has been restricted by the segregated and low-wage character of work in the services, trade, finance and public-administration industries, where almost 80 percent of women are concentrated, and by the relatively small numbers of women working in the historically highly unionized construction, transportation, and manufacturing sectors (where only 20 percent of all working women are employed). The wage gap between male and female workers has actually increased, 1980 statistics pegging the average woman's wage ($9,874) well below that of a man ($17,038).

However, certain well-publicized struggles speak to the emerging prominence of women and women's issues in the labour movement. In 1978, 75 women struck the Fleck Manufacturing auto-parts factory near Exeter, Ontario, in the summer of 1981 paid maternity leave was a major bargaining issue in a strike by the Canadian Union of Postal Workers, and rank-and-file upheavals have occurred in unions like the Hotel, Restaurant, Culinary and Bartenders Union, which recently saw a waitress and a female bartender defeat a well-entrenched male bureaucracy in Vancouver's 14,000-member Local 40. Never before has the demand for equal pay for equal work been so prominently before the public eye, and for the first time, sexual harassment at the workplace is attracting the attention of workers' organizations. At the Steelworkers' 1981 Policy Conference, the third-largest union in the country went on record as supporting affirmative action programs, childcare legislation, paternity-leave provisions for *both* men and women, women's involvement in union education, and the creation of women's committees within the union. Among Quebec's Common Front unionists, such demands have long been supported and are most likely to remain on labour's agenda in spite of the opposition of employers in the public and private sectors.

Both in their homes and in their workplaces, then, female workers have experienced profound changes in the 1960s and 1970s. Moving away from the insular, family-centred cultural constrictions of the 1950s, they have fought their way into the labour movement and redefined the very notion of collectivity. An older woman in Flin Flon (born in 1891) spoke to Meg Luxton of her own experiences and what they told her about historical process:

> Women's politics are like an iceberg. Only the tip shows and it never looks like much. But underneath is a vast mass of women, always moving, usually very slowly. . . . When I was young, women didn't even have the vote. Well, we thought about that and it didn't seem right so finally lots of women got together and worked for it and now we got the vote. Most people assume women will put up with things the way they are. But that isn't so. When women see a thing needs changing, things change.

This woman was undoubtedly overly sanguine, and history reveals that working-class gains are usually won and preserved through struggle. Women's actions in these years, however, were not isolated demands for change cut off from mainstream developments within the working class. On the contrary, the last three decades have seen the women's movement and many other forces unite to revitalize the Canadian workers' movement.

Youth, Popular Culture, and Nationalism

The Canadian labour force, like Canadian society in general, grew younger over the 1960s and 1970s. Whereas people between the ages of 15 and 24 accounted for 15.3 percent of the country's population in 1951, by 1978, 19 percent of all Canadians were in this age group. Within the workforce, this demographic shift had a dramatic impact. In the decade-and-a-half between 1961 and 1975, the numbers of youth participating in wage labour rose dramatically. The percentage of wage earners in the 14 to 19 and 20 to 24 age brackets rose from 36.2 and 68.9, respectively, to 51.1 and 75.9 percent. These figures climbed even higher in the later 1970s before beginning to decline in the post-1978 years. The 1980s will undoubtedly experience declining participation rates for the young, as a post-1957 drop in the birth rate makes its influence felt in the workplace. But throughout the 1960s and 1970s, the average annual participation rate increases of workers under 25 years of age were between 4.4 and 5.3 percent, consistently outpacing the average annual labour force increase of 3.1 percent. This lent an increasingly youthful appearance to the Canadian working class: almost one-quarter, or 4,345,200, of all working Canadians were between the ages of 14 and 24 in 1978.

Some of the youths entering the labour market for the first time in these years continued to live with their parents, sustaining the family's capacity to consume in the face of inflation. For a time this family strategy, so reminiscent of nineteenth-century and immigrant forms of adaptation, allowed the family unit an illusion of "prosperity." However, job satisfaction was low. A work ethic survey recently undertaken by the Department of Employment and Immigration found that young workers under the age of 20 were the least satisfied with their current employment, while in the 20 to 34 age group, there was a notable gap between job aspirations and realizations: as more and more young people crowded into a finite number of jobs, the possibilities for "advancement" became constricted. Within this context of limited potential, youthful grievances found an outlet in cultural developments of the 1960s and 1970s that placed an accent on youth and libertarian antiauthoritarianism. Popular culture, in these decades, fused home and workplace resentments in a populistic assault on the "establishment," an imprecise target that seemed to include the older "generation" and the bastions of social and economic power, both of which seemed rigidly separated out from the experiences of the young.

The antiestablishment wave gained momentum with Elvis Presley, whose "white" renditions of black blues music galvanized youth across North America. None, perhaps, were so enchanted as Presley's own people, the migrants from Appalachia who, together with black Americans, manned the assembly lines in automobile plants in Michigan and Ohio. Presley's 1950s Canadian tour was followed by other entertainers and in the 1960s British rock groups and American folk singers (all of whom, like Elvis, drew upon black jazz and blues artists) followed in his wake. New fashions, scientific advances in birth-control methods, increased sexual permissiveness, and drug experimentation paralleled the transformation in music that was at the centre of the emergence of a "counter-culture." Much of this culture was apolitical, extended well beyond class boundaries, and only supported the consumerism of a pluralist society. But at the same time, in its essential questioning of social convention and defiance of established authority, developments within popular culture easily drifted toward a more explicit challenge to the social order. Quebec's Quiet Revolution was loosely connected to such processes, as was the emergence of the women's movement. One sociological study of sexuality and family planning among low-income urban Québécois married couples revealed how much had changed in the tradition-bound relations of the sexes. Before 1969/70 two-thirds of all pregnancies were unplanned and a mere 25 percent of women used contraceptives after marriage or the first pregnancy; in the 1970s, however, 86 percent of the couples were using some method of birth control, and half the women were taking oral contraceptives. Finally, the emergence of the New Left in Canada, with its explicit ties to the American civil rights movement and opposition to the war in Vietnam, was related to the general cultural climate of dissidence, although it attempted to focus previously incoherent or unarticulated strands of opposition into a more direct challenge.

The rise of a popular culture centred on youth and open expression of discontent was often perceived as a product of campus rebellion: the expanding number of university students necessarily attracted attention to those in the classroom rather than the workplace. But even at the height of university enrolments, less than 20 percent of all Canadians aged 18 to 24 were students, and young workers were caught up in many of the same cultural activities and processes of change that swept so prominently through the ranks of postsecondary educational institutions.

Within Canadian unionism, for instance, a rank-and-file membership that came of age after the anticommunist purges of the 1940s and 1950s was less loyal to its leadership than workers of another generation.

Younger workers were simply less likely to identify closely with an entrenched leadership whose accomplishments in the recognition struggles of the postwar period or the economic and job condition gains of the 1950s meant less to them than they had to their fathers. Moreover, with unions expanding in size (by 1970 well over two million Canadian unionists paid dues of almost $100 million) and with international offices far removed from Canadian memberships, some youthful dissidents accused the labour movement of being too centralized. The results would be felt throughout the 1960s and 1970s.

By the mid-1960s, for instance, illegal "wildcat" strikes were commonplace and in 1965/66, 369 such struggles were waged in defiance of union leaders. Many of these battles were epic confrontations that won workers considerable concessions from capital. Throughout these tense moments of conflict, workers fought their employers, the state, and their unions, rejecting contracts, fighting police, and defying court injunctions. Typical of the complex levels of developing antagonism were strikes of Hamilton and Sudbury steelworkers and Montreal longshoremen in 1966. Negotiations at Inco were disrupted by a 16,000-member wildcat that union officials subdued only after three weeks; nevertheless, it helped to win Sudbury's miners the highest rates in North America. When the contract was eventually approved, however, only 57 percent of the union's membership were in favour of a settlement. To the south, in Hamilton, worker discontent erupted in a violent wildcat at the Steel Company of Canada, where workers fought

TABLE 6.3 Strikes and lockouts in Canada, 1950–66

Year	Number	Workers involved (000s)	Worker-days (000s)	Percentage of estimated working time
1950	160	192.1	1387.5	.15
1951	258	102.8	901.6	.09
1952	219	112.3	2765.5	.29
1953	173	54.5	1312.7	.14
1954	173	56.6	1430.3	.15
1955	159	60.1	1875.4	.19
1956	229	88.7	1246.0	.11
1957	245	80.7	1477.1	.13
1958	259	111.5	2816.8	.25
1959	216	95.1	2226.9	.19
1960	274	49.4	733.7	.06
1961	287	98.0	1335.1	.11
1962	311	74.3	1417.9	.11
1963	322	83.4	917.1	.07
1964	343	100.5	1580.6	.11
1965	501	171.9	2349.9	.17
1966	617	411.5	5047.0	.33

Adapted from Jamieson, *Times of Trouble*, 371, 397.

police and union leaders, destroyed property, and won themselves a reputation for militancy and the highest steelworking wage in the world. On the Montreal docks, the first illegal strike in years was fought by dockers resisting the stevedoring companies' demands that new cargo-handling machinery be used and gangs reduced in size accordingly. Similar developments on the railways forced parliament to guarantee 18 percent wage increases before it ordered strikers back to work, and 12,000 postal workers led one of the largest nationwide wildcats in the 1965/66 upheaval, partly improving the depressed wage environment in which they earned $3,000 less than policemen and firemen of comparable seniority and $2,000 less than unskilled labourers employed by municipalities like Vancouver. Table 6.3 shows the number of strikes and lockouts that occurred in Canada between 1950 and 1966.

Typical of contemporary descriptions of these conflicts was a newspaper account outlining the violence and organization of the four-day "quickie" wildcat of Hamilton's Stelco workers:

> Mob rule shut down the sprawling works of the Steel Company of Canada Limited, putting 16,000 persons out of work. Wildcat strikers defied and mobbed their union leaders, shoved police aside and closed off all access to the company's plant and offices. . . . The strike appeared to be well organized, but neither the union nor the company could identify those behind it. Some attributed it to young hotheads, others to communists and still others to a group of Canadian autonomists within the union.

This confrontation contained many of the sociological characteristics typical of the wildcats of the 1960s: youthful exuberance, the emergence of semiautonomous structures of working-class self-activity, and a history of grievance and frustration vented not only against the company, but also against the union. Throughout the 1960s and 1970s, a part of the Canadian labour-movement effort would be directed toward alleviating this threat to capital, the state, and, in many cases, established trade unions.

Young workers of the 1960s were also members of the youth-oriented mass culture of these years, and, as such, showed open hostility to bureaucratic structures and impersonalized social relations. Ironically enough, much of the imported American dissident culture of the time led Canadians to embrace nationalism as a protest against the American "establishment." Among trade unionists, however, the immediate issues were not the lack of Canadian content in television and radio, the high levels of foreign ownership in the resource and manufacturing sectors, or the number of non-Canadians staffing university faculties. The main issue was that perennial point of contention, international unionism. The national question was manifested within the Canadian trade-union movement in the 1960s and 1970s, as a breakaway movement emerged and a new round of internecine warfare splintered the already fragmented forces of Canadian labour.

Since the 1920s, a strictly Canadian labour movement had been espoused by some in the trade-union movement. By the 1950s, two key figures in the drive to organize workers into autonomous Canadian unions were Kent Rowley and Madeleine Parent. Driven from the United Textile Workers of America in a 1952 purge of a dozen Canadian staffers accused of "disastrous and irresponsible leadership" and "communist" leanings, Rowley and Parent countered by setting up the Canadian Textile Council (CTC), an organization established during their UTWA years, when they anticipated their expulsion. The CTC provided a base for the organization of national textile unions independent of the AFL–CIO, with Brantford, Ontario, acting as a centre of recruitment to the fledgling movement. But throughout the 1950s, progress for the nationalists in the labour movement was limited, and Rowley, Parent, and their followers had little support until the populist and poorly conceived nationalism of the Diefenbaker years (1958–63) and Walter Gordon's Liberal anti-Americanism revived working-class concern with the national question. By the mid-1960s, a number of Canadian locals had broken from American unions to found small independent Canadian bodies.

Rowley orchestrated the founding of the Council of Canadian Unions in 1967, later to be known as the Confederation of Canadian Unions (CCU), a central body offering a home to those national unions that broke from the AFL–CIO-connected Canadian Labour Congress. The Canadian Textile Council was expanded to become the Canadian Textile and Chemical Union (CTCU), and in 1971 Rowley and Parent led a strike at the Brantford Texpack plant. The strike drew public attention to their crusade for national unionism and fused a number of dissident strands into a coherent moment of challenge and opposition to American capital and its incursions upon Canadian economic and social life. The Texpack struggle erupted in the aftermath of an American takeover of the Brantford plant in the 1960s. A large American multinational, the American Hospital Supply Corporation, planned to phase out production at the Ontario factory, using the facilities as a warehouse for distributing goods produced in U.S. and Asian plants, repackaged, and labelled "Made in Canada". The more than 300 workers, many of them women, thus stood to lose their jobs or be channeled into unskilled, low-paying warehouse work. Picket lines at the Texpack plant were thus aimed at resecuring jobs as well as educating the Canadian working class as to the dangers of the branch-plant economy. Unionists affiliated with American internationals, such as the Steelworkers and the Auto Workers, supported the Texpack struggle, as did the women's movement and the nationalistic left wing of the New Democratic Party, the Waffle. Countless young new leftists were also drawn to the daily skirmishes outside the Brantford plant, and local police battled picketers with riot gear and paddy wagons that seldom left the scene without arrested strike supporters. Sympathetic academics took their places beside angry workers, while lawyers refought the day's skirmishes in later courtroom confrontations. In the end, the workers at Texpack won a new contract that would preserve their jobs for the remainder of the decade. Labour unity and youthful support had won Rowley and the cause of national unionism an important victory. Less successful, but equally brutal, was the Artistic Woodwork strike of 1973, where an unorganized immigrant shop was won to the CTCU only to have a dictatorial management insist upon a contract clause that surrendered any vestige of workers' autonomy. As in Brantford, young and old leftists, as well as many in the political centre, united with progressive unionists to back the strikers. As picketers clashed with police in the late summer and early fall of 1973, the owners of the picture-frame factory capitulated and the strike was won. But in the immediate aftermath of this apparent success, victory was turned to defeat: management hounded unionists, foremen threatened leading activitists, and the CTCU Artistic certification vote ended in the crushing of the union and the demoralization of the workers.

Texpack and Artistic involved struggles of workers affiliated with national unions. In both instances, the powerful and established international bodies had shown little interest in organizing these troublesome sectors, where chances of victory were slight and the benefits of drawing such "marginal" workers into the trade-union movement few. But the nationalist mood of the late 1960s and early 1970s probably saw more influential developments within international unionism itself, where discontent with American labour leadership led to breakaways from established unions. Ed Finn, prominent Canadian union figure, noted in 1970 that there was a growing awareness of "nationalist sentiment among Canadian unionists," and that, "Unless the internationals heed these incipient rumblings and grant effective self-government to their branches in this country, the next decade could see a titanic — and ultimately successful — struggle for Canadian union emancipation."

To be sure, Finn wrote at a time when international unionism's control of organized labour was fairly secure, especially in English Canada. As of 1969 there were a mere 124 independent local organizations with a membership of only 56,500, an insignificant 2.7 percent of all unionized workers in Canada. But over the course of the 1970s, the national question persisted, and breakaways and raids made the issue important to labour, particularly in the west. Members of the International Brotherhood of Pulp, Sulphite and Paper Mill Workers seceded amicably to form the Pulp and Paper Workers of Canada, while 15 locals of the Retail, Wholesale and Department Store Union in Saskatchewan successfully disaffiliated. Between 1970 and 1975, the membership of the CCU more than doubled, and joined forces with the Canadian

Association of Industrial, Mechanical and Allied Workers (CAIMAW), and the Canadian Association of Smelter and Allied Workers (CASAW). CASAW led one of the largest successful raids on an international union in the early 1970s, winning jurisdiction rights over the 1,800 Alcan workers at Kitimat, British Columbia, whose previous affiliation had been to the United Steelworkers of America. CAIMAW, formed in 1964, has grown slowly and sporadically over the course of the last fifteen years, attracting 6,000 members to its ranks. These largely western breakaway movements were supplemented by eastern developments within Toronto's immigrant construction-worker community in the Bricklayers, Masons, and Plasterers International Union and among oil, chemical, and atomic workers in Montreal. In 1974, the 52,000 pulpworkers in the United Paperworkers International Union broke their ties with international unionism to found the independent Canadian Paperworkers Union. More recently, rank-and-file upheavals in the United Steel Workers Union and the International Union of Electrical Workers have led to much debate and, in the case of the IUE, formal independence. By 1978, national unions were an important segment of the Canadian labour movement, as revealed in Table 6.4.

The nationalist tide in the labour movement so prevalent during the 1970s may now be receding. Its appeal was never constant, usually fluctuating according to its stand on a particular grievance. National union gains usually occurred because of international unionism's

TABLE 6.4   Union membership by type of union and affiliation, 1978

Type and Affiliation	No. of Unions	Membership Number	Percent
International unions	88	1,553,477	47.4
AFL-CIO/CLC	69	1,281,495	39.1
CLC only	5	165,131	5.0
AFL-CIO only	7	10,573	0.3
Unaffiliated Unions	7	96,278	3.0
National unions	121	1,637,626	50.0
CLC	23	743,886	22.7
CNTU-(CSN)	9	177,239	5.4
CSD	3	25,406	0.8
CCU	13	26,007	0.8
Unaffiliated	73	665,088	20.3
Directly chartered locals	251	26,493	0.8
CLC	111	13,300	0.4
CNTU-(CSN)	4	516	0.1
CSD	136	12,677	0.4
Independent local organizations	170	60,372	1.8
Total	630	3,277,968	100.0

SOURCE: Smucker, *Industrialization in Canada*, 212.

alienating and contemptuous treatment of particular locals. After a decade of breakaways and raids, the large established internationals are realizing that they can not afford to ignore the Canadian membership, which reacts with hostility to indifference, arbitrary decision making, and contracts that do not deliver wage and condition benefits that workers need to survive in an era of unemployment, inflation, and constant assaults upon their health. As public-sector unionism continues to expand, moreover, the bogeyman of international unionism can no longer effectively be thrown in the face of the Canadian Labour Congress. With the rise of PSAC, CUPE, and various government employee unions, moreover, the Canadian Labour Congress now contains a majority of strictly Canadian unions. Indeed, as the recent withdrawal of the building trades unions from the CLC reveals, those at the head of the Congress can, in moments of crisis, don nationalist dress themselves. Nevertheless, as the 1970s give way to the troubled 1980s, with the economic security of Canadian workers in peril because of the stagnation and inflation that is eroding both jobs and purchasing power, the Canadian labour movement has turned toward political solutions to working-class problems. The national question, so critical in the relatively "good times" of the late 1960s and early 1970s, inevitably appears less urgent in the crisis-ridden 1980s, when basic survival engages the attention of more and more Canadian workers.

Politics

As David Lewis' recently published political memoirs record, the early 1940s were the first and most successful years of a labour-social democratic alliance. It was also a time that saw the CCF do daily battle with Communist Party members in the Labor Progressive Party. "All levels of the CCF spent enormous amounts of time and energy fighting off communist pressures to form a united front with them," recalled Lewis. Given what was clearly a social-democratic obsession with the need to purge the left of all communists, it is amazing that the CCF was so successful in courting the working-class voter and gaining union support. When one recognizes that this was achieved in spite of state-supported campaigns of repression, employer hostility, and without financial or personnel resources adequate to the tasks at hand, the accomplishments are even more notable. Much was the product of the tireless effort and remarkable energy of a dedicated corps of moderate socialists, many of whom received their political training in the Co-operative Commonwealth Youth Movement in the 1930s.

The CCF received its first union affiliation in August 1938, when the United Mine Workers of Cape Breton endorsed its reform program. But CCF–labour union connections remained informal, and often quite weak. While many CIO leaders were CCF advocates, few in the more conservative TLC were linked to the cause of reformism. The war provided the catalyst that thrust the divided labour movement into a concerted campaign for political action. In the west, both Saskatchewan and British Columbia provincial CCF parties grew rapidly, and in the former province, the CCF formed the government in 1944, while in the latter, it attained the status of official opposition in 1941. In Alberta one in four voters opted for the CCF in the 1944 provincial election, while in Nova Scotia the percentage of the popular vote cast for CCF candidates almost doubled between 1941 and 1945. In Quebec, the numbers voting CCF increased more than 13 times in the years 1939 to 1944. Much of this increasing CCF vote represented a protest unassociated with working-class constituencies. Farmers in the west, for instance, were attracted to the CCF, which provided an alternative to Liberal, Conservative, and Social Credit politicians.

It was in Ontario that the labour movement was most supportive of social democracy and a 1942 CCF–trade-union conference produced a spate of union affiliations. In the 1943 provincial election, the workers of Ontario's industrial cities, mill towns, and mining communities rallied to the CCF banner, electing 34 members to the provincial legislature; more than half of them were trade unionists. The Liberals were decimated and the Tories narrowly voted into office: the CCF increased its share of the popular vote by 405 percent, and the future looked bright indeed.

But, in fact, many of the union affiliations established at this time were allowed to lapse, large employers bankrolled anti-CCF campaigns, and the now-embittered divisions between communists and socialists split labour constituencies, allowing traditional candidates to emerge victorious. As workers feared the election of antilabour Conservative politicians and as the Labor Progressive Party forged a Communist–Liberal coalition in the closing years of World War II, the labour vote slipped through CCF fingers. By 1945, the CCF was in political retreat. In Ontario, the 34 seats won by the socialists in 1943 dwindled to a mere 8 in 1945. While the CCF vote remained at the level of the 1943 election, the superior (and lavishly funded) Tory machine of George Drew brought out multitudes of Conservative party supporters; the victorious Tories had increased their share of the popular vote from less than 500,000 in 1943 to almost 800,000 a short two years later. One week later, the 1945 federal election ended in another CCF defeat. Industrial Ontario, casting 260,000 votes for the CCF, failed to elect a socialist candidate, and the party became a regional voice of protest: Saskatchewan's 167,000 CCF voters (barely one-fifth of the CCF federal vote) elected 18 MPs (almost two-thirds of all federally elected CCF members). Throughout the country, the CCF had gained 816,259 votes and won 28 seats. This was a distinct improvement over the party's showing in the 1935 and 1940 federal campaigns, but it was nevertheless a great disappointment. Labour, for instance, had responded weakly to the CCF call for votes, and only in areas of established militancy (Cape Breton, British Columbia, Winnipeg) did workers vote the socialist ticket. Divisions within the workers' movement, the Liberal ability to capture working-class votes, and the CCF's underfunded and often amateurish work in the ridings all sealed the fate of social democracy in 1945.

Four years later, in another federal election, the trend continued. The CCF share of the popular vote fell from 15.6 percent to 13.4 percent and the number of seats won by socialists was more than halved, dropping to 13. While the CCF regained a seat in Ontario, its marginal representation in British Columbia and Manitoba declined, and in the traditional stronghold of Saskatchewan, the CCF was decimated, reduced to 5 elected members. "All very depressing," was Lewis' candid recollection.

The situation was worse for the communists. Driven underground in the early years of the war, they contested only ten ridings in the 1940 election and polled fewer than 15,000 votes. In the 1945 federal election, the Communist Party, under the guise of the Labor Progressive Party, capitulated to Mackenzie King liberalism, forging a Liberal–Labour coalition that attracted barely 110,000 votes. Only one communist candidate was sent to the House of Commons, with by far the greatest number of progressive workers voting CCF. But Fred Rose's parliamentary career as member of parliament would soon come to an end, the Gouzenko revelations driving him from office. Tried under the Official Secrets Act in the spring of 1946, Rose was sentenced to six years imprisonment on charges of Soviet espionage. While the communists fared slightly better in Ontario, their overall achievements were negligible and the real victors were the King Liberals.

These years were not ones of total victory for the Liberals, however. The Saskatchewan 1944 election saw the CCF win 47 of 52 seats; the Liberals collapsed in the 1943 Ontario campaign; and some Liberal defeats in federal by-elections of August 1943 saw CCF, communist, and Québécois nationalist candidates capture the voters' allegiances. However, with the election of 1945, the Liberals reestablished their firm hold on the reigns of federal political power. Sustained by "Uncle Louis" St. Laurent, close ties to corporate power, and an astute Ottawa "mandarinate" of senior civil servants, the government party ruled confidently and authoritatively until the electorate grew tired, bored, and eventually outraged enough by the Liberal party's handling of the Trans-Canada Pipeline fiasco to bring Diefenbaker and the Conservatives into office in the election of 1957. Meanwhile, the Cold War and the complacency of the early 1950s nearly eliminated both communist and social democratic oppositions. The CCF met with irreversible lack of support, and, even when the numbers of elected members rose, success was more a consequence of the shifting boundaries of the electoral system than of increased support. In the 1958 federal election, the CCF secured less than ten percent of the popular vote. A change was in order.

At the 1958 convention of the Canadian Labour Congress, union leaders called for "a fundamental realignment of political forces in Canada in . . . a broadly based people's political movement which [would embrace] the CCF, the labour movement, farmer organizations, professional people and other liberally minded persons interested in basic social reform and reconstruction through our parliamentary system of government." A joint CCF–CLC National Committee for the New Party was eventually organized, and New Party clubs emerged, primarily among nonworking-class strata in Ontario and Quebec. The recession of the late 1950s lent strength to the new movement, and within unions thoroughly alienated from both Liberals and Conservatives, but aware of the futility of endorsing the CCF, the threat of rising unemployment was an inducement to action. The resistance of old-guard CCFers was slowly diminished as a Peterborough by-election won a federal seat for a New Party candidate in 1960, as the Quebec Federation of Labour endorsed the New Party early in 1961, and as T.C. Douglas, stalwart CCF leader in Saskatchewan and provincial premier, agreed to run as the New Party's leader.

Thus, social democracy was revitalized, and later in the summer of 1961 the New Democratic Party was founded as 2,084 delegates from unions, the CCF, and the clubs met in the Ottawa Coliseum. Wary of appearing to be a party dominated by labour, the first convention was nevertheless financed and orchestrated by those skilled in the practice of trade-union organization. Moderation was essential to the existence of the New Party, as the interests of the old CCF constituency were to be balanced with those of labour and a new generation of socialists. A relationship of complete equality between the groups was not maintained, however. If labour had given the New Party its first impetus to move into the political arena, it was the experienced leaders of the CCF who maintained their hold on the actual reigns of the New Party's political power, however democratically it was wielded. Many members active in the New Party clubs, envisioning a movement dramatically different than the old CCF, never became members of the NDP that they had helped to bring into being. Others, like Saskatchewan CCF MP Hazen Argue, found the New Party tainted and linked with other political forces. Argue made a critique that seemed to affect social democracy's political fortune for a decade and more, prefacing his defection to the Liberals with these words of warning: "It would be most dangerous to the democratic process to have a party gain power, the effective control of which resided in a handful of labour leaders outside the House of Commons." Even in its most innocuous, subdued, and conciliatory formulation, the ability to resolve class distinctions remained the test of social democracy's success. Perhaps St. Laurent had been right when he characterized CCF partisans as nothing more than "Liberals in a hurry."

Throughout the 1960s and 1970s, the NDP operated in ways that recall its predecessor, the Co-operative Commonwealth Federation. The continuities between the two political formations were marked from the very beginning, when the NDP's share of the popular vote in its first federal campaign in 1962 (13.5 percent) was roughly the same as that captured by the CCF in 1949, although the New Party managed to gain six more seats, electing 19 MPs. Moreover, support for the NDP came from the old radical CCF constituencies (Toronto, northern Ontario, Cape Breton, Winnipeg, and British Columbia). Tommy Douglas' defeat in Regina was a humiliating blow reminding the New Party that the struggle for power was a much more problematic process than the dream of victory. As Diefenbaker's confused mishandling of the nuclear arms question alienated his Cabinet and Canadians in general, casting the country into another election in 1963, the NDP was forced to fight another costly campaign and lost ground to the Liberals. In the provinces, the picture was even more discouraging, with the NDP failing to preserve CCF seats in Manitoba, falling behind an innovative Conservative, John Robarts, in Ontario, and missing a major opportunity to advance in British Columbia, where the old CCF working-class strongholds of the lower mainland seemed unenthusiastic about the arrival of the New Party. The worst defeat lay in the loss of CCF forces in Saskatchewan to the Liberals in 1964. Three brief years after its founding, the New Democratic Party, like the CCF in 1958, had failed to secure a broad base of support.

In the years that followed, the New Party returned to the hard work of organizing in the local constituencies and built the support that it had mistakenly assumed to exist from the beginning. Gains were registered in 1965/66, and particularly in the industrial cities of Ontario, working-class voters were won to the NDP. Trudeau's dramatic and popular emergence as leader of the front-running Liberals slowed the NDP federally, but provincial victories attested to the developing strength of social democracy and its capacity to govern. The accent was on youth and new leadership (precisely the same appeal that worked so well for the Liberals). Ed Schreyer consolidated Manitoba's ethnic communities around the NDP and opposed old-line traditional parties with a program that included medicare, government-controlled automobile insurance, more public housing, and better roads. It was a twentieth-century variant of "gas-and-water socialism," but it won Schreyer, then 33 years old but a veteran campaigner with a decade of political experience behind him, a narrow victory. Canada had acquired its first New Democratic Party government.

Some party members were opposed to Schreyer's unambiguously

socialist campaign, but others, in what came to be known as the Waffle movement, were advocating an even more explicitly radical program. Success, more than anything else, dampened the attempt to push the party to the left, and by the early 1970s, the Waffle had been driven into retreat. As Stephen Lewis pleaded for relief from Ontario Wafflers who challenged him at public meetings and called for clarification of what the party meant when it referred to itself as socialist, two successful western provincial campaigns finally silenced the radicals' demands for a more resolute socialist stand. In Saskatchewan, Allan Blakeney led the NDP to a decisive 1971 victory, reviving faith in the potential of the old CCF farmer–labour alliance. A year later, social worker Dave Barrett resuscitated the flamboyant nonconformism that was once a staple in British Columbia politics and, in the context of unemployment and a sagging resource sector, defeated Social Credit pillar, W.A.C. Bennett.

These provincial victories recast the role of the New Democratic Party as something more than that of a perpetual loser. This provided the background to the NDP's 1972 federal election campaign, in which David Lewis effectively assaulted corporations, styled as "Corporate Welfare Bums" living on Liberal party largesse. With public sentiment turning against Trudeau, the Liberals were dealt a near-defeat. When the votes were counted, Trudeau had survived, but only barely: his party won 109 seats to the Conservative's 107, while Social Credit elected 15 and David Lewis' NDP held the balance of power with 31 members and 18.1 percent of the popular vote.

Workers benefitted from these social democratic victories as western NDP provincial governments introduced legislation that raised minimum wages, protected jobs, and restructured the machinery of labour-capital relations. Labour representatives were hired into government administration and in provinces like Ontario, close links between unions like the Steelworkers and UAW and the NDP were forged. But the real assault on the working class in these years came from a spiralling inflation that, by 1974, settled into an annual rate approaching 13 percent. As the Liberal minority government fell in 1974, working-class voters seemed forced to choose between the Liberals, who campaigned against wage and price controls, and the Stanfield Tories, who demanded them. Trudeau's bluff brought results: a Liberal majority was secured easily and the NDP suffered a serious setback, its share of the popular vote declining to 15.4 percent and its elected representatives nearly halving, to 16. Further provincial defeats in British Columbia (1975) and Manitoba (1977) were in the offing. So, too, were wage controls. Trudeau, who had characterized controls as "a proven disaster looking for a place to happen," now gave them that very space, establishing an Anti-Inflation Board limiting over four million workers to wage increases of eight percent for inflation and two percent for increased productivity.

Controls split the NDP and exacerbated tensions between the party and the labour movement. While Ed Broadbent, acting federal leader, and Stephen Lewis of the Ontario branch, opposed controls, the three provincial premiers in the west all acquiesced to the antiinflationary drive. In British Columbia, where Barrett's government was breaking strikes of pulp-and-paper workers as well as endorsing wage and price controls, the NDP government went down to defeat. Labour was left to its own devices, and mounted a "Day of Protest" on 15 October 1976. Organized by the CLC, this so-called "general strike" saw almost one million Canadian workers leave their jobs in opposition to Trudeau's policies, implemented a year earlier. But as the Anti-Inflationary Board rolled back wage gains won in defiance of controls, the CLC changed its tactics and embraced Liberal party initiatives to restore some of the close connections between labour and Liberals that had prevailed in earlier epochs. Joe Morris of the CLC led a post-1975 drive toward tripartism: a corporatist, King-like vision of government, business, and labour cooperation. But this bureaucratic pipe-dream was opposed by the militant critiques leveled at tripartism from the nationalist Confederation of Canadian Unions, Quebec's CNTU, and various CLC unions, and gained no substantial support from rank-and-file workers who were mystified by the apparent collusion between their leaders and their proverbial enemies, capital and the state.

By late 1978, wage controls were no longer a strict necessity: the government message that inflation was caused by the "wage push" fell on receptive ears outside the working class, and unionism became something of a public enemy. However, both prices and wages began to rise less dramatically, and it became clearer with each passing month that unemployment, rather than inflation, was the major economic problem of the late 1970s. More than a million "official" jobless walked the streets in 1978, and among younger workers, unemployment rates were between 12 and 18.5 percent. Atlantic Canada and Quebec were the most severely affected, with the unemployed comprising 11 to 12 percent of the labour force. The real incomes of unionized workers fortunate enough to hold jobs plummeted during 1977 and 1978 and bargaining power was eroded. When the Sudbury miners, led by the youthful militant Dave Patterson, defied the trend and fought the powerful Inco interests and when postal workers refused to submit to the Liberal state, CLC leader Dennis McDermott issued pious condemnations of these "stupid" confrontations and "ideological ego trips and permanent, perpetual obstruction." McDermott was also unreceptive to those in the labour movement who wanted to fight unemployment with implementation of the four-day week. Labour's leadership no longer used the bluster and militant posturing to which it had resorted during its protests against the Anti-Inflationary Board. But they would return to these tactics as the crisis deepened in the 1980s.

With the 1979 and 1980 elections, the CLC cast its lot, once again, with the NDP. Old arguments about controls and unfulfilled visions of social corporatism faded quickly into the past as the labour movement, led by the largest and most powerful international unions, exhorted its membership to vote the social democrats into office. The NDP won a substantial number of seats (almost one in five people voted NDP in 1980, sending 32 representatives to parliament), but the final results were far from encouraging. Their share of the popular vote seemed to have plateaued at 18 percent. With no seats in Quebec or eastern Canada, and with many NDP supporters in the industrial heartland of Ontario willing to sacrifice their party in order to avoid a return of the Conservatives, the 1980 NDP effort resulted only in a weak voice of regional protest. One of the party's seats was in the Yukon/Northwest Territories, 12 were in British Columbia, and seven each in Saskatchewan and Manitoba. Trudeau seemed to be constantly stealing social democratic thunder. When Lewis' NDP held the balance of power between 1972 and 1974, it was the Liberal, not the NDP, leader who scored political points. Trudeau taunted the social democrats in parliament as "seagulls, squawking and squealing above the ship of state, and pretending to steer it," while Lewis grew obviously irritated at the media's depiction of him as "PET's pet." Later in the decade, Trudeau appointed a defeated NDP Manitoba premier, Ed Schreyer, to the Governor General's post and another Liberal in a hurry was slowed to a ceremonial trot. Small wonder that cynicism began to set in, with some quick to relegate the greying New Party to the retirement home of political dissent.

In spite of setbacks and internal conflict, the NDP remains a political force of considerable consequence, as its 1981 victory in Manitoba suggests. And the labour movement, preparing for another offensive against Ottawa's reigning Liberals, refuses to concede that social democracy is unviable. As interest rates climbed to 22.75 percent in the summer of 1981, with unemployment again over the one million mark, and plant shut-downs eliminating thousands of jobs monthly, labour's leaders understandably turned to the political arena seeking solutions to the depressed economy that left workers jobless, homeless, and often hopeless.

The NDP was held up as the workers' saviour, although McDermott and the CLC underscored their commitment to change with direct action and a return to the bravado of Labour's 1976 "Day of Protest." On 21 November 1981, over 100,000 workers joined a CLC-led Parliament Hill demonstration, which was the largest ever staged. Farmers, consumers, pensioners, and women's groups joined unionists and unorganized workers in a gigantic show of disapproval of suffocating interest rates that were costing Canadians jobs, homes, farms, and any sense of security. McDermott had harsh words for Trudeau and Finance Minister

MacEachen, and promised an occupation of the House of Commons if government did not control interest rates as it had wages in 1974. But for such words to be translated into action, much remains to be done.

Past and Present

As Canadian workers enter the 1980s, some of the most significant events in the history of the trade-union movement are unfolding. Of course, developments are not meeting with equal success in all areas, nor are they receiving uniform support from the rank and file and the leadership. Given the fragmented character of the Canadian workers' movement it is understandable that while certain developments please some labouring people, these same events may be assessed by others as defeats. Region, occupational sector, ethnicity, political orientation, gender, and organizational place all tend to influence the way in which workers and their leaders regard a wide range of contemporary problems and issues. But regardless of perspective, the history of workers in the 1980s is emerging out of a common context of crisis, in which all economic indicators presage the coming depression.

After what was originally hailed as a boom year in 1980, 1981 established itself as the year of the bust. As of September 1981, official Ottawa statistics (generally recognized to understate problems) indicated that one in 12 Canadian workers was unemployed, and the 1.2 percent monthly increase in the unemployment rate was the greatest since the first such figures were compiled in 1945. With inflation running at 12 to 13 percent, workers were caught between a constricting labour market with consequent disappearing jobs and the deteriorating consuming power of the wage. By the end of 1980, the Canadian Labour Congress claimed that the purchasing power of unionized workers' wages had declined 4.5 percent since 1976; for unorganized workers, the figure was a more drastic 10 percent. Industrial relations "experts" predicted "a long, hot summer" that would see a "troubled negotiating climate" as workers in various sectors sought "catch-up" wage increases of 13 percent or more.

Escalating worker discontent was evident a year earlier, late in the summer of 1980. As Chrysler Corporation was rescued by a $500 million U.S. government-guaranteed loan, plants in Ontario, having suffered from Chrysler's financial problems for years, began to close down. To win back their jobs or to negotiate better severance pay, workers at Houdaille (near Oshawa) and Brampton seized their workplaces and occupied the factories. "Maybe this is the way out for workers across Canada," declared one United Electrical Workers spokesman. As the Ford Oakville assembly plant ousted 1,400 workers in 1980, and as thousands of jobs disappeared in the Niagara-Oshawa manufacturing belt, with factory shut-downs continuing into the fall of 1981 (almost

6,000 laid off at General Motors alone), the words of a successful Houdaille sit-down striker echo in the ears of the workers' movement: "We had nothing. All we had were the people outside backing us. We really had to take it."

That is precisely what was attempted across the country in 1981. In British Columbia, where cement strikes, a confrontation at B.C. Tel, municipal workers' militancy, and job actions by the forest workers, hotel employees, Wardair flight attendants, posties, and public-sector unionists in the insurance and transit realms all contributed to the climate of confrontation, more worker days were lost to the strike than ever before: 3,000,000 worker days evaporated as massive and marginal conflicts broke out across the province. 1981 was a year in which, according to Peter Warrian of the United Steelworkers of America, "the companies try us on for size." Steelworkers in Ontario elected rank-and-file militant Dave Patterson as District 6's director, and then went on to wage the largest strike in Stelco's history, closing the Hamilton works for four months, making common cause with coworkers in Quebec and the west.

As provincial labour bodies convened in 1981, the message of militancy was proclaimed from one rostrum to another. "It's trench warfare," one Ontario Federation of Labour delegate said in November 1981. In Quebec, Louis Laberge of the provincial Federation of Labour, long a supporter of the Parti Québécois, warned that his members would no longer swallow restraint from a government that, for all its social democratic promise, delivered little: with the CNTU long alienated from the Lévesque government, which has divided Quebec's labour bodies to keep them subdued, the close relationship between workers and the Péquistes showed signs of ending. Public-sector unionists in the Canadian Union of Public Employees, with a membership of 267,000, announced their intention to build for a general strike should the Liberal government initiate any return to a program of wage controls. At the same time, 49,000 federal clerks in the Public Service Alliance of Canada took on the state with demands for a 15 percent wage increase, a shorter work week, and paid maternity leave. Finally, in November of 1981, the CLC launched its 100,000-strong protest of interest rates, the International Woodworkers of America stormed the provincial legislature in Victoria, British Columbia, and the Grey-Bruce Survival Association, a 600-member farmers' organization in two southwestern Ontario counties, declared itself ready to defend local farms physically from bankers' and sheriffs' attempts to seize them for mortgage-payment defaults.

Other workers reacted to the economic collapse and the increasing alienation of modern work with individualistic flight. Worker absenteeism reached chronic levels, as one business administration professor claimed that it was costing Canadian capital five billion dollars yearly.

According to Jeffrey Gandz, at the University of Western Ontario, this represented 11 times the amount lost to strikes and lockouts, or approximately 100,000,000 worker-days.

Within trade-union circles, the crisis of the economy exacerbated strains and tensions that had long divided segments of the workers' movement. The CLC, numerically dominated by the huge, nationally organized, public-sector unions and the large industrial unions of the CIO era, made more proclamations of intent to bring about internal democracy, national autonomy, and political action. Building and construction trades unions, strongly tied to Washington headquarters, grew resentful of such developments and increasingly discontented with their peripheral place in the central labour body. For almost one year they withheld dues amounting to $675,000. On 1 May 1981 the 12 building trades unions, under threat of suspension from the CLC, took their 230,000 members out of the Congress and announced the formation of the Canadian Federation of Labor. Thus, on a date traditionally reserved for strike action against capital, labour unity, and worker protest in the streets, the building trades unions struck the workers' movement itself. The result was a serious division in labour's ranks that led to a fresh round of raiding and hypocritical posturing on both sides that only weakened the voice of the working class at a moment when, more than ever, strength was needed to combat capital, the anarchy of economic collapse, and the politics of mystification that had relegated unemployment and inflation to the margins as Trudeau continued to be absorbed in repatriating the Constitution.

Unlike any other single event, the secession of the building trades unions emphasized the fragility of the Canadian labour movement, and brought to light again elements that keep workers sectionally rooted and fragmented. Some of these, of course, are consciously erected by capital and the state, while others are merely exploited by them: segmented labour markets, technological changes displacing workers, regional peculiarities, and ethnic-, gender-, and age-related divisions. Historically, such forces have kept workers apart and have reduced their capacity to challenge employers and the state.

There are signs that large numbers of workers and their strategically placed leaders understand this now, as they have not understood it for years. The joint action of the CLC, Quebec labour, and unaffiliated producers in the 21 November 1981 protest rally on Parliament Hill seemed to herald a new era of "common front" agitations placing labour at the forefront of a mass resistance movement. It must not be forgotten, however, that labour leaders took consolidated, militant action only because of pressure at the base — unprecedented and unequivocal discontent. It is far easier for leaders like Dennis McDermott and Jack Munro (of B.C.'s I.W.A.) to make threats and use posturing tactics, than it is for workers to swallow the hard consequence of economic collapse:

the $7,000 the 1981 Stelco strike cost each member of Cec Taylor's Local 1005, or the enforced idleness that threatens entire communities in the B.C. interior, where a summer strike and a slack industry put whole families into a downward slide of economic dependency. Across Canada, in spite of forecasts that 1982 will be a year of reckoning between labour, on the one hand, and capital and the state, on the other, there has never been so much discussion of the negotiated no-strike agreements, rollbacks, and wage cuts that are presented as necessary to corporate survival.

In a period of economic restraint, the trade-union movement's drift toward economistic initiatives is part of an understandable and necessary attempt to preserve the material well-being of the working class. But it is also a jolt to collective memories and a reminder of past struggles and achievements, all of which lend a measure of cultural coherence to working-class experience, even in the face of years of fragmentation and historic losses. Workers across Canada mounting a November 1981 protest against high interest rates recalled the depression years of the 1930s. A train carrying government employees and other opponents of the Liberal state to the country's capital was christened the "Spirit of '35," commemorating the earlier "On to Ottawa Trek" of thousands of unemployed western workers. As Springhill, Nova Scotia's young prepare to go back into the town's coal mines, where an 1891 explosion killed 125 men and two disasters in 1956/57 took 114 lives, miners and widows recall the 450 Springhill miners who have succumbed to this most dangerous of industries over the course of the last century. But in Springhill, as elsewhere, working-class culture is a complex fusion of contradictory processes, a balanced expression of human agency, on the one hand, and a cold and imposed necessity on the other. One part of workers' lives is composed of aspirations, dignity, self-respect, and historically evolved structures and patterns of behaviour that encompass limited forms of autonomy. Dipping into the reservoir of history to cast labour's contemporary struggle for just treatment in the forms and "spirit" of the past is an obvious manifestation of this aspect of experience. In spite of many differences and peculiarities, moreover, similar developments taking place across the vast geographic expanse of Canada, such as the revival of interest in folk/working-class song, indicate that this is not only a regional or sectional phenomenon. There are also, however, the harsh realities of material life. These, too, operate across regions, undercutting the creative and semiautonomous thrusts of working-class culture, subordinating the wants and values of workers to the impersonalities of the market and the cash nexus. Springhill's new mine will obtain its workforce despite much opposition. With unemployment in the town at 16 percent and the humiliation of welfare too much for many young workers to bear, the dangers of the job will seem less important than simply being employed. In the face of dire necessity the collective memory of the working class can be as short as it is long at times of challenge and overt opposition.

But if this book has a message, it is that the workers' movement must develop a memory that reaches even farther back into its past to cultivate an appreciation of those rare moments when workers sustained a movement that thrived because it was able to forge an assertion of opposition that united political, and cultural struggles with the demands of the workplace. For there have been times in the history of Canadian workers when labour has united to reassert itself and to reappropriate what capital and the state have been concerned to suppress or destroy: the sense of potential that workers hold in their productive power and the alternative society that could be created around that capacity and authority. Labour's collective memory, which at certain times reaches back to recall vividly the explicitly political and unambiguously economistic achievements of the post-depression period, needs to be supplemented with the realization that those struggles — of the jobless in the 1930s, of those who battled for a social democratic party and union recognition in the 1940s, of those who built white-collar unions and Quebec's Common Front in the 1960s and 1970s — were also cultural moments of creation and renewal. In an epoch of mass culture and supposed working-class affluence, the cultural has become less prominent relative to the more explicit battlegrounds of the economy and politics. Yet it is intimately related to other battles for reform and change, and without recognition of culture's centrality, the workers' movement cannot avoid emasculation. It will inevitably be drugged into an illusory and temporary sense of its own well-being under the exceptionalism of North American prosperity, forced to react solely to capital's erroneously conceived and implemented economic policy, or attracted toward the welfare state that will, ultimately, reveal its contempt of working-class needs and values.

In the 1880s, when workers newly confronted with industrial capitalism took up their unequivocal stand against it, a hint of solidarity first emerged. No workers' movement since then has so effectively bridged the gaps separating and fragmenting different labour factions, but the achievements and the lessons of that epoch remain foreign to today's workers, who are familiar with the CIO, but not usually with its predecessor, the Knights of Labor. Nor has any workers' movement fought so explicitly within the realm of culture, striving to link inequality and exploitation in the political economy to the oppressions of everyday life. Although a complete reversion to the practice of the 1880s would, of course, be inadequate in light of present-day issues, it will be impossible for workers to renew their collective force to meet the difficulties of the future unless they search the past for ways in which to unite on a cultural, as well as an economic and political, level. The Canadian workers of the 1880s sustained a movement rooted in local initiative, diverse organizational forms, democratic practices, and a commitment to cooperation, political action, self-education, workplace militancy, and cultural autonomy. Such a rich and varied movement culture of resistance and alternative, premised on a wide-ranging solidarity, is precisely what is lacking in Canadian labour's response to the crisis of the 1980s.

First unified in the 1880s, after a century of consolidation, the Canadian working class has been, to some extent, unmade in the century that followed. A state servile to capital's needs has crushed periodic labour upheavals with military force or the enticements of government-supervised conciliation. Technology, the business cycle, segmented labour markets, and fragmented ethnic cultures have been consciously manipulated and unconsciously utilized by employers to undercut whatever strength and power workers have managed to build up over time. Authority has used both carrot and stick to neutralize labour, while jobs have been hierarchically ordered and conventional wisdoms marshalled to keep various working-class strata forever distrustful of each other. And yet, for all of this, the legacy of the 1880s persists. Against the forces of division, so strong throughout the twentieth century, has been the refusal of Canadian workers to renounce their collective destiny, to succumb totally to capital and the state. As problematic and elusive as all of this appears in the 1980s, these years of refusal and the legacies of moments of class action and cultural self-affirmation remain forces upon which workers will be able to draw in future battles. They are a resource to be tapped and extended, perhaps finally fulfilled, in the attempt to realize the aims and dreams that have gathered momentum and been forced into retreat over the course of two centuries of working-class experience.

Appendices

Appendix I

Partial Listing of Early Canadian Strikes, Pre-1850

Date	Place	Occupation	Remarks
Spring 1671	Quebec	Shipyard workers	Slowdown to secure better wages, conditions; victory
October 1741	Quebec	Shipyard workers	Protest for having to work in bad weather; strikers imprisoned
1749 (1739?)	St. Maurice	Forge workers	120 workers protest payment in kind; Quebec council decree grants workers wage payment
3 August 1794	Rainy River	Voyageurs	Demand for wage-condition improvements; some dismissed
June 1815	Quebec	Hatters	12 workmen combine against 2 manufacturers to demand firing of "finishers"; conspiracy charges laid
May 1823	Lachine	Stonecutters-Labourers on canal	Demand for shorter hours; hours held constant but wages increased
August 1825	Lachine	Carpenters	3-day strike; wages increased
April–May 1827	Rideau Canal	Canallers	3 strikes to protest wage cuts
1830	Toronto (York)	Shoemakers	Protest of "scanty wages . . . beds of straw . . . tyrannical oppression"
March 1831	Toronto	Bricklayers, masons, and plasterers	Demand for reduced hours
October 1831	Quebec	Tailors	Demand for wages to be raised above $9–$12 weekly
January 1832	Montreal-Quebec	River pilots	Protest steam boat

Date	Location	Group	Description
18 March 1833	Montreal	Miscellaneous Mechanics led by carpenters	Demand for hours to be reduced from 12 to 10 daily; strike lasted a few weeks; successful, but gains later turned back
May 1833 (?)	Montreal	Seamen	Six jailed in mutiny
June 1833 (October?)	Toronto	Carpenters	Demand for punctual payment of wages
4 March 1834	Montreal	Carpenters-joiners	Demand for reduced hours for all mechanics; successful after a few weeks of lock-out
1 April 1834	Cornwall	Canal labourers	Wage increase demand
May–June 1834	Montreal	Tailors	Wage increase demand
October 1834	Quebec	Sailors	Wage increase demand
December 1834	Cornwall	Canal labourers	Oppose wage reduction of 10s monthly over winter
1834	Montreal	Iron forgers-gunsmiths	Wage increase
September–October 1835	Toronto	Shoemakers	Wage increase
1 April 1835	Cornwall	Canal labourers	Wage increase
April 1836	Montreal	Bakers	Wage increase
22 October 1836	Toronto	Printers	Demand New York piece rates; changes in hours; 2-week strike; defeated
17 November 1836	Toronto	Tailors	Demand share of profits; 2-week strike
February 1837	Kingston	Bakers	One-week strike for wages; new men hired; conspiracy charges; follows earlier (Dec.) defection of journeymen from Counter's shop and establishment of rival bakery
27 February 1838	Newfoundland	Sealers	Strike for berth money; successful

Date	Place	Occupation	Remarks
December 1840	Quebec	Shipwrights-carpenters	2-week strike; demands for 4s for 8 hours; masters offer 3s; committee of 21 established; general combination affecting many yards and as many as 6,000 workers; compromise
1841	Quebec	Painters	Conspiracy charges
19 November 1841–9 February 1842	Pictou County (Albion Mines)	Miners	Resistance of wage reductions (demand 2p more per cubic yard after 4p cut imposed); successful
18 May 1842	Saint John	Labourers	Demand for wages to be raised above 3s daily; intimidation; arrests; sentences of 6-18 months with hard labour
May–June 1842	Kingston (?)	Tailors	Wage-condition demands; masters resist; conspiracy charges
Summer 1842	Pictou County	Miners	Resistance of wage reduction
January 1843	Marshville	Canal labourers	
January–April 1843	Lachine	Canal labourers-borers-blasters	1,300–2,000; demand 2s/6d for labourers and 3s for borers-blasters; wages cut to 2s; followed by rioting
18 March 1843	Newfoundland	Sealers	Berth money
1 June 1843	St. Timothée (Beauharnois Canal)	Canal labourers	1,000–2,500; demand 3s/6d, or 50 cents for 11 hours; 8 killed; riots and arrests
4 November 1843	Quebec	Sailors	Demand for 12–15 pounds monthly; press describes 4–5 pounds as "reasonable"
April 1844	Lachine	Canal labourers	Wages
1 May 1844	West Williamsburg (Mariatown)	Canal labourers	10-day strike; demand for wages to be raised from 2s to 3s; success

Date	Occupation	Location	Description
May 1844	Stonecutters	Montreal	Wage increase demand
August 1844	Canal labourers	Beauharnois	French and Irish unite to demand 3s/6d
1 March 1845	Canal labourers	St. Catharines	Demand 5s; threatened strike in February
March 1845	Carpenters	Montreal	Wage increase demand; conspiracy charges
March 1845	Canal labourers	Welland Canal	Were receiving 3s/6d and demand $1 daily
17 April 1845	Sealers	Newfoundland	Protest reduction of berth money; 3,000 meet at Brigus
November 1845	Canal labourers	Williamsburg	Demand reduced hours; some drift to U.S.; others remain unemployed throughout winter
1846	Miners	Pictou County	Wage increase demand
April 1846	Canal labourers	Williamsburg	Wage increase demand
22 July 1846	Canal labourers	Williamsburg (Rapid du Plat)	1-day strike to secure wage increase from 3s; failure
January 1848	Railway labourers	Hamilton	Demand for higher wages; Great Western Railroad
1849	Hudson's Bay Co. Miners	Fort Rupert	8 Scots 1-day strike; refuse labourers work; 2 chained; some desert to California
July 1849	Seamen	Quebec	—
October/November 1849	Shoemakers	Montreal	Union formed; resisted by masters; conspiracy charges

Appendix II

Partial Listing of Early Canadian Riots, 1820–50

Date	Place	Remarks
17 July 1820	Fredericton	Irish attack mechanics
October 1822	Lachine	Canallers: Protestant vs. Catholic
May 1824	Lachine	Canallers: Protestant vs. Catholic
May 1824 (?)	Perth	Protestant vs. Catholic
17 July 1824	Three Rivers	Irish-Scots vs. French Canadians
12 July 1825	Montreal	Orange
12 July 1825	Kingston	Canallers vs. Orangemen
June 1826 (?)	Lockport (near Montreal)	Labourer killed
7 June 1826 (?)	Nepean Point	Attack on inn where raftsmen's–employer's credit discontinued.
26 June 1826	Nepean Point	Raftsmen attack storekeepers; armed; defiance of constables
July 1826 (?)	Bathurst	Raftsmen
July 1826 (?)	Rideau	Raftsmen
March 1827 (?)	Nepean	3 work stoppages of canal labourers led by leader of 1826 raftsmen's riots; continual street brawls into May
17 September 1827	Kingston	Orange procession: Protestant vs. Catholic
1 October 1827	Toronto (York)	Orange procession: Protestant vs. Catholic

17 March 1828	Bytown	Irish Green procession: attacked
4 August 1829	Brockville	Irish
September 1829	Montreal	Canallers attack constables; free arrested peer
November 1829	Halifax (?)	Jail riot of 23 prisoners about to be transported to Bermuda
January 1830	Bytown	Canallers attack house of contractor who has discharged them
March 1830	Montreal (West Ward)	Election riot
May 1830	Humber	—
July 1830	Montreal	Tailors riot against circus play, "Billy Button", which they feel degrades craft
July 1830	Quebec	Tailors riot against "Billy Button"
January 1831	Bytown	Religious clash; shanty blown up
March 1831	Montreal	Attack on Presbyterian church
April–May 1831	Montreal	Election riots
January 1832	Quebec	Election riots
16 April 1832	Picton	Tailors attack employer and a magistrate
May 1832	Montreal	Election riots
12 July 1832	Picton	Orange vs. Green
7 July 1832	Niagara	Anticholera riot
November 1832	Montreal–Quebec	French vs. Irish on board steamer

Date	Place	Remarks
November 1832	New Liverpool (near Quebec)	Sailors vs. labourers
25 December 1832	Alumberston (Niagara District)	Canallers (10–50) destroy house; armed
9 March 1833	Farmersville	Election riot
April 1833	Brockville	Election riot
1 April 1833	Johnstown District	Election riot
June 1833	Montreal	French carters and labourers vs. Irish militia
12 July 1833	St. Catharines	Protestant vs. Catholic
August 1833 (?)	Brockville	Reform vs. Tory Orange
20 August 1833	Cobourg	Anticholera attack on steamship
September 1833	Montreal	Soldiers attacked
September 1833	Kingston	Blacks attempt to free slaves
1834	St. Lawrence Canal	Canallers: protest reduction of wages
October 1834	Quebec	Soldiers attacked at brothel
October 1834	Johnstown District	Election riot
October 1834	Toronto (York)	Election riot
October–November 1834	Montreal (West Ward)	Election riot (sailors)
October–November 1834	Quebec	Election riot (sailors)

Date	Location	Event
November 1834	Kingston	Tavern riot
November 1834	Sorel	Orangemen attack church
November 1834	Two Mountains	Election riot (400)
November 1834	Kingston	Attack on magistrates
December 1834	Montreal	Political rioting
December 1834	St. Eustache	Election riot
December 1834	Toronto	Election riot
March 1835	Brockville	Orange Gowan supporters riot
March 1835	Toronto (John Street)	English vs. Irish
March 1835	Cornwall	Canallers parade; wage-hour demands
April 1835	Cornwall	Canallers (200) work turn-out; demolition of English church; intimidation of innkeepers
April–August 1835	Bytown	Shiners' War: Irish vs. French Canadian Raftsmen, Farmers, Constituted authority
May–June 1835	Hawkesbury	Shiners' War
18 June 1835	Kingston	Shoemakers daub manufacturers house for curtailment of wages
July 1835	Kingston	Wharf riot (rival ship crews)
July 1835	Long Sault	Canallers: Munster vs. Connaught
July 1835	Bytown	Shiners
July 1835	Grand Calumet Rapids	Shiners

Date	Place	Remarks
12 July 1835	Toronto	Orange
September 1835	Toronto	Soldiers; at brothel
October 1835	Montreal	Irish vs. others at "oyster cellar"
March 1836	Quebec	Election riot
June 1836	Toronto	Election riot
1 June 1836	Montreal	Sailors rescue arrested deserters
10 June 1836	Osnabruck	Menagerie riot: canallers vs. country folk
July 1836 (?)	Cornwall	Canallers turn-out to protest incompetent doctor
12 July 1836	Toronto	Orange (100)
October 1836	London	Election riot
November 1836	St. Thomas	Election riot
January–March 1836	Bytown	Shiners
February 1837	Montreal (St. Edouard St.)	Riot against medical students dissecting bodies in shed
March 1837	Bytown	Orange vs. Green
5 June 1837	Cooksville	Election riot
September 1837	Home District	Orange riots; political opposition to reformers
October 1837	Varrenes	Political
November 1837	Quebec	Patriot meeting draws counterdemonstration
6 November 1837	Montreal	Doric Club vs. Sons of Liberty

April 1838	Brockville	Soldiers riot over political cartoons exhibited in store
19 April 1838	Brockville	Militia riots to protest nonpayment
18–19 May 1838	Toronto	—
September 1838	Montreal	Tavern riot
November 1838	Cramahe (?) (near Trent River)	Attack on court-martial of delinquent militiamen
14 April 1839	Prescott	Antagonism to American steamer
October 1839	East Gwillainbury	Riot against Durham meeting
1840	Amherstburg	Riot against blacks
4 July 1840	Waterdown	Liberty riot: American Independence Day celebration
16 September 1840	Drummondville	Black soldiers and civilians attempt slave rescue
October 1840	Mariposa	Attack on magistrate's house; rebel inspired (?)
January 1841	Abord à Plouffe	Irish labouring stonebreakers vs. French Canadians
January 1841	Belleville	Tavern riot
March 1841	Toronto	Election riot
March 1841	Hamilton	Political tavern riot
March 1841	Montreal County	Election riot
March 1841	Northumberland	Election riot
17–18 March 1841	Ronville	Election riot: French vs. Irish
April 1841	Toronto	Orange

Date	Place	Remarks
24 November 1841	Pictou County (Albion Mines)	Miners, wives, children attack house of company agent in midst of strike to protest cutting off free coal allowance and closing of company store; also riot at public house
December 1841–January 1842	Scugog Lake (near Peterborough)	Opposition to dam that causes flooding, disease
June 1842	Cornwall	Canallers: Cork vs. Connaught
July–August 1842	Broad Creek (Welland Canal)	Canallers: Connaught vs. Munster; 300 arrests
July–August 1842	St. Catharines	Canallers: Connaught vs. Munster
July–August 1842	Drummondville	Canallers: Connaught vs. Munster
10–12 August 1842	St. Catharines	Canallers plunder stores, mills, and schooner; demand "bread or work"
September 1842	Dunnville	Canallers: Connaught vs. Munster
October 1842	Cavan	Protestant vs. Catholic
December 1842	Broad Creek	Canallers
January 1843	Brantford	Canallers intervene in local election
4–5 February 1843	Lachine Canal	Canallers: Connaught vs. Cork; grows out of strike; 2,000 involved
2–4 March 1843	Lachine Canal	Canallers
30 March 1843	Lachine Canal	Canallers: French vs. Irish
June 1843	St. Timothée (Beauharnois Canal)	Canallers: grows out of strike; number killed; 1,000 involved
22 June 1843	Brantford	Canallers: enforce Irishman's attempt to secure toll rights at public bidding

12 July 1843	Kingston	Orange attack on Catholic Church (300)
12 July 1843	Hamilton	Protestant vs. Catholic
31 July 1843	Brantford	Canallers (100) force others (20) to stop work
August 1843	Beauharnois Canal	Canallers: Irish vs. French
September 1843	Bytown	Orange vs. Green; Governor General's visit
October 1843	Charlottetown	Antisoldier protest
November 1843	Thorold	Connaught quarrymen quarrel among themselves
December 1843	Allenburg	Canallers
25–27 December 1843	Stone Bridge (Niagara District)	Canallers: Cork vs. Connaught (1,000–1,200)
27 December 1843	Slabtown (Niagara District)	Canallers: Cork vs. Connaught
27 December 1843	Allansburg (Niagara District)	Canallers: Cork vs. Connaught
27 December 1843	Thorold	Canallers: Cork vs. Connaught
January 1844	Montreal (Duke Street)	Sailors
February 1844	Niagara	Canallers
27 February 1844	Kingston	Orange attack on Irish meeting
March 1844	Montreal (Griffintown)	Political
16–17 March 1844	Montreal	Canallers, others riot in support of election of Drummond
20 June 1844	Thorold	Canallers attack house (300–600)

Date	Place	Remarks
12 July 1844	Drummondville	Canallers: Orange vs. Green
12 July 1844	Montreal	Orange
August 1844	Wardsville	Labourers and inhabitants clash
September 1844	St. Catharines	Canallers: Cork vs. Connaught
September–October 1844	Eastern District (Mariatown, Earrand's Point, Ferrand's Point)	Canallers attack stores, houses
September–November 1844	Osnabruck, Williamsburg, & Matilde Townships	Canallers
22 September 1844	Ferren's Point	Canallers from Connaught attack Munster storekeeper
October 1844	Montreal	Canallers: election riot (also Orangemen and sailors)
10 October 1844	Quebec	O'Connell & Repeal crowd attack houses not illuminated for them
December 1844	Montreal	Election riot
December 1844	Seymour East	Canallers attack store: Connaught vs. Munster
28 December 1844	Rapid du Plat	Canallers attack house
January 1845	West Williamsburg	Canallers protest dismissals and contractor leaving site
January 1845	Cornwall	Canallers seize contractor's wagons; demand employment
January 1845	Stratford	Election riot: Orange vs. Green
February 1845	St. Catharines	Canallers rescue arrested Irishman
April 1845	Rapid du Plat–Point Iroquois	Canallers

April 1845	Welland Canal	Canallers threaten destruction for back wages owed; 2,371
April 1845 (?)	Lachine	Canallers
April 1845 (?)	Williamsburg	Canallers
May 1845	St. Catharines	Canallers free woman arrested for larceny
June 1845	Stone Bridge	Canallers: Tipperary vs. Cork (100)
July 1845	Stone Bridge	Canallers attack house
22 August 1845	Montreal	Tavern–race course riot
September 1845	Kingston	Sailors vs. soldiers
September 1845	Montreal	Sailor factions
October 1845	Lachine	Sailor tavern riot
November 1845	Cornwall	Canallers: Cork vs. Connaught
March 1846	Montreal	Election riot
July 1846	Goderich	Orange riot (200–300)
July 1846	Montreal	House of ill fame
12–13 July 1846	Bytown	Protestant vs. Catholic (80–100)
12–13 July 1846	Pembroke	Protestant vs. Catholic
12–13 July 1846	Lanark & Renfrew	Protestant vs. Catholic
August 1846	Lindsay	Orange
August 1846	Montreal	Protestant vs. Catholic
August 1846	Belleville	Protestant vs. Catholic
August 1846	Quebec	Protestant vs. Catholic

Date	Place	Remarks
2 September 1846	Port Dalhousie	Canallers attack and burn steam dredge
September 1846	Welland Canal	Canallers attack American vessels in reaction to American sailors beating and insulting a priest
March 1847	Montreal	Election riot
March 1847	Belfast County (PEI)	Election riot: Irish vs. Scots
May 1847	Halifax	Soldiers riot at house of ill fame where one of their number found dead
12 July 1847	Woodstock, NB	Orange
October 1847	St. Joseph La Beauce	Antieducation riots
1848	Chatham, NB	Cunard bankruptcy
January 1848	Montreal	Election riot
May 1848	Bytown	Attack on Gatineau Public Works
July 1848	Quebec	Sailors resist police arrest of deserters
February 1849	Quebec	Election riot
6–7 February 1849	Cavan	Orange attack on Catholic households; Cavan's Blasers
22 March 1849	Toronto	Attack on house
28 April 1849	Brockville	Rebellion losses
April 1849	Montreal	Rebellion losses
April–May 1849	Quebec	Rebellion losses

April–May 1849	Bytown	Rebellion losses
July 1849	Quebec	Cholera riot
July 1849	Slabtown	Protestant vs. Catholic; Orangemen vs. Canallers (300)
July 1849	Saint John	Orange vs. Green
11 July 1849	Quebec	Anticholera hospital riot
August 1849	St. François La Beauce	Antieducation riot
October 1849	Toronto	Rebellion losses
November 1849	Quebec	Competing juvenile gangs

A more thorough, ongoing study by Michael Cross has identified over 400 riots in the four mainland colonies of British North America in the years 1800–1850, 50 of which resulted in death.

Appendix III

An Insurrection of Labour: Strikes and Worker Protest in the 1850s

Date	Place	Occupation	Remarks
September 1850	Montreal	Tide-waiters	Protest government wage cut and elimination of winter unemployment allowance; gain wage of $1 daily but no allowance
1850–51	St. Andrews Railway, NB	Labourers	2 strikes; wages of 2s/day; riots
January–April 1851	Hamilton	GWR* labourers	4 strikes; protest wage cuts and hours; demand increases of 6 pence daily; riots; 150
February 1852	Toronto	Tailors	Strikes against machine
March 1852	Quebec–Richmond Railway	Labourers	Protest wages and treatment (2s/6d)
March–April 1852	St. Lambert Railway	Labourers	Wages unpaid; riots; property destroyed; threats against contractors
May 1852	Kingston	Stonecutters	Opposition to convict labour being hired; strike
May 1852	Canada West	GWR labourers	Demand $1 daily; strike for 7s daily in May and raise when navigation season begins in June
July 1852	Quebec	Stonecutters	Wages
February 1853– early 1854	Hamilton	Tailors	2 strikes; wages
15 February 1853– 3 March 1853	Compton	Navvies/labourers	Protest firing of 400 by contractor

Date	Location	Trade	Strike
April 1853	Quebec–Richmond Railway	Labourers	Strike
June 1853	Canada West	GWR labourers	Riots gain $1 day for 12 hours
January–May 1853	Sherbrooke	Railway navvies	Riots; 400
March–April 1853	Hamilton	Carpenters	Wage increase of 1s/3d daily
May 1853	Toronto	Carpenters	Wage increase
May 1853	Kingston	Carpenters	Wage increase
July–August 1853	Toronto	Bricklayers—masons	Wage increase to 8s/9d from 7s/9d daily
June 1853	Toronto	Printers	Increase of overtime rates
August 1853	Toronto	Tailors	Wage increase
September 1853	Quebec City	Tailors	25% wage increase
November 1853	Quebec City	Shoemakers	Wages; nonunion labour
February 1854	Hamilton	Tailors	Protest sewing machine
March 1854	Oshawa	Shoemakers	Wages
April 1854	Montreal	Railway navvies	Hours reduction, 60–58 weekly
May 1854	Georgetown	Stonecutters	Wage increase; hour reduction
May 1854	Montreal	Several trades (shoemakers, bakers?)	Wages
May 1854	Montreal	Stonecutters	—

Date	Place	Occupation	Remarks
May 1854	Toronto	Carpenters	Wages
May 1854	Toronto	Bricklayers	Wages
May 1854	Toronto	Tinsmiths	Wages
May 1854	Toronto	Labourers	Wages
May 1854	Toronto	Bakers (?)	Wages (?)
May 1854	St. Catharines	Shoemakers	Wages
May 1854	Quebec City	Stonemasons	Wages
May 1854	Toronto	Carters/teamsters	Wages
May 1854	Montreal	Carters	Wages; oppose municipal rates
May 1854	Montreal	Waterworks labourers	10-hour day
June 1854	Toronto–Guelph	Stonecutters–masons (Grand Trunk)	Wages
3 June 1854	Toronto	Printers	Wages; conditions; conspiracy charges laid
3 June 1854	Quebec City	Police	Strike for 6s daily in summer; 5s in winter; one day
June 1854	Montreal	River police	Wages
July 1854	Toronto	Tailors	Conspiracy charges laid
June 1854	Quebec City	Printers	Seek Toronto rates; increase of 1s/6d per 1000 ems
June 1854	Montreal	"All trades"	
October 1854	Belleville	Labourers–quarrymen	Increase from 5 to 6s daily

Date	Location	Workers	Description
June 1854	Hamilton	Shoemakers	—
June 1854	Ottawa	25 workers	Poor conditions, treatment; conviction under Master & Servant Act
June 1854	Toronto	Furniture works apprentices	Wages; violent intimidation
30 October 1854	Port Colborne	Railway labourers	Payment back wages
May 1855	Toronto	Carpenters	Maintain wages
May–June 1855	Quebec City	Ship labourers	300–400; wages (8s + 12s daily); and riotous protest of imported labour
January 1855	Buffalo, Brantford, Goderich Railway	Labourers	Ridgeway Riots; repeated strikes to gain back pay; sabotage; American invasion of Canada
March 1855	Quebec	Waterworks labourers	Contractor cannot pay workers; riots at his house
February–April 1855	Ottawa (Chats Canal)	Labourers	Riots; attempt to blow up works; 2 strikes; stables, barns of contractor burned
30 April–5 May 1855	Point St. Charles	Grand Trunk workers	Hours/wages; strike; 500; riotous confrontations; destruction of property and derricks; strikes spread to other Griffintown shops, especially foundries and Redpath refinery
September 1855	Nanaimo	Miners	Hudson's Bay Co.
11 February 1856	London	Printers	Wages; unsuccessful
May 1856	Windsor, NS	Railway labourers	Strike for 3p wage increase; riots; Prot. vs. Cath.

Date	Place	Occupation	Remarks
November–December 1856	London–Hamilton	GWR shop workers	500 strike; possibly members of Amalgamated Association of Engineers involved; protest of shopmate's dismissal; reinstatement
17 December 1856	London	Wood department of GWR shop	Wage reduction from 5s to 4s/4½d protested
November 1857	Quebec City	Unemployed; ship carpenters dominant	Mass meeting of 3,000+ to demand work and relief; followed by another; December 1857 march
November 1857	Montreal	Stonecutters	Wages
April 1858	Quebec City	Unemployed labourers	Protest riot at Board of Works
April–May 1858	St. Marys	Grand Trunk labourers	Riots to secure $1 day
January 1858	Toronto	Shoemakers	Lock-out; men refuse to work with obnoxious workman; intimidation; successful defence against conspiracy charges

* GWR = Great Western Railway

A Bibliography and an Apology

For the nineteenth-century years I have been able to draw upon a literature that confronts the problematic dimensions of plebeian and working-class cultural experience. My own research in original source materials has also been concentrated in this earlier period. Varying assessments of this historiographical context are found in Bryan D. Palmer, "Working-Class Canada: Recent Historical Writing," *Queen's Quarterly* 86 (1979/80), 594–616; David Bercuson, "Through the Looking Glass of Culture: An Essay on the New Labour History and Working-Class Culture in Recent Canadian Historical Writing," *Labour/Le Travailleur* 7 (1981), 95–112; and Gregory S. Kealey, "Labour and Working-Class History in Canada: Prospects in the 1980s," *Labour/Le Travailleur* 7 (1981), 67–94. In the twentieth-century treatments of labour, however, little attention has been paid to culture. For this reason, my argument is weighted toward the institutional/political context of working-class life in the years after 1919. But as I attempted to stress in the introduction, a culture does not exist "above" institutions and politics, and in advanced capitalist societies where the institutional/political forces of repression are highly developed, the union and labour political action are of vital importance, and are themselves part of cultural experience.

What follows is a partial listing of sources relevant to this study. Particular efforts have been made to include reference to the more obscure unpublished works referred to in the text, but this by no means encompasses all of the pertinent writing in the field. See, for instance, Douglas Vaisey, *The Labour Companion: A Bibliography of Canadian Labour History Based on Materials Printed from 1950 to 1975* (Halifax: Committee on Canadian Labour History, 1980). The following abbreviations have been employed: *Canadian Historical Review (CHR); Labour/Le Travailleur (L/LT); Histoire Sociale/Social History (HS)*. The countless economic histories and standard texts drawn upon in discussions of particular social formations cannot be adequately acknowledged but I have relied upon William L. Marr and Donald G. Paterson, *Canada: An Economic History* (Toronto: Macmillan, 1980) most persistently.

This bibliography is arranged according to the sequence of the text, but is prefaced by a preliminary listing of "essential" texts that cover a wide range of working-class history.

Essential Texts

Early and pioneering attempts to locate the place of labour in nineteenth century capitalist social formations are found in H. Clare Pentland, *Labour and Capital in Canada, 1650–1860* (Toronto: Lorimer, 1981), the published version coming to my attention after this study was well underway; and Stanley B. Ryerson, *Unequal Union: Roots of Crisis in the Canadas, 1815–1873* (Toronto: Progress, 1968). Eugene

321

Forsey's *Trade Unionism in Canada, 1812–1902* (Toronto: University of Toronto Press, 1982) provides a detailed listing of trade unions, labour political actions, and strikes in the nineteenth century. A rare and preliminary attempt to catalogue regional strike activity is found in Jean Hamelin, Paul Larocque, and Jacques Rouillard, *Répertoire des grèves dans la province de Québec au XIXe siècle* (Montréal: Presses de l'École des hautes études commerciales, 1971).

Late-nineteenth century community studies include Palmer, *A Culture in Conflict: Skilled Workers and Industrial Capitalism in Hamilton, Ontario, 1860–1914* (Montreal: McGill–Queen's University Press, 1979); and Gregory S. Kealey, *Toronto Workers Response to Industrial Capitalism, 1860–1892* (Toronto: University of Toronto Press, 1980). Martin Robin's now dated study, *Radical Politics and Canadian Labour, 1880–1930* (Kingston: Industrial Relations Centre, Queen's University, 1968) can still be read with profit.

Overviews of the institutional/political history of workers, all of uneven quality, include Harold Logan, *Trade Unions in Canada* (Toronto: Macmillan, 1948); Charles Lipton, *The Trade Union Movement of Canada, 1827–1959* (Montreal: Canadian Social Publications, 1966); Desmond Morton with Terry Copp, *Working People: An Illustrated History of Canadian Labour* (Ottawa: Deneau & Greenberg, 1980). Stuart Jamieson's *Times of Trouble: Labour Unrest and Industrial Conflict in Canada, 1900–1966* (Ottawa: Queen's Printer, 1968) provides an introduction to twentieth-century strike activity, while Pentland, *A Study of the Changing Social, Economic and Political Background of the Canadian System of Industrial Relations* (Ottawa: Task Force on Labour Relations, 1968) serves as a schematic overview of labour–capital relations.

Western labour radicalism receives coverage in A. Ross McCormack, *Reformers, Rebels, and Revolutionaries: The Western Canadian Radical Movement, 1899–1919* (Toronto: University of Toronto Press, 1977); David Bercuson, *Confrontation at Winnipeg: Labour, Industrial Relations, and the General Strike* (Montreal: McGill–Queen's University Press, 1974); and Bercuson, *Fools and Wise Men: The Rise and Fall of the One Big Union* (Toronto: McGraw-Hill, 1978). Kenneth McNaught discusses the rise of the early radical social democrat, J.S. Woodsworth, in *A Prophet in Politics: A Biography of J.S. Woodsworth* (Toronto: University of Toronto Press, 1959). Canada's most persistently radical region, British Columbia, is the object of study in Paul Phillips, *No Power Greater: A Century of Labour in B.C.* (Vancouver: B.C. Federation of Labour, 1967).

Documentary collections of value include Michael S. Cross, ed., *The Workingman in the Nineteenth Century* (Toronto: Oxford University Press, 1974); and Irving Abella and David Millar, eds., *The Canadian Worker in the Twentieth Century* (Toronto: Oxford University Press, 1978). Two significant collections of essays highlight different historiographical traditions. Gregory S. Kealey and Peter Warrian, eds., *Essays in Canadian Working-Class History* (Toronto: McClelland and Stewart, 1976) concentrates on local and cultural aspects of workers' experience, while Irving Abella, ed., *On Strike: Six Key Labour Struggles in Canada, 1919–1945* (Toronto: Lewis and Samuel, 1974) probes the episodic struggles of the twentieth century.

Of the many popular histories of labour, few have influenced this study. Most are either official histories, celebrations of particular events and movements, or explicitly informed by other scholarly studies. One invaluable recent development, however, has emerged out of the McMaster Labour Studies Program. Among the impressive products are Craig Heron et al., *All That Our Hands Have Done: A Pictorial History of the Hamilton Workers* (1981); and a group of pamphlets put together by Wayne Roberts: *Miner's Life: Bob Miner and Union Organizing in Timmins, Kirkland Lake and Sudbury* (1979); *Organizing Westinghouse: Alf Ready's Story* (1979); *Where Angels Fear to Tread: Eileen Tallman and the Labour Movement*

(1981); and *Baptism of a Union: Stelco Strike of 1946* (1981). Derek Reimer of Sound Heritage has edited a similar work for British Columbia: *Fighting for Labour: Four Decades of Work in British Columbia, 1910–1950* (Victoria: Provincial Archives, 1978). For Quebec, see *L'Industrialisation à Hochelaga–Maisonneuve, 1900–1930* (Montréal: Atelier d'Histoire Hochelaga-Maisonneuve, Inc., 1980).

Partisans of the workers' movement have also written histories. The radical orientation is epitomized by Jack Scott's writings, the most well known being *Sweat and Struggle: Working Class Struggles in Canada* (Vancouver: New Star Books, 1974). More conservative is the CLC-centered Jack Williams, *The Story of Unions in Canada* (Toronto: Dent, 1975).

I: Producing Classes, Paternalist Authority, 1800–50

On the character of the social formation, note Richard E. Rice, "Ship Building in British America, 1787–1890: An Introductory Study" (Ph.D. thesis, Liverpool, 1977); Gerald Tulchinsky, *The River Barons: Montreal Businessmen and the Growth of Industry and Transportation, 1837–1853* (Toronto: University of Toronto Press, 1977); Jacob Spelt, *Urban Development in South–Central Ontario* (Toronto: McClelland and Stewart, 1972); and the work of Leo A. Johnson, especially *History of the County of Ontario, 1615–1875* (Whitby, Ontario: County of Ontario, 1973); "Land Policy, Population Growth and Social Structure in the Home District, 1793–1851," *Ontario History* 48 (1971), 41–60. See also, Gary Teeple, "Land, labour, and capital in pre-confederation Canada," in Teeple, ed., *Capitalism and the National Question in Canada* (Toronto: University of Toronto Press, 1972), pp. 43–66. Graeme Wynn's *Timber Colony: A Historical Geography of Early Nineteenth Century New Brunswick* (Toronto: University of Toronto Press, 1981) is a lucid account of the vital importance of one key staple, while his " 'Deplorably Dark and Demoralized Lumberers'? Rhetoric and Reality in Early Nineteenth Century New Brunswick," *Journal of Forest History* 24 (1980), 168–87 is an interesting discussion that came to my attention too late for inclusion in this study.

Quebec's agricultural crisis is analyzed in numerous works by Fernand Ouellet, the most accessible for an English readership being *Economic and Social History of Quebec, 1760–1850* (Toronto: Macmillan, 1980). This interpretation is called into question, but not, in my assessment, convincingly refuted, by R.M. McInnis, "A Reconsideration of the State of Agriculture in Lower Canada in the First Half of the Nineteenth Century," in D.H. Akenson, ed., *Canadian Papers in Rural History* III (1982), 9–49.

Throughout this chapter, I have drawn primarily upon my own research notes from the *Upper Canadian Sundries*, the *Montreal Gazette* (1819–50), the *Kingston Whig* and *Kingston Chronicle and Gazette* (1811–40), and assorted other archival holdings and published sources.

Pentland's notion of feudal social relations is elaborated in "The Development of a Capitalistic Labour Market in Canada," *Canadian Journal of Economics and Political Science* 25 (1959), 450–61, although his recently published book redefines such relations as paternalistic. On paternalism, note the discussions in Patrick Joyce, *Work, Society & Politics: The Culture of the Factory in Later Victorian Britain* (New Brunswick, New Jersey: Rutgers University Press, 1980), and Genovese, *Roll, Jordan, Roll: The World the Slaves Made* (New York: Pantheon, 1974). There are pertinent, although differing, discussions in Gerald Sider, "The Ties that Bind: Culture and Agriculture, Property and Propriety in the Newfoundland Village Fishery," *Social History* 5 (1980), 1–39; David Terence Ruddell, "Colonial Capital and Labour: Principles and Practices in the Quebec District, 1760–1840" (Unpublished paper presented to the McGill Conference on Class and Culture,

1980). Note, as well, Larry MacDonald, "France and New France: The Internal Contradictions," *CH* 52 (June 1971), 121–43. Christian Norman, "A Company Community: Garden Island, Upper Canada at Mid-Century," in Donald H. Akenson, ed., *Canadian Papers in Rural History* II (1980), 113–34 is the best recent treatment of Calvin. Invaluable studies include F.L. Barron, "The Genesis of Temperance in Ontario, 1828–1850" (Ph.D. thesis, University of Guelph, 1976); and Graeme H. Patterson, "Studies in Elections and Public Opinion in Upper Canada" (Ph.D. thesis, University of Toronto, 1970).

Material life is probed in Robert Tremblay, "La formation matérielle de la class ouvrière à Montréal entre 1790 et 1830," *Revue d'histoire de l'Amérique français* 33 (1979), 39–50; Michael Katz, *The People of Hamilton, Canada West: Family and Class in a Mid-Nineteenth Century City* (Cambridge: Harvard University Press, 1975). Wage rates are taken from a range of primary materials and from other studies: Robert F. Gourlay, *Statistical Account of Upper Canada* (Toronto: McClelland and Stewart, 1972); Leo Johnson, "Prices and Wages in Canada West, 1840–41" (Unpublished paper presented to the McGill Conference on Class and Culture, 1980). Judith Fingard charts the pattern of poverty in early Canada in "The Winter's Tale: The Seasonal Contours of Pre-Industrial Poverty in British North America, 1815–1860," Canadian Historical Association, *Papers* (1974), 65–94.

The trauma of Scots immigration can be gleaned from James Hunter, *The Making of the Crofting Community* (Edinburgh: John Donald, 1976), while David Gagan, "Mid-Victorian Rural Canada West: 'A Good Poor Man's Country', " (Unpublished paper presented to McGill Conference on Class and Culture, 1980), has some impressionistic data on immigrants that I have used. The nature of population in French Canada can be drawn out of Fernand Ouellet's *Economic and Social History of Quebec, 1760–1840* (Toronto: Gage, 1980), or *Lower Canada, 1791–1840* (Toronto: McClelland & Stewart, 1980). For material on the Irish, I have relied upon Terrence M. Punch, "The Irish in Halifax, 1836–1871: A Study in Ethnic Assimilation" (M.A. thesis, Dalhousie University, 1977), and the recent study by Donald H. Akenson, "Ontario: Whatever Happened to the Irish?" in Akenson, ed., *Canadian Papers in Rural History* III (1982), 204–56. Other minor studies, most notably T.W. Acheson, "A Study in the Historical Demography of a Loyalist County," *HS* 1 (1968), 53–65, have also been consulted.

On apprenticeship, see David Terence Ruddell, "Apprenticeship in early nineteenth-century Quebec, 1793–1815" (M.A. thesis, Laval University, 1969), which appears in published form in Jean-Pierre Hardy and David Thierry Ruddell, *Les apprentis artisans à Québec, 1660–1815* (Montréal: Les presses de l'Université de Québec, 1977); P.H. Audet, "Apprenticeship in Early Nineteenth Century Montreal" (M.A. thesis, Concordia University, 1976); David Sutherland, "The Stanyan Ropeworks of Halifax, Nova Scotia: Glimpses of a Pre-Industrial Manufactory," *L/LT* 6 (1980), 149–58.

On the respectable, see the important and neglected study by Richard Rice, "A History of Organized Labour in Saint John, New Brunswick, 1813–1890" (M.A. thesis, University of New Brunswick, 1968), as well as Ruddell, "Colonial Capital and Labour"; Catherine Vance, "Early Trade Unionism in Quebec: The Carpenters and Joiners General Strike of 1833–1834," *Marxist Quarterly* 3 (1962), 26–42; F.H. Armstrong, "Reformer as Capitalist: William Lyon Mackenzie and the Printers' Strike of 1836," *Ontario History* 59 (1967), 187–96.

The rough are the subject of important examination in Pentland, "The Lachine Strike of 1843," *CHR* 29 (1948), 255–77; Ruth Bleasdale, "Class Conflict on the Canals of Upper Canada in the 1840s," *L/LT* 7 (1981), 9–89; Raymond Boily, *Les Irlandis et Le Canal de Lachine: La Grève de 1843* (Montréal: Leméac, 1980); Michael

S. Cross, "The Shiners' War: Social Violence in the Ottawa Valley in the 1830s," *CHR* 59 (1973), 1–26.

Comment on law, the penitentiary, and crime can be found in Palmer, "Kingston Mechanics and the Rise of the Penitentiary, 1833–1836," *HS* 13 (1980), 7–82; William R. Teatero, " 'A Dead and Alive Way Never Does': The Pre-Political Professional World of John A. Macdonald" (M.A. thesis, Queen's University, 1978); John Beattie, *Attitudes Towards Crime and Punishment in Upper Canada, 1830–1850: A Documentary Study* (Toronto: University of Toronto Centre of Criminology, 1977); and in Paul Craven, "The Masters-Servants Act in Pre-Confederation Canada" (Unpublished paper presented to the McGill Conference on Class and Culture, 1980). Although I have presented new data in the section on rough justice, my own "Discordant Music: Charivaris and Whitecapping in Nineteenth-Century North America," *L/LT* 3 (1978), 5–62 is a necessary background study. Much remains to be done on the underground history of dissent and insurrection, but note J.B. Walton, " 'An End to All Order': A Study of Upper Canadian Conservative Responses to Opposition, 1805–1810" (M.A. thesis, Queen's University, 1977). One of the best treatments of the rebellion remains Edwin C. Guillet's *The Lives and Times of the Patriots* (Toronto: University of Toronto Press, 1968), while previously cited works by Ryerson and Ouellet deserve mention. John Brewer's *Party Ideology and Popular Politics at the Accession of George III* (Cambridge: Cambridge University Press, 1976) should be required reading for those seeking to understand the nature of ritualistic combat in the political realm.

Alison Prentice, *The School Promoters: Education and Social Class in Mid-Nineteenth Century Upper Canada* (Toronto: McClelland and Stewart, 1977) points out how class seeped into all aspects of social experience. The beginnings of the labour movement in this period are sketched in Stephen Langdon, *The Emergence of the Canadian Working Class Movement* (Toronto: New Hogtown Press, 1975).

II: The Emergence of Class Antagonism, 1850–80

Gustavus Myers, *A History of Canadian Wealth* (Toronto: Lewis and Samuel, 1972), discusses the first railway boom, while Pentland's review of this reprint of a 1914 muck-raking classic, "Were Canadian Capitalists Different? How the West Was Won," *Canadian Forum* (September 1972), 6–9, contains insight. Valuable analytic advances of early capitalist development and the nature of the workplace can be gleaned from essays by Bruce Laurie and Mark Schmitz in Theodore Hershberg, ed., *Philadelphia: Work, Space, Family, and Group Experience in the 19th Century* (New York: Oxford University Press, 1981). Michael Katz, Michael Doucet, and Mark Stern have carried their work forward from the 1851–61 period covered in *The People of Hamilton* into the next decade of the 1860s, and I have drawn upon their forthcoming study. Another unpublished work, Alan Conter's "The Origins of a Working-Class District: A Portrait of St. Ann's Ward in the 1850s," McGill University, 1976, focuses on the capitalist development in a Montreal working-class district, and can be read profitably with John McCallum's *Unequal Beginnings: Agriculture and Economic Development in Quebec and Ontario until 1870* (Toronto: University of Toronto Press, 1980); J.J. Cooper, "The Social Structure of Montreal in the 1850s," Canadian Historical Association, *Annual Report* (1956), 63–73; and Brian Young, *George-Etienne Cartier: Montreal Bourgeois* (Montreal: McGill–Queen's University Press, 1981), which appeared too late to influence this study.

Labour's place in the social formation of this epoch is given attention in J.V. Barkans, "Labour, Capital and the State: Canadian Railroads and Emergent

Social Relations of Production, 1850–1879" (M.A. thesis, McMaster University, 1976); Ian McKay, "The Working Class of Metropolitan Halifax, 1850–1889" (B.A. Honours Essay, Dalhousie University, 1975), part of which appears in a general collection of articles that came to my attention after the completion of this book, Rosemary Ommer and Gerald Panting, ed., *Working Men Who Got Wet* (Saint John: Memorial University Maritime History Group, 1980).

Useful economic histories include O.J. Firestone, *Canada's Economic Development, 1867–1953* (London: Bowes and Bowes, 1958); Firestone, "Development of Canada's Economy, 1850–1900," in *Trends in the American Economy in the Nineteenth Century* (Princeton: Princeton University Press, 1960), 217–52; E.J. Chambers and G.W. Bertram, "Urbanization and Manufacturing in Central Canada, 1870–1890," in Ostry and Rymes, ed., *Papers on Regional Statistical Methods* (Toronto: Canadian Political Science Association, 1966), 205–28.

Paul Campbell Appleton, "The Sunshine and the Shade: Labour Activism in Central Canada, 1850–1860" (M.A. thesis, University of Calgary, 1974) is a yet-to-be-appreciated discussion of mid-nineteenth century strikes and working-class experience. J.I. Cooper, "The Quebec Ship Labourers Benevolent Society," *CHR* 30 (1949), 336–43; Margaret Heap, "La grève des charretiers de Montréal, 1864," in Fernand Harvey, ed., *Le Mouvement ouvrier au Québec* (Montréal: Boréal Express, 1980), 49–68, and Gregory S. Kealey, "Artisans Respond to Industrialism: shoe makers, shoe factories and the Knights of St. Crispin in Toronto," Canadian Historical Association, *Papers* (1973), 137–58 are important studies for the 1860s and 1870s. Charles Bruce Ferguson, *The Labour Movement in Nova Scotia Before Confederation* (Halifax: Public Archives of Nova Scotia, 1964) contains much on the immediate pre-Confederation labour movement, as well as a great deal on earlier years. See also Kenneth Pryke, "Labour and Politics: Nova Scotia at Confederation," *HS* 6 (1970), 33–55.

Associational life is currently drawing more attention. Previously cited studies by Palmer and Kealey contain arguments, as do articles by these authors in Kealey and Warrian, ed., *Essays in Working-Class History*. A significant and sophisticated discussion of the Orange Lodge, at variance in some ways with the interpretation put forward here, is Cecil J. Houston and William J. Smyth, *The Sash Canada Wore: An Historical Geography of the Orange Order in Canada* (Toronto: University of Toronto Press, 1980). Work on the family is just beginning, and I have drawn upon Bettina Bradbury, "The Family Economy and Work in an Industrializing City: Montreal in the 1870s," Canadian Historical Association, *Papers* (1979), 71–96; Bradbury, "The Fragmented Family: Family Strategies in the Face of Death, Illness and Poverty, Montreal, 1860–1885," in Joy Parr, ed., *Childhood and Family in Canadian History* (Toronto: McClelland and Stewart, 1982), 109–128; Chad Gaffield, "Seasonal Labour and Family Formation in Mid-Nineteenth Century Canada West" (Paper presented to the McGill Conference on Class and Culture, 1980); essays in Normand Séguin, ed., *Agriculture et Colonisation au Québec: Aspects Historiques* (Montréal: Boréal Express, 1980); and Michael Katz, "Social Class in North American Urban History," *Journal of Interdisciplinary History* II (Spring 1981), 579–606. Joanne Burgess, "L'industrie de la chaussure a Montréal, 1840–1870: Le Passage de l'artisanat a la fabrique," *Revue d'histoire de l'Amérique français* 31 (1977), 187–210 is the foundation upon which a discussion of family inheritance of craft skill in the leather trades is now developing. David Gagan, *Hopeful Travellers: Families, Land, and Social Change in Mid-Victorian Peel County, Canada West* (Toronto: University of Toronto Press, 1981) came to me too late to be included in the account of family life. I cannot stress too much the significance of Peter de Lottinville's study, "Joe Beef of Montreal: Working Class Culture and the Tavern, 1869–1889," *L/LT* 8/9 (1981–82), 9–40.

Foster Vernon, "The Development of Adult Education in Ontario, 1790–1900" (Ph.D. Thesis, University of Toronto, 1969), provides an introduction to Mechanics' Institutes, while early responses to poverty are outlined in James Pitsula, "The Relief of Poverty in Toronto, 1880–1930" (Ph.D. Thesis, York University, 1979).

Bernard Ostry's "Conservatives, Liberals and Labour in the 1870s," *CHR* 41 (1960), 93–127 stood as the major account of the nine-hour movement for some years. It should now be read in conjunction with the appropriate chapters in the Palmer and Kealey studies of Hamilton and Toronto, and also beside John Battye, "The Nine Hour Pioneers: The Genesis of the Canadian Labour Movement," *L/LT* 4 (1979), 25–56. Langdon's *The Emergence of the Canadian Working Class Movement* places the 1872 struggle at the centre of the process of class formation, but more illuminating is his wider unpublished study, "The Political Economy of Capitalist Transformation: Central Canada from the 1840s to the 1870s" (M.A. thesis, Carleton University, 1972). Another unpublished thesis, Robert Storey, "Industrialization in Canada: The Emergence of the Hamilton Working Class, 1850–1870s" (M.A. thesis, Dalhousie University, 1975) contains much of interest.

Studies of relevance in comprehending the nature of class experience in these years include Dorothy Susanne Cross, "The Irish in Montreal, 1867–1896," (M.A. thesis, McGill University, 1969); Desmond Morton, "Taking on the Grand Trunk: The Locomotive Engineers Strike of 1876–1877," *L/LT* 2 (1977), 5–34; Judith Fingard, "The Decline of the Sailor as a Ship Labourer in 19th Century Timber Ports," *L/LT* 2 (1977), 35–53; Ian McKay, "Capital and Labour in the Halifax Baking and Confectionery Industry During the Last Half of the Nineteenth Century," *L/LT* 3 (1978), 63–108; Debi Wells, " 'The Hardest Lines of the Sternest School': Working-Class Ottawa and the Depression of the 1870s" (M.A. thesis, Carleton University, 1982); and Jin Tan, "In Search of Chinese Labour Militancy: Manifestations of Coolie Protest in British Columbia and the New World, 1850–1855" (Unpublished manuscript, Ontario Institute for Studies in Education, 1982).

III: The Consolidation of Working-Class Culture, 1880–95

A full elaboration of the economic, social, political, and cultural developments in the industrial heartland of Ontario, along with extensive documentation, will be found in Gregory S. Kealey and Bryan D. Palmer, *Dreaming of What Might Be: The Knights of Labor in Ontario* (New York: Cambridge University Press, 1982). T.W. Acheson, "The Changing Social Origins of Canadian Industrialization: A Study in the Structure of Entrepreneurship" (Ph.D. thesis, University of Toronto, 1971), and the major articles drawn from it, are invaluable in understanding capitalist consolidation. Michael Bliss, *A Living Profit: Studies in the Social History of Canadian Business, 1883–1911* (Toronto: McClelland & Stewart, 1974) contains some interesting digressions.

For Quebec, see Fernand Harvey's essay on the Knights of Labor in Harvey, ed., *Le mouvement ouvrier au Québec*; Harvey, *Révolution industrielle et travailleurs: Une enquête sur les rapports entre le capital et le travail au Québec à la fin du 19e siècle* (Montréal: Boréal Express, 1978); Jacques Martin, "Les Chevaliers du travail et le syndicalisme international a Montréal" (M.A. thesis, Université de Montréal, 1965); Victor Oscar Chan, "Canadian Knights of Labor with Special Reference to the 1880s" (M.A. thesis, McGill University, 1949); Robert W. Cox, "The Quebec Provincial Election of 1886" (M.A. thesis, McGill University, 1948).

The Provincial Workmen's Association demands fuller study but important advances have been made with Ian McKay's introduction to "C.W. Lunn, *From*

Trapper Boy to General Manager," *L/LT* 4 (1979), 211–22; Sharon Reilly, "The History of the Provincial Workmen's Association, 1879–1898" (M.A. thesis, Dalhousie University, 1979); and McKay, "Workers' Control in Springhill, 1882–1927" (Unpublished paper presented to the Canadian Historical Association, Halifax, 1981).

Russell Hann, "Brainworkers and the Knights of Labor: E.E. Sheppard, Phillips Thompson, and the *Toronto News,* 1883–1887," in Kealey and Warrian, ed., *Essays in Canadian Working-Class History,* 35–57; Frank W. Watt, "The National Policy, the Workingman, and Proletarian Ideas in Victorian Canada," *CHR* 40 (1959), 1–26; Phillips Thompson, *The Politics of Labor* (New York: Belford, Clark, 1887); Peter de Lottinville, "The St. Croix Cotton Manufacturing Company and Its Influence on the St. Croix Community, 1880–1892" (M.A. thesis, Dalhousie University, 1979); Gerald Henry Allaby, "New Brunswick Profits of Radicalism: 1890–1914" (M.A. thesis, University of New Brunswick, 1973); Gene Homel, " 'Fading Beams of the Nineteenth Century': Radicalism and Early Socialism in Canada's 1890s," *L/LT* 5 (1980), 7–32; Ramsay Cook, "Henry George and the Poverty of Canadian Progress," Canadian Historical Association, *Papers* (1977), 142–57; Edward McKenna, "Unorganized Labour Versus Management: The Strike at the Chaudière Mills, 1891," *HS* 4 (1972), 186–211; Norman J. Ware, *Labor in Modern Industrial Society* (New York: Russell & Russell, 1935); an unpublished Carleton University seminar paper by Debi Wells, " 'Unknown Scribes of Unknown Worth': The Working Class at the Turn of the Century in Canadian Poetry and Novels of Social Criticism," (1979); and Mary Vipond, "Blessed are the Peacemakers: The Labour Question in Canadian Social Gospel Fiction," *Journal of Canadian Studies* 10 (1975), 32–43, are among the many studies drawn upon here. For a rare comment on religion and workers in the late nineteenth century see G. Levine, "In God's Service: The Role of Anglican, Methodist, Presbyterian, and Roman Catholic Churches in the Cultural Geography of Late Nineteenth Century Kingston" (Ph.D. thesis, Queen's University, 1980).

IV: The Indian Summer of Working-Class Culture, 1895–1919

Mackenzie King and the "labour problem" are the subject of a recent discussion in Paul Craven, *"An Impartial Umpire": Industrial Relations and the Canadian State, 1900–1911* (Toronto: University of Toronto Press, 1980). On the merger movement and other aspects of the late nineteenth and early twentieth century economy, see Tom Naylor, *The History of Canadian Business, 1867–1914,* 2 vols. (Toronto: Lorimer, 1975); David Frank, "The Cape Breton Coal Industry and the Rise and Fall of the British Empire Steel Corporation," *Acadiensis* 7 (1977), 3–34; H.G. Stapells, "The Recent Consolidation Movement in Canadian Industry" (M.A. thesis, University of Toronto, 1922). An invaluable study of the war years is Naylor, "The Canadian State, the Accumulation of Capital, and the Great War," *Journal of Canadian Studies* 16 (Fall–Winter 1981), 26–55. The place of American capital in this period can be discerned from Wallace Clement, *Continental Corporate Power: Economic Linkages between Canada and the United States* (Toronto: McClelland & Stewart, 1977); Herbert Marshall, Frank A. Southard Jr., and Kenneth W. Taylor, *Canadian–American Industry* (New Haven: Yale University Press, 1936). American management techniques are the subject of Daniel Nelson, *Managers and Workers: Origins of the New Factory System in the United States, 1880–1920* (Madison: University of Wisconsin Press, 1975).

The immigrant experience has recently received sustained treatment. Donald Avery's *"Dangerous Foreigners": European Immigrant Workers and Labour Radicalism in Canada, 1896–1932* (Toronto: McClelland & Stewart, 1979) tends to homogenize the ethnic experience and should be read in conjunction with more focused studies of particular group and local histories. See, for instance, Bruno Ramirez and Michael Del Balso, *The Italians of Montreal: From Sojourning to Settlement, 1900–1921* (Montréal: Éditions Du Courant, 1980); Robert F. Harney, "Montreal's King of Italian Labour: A Case Study of Padronism," *L/LT* 4 (1979), 57–84; Allen Seager, "A Forecast of the Parliament of Man: Aspects of the Alberta Miners' Movement, 1905–1945" (Paper presented to the McGill Conference on Class and Culture, 1980). An exceptional collection of essays on the Finns, edited by Varpu Lindstrom-Best, *Polyphony: The Bulletin of the Multicultural History Society of Ontario* 3 (1981) appeared too late for discussion in the text, although I had seen Lindstrom-Best's *The Finnish Immigrant Community of Toronto, 1887–1913* (Toronto: Multicultural History Society of Ontario, 1979).

The material circumstances of Canadian workers are scrutinized in Terry Copp, *The Anatomy of Poverty: The Condition of the Working Class in Montreal, 1897–1929* (Toronto: McClelland & Stewart, 1974): Michael J. Piva, *The Condition of the Working Class in Toronto — 1900–1921* (Ottawa: University of Ottawa Press, 1979); David Millar, "A Study of Real Wages: The Construction, Use, and Accuracy Check of a Constant-Dollar Plotter" (Unpublished research paper, University of Winnipeg, 1980); Eleanor A. Bartlett, "Real Wages and the Standard of Living in Vancouver, 1901–1929," *BC Studies* 51 (Autumn 1981), 3–62; and Jacques Rouillard, *Les Travailleurs du Coton au Québec, 1900–1915* (Montréal: Les Presses de l'Université du Québec, 1974). Early attempts to probe the nature of inflation and real wages in these years include R.H. Coat's comments in Canada, Department of Labour, Board of Inquiry into the Cost of Living, *Report* (Ottawa: Government Printer, 1915), and H. Michell, "Statistics of Prices," in *Statistical Contributions to Canadian Economic History*, vol. II (Toronto, 1931). J.S. Woodsworth, *Strangers Within Our Gates* (Toronto: University of Toronto Press reprint, 1972), and Edmund Bradwin, *The Bunkhouse Man: A Study of Work and Pay in the Camps of Canada, 1903–1914* (Toronto: University of Toronto Press reprint, 1972) are early works addressing living and working conditions of immigrant workers.

Robert Babcock, *Gompers in Canada: A Study of American Continentalism Before the First World War* (Toronto: University of Toronto Press, 1975) is an invaluable account of early international unionism's development, though the interpretation diverges from that presented above. For treatment of one union, see James Douglas Thwaites, "The International Association of Machinists in Canada: to 1919" (M.A. thesis, Carleton University, 1966). Desmond Morton, "Aid to the Civil Power: The Canadian Militia in Support of Social Order, 1867–1914," *CHR* 51 (1970), 407–25, examines the use of state force to suppress strikes, while detailed examinations of conflict in the pre-World War I period are found in Ian McKay, "Strikes in the Maritimes, 1901–1914," *Acadiensis* (forthcoming 1983); Craig Heron and Bryan D. Palmer, "Through the Prism of the Strike: Industrial Conflict in Southern Ontario, 1901–1914," *CHR* 58 (1977), 423–58. Henry C. Klassen, " 'The Bond of Brotherhood' and Calgary Workingmen," in Rasporich and Klassen, ed., *Frontier Calgary: Town, City, and Region* (Calgary: University of Calgary, 1975), 267–71, offers some comments on a western city other than Winnipeg or Vancouver. On Alberta miners I have relied upon Allen Seager, "A Proletariat in Wild Rose Country: The Alberta Miners, 1905–1945" (Ph.D. thesis, York University, 1982), while other work sectors are treated in Warren Caragata, *Alberta Labour: A Heritage Untold* (Toronto: Lorimer, 1979). Nova Scotia miners and steelworkers are the subject of Paul MacEwan's work *Miners and Steelworkers: Labour in Cape Breton* (Toronto: Samuel, Stevens Hakkert and Company, 1976), but I have relied more explicitly upon David Alexander Frank, "The Cape Breton Coal Miners, 1917–1926" (Ph.D. thesis, Dalhousie University,

1979), and the many papers and articles drawn from this important study. Frank's arguments are challenged in Ralph Wayne Ripley, "Industrialization and the Attraction of Immigrants to Cape Breton County, 1893–1914" (M.A. thesis, Queen's University, 1980). The Lethbridge 1906 coal strike forms the pivotal event around which William Baker is conducting important research, while the 1916 Hamilton munitions strike receives sustained examination in Myer Siemiatycki, "Munitions and Labour Militancy: the 1916 Hamilton Machinists' Strike," *L/LT* 3 (1978), 130–52. The unskilled receive a rare word in Craig Heron's unpublished discussion of "Hamilton and the Rise of Mass Production."

My discussion of politics draws heavily upon work cited in the "essential texts" section of the bibliography as well as studies listed in later sections. There is some material, as well, in Ian Angus, *Canadian Bolsheviks: The Early Years of the Communist Party of Canada* (Montreal: Vanguard, 1981), while Gene Howard Homel, "James Simpson and the Origins of Canadian Social Democracy (Socialism in Toronto, 1890–1914)" (Ph.D. thesis, University of Toronto, 1978) ranges well beyond the apparent limitations of the title. Also important are the articles drawn from Wayne Roberts, "Labour and Reform in Toronto, 1896–1914" (Ph.D. thesis, University of Toronto, 1978). Socialist activity on the east coast is discussed in David Frank and Nolan Reilly, "The Emergence of the Socialist Movement in the Maritimes, 1899–1916," *L/LT* 4 (1978), 85–114. Labourist thought and its evolution in Winnipeg can be charted in Allen Mills, "Single Tax, Socialism, and the Independent Labour Party of Manitoba: The Political Ideas of F.J. Dixon and S.J. Farmer," *L/LT* 5 (1980), 33–56.

Work on the General Strike and the class conflicts of 1919 makes up an important component of the historiography within the field of working-class studies. Aside from studies that I have mentioned earlier, see D.C. Masters, *The Winnipeg General Strike* (Toronto: University of Toronto Press, 1950); Norman Penner, ed., *Winnipeg 1919: The Strikers' Own History of the Winnipeg General Strike* (Toronto: James, Lewis, and Samuel, 1973); Nolan J. Reilly, "The General Strike in Amherst, Nova Scotia, 1919," *Acadiensis* 9 (Spring 1980), 56–77; Fred Thompson, "A Rebel Voice: Fred Thompson Remembers Halifax, 1919–1920," *This Magazine* 12 (1978), 7–11; S.W. Horrall, "The Royal North-West Mounted Police and Labour Unrest in Western Canada, 1919," *CHR* 61 (June 1980), 169–90; Gerry Kopelow, "Weekend Graffiti: the Winnipeg Strike," *Weekend Magazine* (12 May 1979), 22a–22b; H.C. Pentland, "Fifty Years After," *Canadian Dimension* 6 (1969), 14–17; and A.B. Woywitka, "Drumheller Strike of 1919," *Alberta History* 21 (1973), 1–7. Background to western labour radicalism, aside from McCormack's previously cited study, can be obtained from Joseph Harry Sutcliffe, "The Economic Background of the Winnipeg Strike: Wages and Working Conditions" (M.A. thesis, University of Manitoba, 1972); Allan Donald Orr, "The Western Federation of Miners and the Royal Commission on Industrial Disputes in 1903 with Special Reference to the Vancouver Island Coal Miners' Strike" (M.A. thesis, University of British Columbia, 1976); Alan F.J. Artibise, *Winnipeg: A Social History of Urban Growth, 1874–1914* (Montreal: McGill–Queen's University Press, 1975). The One Big Union is a much-discussed moment in the history of Canadian labour but one of the more significant studies remains unpublished: Peter Warrian, "The Challenge of the One Big Union Movement in Canada, 1919–1921" (M.A. thesis, University of Waterloo, 1971). An interpretation at odds with the one presented here is found in David Bercuson, "Labour Radicalism and the Western Industrial Frontier, 1897–1919," *CHR* 58 (1977), 154–75. The experience of the IWW is probed in A. Ross McCormack, "The Industrial Workers of the World in Western Canada: 1905–1914," Canadian Historical Association, *Papers* (1975), 167–90.

On women workers see Wayne Roberts, *Honest Womanhood: Feminism, Femininity, and Class Consciousness among Toronto Working Women, 1893–1914* (Toronto: New Hogtown Press, 1976); Joan Sangster, "The 1907 Bell Telephone Strike: Organizing Women Workers," *L/LT* 3 (1978), 109–29; Star Rosenthal, "Union Maids: Organizing Women Workers in Vancouver, 1900–1915," *B.C. Studies* 41 (1979), 36–55; Marie Campbell, "Sexism in British Columbia Trade Unions, 1900–1920," and Susan Wade, "Helena Gutteridge: Votes for Women and Trade Unions," in Barbara Latham and Cathy Kess, eds., *In Her Own Right: Selected Essays on Women's History in B.C.* (Victoria: Camosun College, 1980), 167–204; and Deborah Gorham, "Flora MacDonald Denison: Canadian Feminist," in Linda Kealey, ed., *A Not Unreasonable Claim: Women and Reform in Canada, 1880s–1920s* (Toronto: Women's Press, 1979), 47–70.

The emergence of Catholic unionism is discussed in Jacques Rouillard *Les Syndicats Nationaux au Québec de 1900 à 1930* (Québec: Les Presses de l'Université Laval, 1979); Brian Hogan, "Church and Union: The Case of Hull, 1912–1921. An introduction to R.P. Joseph Bonhomme OMI, 'Notes historiques sur l'association ourvriere de Hull'," *L/LT* 7 (1981), 131–49; Allan B. Latham, *The Catholic and National Labour Unions of Canada* (Toronto: MacMillan, 1930).

V: Dissolution and Reconstitution, 1920–39

For discussions of the merger movement and the Americanization of Canadian capitalism note the studies cited earlier. Tom Traves, *The State and Enterprise: Canadian Manufacturers and the Federal Government, 1917–1931* (Toronto: University of Toronto Press, 1979) is an exceedingly important study. The nature of the depression and the imbalance in the economy of the 1920s are the subject of wide-ranging comment. Among the more accessible works are Michiel Horn, *The Dirty Thirties: Canadians in the Great Depression* (Toronto: Copp Clark, 1972); Linda Grayson and Michael Bliss, ed., *The Wretched of Canada* (Toronto: University of Toronto Press, 1972); and the oral histories in Barry Broadfoot, *Ten Lost Years: Memories of Canadians Who Survived the Depression* (Toronto: Doubleday, 1973). An important discussion of workplace relations is Bruce Scott, "A Place in the Sun: The Industrial Council at Massey Harris, 1919–1929," *L/LT* 1 (1976), 158–92.

On the defeat of labour and the rise of the communists see Angus, *Canadian Bolsheviks*; William Rodney, *Soldiers of the International: A History of the Communist Party of Canada, 1919–1929* (Toronto: University of Toronto Press, 1968). Labour's decline in the west is outlined in Kathleen O'Gorman Wormsbecker, "The Rise and Fall of the Labour Political Movement in Manitoba, 1919–1927" (M.A. thesis, Queen's University, 1977); and W.J.C. Cherwinski, "Organized Labour in Saskatchewan: The T.L.C. Years, 1905–1945" (Ph.D. thesis University of Alberta, 1972). The demise of the craft worker is explored in Craig Heron, "The Crisis of the Craftsman: Hamilton's Metal Workers in the Early Twentieth Century," *L/LT* 6 (1980), 7–48.

For material life in the 1920s, see the previously cited studies by Bartlett, Copp, Millar, and others, as well as Leonard Marsh's studies in the McGill Social Research Series, which are an invaluable source, as is M.C. Urquhart and K. Buckley, eds., *Historical Statistics of Canada* (Toronto: MacMillan, 1965). My speculative assertions on the Americanization of mass culture in the 1920s draw upon lecture notes graciously made available to me by Professor John Herd Thompson of McGill University. An exceptional source is E.R. Forbes and A.A. MacKenzie, eds., (Clifford Rose), *Four Years with the Demon Rum* (Fredericton: Acadiensis Press, 1980).

Veronica Strong-Boag, "The Girl of the New Day: Canadian Working Women in the 1920s," *L/LT* 4 (1979), 131–64 is a pioneering breakthrough in delineating the structural contours of women's working experience in the 1920s. Mary Vipond, "The Image of Women in Mass Circulation Magazines in the 1920s," *Modernist Studies* 1 (1974–75), 5–13 is noteworthy, as is the Quebec study, Marie Lavigne and Jennifer Stoddart, "Ouvrières et travailleuses Montréalaises, 1900–1940," in Lavigne and Pinard, ed., *Les Femmes dans la Societe Québeçois* (Montréal: Boréal Express, 1977), 125–44. See, as well, Catherine Macleod, "Women in Production: The Toronto Dressmakers' Strike of 1931," in Janice Acton, Penny Goldsmith, and Bonnie Sheppard, ed., *Women at Work: Ontario, 1850–1930* (Toronto: Women's Press, 1974), 309–30.

On coal miners and communism, I have relied most upon the studies of Seager, Frank, and Angus, mentioned above. See, as well, A.B. Woywitka, "A Pioneer Woman in the Labour Movement," *Alberta History* 26 (1978), 10–16. It is on the "Third Period" of communist activity (1928–35) when the Communist Party led the fight against unemployment and established the Workers Unity League that I depart from the interpretation in Angus. June MacPherson, " 'Brother can you spare a dime?' The Administration of Unemployment Relief in the City of Montreal, 1931–1941" (M.A. thesis, Concordia University, 1975), and Bettina Bradbury, "The Road to Receivership: Unemployment Relief in Burnaby, North Vancouver district, and West Vancouver" (M.A. thesis, Simon Fraser University, 1976) provide some local detail on processes outlined in national studies. Kingston data is drawn from an undergraduate essay, Gudron Leys, "The Impact of the Great Depression on Kingston and the Response of the Propertied Class" (Queen's University, 1979), while the comments on Newfoundland rely upon material found in S.J.R. Noel, *Politics in Newfoundland* (Toronto: University of Toronto Press, 1971). Ronald Liversedge, *Recollections of the On-to-Ottawa Trek* (Toronto: McClelland and Stewart, 1973); Lorne A. Brown, "Unemployment Relief Camps in Saskatchewan, 1933–1936," *Saskatchewan History* 23 (1970), 81–104; Richard McCandless, "Vancouver's Red Menace of 1935: The Waterfront Situation," *B.C. Studies* 22 (1974), 56–71; James D. Leach, "The Workers Unity League and the Stratford Furniture Workers: The Anatomy of a Strike," *Ontario History* 60 (June 1968), 39–48 are indispensable. On relief activities see Pierre Berton, "Bloody Sunday in Vancouver," in *My Country: The Remarkable Past* (Toronto: McClelland & Stewart, 1976), 177–96; Patricia V. Schulz, *The East York Workers' Association: A Response to the Great Depression* (Toronto: New Hogtown Press, 1975); and sections of Fern Sayles, ed., *Welland Workers Make History* (Welland, 1963).

The social democratic experience is analyzed in Norman Penner, *The Canadian Left: A Critical Analysis* (Toronto: Prentice-Hall, 1977), and Penner, "Social Democracy in Canada" (Unpublished paper presented to the Commonwealth Labour History Conference, Warwick University, 1981). Understanding of this milieu requires knowledge of the social gospel, explored in Richard Allen, *The Social Passion: Religion and Social Reform in Canada, 1914–1928* (Toronto: University of Toronto Press, 1971). Besides McNaught's biography of Woodsworth, another important statement is found in Anthony Mardiros, *William Irvine: The Life of a Prairie Radical* (Toronto: Lorimer, 1979), while Irvine's *The Farmers in Policics* (Toronto: McClelland and Stewart, 1976) remains an important contemporary statement. The League for Social Reconstruction can be understood through reading its major statement, *Social Planning for Canada* (Toronto: University of Toronto Press reprint, 1975) and the recently published Michiel Horn, *The League for Social Reconstruction: Intellectual Origins of the Democratic Left in Canada, 1930–1942* (Toronto: University of Toronto Press, 1980). David Lewis has offered his comments on the CCF experience in *The Good Fight: Political Memoirs, 1909–1958* (Toronto: Macmillan, 1981).

The standard account of the CIO in Canada is Irving Abella, *Nationalism, Communism and Canadian Labour: The CIO, The Communist Party of Canada and the Canadian Congress of Labour, 1935–1956* (Toronto: University of Toronto Press, 1973). See, also, Duart Snow, "The Holmes Foundry Strike of March, 1937: 'We'll give their jobs to white men'," *Ontario History* 69 (1977); and, for Quebec, Evelyn Dumas, *The Bitter Thirties in Quebec* (Montreal: Black Rose, 1975); Conrad Black, *Duplessis* (Toronto: McClelland and Stewart, 1977). An exemplary study, yet to be equalled in Canada, is Peter Friedlander, *The Emergence of a UAW Local, 1936–193a: A Study in Class and Culture* (Pittsburgh: University of Pittsburgh Press, 1975).

Agitational propaganda and cultural activity is the subject of Frank Watt, "Literature of Protest," in Klinck, ed., *Literary History of Canada* 1 (Toronto: University of Toronto Press, 1965), 473–92; Richard Wright and Robin Endres, eds., *Eight Men Speak and Other Plays from the Canadian Workers' Theatre* (Toronto: New Hogtown Press, 1976); Dawn Fraser, *Echoes from Labor's War: Industrial Cape Breton in the 1920s* (Toronto: New Hogtown Press, 1978); Bettina Bradbury and Yolanda Kingsmill, "Poverty, Politics and the Press: A Cartoon History of the Depression Years in British Columbia" (Unpublished manuscript, Vancouver 1977); John Bentley Mays, "A Visual Trip to the Depression," *Globe and Mail* (14 November 1981); and Donna Phillips, ed., *Voices of Discord: Canadian Short Stories from the 1930s* (Toronto: New Hogtown Press, 1979). I have also drawn upon an undergraduate essay, Anne MacLennan, "Food for Thought: The Changing Mood of the Depression as Indicated by Selected Urban Literary Works" (McGill University, 1980).

An overview of Catholic unionism is found in the introduction to *Quebec Labour* (Montreal: Black Rose, 1972), while the Antigonish movement is explored in Robert James Sacouman, "Social Origins of Antigonish Movement Co-operative Associations in Eastern Nova Scotia" (Ph.D. thesis, University of Toronto, 1976), and a number of published articles based upon this dissertation. Racial fragmentation in British Columbia is the subject of W. Peter Ward, "Class and Race in the Social Structure of British Columbia, 1870–1939," *B.C. Studies* 45 (1980), 17–36.

VI: Class and Movement, 1940–80

There is still no adequate contemporary history of Canada although Robert Bothwell, Ian Drummond, and John English, *Canada Since 1945: Power, Politics, and Provincialism* (Toronto: University of Toronto Press, 1981) can be used to obtain some insights and empirical data. But it requires great patience to separate the relevant from the ridiculous. On the most successful political leader of the period, see Richard Gwyn, *The Northern Magus: Pierre Trudeau and the Canadians* (Toronto: McClelland and Stewart, 1980). Robert Bothwell and William Kilbourn, *C.D. Howe, A Biography* (Toronto: McClelland and Stewart, 1979), tells us something of a strategically placed political-economic figure, while an understanding of the Liberal party emerges from a reading of Reginald Whitaker, *The Government Party: Organizing and Financing the Liberal Party of Canada, 1930–1958* (Toronto: University of Toronto Press, 1978).

The nature of concentrated economic power is addressed in a voluminous literature that now includes John Porter, *The Vertical Mosaic* (Toronto: University of Toronto Press, 1965); Clement, *The Canadian Corporate Elite: An Analysis of Economic Power* (Toronto: McClelland & Stewart, 1975); Clement, *Continental Corporate Power: Economic Linkages Between Canada and the United States* (Toronto: McClelland and Stewart, 1977); Jorge Niosi, *The Economy of Canada: Who Controls It?* (Montreal: Black Rose, 1978); Robert Sweeney, "The Evolution of Financial

Groups in Canada and the Capital Market since the Second World War" (M.A. thesis, Université de Québec à Montréal, 1980).

Railway labourers in the period are the subject of a useful study, Rosemary Ellen Speirs, "Technological Change and the Railway Unions, 1945–1972" (Ph.D. thesis, University of Toronto, 1974), while Inco's miners and their experience are the center of Wallace Clement's study, *Hardrock Mining: Industrial Relations and Technological Changes at Inco* (Toronto: McClelland & Stewart, 1981). An important assessment of labour in the World War II years is Laurel Sefton MacDowell, "The Formation of the Canadian Industrial Relations System during World War Two," *L/LT* 3 (1978), 175–96; a wider-ranging study is H.C. Pentland, "The Canadian Industrial Relations System: Some Formative Factors," *L/LT* 4 (1979), 9–24. On the IWA I have drawn most heavily from Jerry Lemcke, "The International Woodworkers of America in British Columbia, 1942–1951," *L/LT* 6 (1980), 113–48, which should be read against Abella's *Nationalism, Communism, and Canadian Labour*.

Differing assessments of industrial unionism and the anticommunist drive in the labour movement can be gleaned from Terry Copp, *The I.U.E. in Canada* (Elora, Ontario: Cumnock Press, 1980); Copp, ed., *Industrial Unionism in Kitchener, 1937–1947* (Elora, Ontario: Cumnock Press, 1976); and James Turk, "Labour During the Cold War: Oral History in the Study of the Survival of the United Electrical Workers in Canada" (Unpublished paper presented to the Canadian Oral History Association, Montreal 1980). The development of the 1946 steel strike in Hamilton, which I have neglected here because of the existence of other accessible sources, is explored in an unpublished paper by Robert Storey, "Unions, Workers and Steel: The Blurring of the Picket Lines," University of Toronto, 1979. I have benefited from seeing a lengthy unpublished research paper on the Penman's Ltd. Paris, Ontario strike of 1949 that was forwarded to me by D.A. Smith. The sordid history of the CSU is examined in John Stanton, *Life and Death of a Union: The History of the Canadian Seamen's Union, 1936–1949* (Toronto: Steel Rail, 1978). On Newfoundland see Peter Neary, " 'Traditional' and 'Modern' Elements in the social and economic history of Bell Island and Conception Bay," Canadian Historical Association, *Papers* (1973), 105–36; Peter Neary, "Canada and the Newfoundland Labour Market, 1939–1949," *CHR* 62 (1981), 470–95. Ernest Bugya Akyeampong, "Labour Laws and the Development of the Labour Movement in Newfoundland, 1900–1960" (M.A. thesis, Memorial University of Newfoundland, 1968) is countered by William E. Gillespie, "A History of the Newfoundland Federation of Labour, 1936–1963" (M.A. thesis, Memorial University, 1980), which challenges Akyeampong's argument that the regional labour movement thrived in the aftermath of Confederation.

Quebec is the subject of much study, most of it focusing upon the institutional and ideological evolution of labour. See Alexander Fraser Isbester, "A History of the National Catholic Unions in Canada, 1901–1965" (Ph.D. thesis, Cornell University, 1965); Samuel Henry Barnes, "The Ideologies and Policies of Canadian Labor Organizations" (Ph.D. thesis, Duke University, 1957); Pierre Elliott Trudeau, ed., *The Asbestos Strike* (Toronto: James, Lewis, and Samuel, 1974); and Daniel Drache, ed., *Quebec — Only the Beginning: The Manifestoes of the Common Front* (Toronto: New Press, 1972).

White-collar unionism occupies a prominent place in Robert Laxer, *Canada's Unions* (Toronto: Lorimer, 1976), while its historical origins are the subject of recent historical and sociological inquiry in studies such as Graham Lowe, "The Administrative Revolution: the Growth of Clerical Occupations and the Development of the Modern Office in Canada, 1911–1931" (Ph.D. thesis, University of Toronto, 1979); David Coombs, "The Emergence of a White Collar

Work Force in Toronto, 1895–1911" (Ph.D. thesis, York University, 1978). White collar inhibition concerning unionism is the subject of Janet J. Mayer, "Hegemony and Class Imagery: A Study of Monopoly-Sector White-Collar Labour" (Unpublished paper presented to the Canadian Political Science Association, Montreal, 1980), and is also an issue in Michael Katzemba, "Working in an Office," in Walter Johnson, ed., *Working in Canada* (Montreal: Black Rose, 1975), 122–30.

On women workers, see Ruth Roach Pierson, "Women's Emancipation and the Recruitment of Women into the Labour Force in World War II," in Susan Mann Trofimenkoff and Alison Prentice, ed., *The Neglected Majority: Essays in Canadian Women's History* (Toronto: McClelland and Stewart, 1977), 125–45; Veronica Strong-Boag, "Working Women and the State: the case of Canada, 1899–1945," *Atlantis* 6 (Spring 1981), 1–9; Hugh and Pat Armstrong, "The Segregated Participation of Women in the Canadian Labour Force, 1941–1971," *Canadian Review of Sociology and Anthropology* 12 (November 1975), 370–84; Martin Meissner et al., "No Exit for Wives: sexual division of labour and the cumulation of household demands," *Canadian Review of Sociology and Anthropology* 12 (November 1975), 424–39. On the role of wives in the Sudbury strikes, I have utilized Bill Pentney, "Mine-Mill versus Inco, Sudbury 1958: A Study in Class, Culture, and Conflict" (Undergraduate essay, Queen's University, 1979), and Meg Luxton, *More than a Labour of Love: Three Generations of Women's Work in the Home* (Toronto: Women's Press, 1980), a study I have drawn upon for other material as well. Note, too, Gail Cuthbert Brandt, " 'Weaving it Together': Life Cycle and the Industrial Experience of Female Cotton Workers in Quebec, 1910–1950," *L/LT* 7 (1981), 113–26; Nicolas Zay, "Analyse statistique du travail de la femme mariée dans la province de Quebéc," in Michèle Jean, ed., *Québécoises du 20e siècle* (Montréal: Éditions du Jour, 1974), 124–40. The most thorough contemporary statement on women, work, and unionization remains Julie White, *Women and Unions* (Ottawa: Canadian Advisory Council on the Status of Women, 1980).

Nationalism and the breakaway movement are addressed in R.B. Morris, "The reverter clause and breakaways in Canada," in Teeple, ed., *Capitalism and the National Question in Canada*, 89–100; Philip Resnick, "The Breakaway Movement in Trail," and Paul Knox, "Breakaway Unionism in Kitimat," in Resnick and Knox, ed., *Essays in B.C. Political Economy* (Vancouver: New Star, 1974); Rick Salutin, *Kent Rowley: The Organizer; a Canadian Union Life* (Toronto: Lorimer, 1980).

Politics and labour's involvement in the CCF–NDP has drawn extensive comment, starting with Gad Horowitz, *Canadian Labour in Politics* (Toronto: University of Toronto Press, 1968). David Lewis, *The Good Fight*, is essential reading, and an institutional overview of social democracy's experience can be developed from G.L. Caplan, *The Dilemma of Canadian Socialism: The CCF in Ontario* (Toronto: McClelland & Stewart, 1973); Leo Zakuta, *A Protest Movement Becalmed: A Study of Change in the CCF* (Toronto: University of Toronto Press, 1964); Walter Young, *Anatomy of a Party: The National CCF, 1932–1a61* (Toronto: University of Toronto Press, 1969); Desmond Morton, *NDP: The Dream of Power* (Toronto: Hakkert, 1974); Morton, *Social Democracy in Canada* (Toronto: Samuel Stevens, 1977). The Communist experience is less well served, but see Ivan Avakumovic, *The Communist Party in Canada: A History* (Toronto: McClelland & Stewart, 1975).

I have drawn much of the more current material from my own files from Vancouver, Toronto, and Montreal newspapers and from W.D. Wood and Pradeep Kumar, eds., *The Current Industrial Relations Scene in Canada* (Kingston: Queen's University Industrial Relations Centre, 1979). See also Jenny R.

Podoluk, *Incomes of Canadians* (Ottawa: Dominion Bureau of Statistics, 1968); Warren E. Kalbach, *The Impact of Immigration on Canada's Population* (Ottawa: Dominion Bureau of Statistics, 1970).

Index

DUE DATE